Material Culture and Queenship in 14th-century France

The Testament of Blanche of Navarre (1331–1398)

By

Marguerite Keane

BRILL

LEIDEN | BOSTON

Cover illustration: Blanche of Navarre presenting the chapel of Saint Hippolyte, with family and saints, 1372. Paris, Archives nationales, K 49, no. 76A. PHOTO CREDIT: ARCHIVES NATIONALES.

Publication of this volume was made possible by a Kress research & publication grant from the International Center of Medieval Art.

Library of Congress Cataloging-in-Publication Data

Names: Keane, Marguerite A., author.
Title: Material culture and queenship in 14th-century France : the testament of Blanche of Navarre (1331-1398) / by Marguerite Keane.
Description: Leiden ; Boston : Brill, [2016] | Series: Art and material culture in medieval and Renaissance Europe, ISSN 2212-4187 ; volume 5 | Includes bibliographical references and index.
Identifiers: LCCN 2016011390 (print) | LCCN 2016019258 (ebook) | ISBN 9789004248366 (hardback : acid-free paper) | ISBN 9789004318830 (e-book) | ISBN 9789004318830 (E-book)
Subjects: LCSH: Blanche, de Navarre, Queen, consort of Philip VI, King of France, 1331-1398--Art collections. | Blanche, de Navarre, Queen, consort of Philip VI, King of France, 1331-1398--Will. | Queens--France--Biography. | France--Kings and rulers--Biography. | Material culture--France--History--To 1500. | Personal belongings--France--History--To 1500. | Wills--France--History--To 1500. | Patronage, Political--France--History--To 1500. | France--History--Philip VI, 1328-1350. | France--History--14th century.
Classification: LCC DC98.7.B63 K43 2016 (print) | LCC DC98.7.B63 (ebook) | DDC 707.4/44--dc23
LC record available at https://lccn.loc.gov/2016011390

Want or need Open Access? Brill Open offers you the choice to make your research freely accessible online in exchange for a publication charge. Review your various options on brill.com/brill-open.

Typeface for the Latin, Greek, and Cyrillic scripts: "Brill". See and download: brill.com/brill-typeface.

ISSN 2212-4187
ISBN 978-90-04-24836-6 (hardback)
ISBN 978-90-04-31883-0 (e-book)

Copyright 2016 by Koninklijke Brill NV, Leiden, The Netherlands.
Koninklijke Brill NV incorporates the imprints Brill, Brill Hes & De Graaf, Brill Nijhoff, Brill Rodopi and Hotei Publishing.
All rights reserved. No part of this publication may be reproduced, translated, stored in a retrieval system, or transmitted in any form or by any means, electronic, mechanical, photocopying, recording or otherwise, without prior written permission from the publisher.
Authorization to photocopy items for internal or personal use is granted by Koninklijke Brill NV provided that the appropriate fees are paid directly to The Copyright Clearance Center, 222 Rosewood Drive, Suite 910, Danvers, MA 01923, USA. Fees are subject to change.

This book is printed on acid-free paper and produced in a sustainable manner.

Printed by Printforce, United Kingdom

Contents

Acknowledgements   VII
List of Figures and Tables   IX
Notes on Translation, Citation, and Names   XI

Introduction   1

1   The Life and Patronage of Blanche of Navarre   19
    Conflict with the Monks of Saint-Denis   33
    Childhood and Marriage   41
    Widowhood and Early Commissions   44
    The Dowager Queen as Mediator: Charles of Navarre and the Hundred
        Years War   52
    The Dowager Queen at Home and at Court   56

2   The Testament: Legal Document and Sentimental Autobiography   61

3   Books as Evidence to Perpetuate Memory   77

4   Reliquaries, Altarpieces, and Paintings   116
    Devotional Spaces within the Household   119
    Reliquaries   126

5   Wearable Reliquaries, Metalwork, and Gems   151
    The Reliquary Belt of Philip VI   153
    Reliquary Brooches   156
    Heirloom Diamonds   159
    Heirloom Paternoster Beads   166
    The Queen's Crowns and Sealing Ring   169

6   Textiles: Vestments, Wall Hangings, and Clothing   178

Conclusions   202

Appendices: Gifts and Their Recipients   206
    1   Gifts of Books   206
    2   Gifts of Reliquaries, Altarpieces, and Paintings   212
    3   Gifts of Wearable Reliquaries, Metalwork, and Gems   220
    4   Gifts of Textiles   226

Bibliography   231
Index   255

Acknowledgements

At the beginning of this book about Blanche of Navarre, an assiduous curator of her connections to the past and to other people, it is a pleasure to acknowledge those who have helped me bring the project to completion. I recognize their contributions here, knowing that this book stands as the final product of their innumerable acts of generosity and kindness.

The project would not have been possible without the support of my friends and colleagues in the Art History Department at Drew University, Margaret Kuntz and Kimberly Rhodes. Sonja Sekely-Rowland and Şan Solu provided valuable assistance with image editing. Drew University contributed a semester-long sabbatical, a one-semester course release, several research grants for trips to France, and funds for copyediting. A generous publication grant from the Kress Foundation in conjunction with the International Center of Medieval Art substantially offset the publication costs of the book. My colleagues in the Interlibrary Loan office at Drew, Kathleen Juliano and Madeline Nitti-Bontempo, obtained innumerable obscure volumes and images from libraries all over the country during the six years I worked on this project. I am most grateful to all these individuals and institutions.

For discussing my research on Blanche of Navarre with me and offering research assistance and insights, I thank Brigitte Bedos-Rezak, Cynthia Brown, Brigitte Buettner, Keith Busby, Kristen Collins, Laura Gathagan, Jim Hala, Louis Hamilton, Tracy Chapman Hamilton, Melissa Katz, Jim Keane, Genevra Kornbluth, Thomas Kren, Therese Martin, Kathleen Nolan, Mariah Proctor-Tiffany, Maureen Quigley, Miriam Shadis, Anne Rudloff Stanton, and Elena Woodacre. I owe a special debt of gratitude to Joan Holladay, who has been a kind mentor and friend from the beginning of the project. Peggy Brown's generosity with her unparalleled knowledge of 14th-century French archival sources has made her an invaluable help to me and to this project. S.C. Kaplan vetted my English translation of the testament of Blanche of Navarre, and Maura Heyn assisted with Latin translations. The anonymous external reviewer engaged by Brill furnished me with a detailed critique, thereby contributing to the strength of the analysis in the book. Series editors Sarah Blick and Laura Gelfand offered useful suggestions and feedback throughout the process. I also thank my Brill editor, Marcella Mulder, for her guidance, and my copy editor, Sharon Herson, for her thoughtful and careful work on the text.

I have depended heavily on the expertise and kindness of the curators, archivists, and librarians at the American and European institutions where I did my research, in particular, the Archives nationales and the Bibliothèque nationale in Paris, the British Library, the Archives départementales des Pyrénées-Atlantiques in Pau, the Princeton University libraries, and the Drew University library.

Sarah Thompson, fellow medievalist and Francophile, intrepid traveling companion, and talented photographer, provided several of the images for this book. I am very grateful to her, and to my family as well, especially my parents, Robert and Maureen Keane. I dedicate this book with love and gratitude to my beloved immediate family: Patrick, Kathleen, and Thomas Ott de Vries.

List of Figures and Tables

Figures

1.1   Blanche of Navarre presenting the chapel of Saint Hippolyte, with family and saints, 1372   20

1.2   Chapel of Saint Hippolyte, Saint-Denis   21

1.3   Blanche of Navarre presenting the chapel of Saint Hippolyte, with family and saints, 1372   22

1.4   Tomb of Blanche of Navarre and her daughter Jeanne of France at Saint-Denis   24

1.5   Tomb figures of Jeanne of France and Blanche of Navarre, chapel of Saint Hippolyte, Saint-Denis, *c.* 1372   26

1.6   Tomb figure of Blanche of Navarre, Saint-Denis, detail   27

1.7   Tomb figure of Jeanne of France, Saint-Denis, detail of dogs   27

1.8   Tomb figure of Jeanne II, queen of Navarre, *c.* 1350   28

1.9   Philip VI with Saint Hippolyte   30

1.10   Blanche of Navarre and Jeanne of France with Saint Louis   31

1.11   Crucifixion with Saint Louis, Philip VI, Charles V as dauphin, Blanche of Navarre, and Saint Denis   46

1.12   Entrails tomb of Philip VI at the church of the Jacobins   48

1.13   Head of Philip III, count of Evreux, king of Navarre, from his heart tomb at the church of the Jacobins, *c.* 1350   49

1.14   Head of Jeanne II, countess of Evreux and queen of Navarre, from her heart tomb at the church of the Jacobins, *c.* 1350   49

1.15   Pardon of Charles II, king of Navarre, *Grandes chroniques*, 1375–80   54

1.16   Château of Blanche of Navarre, Neaufles   59

2.1   Testament of Blanche of Navarre, *c.* 1398   63

2.2   Map of the churches and other religious foundations in France (outside Paris) given bequests of devotional objects or vestments in the testament of Blanche of Navarre   69

3.1   Miraculous return of the breviary of Saint Louis, *Hours of Jeanne of Evreux*, *c.* 1325–28   84

3.2   Miraculous return of the breviary of Saint Louis, *Hours of Marie of Navarre*, *c.* 1340   85

3.3   *Psalter of Saint Louis*, *c.* 1200   90

3.4   Education of Saint Louis, *Hours of Jeanne of Navarre*, *c.* 1330–40   96

3.5   Humility and Pride, a sinner and a hypocrite, *La Somme le roi* of Philip the Fair, *c.* 1295   108

4.1	John, duke of Berry, at prayer, *Belles Heures*, 1405–1408/1409	123
4.2	Jeanne of Auvergne, duchess of Berry, at prayer, *Belles Heures*, 1405–1408/1409	124
4.3	Philip the Good attending Mass, from Jean Miélot, *Traité sur l'oraison dominicale*, after 1457	125
4.4	Virgin and Child reliquary statue, *c.* 1324–39, donated to Saint-Denis by Jeanne of Evreux in 1339	132
4.5	Reliquary commissioned by Blanche of Navarre for the church of Vernon, after 1396	133
4.6	Saint Catherine in her study, *Belles Heures*, 1405–1408/1409	137
4.7	Reliquary of Saint Lawrence, *c.* 1300	138
4.8	Reliquary of the Trinity, *c.* 1400	147
6.1	Chasuble of Blanche of Navarre, second half of the 14th century	187
6.2	Chasuble of Blanche of Navarre, detail	188
6.3	Chasuble of Blanche of Navarre, detail of the heraldic device	188

Tables

0.1	Genealogical table of the family of Blanche of Navarre, part 1	16
0.2	Genealogical table of the family of Blanche of Navarre, part 2	17

Notes on Translation, Citation, and Names

I have translated the relevant bequests of Blanche's testament and codicils into English and included the translation in brackets after the original French.* The text of the will was divided into sections numbering 1–534 by Léopold Delisle in "Testament de Blanche de Navarre, reine de France," *Mémoires de la Société de l'histoire de Paris et de l'Ile de France* 12 (1885), 1–64 (cited below as Delisle followed by the pertinent number). I have included only the bequests relevant to objects in this book, about half the total number. In the case of other wills or inventories used for comparison (those of Jeanne of Evreux or Blanche of Orléans, for example), the English translation appears in the text and the original French in a footnote.

In scholarship written in English on 14th-century France, the use of names for individuals varies, for example, Jean, duc de Berry, or John, duke of Berry. Whenever possible I have used the English version of names, except when it would deviate too much from accepted usage (so John II, king of France, but Jeanne of Evreux, not Joan of Evreux).

---

* The translation of Blanche's will into English is my own; I am grateful to S.C. Kaplan for reviewing it and discussing it with me. All errors are my own.

Introduction

In her testament of 1396, Blanche of Navarre (1331–98) wrote about a diamond that her late husband, the French king Philip VI (r. 1328–50), had greatly loved; noted that she wanted to give a set of bedclothes that she used for women in labor in her household to her niece (a future queen of England); said that her book, now more than 150 years old, which had once been owned by Saint Louis and returned to him by an angel, should be given to her nephew, Charles III, king of Navarre; and made known that the reliquary belt for protection in battle of her late husband (a belt that presumably had been put away in the 46 years since Philip's death, unless it was efficacious for more than just battle) was intended for the present king of France, Charles VI.[1] The object collection of Blanche of Navarre, in other words, is an irresistible topic for further research. Blanche herself made her objects irresistible through these testamentary descriptions; she wanted her heirs to cherish her gifts, and by extension, her memory.

Blanche, like so many of her contemporaries, used cultural patronage for spiritual benefit, to exercise power, maintain and display status, and bolster family relationships. This book, however, is atypical as a patronage study because the extant evidence of her possessions includes her remarkable testament and codicils. In what follows, I consider Blanche's commissions of funerary monuments for herself and her daughter at Saint-Denis, and for her parents at the church of the Jacobins, as well as scattered other commissions, along with the usual kinds of information employed to elucidate patronage, such as surviving works of art, household accounts, and other payment records. Blanche's testament does not provide the kind of evidence that typically illuminates patronage, like the cost of items or the names of the artists who were hired to create works of art; nevertheless, it conveys a great deal of information. Blanche draws connections between people and between persons and things that she intended to be meaningful, so that we see what she thought was

---

1   Following the example of other scholars, I use the terms 'testament' and 'will' interchangeably in this book. For discussion of these terms, see Clive Burgess, "Late Medieval Wills and Pious Convention: Testamentary Evidence Reconsidered," in *Profit, Piety, and the Professions in Later Medieval England*, ed. Michael Hicks (Gloucester, 1990), pp. 14–33, esp. p. 30; and Anne M. Dutton, "Passing the Book: Testamentary Transmission of Religious Literature to and by Women in England, 1350–1500," in *Women, the Book and the Godly: Selected Proceedings of the St. Hilda's Conference, 1993*, ed. Lesley Smith and Jane Taylor (Woodbridge, UK, 1995), vol. 1, pp. 41–54, esp. p. 41, n. 2.

© KONINKLIJKE BRILL NV, LEIDEN, 2016 | DOI 10.1163/9789004318830_002

important, as well as what she valued about her possessions. The testament also tells us about her aesthetic choices and what she appreciated about her objects, revealing the accoutrements of a dowager queen's household in the 14th century, from her bedding to her kitchen to her chapel.

In this study about objects and relationships between people, it seems appropriate to begin with a story about a wedding, a ceremony marking status and transition that also calls for gifts of objects and the celebration of old and new family ties. The wedding was that of Jeanne, the only child of Blanche and Philip VI; her intended spouse was John, son of the king of Aragon. The archival material on which we depend to reconstruct the wedding events is from the payment records kept by King Charles V (1332–80), grandson of Philip VI; out of obligation or affection, he paid for at least some of the expenses of the wedding of this French princess. From these payment records we learn that the 20-year-old Jeanne set out on her journey to Perpignan, the wedding site in July or August 1371, accompanied by an entourage that included the countess of Porcien, Jacqueline de Dammartin, the bishop of Auxerre, Pierre Aymé, and a knight, Philippe de Villiers.[2] Just prior to her departure, in June 1371, Charles V gave Jeanne 200 francs to distribute on visits (*pèlerinages*) to churches in Paris and to Saint-Denis.[3] At Saint-Denis she would have visited her father's grave as well as the tombs of her Capetian ancestors; the visits to other churches in Paris enabled her to marshal the spiritual aid of the clergy, the patron saints, and the relics of the churches of her native city before she embarked upon her life in Aragon.

By mid-August, Jeanne and her companions were in southern France; a chronicler recorded her entry into Montpellier on 23 August and her departure six days later.[4] Subsequently, her entourage was delayed at Béziers, 95 kilometers north of Perpignan, because Jeanne had fallen ill. She would die in Béziers on 16 September 1371, and her body was taken to the cathedral of Saint-Nazaire

---

2 The exact date of her departure is not known. Pierre Aymé was paid 300 francs for each month of the trip by order of 25 June 1371; see *Mandements et actes divers de Charles V*, ed. Léopold Delisle (Paris, 1874), p. 404. On 2 July 1371, Charles V paid the knight Philippe de Villiers 400 francs for the expenses of accompanying her; *Mandements de Charles V*, p. 407. On the details of this trip and the participation of Jacqueline de Dammartin, see Roland Delachenal, *Histoire de Charles V*, 5 vols. (Paris, 1909–31), 4:389–90.

3 *Mandements de Charles V*, p. 403.

4 *Thalamus parvus. Le petit thalamus de Montpellier*, ed. La Société Archéologique de Montpellier (Montpellier, 1841), p. 386.

INTRODUCTION

there.[5] Sometime in the fall of 1371, Jeanne's body was transported to Paris for burial at the abbey church of Saint-Denis, where her mother furnished a chapel for Jeanne and herself among her Capetian ancestors (see chap. 1 below). Despite having moved her daughter's body to Paris, Blanche of Navarre commissioned a tomb or a memorial for her at Saint-Nazaire in Béziers.[6] This memorial monument was destroyed in 1562; its presence in the church nearly 200 years later despite the transfer of Jeanne's remains to Saint-Denis suggests that a part of her body may have been left at Saint-Nazaire for burial, perhaps her entrails.[7] The commission of a tomb or a memorial in Béziers might seem odd, considering this distant town had no other evident familial or devotional significance for Blanche. But once her daughter had died there, it seems that the church of Saint-Nazaire became part of the biography of Blanche and her daughter; she commemorated its significance in her life and the memory of her daughter through a visual marker of her daughter's passing there. This practice is reminiscent of Jeanne's pilgrimages to the churches of Paris to distribute money; by her patronage, funded by Charles V, Jeanne had demonstrated her change in status and identity, from a French princess to a new bride and a future queen of Aragon.

At some point in their journey, the entourage of Jeanne of France ran into financial difficulties, likely a result of the funds expended on the unexpected stay at Béziers, and some of the bride's wedding gifts had to be pawned. The unlucky travelers have left a serendipitous record, however, because some of the pawned gifts are described in an April 1372 act by King Charles V, who wanted to retrieve them.[8] They included a large silver-gilt *nef* (an elaborate metal table vessel in the form of a ship) from Jeanne's half-brother, Philip, duke of Orléans, as well as a set of silver tableware that included four cups, four ewers, two large basins for spices, and a silver-gilt vessel for alms. This set is

---

5   *Thalamus parvus. Le petit thalamus de Montpellier*, p. 386. Blanche left money to Saint-Nazaire in her will, indicating it was the church in which her daughter had initially been buried; Léopold Delisle, "Testament de Blanche de Navarre, reine de France," *Mémoires de la Société de l'histoire de Paris et de l'Ile de France* 12 (1885), 1–64, no. 527.

6   The tomb memorial was destroyed on 6 May 1562; Claude de Vic and Joseph Vaissete, *Histoire générale de Languedoc, avec des notes et les pièces justificatives*, 5 vols. (Toulouse, 1872), 4:271.

7   Étienne Sabatier called it an entrails tomb and said it was supported by columns with fleur-de-lis; *Histoire de la ville et des évêques de Béziers* (Paris, 1854), p. 336. For the practice of dividing the body at burial, see Elizabeth A.R. Brown, "Death and the Human Body in the Later Middle Ages: The Legislation of Boniface VIII on the Division of the Corpse," *Viator* 12 (1981), 221–70.

8   *Mandements de Charles V*, pp. 453–54.

described as a gift from the pope, Gregory XI, at this time resident himself in Avignon. These goods were pledged for 1,000 francs, which Charles V had already repaid at the writing of the June 1372 document, and he wanted the objects returned to Blanche of Navarre.

The documentary traces of this ill-fated wedding voyage reveal the kind of gift, silver tableware, that might be expected for a royal wedding in the 14th century. The records also demonstrate that the pope was generous in his gifts to the French princess because his silver items were among those valuable enough to be pawned. We discover that Charles V worked to ensure that Jeanne's wedding gifts were returned to her mother, probably at Blanche's request. That the objects themselves were to be returned, not just financial remuneration for them, is an indication that the objects had value beyond the monetary, whether emotional, because they were a deceased daughter's possessions, or symbolic, because of the elevated status of those who gave, such as the pope.

Another important point should be highlighted in this narrative. None of these works survives, neither the Béziers tomb nor any of the tableware; we know about them only through written descriptions. If pieces of the silver survive in a museum or private collection, they are not still associated with the name of Jeanne of France or Blanche of Navarre. A reconstruction of Blanche's collection from documentary evidence like the records of Charles V, or from the evidence of her testament, adds these objects to the history of art even if they do not exist in physical form.

Blanche of Navarre was an important figure of her era at the French court, a dowager queen, an advisor to the kings of France, and to her brother, Charles II (1332–87), king of Navarre, and a mediator in times of crisis during the Hundred Years War, though histories of the 14th century in France have mostly neglected her life. She was born in 1331, married to Philip VI at 18 in 1350, and a widow seven months later. She was pregnant at her husband's death and her daughter Jeanne was born in May 1351. She lived in and near Paris with her daughter and a community of women that variously included her sister Jeanne of Rohan, her aunt Jeanne of Evreux, as well as the wife of her brother Charles, another Jeanne. Her oldest brother is known to history as Charles the Bad because of his attempts in the 1350s and 1360s to unseat the French kings. These crises and Blanche's role in resolving them are described more fully in the first chapter. Since there is so much surviving documentary evidence about Blanche of Navarre, it would be possible to write a fairly complete biography; for this project, however, I am interested in her biography as it intersects with her patronage and her possessions.

INTRODUCTION

As a widow with substantial land holdings, Blanche had the resources to commission works of art that are associated only with her, not with a husband whose motivations and interests might obscure those of his wife. Of the hundreds of works of art that must have passed through Blanche's hands or been commissioned by her, only a small number survive, and a handful more are known through later copies. These works are illustrated in the chapters that follow. The Saint-Denis tomb sculptures are kept today in the chapel she founded at Saint-Denis (Fig. 1.2), and the documents founding this chapel with their historiated initials showing Blanche and her family are in the Archives nationales in Paris (Figs. 1.1, 1.3). Two funerary monuments surviving only in fragmentary form are the heart tombs of Blanche's parents that were sculpted for the church of the Jacobins in Paris; only the heads are extant (Figs. 1.13, 1.14). Of Blanche's many textiles, a single vestment in the collection of the treasury of the cathedral of Sens is still associated with her (Figs. 6.1–6.3). The stained-glass windows that she may have commissioned for the cathedral of Evreux are also still *in situ*.[9]

One manuscript that passed through her collection survives: the psalter of Saint Louis today in the library of Leiden University in the Netherlands (Fig. 3.3). The *Somme le roi* manuscript of Philip the Fair in the British Library may also have been in Blanche's collection (Fig. 3.5). Some of Blanche's commissions survive in reproductions made for French antiquarians in the 17th and 18th centuries: François Roger de Gaignières commissioned copies of the tomb and paintings in her chapel at Saint-Denis and the heart tomb for her husband Philip VI from the church of the Jacobins (Figs. 1.4, 1.9–1.10, 1.12); Aubin-Louis Millin reproduced a reliquary that Blanche commissioned for the church of Vernon showing herself with the Virgin Mary (Fig. 4.5);[10] Gaignières also had a copy made of a no-longer-extant painting in the chapel of Saint Michel in the Palais de la Cité in which Blanche is shown kneeling across from her husband (Fig. 1.11); I argue below that it seems unlikely that she commissioned this work. Another image that represents Blanche, not commissioned by her, is in the *Grandes chroniques* of Charles V; Blanche is shown with Jeanne of Evreux facilitating a reconciliation between her brother Charles of Navarre and King Charles V. In this book, I consider this corpus of works as well as

---

9   For the windows, see below, chap. 1, n. 114.

10   Aubin-Louis Millin, *Antiquités nationales, ou Recueil des monumens pour servir à l'histoire générale et particulière de l'empire françois*, 5 vols. (Paris, 1791), vol. 3; the image is reproduced on the page between pages 18 and 19.

6   INTRODUCTION

those that are known only through textual evidence, reconstructing them from written descriptions in testaments, inventories, and other records.

The most important evidence about Blanche's life and object ownership comes from her testament and codicils of 1396 and 1398 in which she described her possessions in detail.[11] In chapter 2, I emphasize the importance of the testaments not just for their contents, but also as a genre of discourse. In other words, Blanche's testament, though primarily a legal document, might also serve as a historical source, as an inventory of a queen's collection, and ultimately, as a kind of autobiography.[12] To give a picture of patronage, a scholar typically must assemble all the archival records related to works of art owned by the patron and then interpret them for intention, but in her testament Blanche herself gave this summary of what she thought of her collection at a particular time in her life. Katherine Lewis has written about testaments as autobiographical compositions, noting their importance particularly considering the relatively sparse documentation left by women.[13] One of the goals of autobiography was to establish posthumous reputation; and, indeed, throughout Blanche's testament she indicated her interest in being remembered fondly by the recipients of her possessions.[14] Like an autobiographical narrative, the details of Blanche's testament corroborate those of her life known through other evidence, such as her close relationship with Pierre Basin, her confessor. The archival record shows that he was acting on her behalf (with regard to the testament of her brother, Philip) as early as March 1364. That he was still in her service at the end of her life is one indicator of their close relationship; another is the intimacy of the gifts she left him, such as a reliquary statuette of Saint Catherine that she kept by her bed (analyzed further in chap. 4).[15]

---

11   The surviving wills from 1396 and 1398 are in Pau, Archives départementales des Pyrénées-Atlantiques, E 525. They were published by Léopold Delisle, "Testament de Blanche de Navarre," pp. 1–64. Blanche probably made other wills that do not survive; I consider this question in chapter 2.

12   A model for the use of wills and other legal documents to understand social history and gender roles is Martha Howell's *The Marriage Exchange: Property, Social Place, and Gender in Cities of the Low Countries, 1300–1550* (Chicago, 1998).

13   Katherine Lewis, "Female Life-writing and the Testamentary Discourse: Women and Their Wills in Later Medieval England," in *Medieval Women and the Law*, ed. Noël James Menuge (Woodbridge, UK, 2003), pp. 57–75.

14   Lewis, "Female Life-writing and the Testamentary Discourse," p. 63.

15   I use the definition of 'service' offered by Anne Curry and Elizabeth Matthew: "the word commonly used for the work, whether paid or unpaid, performed by a servant, attendant or official for his or her lord or lady, master or mistress"; "Introduction," in *Concepts and*

INTRODUCTION

After establishing in chapter 2 the genre and context of the testament as a discourse about ownership and memory, I consider in the last four chapters those objects described in Blanche's testament, with some additional objects that can be added to Blanche's collection based on evidence from other inventories or testaments. There are a number of ways to separate Blanche's possessions into productive categories for analysis; I have chosen to divide the material by medium and use. Books, the largest single type of item described in Blanche's testament, are discussed in chapter 3. The analysis of her metalwork objects and paintings follows in the next two chapters, first reliquaries and paintings, and then jewelry and precious stones. The term I will use to describe metalwork objects is *joyaux*, the word used to describe them in medieval inventories.[16] Finally, the last chapter is devoted to Blanche's textiles, such as vestments, room hangings that decorated her household, and her clothing.

Blanche's motivations for patronage aligned her with those of many other medieval women who sought benefit – political, social, and spiritual – through participation in the creation and dissemination of the visual arts.[17] Particularly important for this study is the historiography of the patronage of royal women, who had the resources to commission works of art much more ambitiously than did most medieval women.[18] These queenship studies have developed

---

      Patterns of Service in the Later Middle Ages, ed. Anne Curry and Elizabeth Matthew (Woodbridge, UK, 2000), p. xiv.

16   Timothy Husband, in his discussion of John, duke of Berry's collecting practices, defined *joyaux* as: "any object of goldsmiths' works generally studded with gemstones and often decorated with enamels ... Joyaux also included vessels of cut and polished rock crystal or a variety of semiprecious hardstones mounted in gold and likewise enameled and studded with gems"; *The Art of Illumination: The Limbourg Brothers and the* Belles Heures *of Jean de France, Duc de Berry* (New York, 2008), p. 19.

17   For case studies of female patronage, see the essays in *The Cultural Patronage of Medieval Women*, ed. June Hall McCash (Athens, Ga., 1996).

18   A model for my study of the material culture of Blanche of Navarre is the analysis of the patronage of Mahaut of Artois by Jules-Marie Richard, who linked Mahaut's patronage to her biography using the plentiful documentary evidence in the Archives of the Pas-de-Calais; *Une petite-nièce de Saint Louis, Mahaut, comtesse d'Artois et de Bourgogne (1302–1329). Étude sur la vie privée, les arts et l'industrie, en Artois et à Paris au commencement du XIVe siècle* (Paris, 1887). An early study of a queen's image in the visual arts with an explicitly feminist motivation is Claire Richter Sherman's "Taking a Second Look: Observations on the Iconography of a French Queen, Jeanne de Bourbon (1338–1378)," in *Feminism and Art History: Questioning the Litany*, ed. Norma Broude and Mary Garrard (New York, 1982), pp. 100–117. The collected essays in *Capetian Women*, ed. Kathleen Nolan (New York, 2003), offer varied models and case studies for understanding the patronage of medieval women associated with this dynasty. Kathleen Nolan studied the ways in which 12th- and

theoretical models for understanding how queens accessed and exercised power. If we consider, according to Theresa Earenfight's model, that queenship was a "discursive practice" and "a daily act of reconstruction and interpretation," Blanche's identity – and her status and privileges that came with it – was in part dependent on her choices and the way she presented her identity as a dowager queen.[19] Scholars have suggested that two roles in particular were important for medieval dowager queens, that of mediator and that of mother, both of which offered access to power.[20] An analysis of Blanche's testament and patronage of the visual arts demonstrates that she sought to emphasize her identification with each of these roles.

13th-century Capetian queens asserted their identities visually through seals and tombs in *Queens in Stone and Silver: The Creation of a Visual Imagery of Queenship in Capetian France* (New York, 2009). Recently, Therese Martin has edited a two-volume set of essays with many significant contributions to the study of the patronage of medieval queens: *Reassessing the Roles of Women as 'Makers' of Medieval Art and Architecture*, 2 vols. (Leiden, 2012). The essays in this publication address queens from different areas in Europe, including France, Iberia, and England, a valuable cross-cultural comparison. Finally, for a recent synthetic survey of the field of queenship studies, see Theresa Earenfight, *Queenship in Medieval Europe* (Basingstoke, 2013); for the kingdom of Navarre, see Elena Woodacre, *The Queens Regnant of Navarre: Succession, Politics, and Partnership, 1274–1512* (New York, 2013); and for 14th-century England, see Lisa Benz St. John, *Three Medieval Queens: Queenship and the Crown in Fourteenth-century England* (Basingstoke, 2012).

19   Earenfight, *Queenship in Medieval Europe*, p. 25.

20   For a recent study of the roles of mother and intercessor in 14th-century conceptions of queenship, see Benz St. John, *Three Medieval Queens*, pp. 19–63, 95–131. On the queen as mediator, see Lois Honeycutt, "Intercession and the High Medieval Queen: The Esther Topos," in *Power of the Weak: Studies on Medieval Women*, ed. Jennifer Carpenter and Sally-Beth McLean (Urbana, Ill., 1995), pp. 126–46; John Carmi Parsons, "The Queen's Intercession in Thirteenth-century England," in *Power of the Weak*, pp. 147–77; Paul Strohm, "The Queen's Intercession," in his *Hochon's Arrow: The Social Imagination of Fourteenth-century Texts* (Princeton, 1992), pp. 95–119. On Isabeau of Bavaria as a mediator queen, see Tracy Adams, *The Life and Afterlife of Isabeau of Bavaria* (Baltimore, 2010), pp. 73–112. For the importance of a familial context for medieval queens, see John Carmi Parsons, "Introduction: Family, Sex, and Power: The Rhythms of Medieval Queenship," and his "Mothers, Daughters, Marriage, Power: Some Plantagenet Evidence," both in *Medieval Queenship*, ed. John Carmi Parsons (New York, 1993), pp. 1–11, 63–78. For an analysis of the significance of the representation of motherhood in a queen's book, see Anne Rudloff Stanton, "From Eve to Bathsheba and Beyond: Motherhood in the Queen Mary Psalter," in *Women and the Book: Assessing the Visual Evidence*, ed. Lesley Smith and Jane H.M. Taylor (London, 1997), pp. 172–89.

INTRODUCTION

Blanche was one among many patrons of works of art at the French court in the second half of the 14th century. Without question, the most important patron to consider for framing the analysis of Blanche of Navarre's patronage is Jeanne of Evreux, her aunt. Blanche was married at the queen's château in 1350, they worked in unison as mediators between Charles of Navarre and the French kings, they both furnished objects for chapels at Saint-Denis, and Blanche left instructions for her funeral to follow the model of Jeanne's. The surviving testamentary acts of Jeanne of Evreux help to contextualize Blanche's testament, as well as assist in the tracing of objects that passed through the collections of each queen.[21] The patronage and object ownership of Jeanne has been extensively published, a result of the fame of her book of hours today at The Cloisters (Fig. 3.1) and her Virgin and Child reliquary statuette (Fig. 4.4), given to Saint-Denis in 1339 and today part of the collection of the Louvre; both items will be discussed below.[22]

The larger context for Blanche's object ownership is the ambitious and wide-ranging patronage of works of art by members of the French royal family in the second half of the 14th century.[23] Blanche knew personally nearly all the

---

21 Jeanne of Evreux's final testament and two codicils are lost but were copied in the 17th century by Jacques Menant: Rouen, Bibliothèque municipale, MS 3403, Leber 5870. An excerpt of the Menant manuscript was copied by Constant Leber and published in *Collection des meilleurs dissertations, notices et traits particuliers relatives à l'histoire de France*, 20 vols. (Paris, 1838), 19:120–69. For the queen's astute control over her testaments and memory, see Elizabeth A.R. Brown, "The Testamentary Strategies of Jeanne d'Évreux: The Endowment of Saint-Denis in 1343," in *Magistra Doctissima: Essays in Honor of Bonnie Wheeler*, ed. Dorsey Armstrong, Ann W. Astell, and Howell Chickering (Kalamazoo, Mich., 2013), pp. 217–47.

22 For an overview of Jeanne's patronage and collection, see Barbara Drake Boehm, "Jeanne d'Évreux: Queen of France," in *The Hours of Jeanne d'Évreux. Acc. No. 54.I.2 The Metropolitan Museum of Art, The Cloisters Collection, New York: Commentary* (Lucerne, 2000), pp. 35–87, and Boehm, "Le mécénat de Jeanne d'Évreux," in *1300 ... l'art au temps de Philippe le Bel. Actes du colloque international, Galeries nationales du Grand Palais, 24 et 25 juin 1998*, ed. Danielle Gaborit-Chopin and François Avril, with Marie-Cécile Bardos (Paris, 2001), pp. 15–31. For specific aspects of her patronage, see Carla Lord, "Jeanne d'Évreux as a Founder of Chapels: Patronage and Public Piety," in *Women and Art in Early Modern Europe: Patrons, Collectors, and Connoisseurs*, ed. Cynthia Lawrence (University Park, PA, 1997), pp. 21–36, and Joan Holladay, "Fourteenth-century French Queens as Collectors and Readers of Books: Jeanne d'Evreux and Her Contemporaries," *Journal of Medieval History* 32 (2006), 69–100.

23 This period and the gifting practices of the Valois princes has been studied by Brigitte Buettner, "Past Presents: New Year's Gifts at the Valois Courts c. 1400," *Art Bulletin* 83, no. 4 (Dec. 2001), 598–625. The competition among Valois princes for lavish works of art is also

10   INTRODUCTION

great art patrons in France in the decades between 1350 and 1400, among them the French king Charles V, and his brothers Louis of Anjou, John of Berry, and Philip of Burgundy.[24] The collections of these individuals were vast, they were well inventoried, and many of their works survive; they serve therefore as valuable comparative evidence for Blanche's collection. The scholarly patronage studies of men like John of Berry and women like Jeanne of Evreux have linked the patrons' personalities to their object collecting, seeking to elucidate taste and aesthetic preferences; this model is important to my interpretation of Blanche's testament.[25] The smaller collections and patronage practices of royal women like Jeanne of Burgundy, Blanche of Orléans, and Jeanne of Rohan will also serve as important comparative material, especially with regard to their testamentary practices and the evidence of their motivations in commissioning and disseminating works of art.

Recent patronage studies, particularly those that consider medieval women, have complicated the traditional definition of a patron: the person who paid for the work.[26] Though payment records for Blanche of Navarre do survive in

---

considered by Timothy Husband as one of the defining markers of their patronage; "Jean de France, duc de Berry," in *The Art of Illumination*, pp. 10–31. The increase in the number of books collected by the Valois beginning with Charles V is noted by Joan Holladay, who suggests that "a library of a certain size was considered a necessary accoutrement for a prince of a certain status"; "Fourteenth-century French Queens," p. 96.

24 Among the many publications on these figures, those associated with exhibitions have offered substantive overviews of their patronage, such as *Paris 1400: les arts sous Charles VI* (Paris, 2004); *Art from the Court of Burgundy: Patronage of Philip the Bold and John the Fearless, 1364–1419* (Cleveland, 2004); Husband, *The Art of Illumination*, as well as the older *Les fastes du gothique: le siècle de Charles V* (Paris, 1981).

25 In his recent study of the duke's patronage, Timothy Husband noted that it is possible to describe the duke's taste in objects, a taste he describes as "conspicuous extravagance"; "Jean de France, duc de Berry," in *The Art of Illumination*, pp. 10–31. Michael Camille also studied the connections between the duke's personality and his patronage of works of art: "'For Our Devotion and Pleasure': The Sexual Objects of Jean, Duc de Berry," in *Other Objects of Desire: Collectors and Collecting Queerly*, ed. Michael Camille and Adrian Rifkin (Oxford, 2001), 7–32. For the patronage of Jeanne of Evreux, see Boehm, "Le mécénat de Jeanne d'Évreux," pp. 15–31.

26 For a discussion of the paradigm of medieval patronage, see Holly Flora, "Patronage," in *Medieval Art History Today: Critical Terms*, ed. Nina Rowe, special issue of *Studies in Iconography* 33 (2012), 207–18. Madeline Caviness has analyzed some of the implications of the role of patron or recipient for medieval women in "Anchoress, Abbess and Queen: Donors and Patrons or Intercessors and Matrons?" in *The Cultural Patronage of Medieval Women*, 105–54. For a historiographic overview, see Jill Caskey, "Whodunnit? Patronage, the Canon, and the Problematics of Agency in Romanesque and Gothic Art," in *A*

INTRODUCTION

fragmentary form, none is thorough enough to create a full picture of how and when she spent her funds on works of art. Indeed, for one of the most important monuments of her life, the funerary chapel of herself and her daughter Jeanne, discussed above, she collaborated at least in part with the French king Charles V.[27] At the same time, the charter initial shows Blanche of Navarre presenting the chapel; she holds the model of the chapel firmly in her own hands (Fig. 1.1). Other objects, like the room hangings decorated with the letter B that Blanche acquired between 1396 and 1398 (discussed in chap. 6), might have been gifts rather than purchases. In her study of Blanche's testament, Brigitte Buettner suggested that it should serve as an impetus for reconsideration of paradigms of medieval patronage, arguing that a notion of patronage that involves a contract between two persons does not sufficiently characterize the patterns of object movement memorialized in Blanche's will.[28] Therese Martin has proposed that a model for understanding medieval patronage might focus on the 'maker': "a person without [whom] the work would not exist."[29] Martin's example to illustrate the role of the maker is the Eleanor Vase, which has an inscription noting its ownership by Eleanor of Aquitaine before it came into the possession of Abbot Suger and Saint-Denis. Martin writes that "Eleanor 'made' neither the original vase nor its metalwork additions, but her prestige was such that the object was considered to have proceeded more from her than from any of the men through whose hands it also passed."[30] In this book,

---

    Companion to Medieval Art: Romanesque and Gothic in Northern Europe, ed. Conrad Rudolph (Oxford, 2006), pp. 193–212.

27   A document dated 4 November 1371, arranging the transport of the body of Jeanne of France back to Paris, stated in part the king's obligation, which seems to have included having Jeanne's tomb created: "Item, le Roy fera apporter le corps de ledite madame Jehanne à Saint-Denys en France où elle a esleve sa sepultre et fera faire tous les services, obsèques et solennitez à cause de ce dedenz la Toussains prouchain venant ou plus tost s'il puer estre fait bonnement. Item fera faire le Roy la tumbe et sépultre de ladicte madame Jehanne selon l'estat d'elle"; Léon de Laborde, *Musée des Archives (de l'Empire) nationales, Actes importants de l'histoire de France* (Paris, 1867), pp. 224–25, citing Archives nationales J 405, no. 15.

28   Brigitte Buettner, "Le système des objets dans le testament de Blanche de Navarre," *CLIO: Histoire, Femmes et Sociétés* 19 (2004), 37–62. Professor Buettner and I discussed our mutual interest in Blanche of Navarre in 2002 when I shared my dissertation chapter with her. Her theoretical model for patronage proposed in this article has been an important influence on my own study of Blanche's collection.

29   Therese Martin, "Exceptions and Assumptions: Women in Medieval Art History," in *Reassessing the Roles of Women as 'Makers' of Medieval Art and Architecture*, 1:1–33.

30   Martin, "Exceptions and Assumptions," p. 8.

Blanche is the patron and the 'maker,' because the objects she owned are associated with her and her ancestors; she was the conduit for their dissemination.

To be a conduit for a work of art, or a gift-giver, was also an avenue for the exercise of power.[31] It was particularly important for medieval queens, whose access to political power might otherwise be relatively limited. In the next chapter, I analyze the implications for Blanche of inheriting the *joyaux* of her husband, Philip VI. Though the *joyaux* are not named individually in the will of Philip VI (with the exception of a crown, analyzed further below), among them must have been the reliquary belt and the beloved diamond discussed in the first paragraph of this introduction. At the end of her life she still had five of his metalwork items, an indication also that she had utilized this agency by giving away most of the metalwork. By giving Blanche his *joyaux*, Philip VI bestowed on her a lifelong gifting agency, raising her status and making her a particularly potent force in the heated competition for works of art of the Valois court. The five objects remaining – a reliquary belt and brooch, a sealing ring, a diamond ring, and a diamond that he loved (all discussed in chap. 5) – went to the French king, Charles VI, and to the dukes of Bourbon, Burgundy, and Berry. Blanche could garner influence with the French king and his uncles by giving them these objects owned by her late husband and their ancestor.[32]

An analysis of Blanche as a patron raises the related issue of visual display and the role of works of art in creating and reifying status, especially for someone whose power and influence depended on the continued assertion of her position as dowager queen. In addition, Blanche may have been insecure as a result of not having been crowned, a factor that will be analyzed in the next chapter. Blanche owned and commissioned a number of works that were meant to display her status to others, such as the reliquary belt and sealing ring from her husband. These two objects are quite clearly about power associated with visual display since a belt is part of the regalia of a king and a ring is used

---

31   Brigitte Buettner has studied the annual ritual of gift-giving known as the *étrennes* during the reign of Charles VI in "Past Presents: New Year's Gifts at the Valois Courts c. 1400," pp. 598–625.

32   Another queen who used gifts to leverage power was Blanche of Castile; Miriam Shadis has described this queen's collecting and gifting practices as part of her duties as mediator and a kind of 'undocumented' source of power; see Miriam Shadis, "Blanche of Castile and Facinger's 'Medieval Queenship'; Reassessing the Argument," in *Capetian Women*, pp. 137–61; for this argument specifically, see p. 145. Mariah Proctor-Tiffany has analyzed the gift strategies of Clémence of Hungary in "Transported as a Rare Object of Distinction: The Gift-giving of Clémence of Hungary, Queen of France," *Journal of Medieval History* 41, no. 2 (2015), 208–28.

INTRODUCTION 13

to seal documents and to confer official approval. Beyond these objects, the tomb project at Saint-Denis is also part of a visual display of status: the figures on the tomb were arrayed to emphasize Blanche's descent from Saint Louis. The importance of regalia and royal identity recurs as a theme, both in its celebration and in the piety or humility that was occasionally signaled when such regalia was sold or given away.

I also consider gender analysis with regard to the acquisition and dissemination of works of art.[33] Blanche constructed gender for her recipients (in other words, she thought particular objects were suited to men or women, something that will be particularly evident in the chapter on books), and she made reference to gender roles. For example, a book from which her daughter learned to read was given to a woman; in this way Blanche commemorated the role of women as educators of young family members. A series of crowns given to her goddaughters described Blanche's obligation to provide financially for these girls on the occasion of their marriages (the gifts of the crowns are analyzed in chap. 5). A gendered provenance (if a man or a woman had owned an object previously) might have been another way for Blanche to direct her possessions, but she did not seem to privilege the dissemination of objects in this way.[34] It seems more likely that the gendered identity created by the gift of an object depended on the intention of the giver and the content (the subject matter of a book, for instance) rather than on any gendered quality associated with an object by its provenance; an example would be Blanche's gift of the psalter of Saint Louis, which had been owned by Agnes and Jeanne of Burgundy, to Philip of Burgundy (Fig. 3.3).

As a result of having so much textual information in the testament about what objects looked like, this project also has a distinctive focus on the materiality of the objects in Blanche's collection. Analysis of materials and the symbolic importance assigned to them help to elucidate patterns of meaning. For example, Blanche gave away twenty-eight reliquaries in her will: eighteen were given to churches, ten to individuals. The reliquaries given to churches were nearly all silver or silver-gilt, whereas those given to individuals are described as gold. None given to churches have precious stones on them, but

---

33   The ways in which gender might be used as a category for analyzing medieval art have been described by Sherry C.M. Lindquist, "Gender," in *Medieval Art History Today: Critical Terms*, pp. 113–30. See also Rachel Dressler, "Continuing the Discourse: Feminist Scholarship and the Study of Medieval Visual Culture," *Medieval Feminist Forum* 43, no. 1 (2007), 15–34.

34   For a different perspective on gendered objects in Blanche's will, see Brigitte Buettner's discussion of "le sexe des objets" in "Le système des objets," pp. 37–62.

nearly all of the objects given to individuals do. What can we learn about the value and meaning of materials like gold, silver, and precious stones in the Middle Ages by studying Blanche's collecting and gifting practices? Beyond meaning and appearance, I also consider use and storage. Why might one work rather than another be kept near Blanche's bed, for example? Blanche's testaments offer a trove of evidence for such analysis.

The discussion of materials reflects another important methodological interest, namely, in material culture. The interdisciplinary method is complex and encompasses a number of different areas of study, but here I am interested in the dissolution of traditional differentiations in art-historical study between high art and 'minor arts,' such as metalwork or domestic textiles.[35] My approach foregrounds the analysis of the life of the object as it was acquired, used and enjoyed, and redeployed by its owner.[36] I also consider how Blanche described her objects and what that may indicate about how she valued them. A related methodological approach to material culture is the study of collecting. What might a manuscript owned by Saint Louis have signified for him and how would this meaning have been altered for a later owner? In other words, how does a change in the context in which the same work of art is perceived over generations create new meaning? Should Blanche of Navarre be considered a 'collector' or is such a designation anachronistic? Did Blanche perceive the things she commissioned or owned to be part of a collection, or is that term

---

35   See Michael Yonan, "Toward a Fusion of Art History and Material Culture Studies," *West 86th: A Journal of Decorative Arts, Design History, and Material Culture* 18, no. 2 (Fall 2011), 232–48, and Christopher Tilley, "Introduction," in *Handbook of Material Culture* (London, 2006), pp. 1–6. An important study of the material culture of medieval courts is Malcolm Vale, *The Princely Court: Medieval Courts and Culture in North-West Europe, 1270–1380* (Oxford, 2001). For recent discussions of material culture particularly relevant to art history, see Beth Williamson, "Material Culture and Medieval Christianity," in *The Oxford Handbook of Medieval Christianity* (Oxford, 2014), pp. 60–75, and the essays in *Everyday Objects: Medieval and Early Modern Material Culture and Its Meanings*, ed. Tara Hamling and Catherine Richardson (Farnham, Surrey, UK, 2010), as well as Katherine McIver, "Material Culture: Consumption, Collecting and Domestic Goods," in *The Ashgate Research Companion to Women and Gender in Early Modern Europe*, ed. Allyson Poska, Jane Couchman, and Katherine McIver (Farnham, Surrey, UK, 2013), pp. 469–88.

36   For this I depend on the theoretical model proposed by Arjun Appadurai, "Introduction: Commodities and the Politics of Value," in *The Social Life of Things: Commodities in Cultural Perspective*, ed. Arjun Appadurai (Cambridge, 1986), pp. 3–63. For a perceptive application of Appadurai's ideas to the history of ownership of works of art, see Anne Higonnet, "Afterword: The Social Life of Provenance," in *Provenance: An Alternate History of Art* (Los Angeles, 2012), pp. 195–209.

INTRODUCTION

more appropriate for post-Renaissance history? For this project, I use Pierre Alain Mariaux's definition of collecting: "the collection is an assembly of *chosen* objects (for their beauty, rarity, curious character, documentary value, or expense), and it presupposes the presence of an individual, a collector. It is he or she who makes a deliberate choice."[37] By this definition, the implications of which are evident throughout the book, Blanche was a collector.

In this study I consider all of this evidence, combining several approaches: art historical and material (interpreting the objects); historical (reconstructing Blanche's milieu and analyzing archival evidence); and literary (analyzing the text of the testament as an autobiographical document). From this extensive evidence emerges a portrait of a female patron in the Middle Ages; on view are her aesthetic choices, exercises of power and authority, visual display of identity, and relationships with relatives and members of her household. The strength of this cross-media approach to objects permits the analysis of commissions like the tomb project at Saint-Denis with the descriptions of the testament, considering the elements that tie these different projects together and how they speak to each other. I want to look at the constellation of objects – a personal visual culture – that radiates out from one person. The division of the book by material is unfortunately artificial and downplays Blanche's relationships with people and her desire to link gifts; only occasionally in each chapter do I discuss the gifts to a single person as a group. But in a book about material culture it seems crucial to focus on the objects themselves, and the analysis of the diamond that Philip VI "loved a lot" is more compelling when it is paired with the study of Blanche's other diamonds and precious stones, rather than with the book of hours that was the other gift Blanche gave to the duke of Berry. Separating the items by material is also beneficial to modern scholars because it abides by the boundaries of disciplinary research, so that a discussion of textiles, for example, is easier to find in chapter 6 than if it were scattered throughout the book. One of my primary goals is to make Blanche's testament, an extraordinary document that is still too little-known, more accessible, and it seems to me that this organization of the material is one of the best ways to do this.

To assist the reader in understanding the stakes and the larger implications of the family ties that were marked with objects, a brief overview of family relationships at the French court follows. Blanche's life spanned the rule of four French kings, all members of the Valois dynasty: Philip VI (r. 1328–50), John II (r. 1350–64), Charles V (r. 1364–80), and Charles VI (r. 1380–1422). These

---

37   Pierre Mariaux, "Collecting (and Display)," in *A Companion to Medieval Art*, pp. 213–32.

TABLE 0.1   *Genealogical table of the family of Blanche of Navarre, part 1.* TABLE BY SONJA SEKELY-ROWLAND.

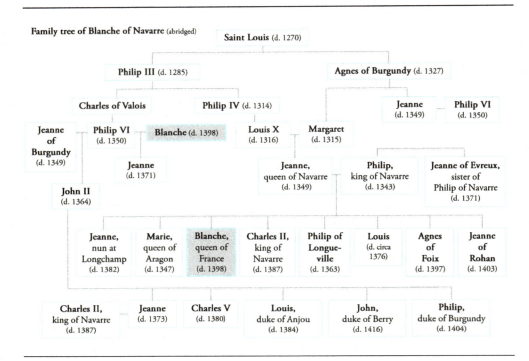

kings were descended from the French king Philip III (r. 1270–85) through his son Charles of Valois (see Tables 1 and 2: genealogical tables). Also of high status at court were those individuals descended from Philip IV (r. 1285–1314), such as Jeanne of Evreux, as well as Blanche herself and her brothers and sisters. I argue that Blanche saw herself as the repository of this family history and that the testament bestowed this authority and identity, through objects, on the family members still alive in 1396. Included in this group were King Charles VI, his wife, Isabeau of Bavaria, and the king's uncles, John, duke of Berry, Philip, duke of Burgundy, and Louis, duke of Bourbon, as well as the brother of Charles VI, Louis, duke of Orléans, and the wives of all of these dukes. The fraying of these family ties was an impetus for the crises of the Hundred Years war, which dragged on with various levels of intensity throughout Blanche's life; I discuss her involvement in it in the next chapter.

INTRODUCTION

TABLE 0.2   *Genealogical table of the family of Blanche of Navarre, part 2*. TABLE BY SONJA SEKELY-ROWLAND.

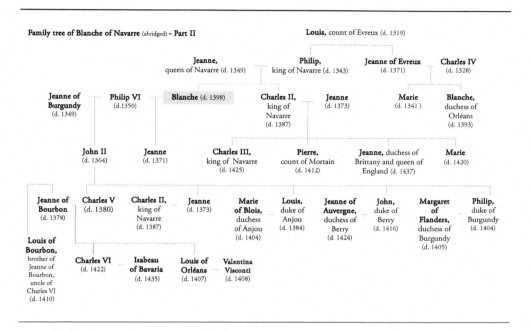

Another family wedding is crucial in this narrative, that of Blanche's niece Marie of Navarre, daughter of her brother Charles, who was married in 1396. In her testament, Blanche left her a hat that was still unfinished (the only object so described in the testament) and a book of hours that she said she had bought in Paris (again, it was rare that she would indicate that an item was purchased). These gifts, along with bedsheets and another book, full of advice, were intended surely for the bride on the occasion of her wedding; they are all considered in the analysis that follows. In addition to revealing the gifts that Blanche thought appropriate for a wedding gift for a niece, this bequest also tells us about the use of clothing, bedding, and books, as well as the distinction between things that had to be purchased and things that she owned that she would give the bride. This evidence is available not through payment records, as in the wedding of Jeanne of France discussed at the beginning of this introduction, but through the bequests of the testament. The study of Blanche's collection is of value for the history of art, for the history of queens, of medieval women, of books and their owners, of the medieval household, of textiles and clothing, of the use of reliquaries in devotion. It shows us Blanche's obligations, how she constructed gender for her recipients, and what objects might mark an important transition in status for a medieval woman.

CHAPTER 1

The Life and Patronage of Blanche of Navarre

In 1372, Blanche furnished the two-bay chapel of Saint Hippolyte, the first chapel west of the south transept at the abbey church of Saint-Denis, to serve as a burial site for her recently deceased daughter, Jeanne (Fig. 1.2).[1] This chapel is the best-known of her commissions because Saint-Denis, wealthy abbey and privileged royal burial site, has been abundantly documented relative to other medieval monuments, even if very few objects survive from Blanche's chapel today.[2] The chapel exhibits many of the same interests and strategies that recur in Blanche's will and in the other evidence of the material culture of her household – her devotional interests, her desire to be remembered after death, and her association of herself with illustrious family members. In this first chapter, I consider the biography of Blanche of Navarre as it can be reconstructed from medieval documentary sources and as it intersected with her commission of works of art.[3] The analysis of the 1396 and 1398 testaments, the most substantive evidence we have for Blanche's patronage, is reserved for the second chapter; the testaments, because they were written from Blanche's viewpoint, offer a perspective different from those of the other documentary sources for

---

1 Though the documents related to the planning of the chapel foundation date to the early 1370s, Damien Berné has suggested that it is likely that Blanche had conceived of the chapel as an appropriate funerary site in the early 1350s, after the death of her husband, who had died on the feast day of Saint Hippolyte; "L'action mémorielle des princesses capétiennes à Saint-Denis au XIVe siècle," *Histoire de l'art* 63 (Oct. 2008), 35–44; for this material, pp. 39–40.

2 This material was published in part in my essay "Memory and Identity in the Chapel of Blanche of Navarre at Saint-Denis," in *Citation, Intertextuality and Memory in the Middle Ages and Renaissance*, vol. 2: *Cross-Disciplinary Perspectives on Medieval Culture*, ed. Yolanda Plumley and Giuliano di Bacco (Liverpool, 2013), pp. 123–36.

3 Two publications by André Lesort provide the most detailed sources for Blanche's biography: "La Reine Blanche dans le Vexin et le Pays de Bray," *Mémoires de la Société historique et archéologique de l'arrondissement de Pontoise et du Vexin* 54 (1948), 35–67 and 55 (1954), 9–88. Her biography is also considered by María Narbona Cárceles, "La 'Discreción hermosa': Blanca de Navarra, reina de Francia (1331?-1398). Una dama al servicio de su linaje," in *La dama en la corte bajomedieval*, ed. Martí Aurell et al. (Pamplona, 2001), pp. 75–116. Two books that include the life of Blanche as part of a broader study of the biographies of other queens are Catherine Bearne, *Lives and Times of the Early Valois Queens: Jeanne de Bourgogne, Blanche de Navarre, Jeanne d'Auvergne et de Boulogne* (London, 1899) and Jean-Marie Cazilhac, *Jeanne d'Evreux, Blanche de France, deux reines de France, deux douairières, durant la Guerre de Cent Ans* (Paris, 2010).

© KONINKLIJKE BRILL NV, LEIDEN, 2016 | DOI 10.1163/9789004318830_003

FIGURE 1.1 *Blanche of Navarre presenting the chapel of Saint Hippolyte, with family and saints, 1372.* PARIS, ARCHIVES NATIONALES, K 49, NO. 76A. PHOTO CREDIT: ARCHIVES NATIONALES.

her patronage, such as chronicles, letters, payment records, and household accounts.

The historiated initials from the two chapel foundation documents show Blanche carrying a model of her chapel, accompanied by her daughter Jeanne, Philip VI, and a group of saints: Denis, Hippolyte, John the Baptist, Peter, and Paul (Figs. 1.1, 1.3).[4] The texts of the two documents are identical; one is a copy of the other.[5] The miniatures in the initial B of each document are also quite

---

4 The two documents are in Paris, Archives nationales, K 49, nos. 76A and 76B. For the foundation charters, see Ghislain Brunel, *Images du pouvoir royal: les chartes decorées des Archives nationales, XIIIe-XVe siècle* (Paris, 2005), pp. 192–99.

5 Brunel believes that 76B (acte no. 30) is the copy, with 76A (acte no. 29) the original; Brunel, *Images du pouvoir royal*, p. 192.

FIGURE 1.2 *Chapel of Saint Hippolyte, Saint-Denis.* PHOTO CREDIT: SARAH THOMPSON.

FIGURE 1.3 *Blanche of Navarre presenting the chapel of Saint Hippolyte, with family and saints, 1372.* PARIS, ARCHIVES NATIONALES, K 49, NO. 76B. PHOTO CREDIT: ARCHIVES NATIONALES.

similar.[6] In each, a kneeling Blanche wears a long mantle and a wimple with a crown.[7] Jeanne, her hair uncovered and clothed in a cloak with a hood hanging down her back, kneels behind her mother. Opposite the two women is Philip VI, also kneeling, wearing the loose hooded garment with wing sleeves known as a *houce*.[8] Saint Hippolyte, distinguished by his bishop's miter, presents Philip VI, reaching out with his hand to touch the king's back. In both charter

---

6 It seems likely to have been the same artist for each, but Brunel suggests that it is possible there were two artists. For his reasoning, see *Images du pouvoir royal*, p. 198.

7 The wimple was a headdress worn around the head by married women; it covered the chin, neck, and chest; a widow wore a white wimple; Desirée Koslin, "Wimple," in *Encyclopedia of Dress and Textiles in the British Isles, c. 450–1450*, ed. Gale R. Owen-Crocker, Elizabeth Coatsworth, and Maria Hayward (Leiden, 2012), pp. 629–30; see also the many examples of wimples illustrated in Anne van Buren, *Illuminating Fashion: Dress in the Art of Medieval France and the Netherlands, 1325–1515* (New York, 2011).

8 For the description of the *houce* and additional examples, see van Buren, *Illuminating Fashion*, p. 307.

THE LIFE AND PATRONAGE OF BLANCHE OF NAVARRE   23

initials Blanche holds out a rather substantial chapel, her arms rigid with its
weight and her hands clearly and firmly grasping its foundation; the viewer
recognizes her as the person with agency in this image, the patron of this chapel. The two initials differ only slightly. The design of the crown atop the letter
B has fleur-de-lis in the first and leaf fleurons in the second; the two documents differ as well in the marginal characters inhabiting the shapes of the
initial B.[9] Both initials have a large heraldic device in the left margin showing
Blanche's coat of arms: France, Evreux, and Navarre. This heraldic device provides the 'portrait' of the image; it is not a physiognomic likeness of Blanche,
Philip, or Jeanne, but, as is typical of the 14th century, names, heraldry, and
family relationships are used to establish identity.[10]

The paintings, sculpture, and metalwork of Blanche's chapel followed some
of the same themes of the charter initials, such as an emphasis on identity
linked to family, but none of the works survive beyond the marble tomb *gisants*
(Fig. 1.5). The appearance of the chapel can be reconstructed in part, however,
from 17th- and 18th-century descriptions.[11] Opposite the altar of Saint Hippolyte
in the two-bay chapel was a black marble tomb with white marble tomb
figures; these were recorded for the antiquarian François Roger de Gaignières
in the late 17th century (Fig. 1.4).[12] Only these tomb figures survive today; they
are now grouped in the chapel of Saint Hippolyte with a number of other tomb
figures that were not originally intended for this chapel. There were also
twenty-four standing statues made of white stone arrayed around the tomb,
Blanche's relatives both living and dead.[13] These figures were organized

---

9   In the 'original,' a soul is carried by angels in a cloth above a figure in a miter with soldiers
in the curves of the letter B. In the copy, a seated solder is at the bottom left in the letter
B, while a one-legged beast and disembodied faces inhabit the rest of the spaces of the
letter.

10   For a consideration of likeness or portaiture in such illustrated charters in the second half
of the 14th century, see Stephen Perkinson, *The Likeness of the King: A Prehistory of Portraiture in Late Medieval France* (Chicago, 2009), pp. 231–38.

11   For the later descriptions of the chapel, Jacques Doublet, *Histoire de l'abbaye de S. Denys
en France* (Paris, 1625), pp. 329 and 1333–34, and Michel Félibien, *Histoire de l'abbaye
royale de saint Denys en France* (Paris, 1706), p. 560. There was also a 1634 inventory that
recorded objects at Saint-Denis with Blanche's coat of arms; these are described in Blaise
de Montesquiou-Fezensac and Daneille Gaborit-Chopin, *Le trésor de Saint-Denis*, 3 vols.
(Paris, 1973), 1:276–77.

12   The Gaignières images are Paris, Bibliothèque nationale de France, Département des
Estampes, Pe 11 C, fol. 95r.

13   Doublet identified the material of the standing figures as white marble; *Histoire de
l'abbaye de S. Denys*, p. 1333, whereas Félibien said that the small figures decorating the
tomb were alabaster; *Histoire de l'abbaye royale de saint Denys*, p. 560.

FIGURE 1.4   *Tomb of Blanche of Navarre and her daughter Jeanne of France at Saint-Denis, late 17th- or early 18th-century watercolor made for François Roger de Gaignières (compare fig. 1.5).* PARIS, BIBLIOTHÈQUE NATIONALE DE FRANCE, DÉPARTEMENT DES ESTAMPES, PE 11 C, FOL. 95R. PHOTO CREDIT: CLICHÉ BIBLIOTHÈQUE NATIONALE DE FRANCE.

according to their descent from Saint Louis, according to the early 17th-century account by Jacques Doublet, though he was unfortunately not more specific about how this genealogical organization was made clear to the viewer. Though Doublet could not identify all the statues because some were damaged, the figures included the saint's daughter Agnes of Burgundy, Philip III, Philip IV, Louis X, Blanche's parents Jeanne and Philip of Navarre, her sisters Marie and Agnes, and her brother Louis.[14] The brothers of Charles V were also represented on the tomb: John, duke of Berry; Philip, duke of Burgundy; and Louis, duke of Anjou. Of the identified statues, only Blanche's sister Agnes, her brother Louis, and the brothers of Charles V were still living in 1372.

The white marble *gisants* of Blanche and her daughter are among the very few 14th-century images of the two women that survive (Fig. 1.5). The sculptor of these *gisants* has been identified as a follower of Jean de Liège.[15] In the recumbent figure, Blanche is shown wearing a wimple, a long-sleeved cote or kirtle, and over this garment the sleeveless, open-sided surcote, called the sur-cote-ouverte, associated with women of high status in the second half of the 14th century.[16] Her daughter also wears a surcote, with panels in the front, perhaps intended to indicate the decoration of the garment in a different fabric. Jeanne's hair is visible; it is parted in the middle and partially braided, with the braids crossing over the top of of her head and looping on either side of her face, a fashionable mid-14th-century hairstyle.[17] The ridge and indentations where a metal crown was once attached are visible on the head of Blanche

---

14 Doublet lists the figures: "Premierement, la Duchesse de Bourgogne Agnes, fille de Saint Louys, beseole de la Reyne; Le Roy Charles de Sicile; le Roy saint Louys; le Roy Philippe son fils; Messire Louys de Navarre Duc de Duras Comte de Beaumont le Roy; S. Louys de Marseille; la Reyne de France Madame Agnes Comtesse de Brie, soeur de la Reyne; le Roy Philippes le Bel; le Roy Louys son fils, Pere de la mere de cette Reyne; le Duc de Bourgogne; le Duc de Berry; le Duc d'Anjou; le Roy de Navarre Pere de cette Reyne; la Reyne Marie d'Aragon, soeur de cette Reyne; la Reyne de Navarre, mere de cette Reyne; la Reyne de Navarre, Tente"; *Histoire de l'abbaye de S. Denys en France*, p . 1334. The last queen of Navarre in Doublet's list may refer to Jeanne of Evreux, who was queen of Navarre by virtue of her marriage to Charles IV, or alternately to Jeanne of France, the wife of Charles II. There are errors in Doublet's transcription: Blanche's sister Agnes was not the countess of Brie but the countess of Foix and her brother Louis was the count of Beaumont-le-Roger.

15 Stephen Scher, "Bust of Marie de France," in *Set in Stone: The Face in Medieval Sculpture*, ed. Charles T. Little (New Haven, 2006), p. 140, n. 5.

16 Van Buren, *Illuminating Fashion*: for cote/kirtle, see p. 310; for surcote, see pp. 28, 311–12. See also Mark Chambers, "Surcote/surcoat," in *Encyclopedia of Dress and Textiles in the British Isles*, pp. 566–67. For the association of the surcote with aristocratic status, see also Margaret Scott, *Medieval Dress and Fashion* (London, 2007), p. 116.

17 Van Buren, *Illuminating Fashion*, pp. 66–67.

FIGURE 1.5 *Tomb figures of Jeanne of France and Blanche of Navarre, chapel of Saint Hippolyte, Saint-Denis, c. 1372.* PHOTO CREDIT: SARAH THOMPSON.

(Fig. 1.6); her daughter perhaps had only a simple metal band.[18] Both also have a pair of dogs at their feet; Blanche's dogs face away from each other and are posed alertly, as if keeping guard, while those at the feet of her daughter's effigy seem more playful with heads together (Fig. 1.7).[19] Blanche holds a scepter, while her daughter's hands are pressed together in prayer.

In her clothing and pose, and in the inclusion of a pair of dogs facing away from each other, Blanche's *gisant* is similar to that of her mother, Jeanne, queen of Navarre, buried in Saint-Denis after her death in October 1349 (Fig. 1.8). Whether Blanche herself commissioned this tomb is a question considered below. Jeanne also wears a surcote, long-sleeved cote, a wimple, and a crown. They differ in the details of the crown, which for Jeanne was sculpted in marble rather than added in metal, and in the scale of the figures, as Jeanne's is under life-size. In their recumbent pose and in the choice of white marble, they are

---

18 For the question of what Jeanne wore on her head, see the discussion by Stephen Scher of the coronet on the head of the tomb figure of Marie of France at Saint-Denis, in "Bust of Marie de France," pp. 138–40.

19 Dogs are typically depicted in pairs on women's tombs; Kathleen Walker-Meikle, *Medieval Pets* (Woodbridge, UK, 2012), pp. 75–78.

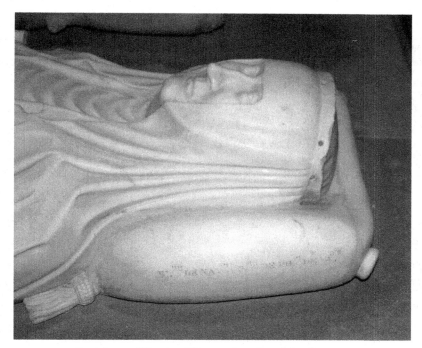

FIGURE 1.6 *Tomb figure of Blanche of Navarre, Saint-Denis, detail.* PHOTO CREDIT: MARGUERITE KEANE.

FIGURE 1.7 *Tomb figure of Jeanne of France, Saint-Denis, detail of dogs.* PHOTO CREDIT: MARGUERITE KEANE.

FIGURE 1.8 *Tomb figure of Jeanne II, queen of Navarre, c. 1350, Saint-Denis.*
Note: the small figure next to her is a gisant of John, the infant son of Louis X.
PHOTO CREDIT: MARGUERITE KEANE.

much like the other *gisants* at Saint-Denis, such as those of Philip VI, John II, and Charles V, commissioned by Charles himself in 1364.[20]

The chapel also contained painted column-statues of Philip VI, Blanche of Navarre, and their daughter Jeanne, as well as painted alabaster statues of the saints to whom the chapel was also dedicated: John the Baptist, Peter, and Paul (who also appear in the charter initials).[21] A chalice and candlesticks with Blanche's coat of arms were intended for the celebration of Mass in the chapel.[22] Two paintings in the chapel were displayed on either side of a central image, probably a Crucifixion.[23] One shows Philip VI presented by Saint

20 On these tombs, see Pierre Pradel, "Les tombeaux de Charles V," *Bulletin monumental* 109 (1951), 273–96; Claire Richter Sherman, *The Portraits of Charles V of France* (New York, 1969), pp. 64–71; Elizabeth A.R. Brown, *Saint-Denis: la basilique* (Paris, 2001), pp. 413–22; and Susie Nash, "'Adrien Biaunevopt ... faseur des thombes': André Beauneveu and Sculptural Practice in Late Fourteenth-century France and Flanders," in *"No Equal in Any Land," André Beauneveu: Artist to the Courts of France and Flanders*, ed. Susie Nash, with contributions by Till-Holger Borchert and Jim Harris (London, 2007), pp. 30–65.

21 Doublet, *Histoire de l'abbaye de S. Denys*, p. 329.

22 Montesquiou-Fezensac and Gaborit-Chopin, *Le trésor de Saint-Denis*, 1:276–77.

23 The copies for Gaignières are Paris, Bibliothèque nationale, Département des Estampes, Oa 11, fols. 90r and 91r. These paintings are presumably copies of those described by Doublet, *Histoire de l'abbaye de S. Denys*, p. 329.

THE LIFE AND PATRONAGE OF BLANCHE OF NAVARRE

Hippolyte (Fig. 1.9), and the other Blanche and her daughter with their ancestor Saint Louis (Fig. 1.10).[24] Blanche and her daughter are again shown in the same clothing that they wear in the marble tomb figures, though in this case color is present to further elucidate the appearance of the garments, if the Gaignières painted copy is to be trusted with regard to the colors represented. Philip VI again wears a *houce*, in this case red, while Blanche and Jeanne wear the surcotes-ouvertes.[25] Blanche wears a white wimple, as expected for a widow. Jeanne's surcote is decorated with fleur-de-lis and the heraldic devices of Evreux and Navarre. These devices function primarily to convey identity; whether a surcote might indeed be decorated in this way is difficult to determine from this evidence alone.[26]

Blanche's chapel included another element that might have drawn Saint-Denis visitors to her chapel and better perpetuated her memory: a copy of the well-known medieval Italian pilgrimage image, the *Volto Santo* of Lucca.[27] Copies of the *Volto Santo*, an image of the risen Christ on the cross, were popular at the French court in the late 14th century.[28] For the uninitiated, a painted inscription on a pillar in the chapel described the miracles that were associated with the *Volto Santo*, reinforcing the importance of this copy at the abbey.[29] Blanche's copy, probably emblazoned with her coat of arms, as in the early 18th century Félibien described it as a "present of this queen," would have attracted the fashionable and the curious, all of whom, ideally, would then have remem-

---

24   There is some debate over who is depicted in these paintings. Since the paintings were in the chapel of Saint Hippolyte, almost certainly depicted here are Philip VI, Blanche of Navarre, and their daughter Jeanne. The question is considered by Hervé Pinoteau, "Tableaux français sous les premiers Valois," *Cahiers d'héraldique* 2 (1975), 119–76, especially pp. 132–33. See also Charles Sterling, *La peinture médiévale à Paris*, vol. 1, *1300–1500* (Paris, 1987), pp. 203–8.

25   For an association of the *houce* with scholarly identity, see Scott, *Medieval Dress and Fashion*, p. 110.

26   For this caveat about the representation of heraldic devices on medieval clothing, see Scott, *Medieval Dress and Fashion*, pp. 100–101.

27   Félibien described on the altar a "grand crucifix, present de la reine Blanche ... copie du fameux crucifix de la ville de Lucques"; *Histoire de l'abbaye royale de saint Denys*, p. 533.

28   See Hilary Maddocks, "The Rapondi, the Volto Santo di Lucca, and Manuscript Illumination in Paris c. 1400," in *Patrons, Authors, and Workshops: Books and Book Production in Paris around 1400*, ed. Godfried Croenen and Peter Ainsworth (Louvain, 2006), pp. 91–122.

29   The inscription is described by Doublet, *Histoire de l'abbaye de S. Denys*, p. 328, as authored by "Frère Henry de Godefoy, Religieux Chantre de S. Denys, Commandeur, & Docteur en Theologie."

FIGURE 1.9   *Philip VI with Saint Hippolyte, late 17th- or early 18th-century copy made for François Roger de Gaignières of a painting made c. 1372 from the chapel of Saint-Hippolyte at Saint-Denis.* PARIS, BIBLIOTHÈQUE NATIONALE DE FRANCE, DÉPARTEMENT DES ESTAMPES, OA 11, FOL. 90R. PHOTO CREDIT: BIBLIOTHÈQUE NATIONALE DE FRANCE.

THE LIFE AND PATRONAGE OF BLANCHE OF NAVARRE 31

FIGURE 1.10 *Blanche of Navarre and Jeanne of France with Saint Louis, late 17th- or early 18th-century copy made for François Roger de Gaignières of a painting made c. 1372 from the chapel of Saint Hippolyte at Saint-Denis.* PARIS, BIBLIOTHÈQUE NATIONALE DE FRANCE, DÉPARTEMENT DES ESTAMPES, OA 11, FOL. 91R.
PHOTO CREDIT: BIBLIOTHÈQUE NATIONALE DE FRANCE.

32   CHAPTER 1

bered the queen, illustrious descendant of the beloved Saint Louis, as they prayed before the image.[30]

In her study of such commemorative chapels, Mailon Doquang has noted the necessity of repetition for the efficacy of memorial.[31] In contrast to the fleeting funeral and anniversary Masses, the collected objects in Blanche's chapel, with their repetitive monologue about the devout queen and her illustrious family, made the practice of commemoration permanent. The images of Blanche, her daughter, and her husband (who was not himself buried in the chapel but in the crossing at Saint-Denis) were repeated in the painted column-statues, as well as in the paintings and on the tomb. Images of Saint Louis appeared both in the painting and on the tomb, and the tomb of Saint Louis himself was not far from the chapel, in the crossing at Saint-Denis. The images of Blanche and her family members and her coat of arms labeled on object after object would have emphasized the purpose of the chapel: the care of the souls of Blanche, her husband, and her daughter, through the prompting of prayers by visitors to the chapel.

These strategies of repetition in the chapel were not just to make permanent the immateriality of memorial; they were also a sign of anxiety that the queen and her family would not be properly remembered in the prayers of those visiting the chapel, or that they might be remembered inaccurately. It was a particularly acute issue for Blanche of Navarre, who was furnishing her chapel in 1372 after two decades in which her brother Charles was nearly constantly at war with the French kings. The chapel served as a way for Blanche to dictate the presentation of her memory. Visitors to the chapel would not remember her rebellious brother Charles of Navarre (the question of whether he was represented on the tomb cannot be answered, as the identities of several damaged figures are not known and he may have been among them); rather, they would have seen images of a virtuous and devout queen surrounded by the French kings and other esteemed family members.

Blanche's chapel was one of many that were thus endowed and furnished in the 14th century at Saint-Denis; there was a fashion for endowing tomb chapels

---

30   Though, as Mailon Doquang notes, we cannot be certain that the chapels' contents were
      visible; she argues that it was likely they were secured by visually permeable gates or were
      left open occasionally; the many representations of identity in the chapel would have
      been much less worthwhile for memorialization if the chapel were not accessible;
      Doquang, "Status and the Soul: Commemoration and Intercession in the Rayonnant Chapels of Northern France in the Thirteenth and Fourteenth Centuries," in *Memory and Commemoration in Medieval Culture*, ed. Elma Brenner, Meredith Cohen, and Mary Franklin-Brown (Farnham, Surrey, UK, 2013), pp. 93–118, this material from p. 103.
31   Doquang, "Status and the Soul: Commemoration and Intercession," p. 104.

THE LIFE AND PATRONAGE OF BLANCHE OF NAVARRE

at this time.[32] Charles V had selected the chapel of Saint John the Baptist, diagonally across the transept from the chapel of Saint Hippolyte, to serve as a tomb site for himself and his family in 1362. Margaret of Artois, the daughter of Philip V and Jeanne of Burgundy, and the widow of Louis II, count of Flanders, endowed the chapel of Saint Michel on the south side of the nave in 1363.[33] Blanche's chapel was most similar to the one furnished by the dowager queen Jeanne of Evreux in the 1340s – not surprising, considering that this queen had consistently served as a model for Blanche. It was just across the transept from Blanche's chapel, and was also meant to serve as a memorial to her family.[34] Fourteenth-century viewers would clearly have seen the visual parallels between the two chapels: Jeanne of Evreux's chapel also had column-statues of herself, her husband Charles IV, and their two daughters.[35] And although she herself was buried next to her husband in the crossing at Saint-Denis, the tombs of her daughters, Blanche and Marie, were in the chapel.[36] The artist of the tomb figures of Blanche and Marie was Jean de Liège, a sculptor active in Paris in the 1360s and 1370s who had also worked for other royal patrons.[37]

Conflict with the Monks of Saint-Denis

The furnishing of Blanche's chapel was likely completed by the mid-1370s and therefore served as a site for prayer and memorial for her daughter alone for more than twenty years, until Blanche's own death, in 1398. She left detailed instructions in her will for the care of her body after death. If she died at her château at Neaufles (her residence for the last few decades of her life, near Gisors in Normandy), her body was to be taken to Saint-Denis, stopping only along the way at churches if the entourage needed to rest.[38] If she died in Paris, her body was to be taken first to Saint-Jean-en-Grève, a parish church near her

---

32 For this phase of chapel decoration, see Berné, "L'action mémorielle," pp. 1–10, and Eva Leisterschneider, *Die franzöische Königsgrablege Saint-Denis. Strategien monarchischer Repräsentation, 1223–1461* (Weimar, 2008).

33 Brown, *La basilique Saint-Denis*, p. 415.

34 For this chapel, see Carla Lord, "Jeanne d'Évreux as a Founder of Chapels," in *Women and Art in Early Modern Europe: Patrons, Collectors, and Connoisseurs*, ed. Cynthia Lawrence (University Park, PA, 1997), pp. 21–36.

35 Doublet, *Histoire de l'abbaye de S. Denys*, p. 329.

36 Marie died in 1341, and Blanche died in 1393.

37 Scher, "Bust of Marie de France," pp. 138–40.

38 Delisle 6.

house in Paris, then to Notre-Dame for a service, and finally to Saint-Denis.[39] Blanche also referred to Jeanne of Evreux in her detailed instructions for her funeral, as she wished Jeanne's funeral to serve as a model for her own. According to her instructions, she was to be clothed in purple velvet on a bier hung with cloth-of-gold, with the service at every church to have twelve candles weighing four livres each. For the services said at the mendicant orders of Paris (the Cordeliers, Jacobins, Augustines, and Carmelites), and at Bourgfontaine, each Mass was to have twelve wax candles, each weighing six livres, "around the representation of my body that will be there."[40] For the burial, she wrote:

> Item pour ce que après nostre trespassement nostre corps ne puet bonnement miz ne enterré de lez nostre très chier seigneur et espoux le roy Phelippe, que Diex absoille, où il n'a pas place pour ce faire, nous ordonnons et voulons que, tantost après nostre trespassement, nostre corps soit mis et enterré tout entier en l'eglise de l'abbaye de monseigneur saint Denis en France, en la chapelle de monseigneur Saint Ypolite, que nous avons fondée, où nous [avons] fait mettre le corps de Jehanne de France, nostre fille, dont Diex ait l'ame, sanz faire nostre corps aucunement diviser, ne en icellui faire aucune incision, pour y estre enterrée en ensuivant, pour celle maniere, humblement et devotement, le commun usaige d'ensevelir et enterrer corps humains.[41]

> [Because after my death my body cannot be buried near my very dear lord and spouse the king Philip, may God pardon him, because there is not space there, my body should be buried whole in the abbey of Saint-Denis, in the chapel of Saint Hippolyte that I have founded, where I have buried my daughter, Jeanne, may God pardon her, without dividing my body, without making any incision, following the common usage of shrouding and burying corpses.]

It would have presumably been obvious to the monks that Blanche intended to be buried in the chapel of Saint Hippolyte, as she had already donated the funds and furnished the chapel two decades before. These funeral arrangements – reminding all that she knew she could not be buried next to Philip VI but wished to be buried next to her daughter – demonstrate a desire to control

---

39 Delisle 7.
40 Delisle 11.
41 Delisle 5.

THE LIFE AND PATRONAGE OF BLANCHE OF NAVARRE   35

what would happen in the few days after death, and provide strong evidence
that funerals often did not go the way they were intended.[42]

Indeed, despite Blanche's careful instructions, her funeral was not quite
what she had hoped. The funeral ceremony was described, probably retrospec-
tively, by the chronicler called the Religieux of Saint-Denis, who has been
identified as Michel Pintoin (*c.* 1350-*c.* 1421), the chanter of the abbey; he wrote
a history of the reign of Charles VI in which Blanche's activities were occasionally of note.[43] His characterization of Blanche is typical for a medieval queen,
in that he described her as pious, generous, and a good mother. For him,
Blanche was a repository of tradition at the court – he noted that Blanche, of
great age and reputation, was consulted for the planning of the 1389 coronation of Isabeau of Bavaria; according to Pintoin, Blanche depended both on her
memory of past coronations and on the historical records kept at Saint-Denis.[44]
In his description of her death in 1398, he wrote that she was a model of chas-
tity and virtue, exemplary qualities of mothers.[45] But in the next sentence
Pintoin deviated suddenly from his anodyne stereotype of the medieval queen,
writing:

> Because she was never crowned, the officers of the court asked the dukes
> of Burgundy, Orléans and Bourbon and others, if they should bring her to
> the church of Saint-Denis and bury her with the pomp and ornaments
> used for royal funerals.[46]

The dukes of the royal court did not seem to share this concern for Blanche's status as an uncrowned queen, as they assented to her royal funeral at Saint-Denis.

---

42   Elizabeth A.R. Brown has argued that the testamentary strategies of Jeanne of Evreux
      demonstrate her shrewd recognition that her testament was best executed in her lifetime;
      it would be her only guarantee that her wishes were carried out; "The Testamentary Strat-
      egies of Jeanne d'Évreux: The Endowment of Saint-Denis in 1343," in *Magistra Doctissima:
      Essays in Honor of Bonnie Wheeler*, ed. Dorsey Armstrong, Ann W. Astell, and Howell
      Chickering (Kalamazoo, MI, 2013), pp. 217–47.
43   Nicole Grévy-Pons and Ezio Ornato, "Qui est l'auteur de la chronique latine de Charles VI
      dite Religieux de Saint-Denis?" *Bibliothèque de l'École des Chartes* 134 (1976), 85–102.
44   *Chronique du Religieux de Saint-Denys, contenant le règne de Charles VI, de 1380 à 1422*, ed.
      L. Bellaguet, 6 vols. (Paris, 1839–52), 1:611.
45   *Chronique du Religieux de Saint-Denys*, 2:657.
46   "Comme elle n'avait point été couronnée, les principaux officiers de sa cour demandèrent
      à messeigneurs les ducs de Bourgogne, d'Orléans et de Bourbon et aux autres seigneurs,
      s'ils devaient la faire porter à l'église de Saint-Denys et l'enterrer avec la pompe et les orne-
      ments usités pour les funérailles royales"; *Chronique du Religieux de Saint-Denys*, 2:657.

This was done, according to Pintoin, out of respect for Blanche's husband, Philip VI.[47] Pintoin's questioning here not just of Blanche's right to a royal funeral but also her burial at Saint-Denis is perplexing considering the extensive preparations that Blanche had already made at Saint-Denis to be buried with her daughter. It seems likely that Pintoin, writing after the funeral ceremony had taken place, was not recording any serious contemporary concern about the burial of Blanche at Saint-Denis, but rather seized an opportunity to denigrate her status, the motivation for which I suggest below. It is clear from the detailed instructions left in the will that Blanche knew she might have to convince the monks that she was entitled to be buried at Saint-Denis.

Pintoin's pettiness about Blanche of Navarre's status persisted in his description of the funeral, on 11 October 1398. He noted:

> The lighting furnished for the funeral ceremony was very paltry, and was only sufficient for a person of obscure condition. It was the testamentary executors of the queen who determined this expense. One can blame them generally for their greed, because one knew that Blanche had left great treasures.[48]

Blanche's executors were the primary objects of Pintoin's disdain here, but the dim lighting and inglorious conditions also afforded Pintoin an opportunity to disparage Blanche's prestige: she might as well have been someone of obscure condition. It was presumably precisely to avoid such a condition that Blanche had so extensively decorated her chapel with images of herself and her family.

At least one motivation for Pintoin's derision about Blanche's status as queen and her funeral is evident in his discussion of the disposition of Blanche's possessions. He wrote that Blanche had given to the convent of the Carmelites in Paris a relic of a nail from the Crucifixion.[49] The monks of Saint-Denis were outraged at this bequest because they owned the only nail relic in the French kingdom. Pintoin wrote:

---

47   "Ces princes, par respect pour la mémoire de son magnanime époux, qui était la tige de leur race, jugèrent convenable de lui accorder tous ces honneurs"; *Chronique du Religieux de Saint-Denys*, 2:657.

48   "Le luminaire fourni pour la cérémonie funèbre fut très mesquin, et eut à peine suffi pour une personne de condition obscure. C'étaient les exécuteurs testamentaires de la reine qui avaient réglé cette dépense. On les blama généralement de leur avarice; car on savait que madame Blanche avait laissé d'immenses trésors"; *Chronique du Religieux de Saint-Denys*, 2:659.

49   *Chronique du Religieux de Saint-Denys*, 2:661.

THE LIFE AND PATRONAGE OF BLANCHE OF NAVARRE

Madame Blanche ... honored with particular affection the house of the Carmelites, and offered to it a very precious jewel, containing an iron nail that she claimed to be one of the nails of Our Lord Jesus Christ, and that she had bought, she said, from Venetian merchants who assured [they had] brought it from Constantinople. She was persuaded by the vain and false words of these merchants, despite the falseness of their claim, and had helped to spread this error and scandal in the kingdom. Because, following the witness of our old annals, it is the church of Saint-Denis in France which possesses this sacred jewel, and the equal does not exist elsewhere; this fact is proven by the history of Charlemagne and by the continuous miracles that have occurred for five hundred years with contact with this relic.[50]

The monks had recently celebrated their own nail relic; in 1397, Charles VI had donated a lavish reliquary for it, embellished with figures in gold of himself, Queen Isabeau of Bavaria, and the French dynastic saints Charlemagne and Saint Louis.[51] The surfacing of another nail relic at another monastic house in Paris given by a royal donor was an intolerable slight to the prestige of the abbey. Pintoin's strategy in his narrative was to paint Blanche as both too trusting (she was persuaded by the false words of the merchant) and unreliable (she had bought it, 'she said,' from Venetian merchants).

Blanche anticipated the objections of the monks of Saint-Denis to her relic, as in her will she gave a detailed provenance for it:

Item nous laissons au couvent des frères du Carme de Paris un reliquaire d'or qui pent en nostre clotet, où il y a un clouet qui fu fait d'un des cloux Nostre Seigneur, lequel nostre dicte fille la duchesse d'Orleans nous lessa en son testament; et fu a madame la royne Jehanne. Et voulons et

---

50   "Madame Blanche aimait en effet beaucoup ces églises; mais elle honorait d'une affection toute particulière la maison des Carmélites, et lui avait solonellement offert un joyau très précieux, contenant un clou de fer, qu'elle prétendait être un des clous de Notre-Seigneur Jésus Christ, et qu'elle avait acheté, disait-elle, à des marchands vénitiens qui assuraient l'avoir apporté de Constantinople. Elle s'était laissé persuader par les vaines et mensongères paroles de ces marchands, malgré la fausseté de leur allégation, et avait contribué à repandre l'erreur et le scandale dans le royaume. Car, suivant le témoignage de nos antiques annales, c'est l'église de Saint-Denys en France qui possède ce joyau sacré, et le pareil n'existe nulle autre part; ce fait est prouvé par l'histoire de Charlemagne et par les miracles continuels que depuis cinq cents ans opère le contact de cette relique"; *Chronique du Religieux de Saint-Denys*, 2:661.

51   Jenny Stratford, *Richard II and the English Royal Treasure* (Woodbridge, UK, 2012), p. 87.

ordonnons que ilz le gardent en leur dicte eglise perpetuelment comme digne saintuaire et pour l'amour d'elles et de nous.[52]

[I leave the brothers of the Carmelites in Paris a gold reliquary that hangs in my *clotet*, where there is a nail which was made of one of the nails of Our Lord, which my daughter the duchess of Orléans left me in her testament; and it belonged to the queen Jeanne. And I wish and order that they keep it in their church perpetually for love of them (Blanche of Orléans and Jeanne of Evreux) and of us.]

The nail was indeed mentioned in the 1392 testament of Blanche of Orléans:

Item, elle laissa à sa très chière Dame Madame la Royne Blanche, son bréviaire où elle disoit ses heures, un petit livret d'oroisons qui fu à la Royne Jehanne sa mère, avecques son petit reliquiaire ou il a du clou Notre-Seigneur, et se elle aloit de vie à trespassement avant que la ditte Madame la Duchesse, ycelle Madame la Duchesse volt que le dit reliquiaire soit et demoure à l'église Nostre-Dame du Carme à Paris, et ou cas que la ditte Madame la Royne Blanche survivra ycelle Madame la Duchesse, elle lui supplie quel dit reliquiaire après son décès, elle vueille laisser à la ditte église.[53]

[She leaves to her very dear lady Madame the queen Blanche, her breviary with which she says her hours, a little prayerbook that belonged to the queen Jeanne her mother, with her small reliquary which has the nail of Our Lord, and if she dies before the Duchess, the Duchess wants the reliquary to be and remain in the church of Our Lady of the Carmelites in Paris, and in the case that the queen Blanche survives her she requests that this reliquary be left to this church after her death.]

A notable difference between these two bequests is that Blanche of Orléans did not mention her mother Jeanne of Evreux as a previous owner, though Blanche of Navarre did, effectively giving the nail reliquary an even longer and more prestigious ownership history. The transfer of this object was unusually complex. Blanche of Navarre was to be given the little reliquary with the nail

---

52   Delisle 395.

53   Gaston Vignat, "Testament de Blanche, duchesse d'Orléans," *Mémoires de la Sociéte archéologique de l'Orléanais* 9 (1866), 115–44; this bequest on p. 131. The book mentioned in the first part of the bequest is considered in chapter 3 below.

THE LIFE AND PATRONAGE OF BLANCHE OF NAVARRE

from the Crucifixion with a condition: if Blanche of Navarre were dead at the time the will was executed, the duchess wanted the reliquary to go to the Carmelites. In the case that the queen Blanche survived the duchess, as she did, Blanche was to leave the reliquary to the monastery. The nail reliquary was valuable enough that Blanche of Navarre wanted it for the short years she would be alive after Blanche of Orléans, even though Blanche of Navarre was already over sixty in 1392. The bequest of Blanche of Orléans was truly more a loan than a gift, she had probably already promised the reliquary to the Carmelites, and Blanche of Navarre dutifully followed her wishes by leaving it to the monks in her will.

According to this testamentary evidence, Blanche had not purchased the nail relic that she gave to the Carmelites; it came from Blanche of Orléans and before Blanche from her mother Jeanne of Evreux. But Blanche must have been aware that the monks of Saint-Denis would cause a fuss over the relic bequest because her executors supplied the Carmelites with a document authenticating the relic's history. This document, kept at the monastery presumably to head off further questioning of the authenticity of the relic, recorded that the Carmelite monk Louis of Vernon witnessed the transfer of the relic in 1398.[54] The arrival of the nail relic at the Carmelites was also described by Félibien in the early 18th century; he does not give a source, but it seems likely he is basing his narrative on this document:

> This queen [Blanche] died on 5 October 1398 and on 24 November of the same year, Pierre Basin, a Franciscan, who was her confessor, Renaud de Braquemont, a knight, Estienne Joffroy, Oudart le Gendre, and Thibaud Roussel, all executors of the queen Blanche's will, declared to the Carmelites that she had left them this precious relic. The Carmelites begged to be told in which manner it had come to the possession of the queen Blanche, so that they could with confidence expose it to public veneration. The testamentary executors affirmed that the queen Jeanne

---

54 I have not been able to see the original document on which this narrative is based. In the 19th century it was in the Archives nationales in Paris in the carton numbered L928; it was described by Jean Lebeuf, who called it "un authentique du saint clou laissé par le testament de la reine Blanche et qui fut solenellement transporté en 1398"; *Histoire de la ville et de tout le diocèse de Paris*, 3 vols. (Paris, 1863–67), 2:721. The transfer of the relic was also noted by Edmond Meyer, *Histoire de la ville de Vernon et de son ancien chatellenie*, 2 vols. (Les Andelis, 1876), 2:167, who gave the name of the monk Louis of Vernon as a witness to it. In September 2012 and again in April 2015 it was verified that the document was not in carton L928. I am grateful to the curators of the Archives nationales and to Elizabeth A.R. Brown for their assistance in trying to locate it.

d'Evreux, third wife of Charles IV, king of France and Navarre, had this part of the holy nail from the king her husband, and had enriched it with gold, with five balas rubies, four sapphires, six diamonds, and twelve pearls, with a figure of Jesus Christ in gold, holding in his hands this part of the nail; that the queen Jeanne d'Evreux had given this precious jewel to Blanche, her daughter, the duchess of Orléans; and that Blanche had given it to the late queen Blanche, who by her testament left it to the Carmelites. Their community soon came to the house where the queen had died. Six between them carried the ornaments of the church and all the others had lit candles. They received the holy relic, and carried it with solemnity into their church, singing. At the entry of the church, Girard bishop of ... took the holy nail and put it on the principal altar, in the presence of Eustache, abbot of Saint Germer, of Estienne de Cherité, secretary of the king, and of Jean Mauger and of Guillaume de la Porte, notaries.[55]

Félibien's discussion of the transfer of the nail has new information not conveyed by the wills of either Blanche of Orléans or Blanche of Navarre. It was in a reliquary laden with precious stones and with a gold figure of Christ. It was not first owned by Jeanne of Evreux, but by her husband, the French king, Charles IV; this knowledge of an owner even prior to Jeanne of Evreux must

---

55 "Cette reine mourut le 5 octobre 1398 et le 24 novembre de la meme année Pierre Bazin Cordelier, qui avoit esté son confesseur, Renaud de Braquemont chevalier, Estienne Joffroy, Oudart le Gendre, et Thibaud Roussel, tous executeurs des derniers volontez de la reine Blanche, déclarèrent aux Carmes qu'elle leur avoit legué cette précieuse relique. Les Carmes les supplièrent de voulour bien déclarer de quelle manière ce saint clou estoit venu au pouvoir de la reine Blanche, afin qu'on pust avec d'autant plus de sureté l'exposer à la veneration publique. Les executeurs testamentaires affirmèrent que la reine Jeanne d'Evreux, troisième femme de Charles IV, roy de France et de Navarre, avoit eu cette partie du saint clou du roy son mari, et l'avoit fait enrichir d'or, de cinq rubis balais, quatre saphirs, six diamans et douze perles, avec une figure de J.C. en or, qui tenoit en ses mains cette partie du clou; que la reine Jeanne d'Evreux, avoit donné ce joyau précieux à Madame Blanche de France, la fille, duchesse d'Orléans; et que madame Blanche l'avoit donné à la feue reine Blanche, laquelle par son testament l'avoit legué aux Carmes. Aussitot leur communauté vint à l'hôtel où la reine estoit décédée. Six d'entr'eux estoient revestus d'ornemens d'église, et tous les autres avoient des cierges allumez. Ils réceurent la sainte relique, et la portèrent avec solemnité dans leur église, en chantant un cantique fait exprès. A l'entrée de l'église, Girard évesque d ... prit le saint clou, et le déposa sur l'autel principal, en présence d'Eustache abbé de S. Germer, d'Estienne de Cherité secretaire du roy, de Jean Mauger, et de Guillaume de la Porte notaires"; Félibien, *Histoire de l'abbaye royale de saint Denys*, pp. 357–58.

THE LIFE AND PATRONAGE OF BLANCHE OF NAVARRE

have come from Blanche's executors, though Blanche did not know it at the time she wrote the will or she surely would have included it. Throughout the narrative there is an insistence on authenticity; we see the chain of custody of the nail, from Blanche's house to the hands of the Carmelites and finally to their altar, and this transfer was witnessed by an audience with a reputation beyond question, a bishop and a secretary of the king.

Two scenarios are possible here. Blanche acquired a nail relic in the way that Pintoin described, but disposed of it without Pintoin being aware that she no longer owned it, and the nail relic of Blanche of Orléans was unfairly disparaged as the fake relic. Or Pintoin or his sources were fabricating the story to undermine the authenticity of a competing monastic house's relic. It seems very unlikely that Blanche was attempting to pass off a fake relic by manufacturing a provenance, as this would have also required the collusion of Blanche of Orléans. Nevertheless, her story cannot help but inspire skepticism, as a longer and more prestigious provenance is attached to the relic each time it was newly described, first in 1396, the ownership of Jeanne of Evreux, and then, in 1398, the even more unassailable provenance dating to Charles IV.

This story of the nail relic depends on three kinds of evidence: the will, historical chronicles, and other documentary historical evidence like the relic authentication written for the Carmelites. Another most valuable category of historical evidence, the object itself, is lost; this will be true for most of the works discussed in this book with some happy exceptions. A history of the material culture of the court and household of Blanche of Navarre depends on all of these kinds of evidence, and indeed, there is abundant documentation of her life and activities, vastly more than might be expected considering how little the life of this queen has been treated in modern scholarship. I turn now to a short narrative of the life of Blanche to serve as a context for her artistic patronage and the material culture of her court.

Childhood and Marriage

The month and day of Blanche's birth are known, 2 April, because Blanche commemorated it with anniversary Masses at Saint-Germer-de-Fly, an abbey church not far from her château at Neaufles, and at Saint-Martin of Pontoise.[56]

---

56   For Saint-Germer-de-Fly: Léopold Delisle, "Testament de Blanche de Navarre, reine de France," *Mémoires de la Société de l'histoire de Paris et de l'Ile de France* 12 (1885), 20, n. 1, citing a document of June 1398 that founded a Mass in the abbey of Saint-Germer, "le second jour d'avril, que nous fusmes née." For the Mass at Saint Martin, see M.J. Depoin, "La

42   CHAPTER 1

If a chronicler was correct that Blanche was eighteen at her wedding in January
1350, her birthdate was 2 April 1331.[57] She was the fourth child of her parents.[58]
She had two older sisters, Jeanne and Marie, and one older brother, Louis, born
in 1330, who did not survive early childhood. Her next-youngest sibling, Charles,
was born in Evreux in 1332.[59] Two more boys (Philip and Louis) and two more
girls (Agnes and another Jeanne, called Jeanne la Jeune to distinguish her from
her older sister) followed in the family.

Blanche's mother, Jeanne, was the daughter of the French king Louis X and
the ill-fated Margaret of Burgundy, who was accused of adultery and died in
prison in April 1315. In the succession crises of the last Capetians, Jeanne was
excluded twice from inheriting the French throne, in 1317 and in 1328. The historical events that led to her exclusions have been much analyzed because the
setting aside of her rights to the French throne in 1317 formed the basis for the
14th-century ban on inheritance of the French throne by women that later
came to be called the Salic law. The throne of Navarre was not subject to the

---

reine Blanche à Pontoise," *Bulletin de la Commission des Antiquités et des Arts de Seine-et-Oise* 11 (1889), 161–62, citing Archives départementales de Seine-et-Oise, fonds Saint Martin de Pontoise, carton 2.

57 Continuator of Guillaume de Nangis, cited by Paulin Paris, *Le premier volume des Grandes chroniques de France. Selon que elles sont conservées en l'église de Saint-Denis en France* (Paris, 1836), p. 1397, n. 2.

58 There is some debate over the birth order of Blanche relative to her siblings. There were at least nine children in the family: Jeanne, Marie, Louis (died early childhood), Blanche, Charles, Philip, Louis, Agnes, and Jeanne la Jeune. Jeanne and Philip had Jeanne and Marie by 1330; they were mentioned by name in a list of expenses from that year; Pau, Archives départementales des Pyrénées-Atlantiques, E 519. This payment record has also been published in *Inventaire-sommaire des Archives départementales antérieures à 1790: Basses-Pyrénées*, ed. Paul Raymond, 6 vols. (Paris, 1863–79), vol. 4: *Archives civiles*, série E, nos. 1-1765, pp. 141–42. Jeanne entered the convent of Longchamp in 1337. Marie married Peter of Aragon in 1338 and had four children by 1346, so a birthday between 1327 and 1329 is likely, placing her older sister Jeanne's birth between 1326 and 1328. Blanche's brother Louis was born in 1330; Fermín Miranda García, *Reyes de Navarra: Felipe III y Juana II de Evreux* (Pamplona, 1994), pp. 212–14, citing Pamplona, Archivo General de Navarra, Comptos, Rep. 26, fols. 54v, 114v. Blanche was born the following year, followed by Charles in 1332. Philip of Navarre was probably born soon after Charles; that his brother named him administrator of his properties in Normandy suggests that Philip was older than Louis. Louis and one other daughter, Agnes or Jeanne, were born before 1342, because clothing was made that year for three sons and two daughters of the king of Navarre in Paris; this clothing purchase is analyzed in greater detail below. Jeanne la Jeune was probably the youngest, born between 1342 and her mother's death in 1349.

59 Denis-François Sécousse, *Mémoires pour servir à l'histoire de Charles II, roi de Navarre et comte d'Évreux, surnommé le Mauvais* (Paris, 1758), p. 5.

THE LIFE AND PATRONAGE OF BLANCHE OF NAVARRE 43

same ban on female succession, and Jeanne was crowned with her husband in 1329.[60] They held significant properties in Normandy as count and countess of Evreux, and Blanche was likely more at home in Paris than in Navarre.[61]

Records of clothing purchased by the French king in 1342 capture the presence of Blanche's family in Paris.[62] For Pentecost, the king paid for a suit of clothing to be worn by Blanche's father, Philip. That same year clothes were also made to celebrate the churching (re-entry into society after the birth of a child) of Blanche's mother; items were made for two daughters and three sons of the king of Navarre.[63] Since the children are not named, we cannot be certain of their identity, but likely the two daughters were Blanche and Agnes, and the sons Charles, Philip, and Louis. The new baby may have been Jeanne la Jeune or another child whose name was not recorded because he or she did not live past childhood. The eldest daughter of Jeanne and Philip, the older Jeanne was in the convent at Longchamp from 1337, and another daughter, Marie, was married and living in Aragon in 1342.[64] The clothes to celebrate the occasion were lavish: among their garments the three boys wore chemises with 'Navarre embroidery' as well as belts with pearls, emeralds, and rubies; hung from their clothing were small golden wafers, or bezants, that would have created a shimmering effect.[65]

The devastating outbreaks of bubonic plague in Paris in 1348 and 1349 were to dictate the next phase of Blanche's life.[66] Blanche's mother Jeanne died in October 1349 at her château of Conflans near Paris; the same outbreak killed Jeanne of Burgundy, wife of Philip VI, and Bonne of Luxembourg, wife of the dauphin John, that same autumn.[67] In January 1350, Blanche married the wid-

---

60 For Jeanne and Philip of Navarre, see Elena Woodacre, *The Queens Regnant of Navarre: Succession, Politics, and Partnership, 1274–1512* (New York, 2013), pp. 51–75.

61 Jeanne and Philip were in Navarre together February 1329-September 1331 and April 1336-October 1337, and Philip made solo trips there in 1342 and 1343; Woodacre, *The Queens Regnant of Navarre*, pp. 65–66.

62 Stella Mary Newton, *Fashion in the Age of the Black Prince: A Study of the Years 1340–1365* (Woodbridge, UK, 1980), pp. 22–24.

63 Newton, *Fashion in the Age of the Black Prince*, p. 25.

64 For Marie, see J.R. Castro, "El matrimonio de Pedro IV de Aragón y María de Navarra," *Estudios de Edad Media de la Corona de Aragon* 3 (1947–48), 55–102.

65 Newton, *Fashion in the Age of the Black Prince*, pp. 25–26.

66 For effects of plague in Paris in this period, see Raymond Cazelles, *La société politique et la crise de la royauté sous Philippe de Valois* (Paris, 1958).

67 Jeanne's death date is occasionally given as 12 September 1348, an error that Patrick van Kerrebrouck attributes to the author of the *Chronique des quatre premiers Valois*. The date of December 1349 is from the *Grandes chroniques* (see note 70 below); see van Kerrebrouck, *Les Valois* (Villeneuve d'Ascq, 1990), p. 83, 90 n. 24. In her recent study of the

44   CHAPTER 1

owed Philip VI.[68] The chronicler Jean Le Bel claimed that the dauphin John wanted to marry Blanche and was angry over his father's choice.[69] John himself was married less than a month later, to Jeanne of Auvergne and Boulogne, mother of the heir to the duchy of Burgundy, a territory that Philip VI was keen to keep close to the French monarchy.

The *Grandes chroniques de France* reported that the wedding of Philip VI and Blanche, on 19 January 1350, was quiet, "privéement plus que en appert," and took place in Brie-Comte-Robert, where Blanche's aunt Jeanne of Evreux had a château.[70] Whatever the reason for the wedding's privacy and the chronicle's emphasis on it – perhaps the feud between Philip and his son over Blanche, or more likely, lingering fear of plague in Paris – the privacy also facilitated a potentially negative assessment of Blanche's status.[71] Although she had married the king, she had done so nearly secretly. It is possible that the same reasons that caused the wedding to be private affected the planning of Blanche's coronation, as she was not crowned during the seven months of her marriage. As noted above, her lack of coronation would be cited more than fifty years later by the Religieux of Saint-Denis when he questioned her legitimacy as a queen.

Widowhood and Early Commissions

Philip died on 22 August 1350. His will of July 1350 left to Blanche all his *joyaux*: crowns, belts, brooches, and rings.[72] He excluded only one metalwork object,

---

testaments of Jeanne of Burgundy, Murielle Gaude-Ferragu also cites 12 December 1349 as Jeanne's death date; "Les dernières volontés de la reine de France. Les deux testaments de Jeanne de Bourgogne, femme de Philippe VI de Valois (1329, 1336)," *Annuaire-Bulletin de la Société de l'histoire de France, année 2007* (2009), 23–66.

68   Blanche was supposed to be married twice before, to Louis of Flanders and Peter of Castile; both engagements were called off. For analysis of the marriage alliances planned by Blanche's parents, see Woodacre, *The Queens Regnant of Navarre*, pp. 67–71.

69   *Chronique de Jean le Bel*, ed. Jules Viard and Eugène Déprez, 2 vols. (Paris, 1905), 2:183–84.

70   *Grandes chroniques de France*, ed. Jules Viard, 10 vols. (Paris, 1920–53), 9:322. Viard notes that the date of 11 January indicated by the chronicler was wrong; a letter of Charles of Navarre confirmed that his sister's wedding was 19 January 1350.

71   Edmond Michel argued that it was the outbreak of plague that had caused Philip VI and the court to flee Paris in the autumn of 1349; "La reine Jeanne d'Evreux à Brie-Comte-Robert," *Bulletin et compte-rendu des travaux de la Société d'histoire et d'archéologie de Brie-Comte-Robert* (Brie-Comte-Robert, 1898), 9–16.

72   I depend on Elizabeth A.R. Brown's transcription of the testaments: Paris, Archives nationales J 406, no. 33 (the testament of 23 May 1347) and no. 34 (the testament of 2 July 1350).

THE LIFE AND PATRONAGE OF BLANCHE OF NAVARRE

the crown that he wore on great feast days and that he had worn to his son's celebration of knighthood; this crown was to go to his son John. Blanche was also entitled to keep the gold, silver, and enameled serving ware of the household, such as ewers, dishes, and *nefs*. It is from the king's will that we see how Blanche acquired the objects analyzed in this book that she attributed to the ownership of her husband. It is possible that Philip gave the objects to Blanche during their seven-month marriage, and not as part of the testament. But Blanche's descriptions of the objects (such as a diamond that he loved, a reliquary brooch that he wore every day, and a reliquary belt that Jeanne of Burgundy gave him to wear into battle) suggest that these objects were precious to him and not things he would likely have given away before he died. That she had so few objects left at the end of her life that belonged to him is a sign that she gave away many of these objects in her lifetime. Indeed, in the gift-giving culture of the French court, Philip VI awarded Blanche a kind of gifting agency by leaving her these *joyaux* that she then gave away as objects once owned by the king and burnished by this provenance.[73] Blanche also owned several books that once belonged to Philip's first wife, Jeanne, but these are not mentioned in the will of Philip VI; the king likely gave them to Blanche during their short marriage (this was the case with the psalter of Saint Louis, discussed in chap. 3). Blanche also shared a confessor with Jeanne of Burgundy, the Franciscan Robert Boisseau; he may have been another conduit for the queen's books.[74]

An image of Blanche from this period survives in a copy of a painting that was in the chapel of Saint Michel at the Palais de la Cité, known today only through a watercolor made for the antiquarian Gaignières (Fig. 1.11).[75] The queen kneeling to the right of a Crucifixion and presented by Saint Denis must be identified as Blanche, the only queen of France to have held the coat of arms represented. Opposite Blanche are Philip VI and a smaller figure with the coat of arms of a dauphin, probably Charles, the grandson of Philip VI; both

---

I am grateful to her for sharing her transcription of these testaments with me.

73   For the gift-giving practices of the Valois, see Brigitte Buettner, "Past Presents: New Year's Gifts at the Valois Courts c. 1400," *Art Bulletin* 83, no. 4 (Dec. 2001), 598–625.

74   Xavier de la Selle, *La service des âmes à la cour: confesseurs et aumôniers des rois de France du XIIIe au XVe siècle* (Paris, 1995), pp. 312–13.

75   For the debate about the identity of the male figures represented and the occasion for the commission, see Raymond Cazelles, "Peinture et actualité politique sous les premiers Valois. Jean le Bon ou Charles, dauphin," *Gazette des Beaux Arts* (September 1978), 53–65; Pinoteau, "Tableaux français sous les premiers Valois," 119–76; and Jean-Bernard de Vaivre, "Sur trois primitifs français du XIVe siècle et le portrait de Jean le Bon," *Gazette des Beaux-Arts* (April 1981), 131–56.

FIGURE 1.11 *Crucifixion with Saint Louis, Philip VI, Charles V as dauphin, Blanche of Navarre, and Saint Denis*, late 17th- or early 18th-century copy made for François Roger de Gaignières of a painting made c. 1350 for the chapel of Saint Michel at the Palais de la Cité. PARIS, BIBLIOTHÈQUE NATIONALE DE FRANCE, DÉPARTEMENT DES ESTAMPES, OA 11, FOL. 89R. PHOTO CREDIT: BIBLIOTHÈQUE NATIONALE DE FRANCE.

men are presented by Saint Louis. The painting must postdate Blanche's marriage to Philip VI in January 1350, but predate his death in August 1350 because she is not shown as a widow. The composition depicts a relatively standard representation of donors, with a husband and wife facing each other across a sacred scene. What is unusual is the inclusion of the dauphin Charles, suggesting that the commission of the painting related to him. The trio of the king, the dauphin, and Saint Louis, placed together in a tight pyramidal form, suggests that what is celebrated here is dynastic continuity and sacred kingship; it seems most likely in this case that the patron was Philip VI.

The deaths of Blanche's mother and husband nine months apart, in October 1349 and August 1350, meant that their tomb memorials were likely among her

THE LIFE AND PATRONAGE OF BLANCHE OF NAVARRE

earliest commissions as queen.[76] As with many royal burials, both chose to have their organs buried separately from their bodies in order to honor different churches and maximize the potential for memorialization. The body of Philip VI was buried at Saint-Denis in the crossing next to his first wife, Jeanne, while his heart was buried at Bourgfontaine, where he and his father had founded a chapel, and his entrails at the church of the Jacobins in Paris, an important French royal burial site.[77] Among many royal burials there were the entrail tombs of Philip III and Marie of Brabant, as well as the body of Philip's father Charles of Valois.[78] Louis of Evreux and Margaret of Artois, Blanche's grandparents on her father's side, were also buried there. When Blanche's father Philip of Navarre died in 1343, his body was buried at the cathedral of Pamplona and his heart at the Jacobins.

The entrails tomb of Philip VI does not survive, but it was painted for Gaignières; Aubin-Louis Millin recorded the epitaph, which indicated Blanche's patronage: "this burial was commissioned by the queen Blanche, his wife" (Fig. 1.12).[79] The heart tombs of Blanche's parents for the Jacobins survive in fragmented form in the Louvre (Figs. 1.13, 1.14).[80] Philip of Navarre's tomb may already have been extant in 1350, as he had been dead since 1343, but Blanche certainly commissioned the heart tomb of her mother, as recorded in the epitaph on the tomb:

> Here lies the heart of Jeanne, by the grace of God queen of Navarre and countess of Evreux, daughter of Louis, king of France, eldest son of the

---

76 But the payment records of Charles V to the artist André Beauneveu for the tombs of Philip VI and Jeanne of Burgundy at Saint-Denis date from 1364; this is evidence that considerable time might elapse between death and the commission of a sculpted tomb; Jim Harris, "Digest of Documents," in *"No Equal in Any Land": André Beauneveu, Artist to the Courts of France and Flanders*, pp. 191–93.

77 For the Bourgfontaine chapel, see Sheila Bonde and Clark Maines, "The Heart of the Matter: Valois Patronage of the Charterhouse at Bourgfontaine," in *Patronage: Power & Agency in Medieval Art*, ed. Colum Hourihane (Princeton, 2013), pp. 77–98.

78 For the burials at the Jacobins, see Aubin-Louis Millin, *Antiquités nationales, ou Recueil des monumens pour servir à l'histoire générale et particulière de l'Empire françois*, 5 vols. (Paris, 1791), 4:69–70, 74–75; see also Tracy Chapman Hamilton, "Pleasure, Politics, and Piety: The Artistic Patronage of Marie de Brabant" (Ph.D. diss., University of Texas, Austin, 2004), pp. 299–300.

79 The inscription reads: "Cy-gissent les entrailles du roy Philippe-le-Vrai, Catholique, qui régna 22 ans, et trépassa le 28 d'août, l'an mil 1350. Priez dieu qu'il en ait l'ame, amen. A fait faire ceste sépultre la royne Blanche, son épouse." Other sources place the death date of Philip VI on 22 August, not 28 August; Millin, *Antiquités nationales*, 4:70, n. 133.

80 Françoise Baron, *Sculpture française: Moyen Âge* (Paris, 1996), p. 146.

FIGURE 1.12   *Entrails tomb of Philip VI at the church of the Jacobins, late 17th- or early 18th-century copy made for François Roger de Gaignières of a sculpted tomb made c. 1350.* BIBLIOTHÈQUE NATIONALE DE FRANCE, DÉPARTEMENT DES ESTAMPES, PE 11A, FOL. 199R. PHOTO CREDIT: BIBLIOTHÈQUE NATIONALE DE FRANCE.

FIGURE 1.13
Head of Philip III, count of Evreux and king of Navarre, from his heart tomb at the church of the Jacobins, marble, c. 1350. PHOTO CREDIT: RMN (MUSÉE DU LOUVRE).

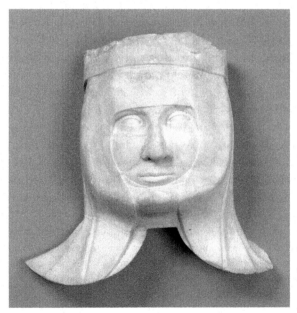

FIGURE 1.14
Head of Jeanne II, countess of Evreux and queen of Navarre, from her heart tomb at the church of the Jacobins, marble, c. 1350. PHOTO CREDIT: RMN (MUSÉE DU LOUVRE).

king Philip the Fair, who died at Conflans near Paris, the year 1349, the sixth day of October, and this tomb was made by the queen Blanche, her daughter, queen of France.[81]

This inscription on the tomb of Blanche's mother at Saint-Denis notes her daughter's name, if not explicitly her patronage ("this tomb was made by ...") as it did at the Jacobins:

> Here lies Jeanne, by the grace of God queen of Navarre, countess of Evreux, daughter of Louis, king of France, eldest son of the king Philip the Fair, mother of the queen Blanche queen of France, who died at Conflans near Paris in 1349, the sixth day of October.[82]

The citation of Blanche's name on these three funerary monuments of her husband and mother is prominent; in two, she indicated that the tomb was made by her, and in the last, though she does not take credit for the commission, her name was cited, indicating her involvement in some way in its production. The motivation for 'signing' the works in this way was twofold. First, and primarily, she was demonstrating that she was honoring the memory of those who had died and those whom she was obligated to memorialize. She was fulfilling her obligation to them and marking it by including her name on the epitaphs. Also she derived prestige from her association with her husband the king of France and her mother the queen of Navarre, and these inscriptions reminded of the viewer of her illustrious relatives. This commemoration of the deceased was also the motivation for the tomb for her daughter at Béziers, discussed in the introduction, which was itself perhaps an entrails tomb.

In September 1350, Pope Clement VI wrote to Blanche to express his condolences and to encourage her to remarry (the pope's candidate was Peter of Castile).[83] Blanche declined; she had discovered that she was pregnant and her daughter, named Jeanne, was born by May 1351.[84] Her motivation to marry a king in faraway Castile was small, as she was a wealthy widow with the means

---

81   "Cy-gist le cuer de Jehanne, par la grace de dieu, royne de Navarre, et comtesse d'Evreux, fille de Loys, roy de France, ainé fils du roi Phelippe-le-Bel, laquelle trèpassa à Conflans-lez-Paris, l'an M CCC XLIX, le VI jour d'octobre, et a fait faire cette sépultre la royne Blanche, leur fille, royne de France"; Millin, *Antiquités nationales*, p. 80.

82   Félibien, *Histoire de l'abbaye royale de saint Denys*, p. 552.

83   Guillaume Mollat, "Clément VI et Blanche de Navarre, reine de France," *Mélanges d'Archéologie et d'Histoire* 71 (1959), 377–80.

84   An account of John the Good, dated May 1351, noted that a girl was born to Blanche of Navarre; Paris, Bibliothèque nationale, MS fr. 20684, pièce 214.

THE LIFE AND PATRONAGE OF BLANCHE OF NAVARRE 51

to create an independent household, and she was surrounded in Paris by her family. In her household, in addition to her infant daughter, was her sister Jeanne la Jeune, still a young child (nine years old if she were the baby born to Jeanne of Navarre in 1342, discussed above), and her eldest sister Jeanne was at the nearby convent of Longchamp. Her aunt Jeanne of Evreux was another close female relative; the two were united not just by family ties, but by their status as dowager queens. The older queen served as a model for Blanche, as can be seen by the chapel at Saint-Denis and Jeanne's funeral that Blanche wished to replicate for herself. Jeanne had also been widowed young; her husband Charles IV had died in 1328, and she and Blanche had the same queenly responsibilities: to administer their lands, to give charity to the poor and sick, to patronize religious organizations, and to occasionally serve as mediator for the French king and his enemies. A commemoration of their close relationship can be seen in the number of objects she gave to Blanche that will be analyzed in the following chapters.

The connections between Blanche's female relatives will be evident throughout this book, but examples of these connections were those between the queens Jeanne of Evreux and Blanche and the royal princesses who were nuns at the convent of Longchamp. Founded in the mid-13th century by another royal princess, Isabelle, sister of Louis IX, the convent was just west of Paris, today part of the Bois de Boulogne.[85] The two princesses who lived at Longchamp were Jeanne, Blanche's sister, who had entered in 1337, and Blanche of France, daughter of Philip V, who had lived there since 1315 and taken vows in 1318. Jeanne of Evreux gave a book to her niece Jeanne at Longchamp called the *"beau livre,* which is of sermons and teachings,"* one of only a few books that she explicitly bequeathed to heirs beyond her daughter.[86] Blanche owned two of these nuns' books, analyzed in chapter 3, likely left to her at their deaths. That she associated the books with their ownership in her will meant that she wished to mark her family ties to these nuns and that their ownership added some value to the bequests (the books were given to the duchesses of Berry and Brittany).[87]

---

85 For the convent, see Anne-Hélène Allirot, "Longchamp and Lourcine: The Role of Female Abbeys in the Construction of Capetian Memory (Late Thirteenth Century to Mid-Fourteenth Century)," in *Memory and Commemoration in Medieval Culture,* ed. Elma Brenner, Meredith Cohen, and Mary Franklin-Brown (Farnham, Surrey, UK, 2013), pp. 243–60, and Sean Field, *Isabelle of France: Capetian Sanctity and Franciscan Identity in the Thirteenth Century* (South Bend, IN, 2006).

86 Joan Holladay, "Fourteenth-century French Queens as Collectors and Readers of Books: Jeanne d'Evreux and Her Contemporaries," *Journal of Medieval History* 32 (2006), p. 88.

87 Delisle 209, 218.

The Dowager Queen as Mediator: Charles of Navarre and the Hundred Years War

Much of our historical information about Blanche derives from the documentation of the actions of her brothers, Charles and Philip of Navarre. Charles of Navarre believed that he was entitled to the kingdom of France through his mother's descent from Louis X, and in the decades of the 1350s and 1360s, he tilted between the extremes of close ally to the French kings, John II and Charles V, and worst enemy, with occasionally only a day or two separating these states.[88] They had strong family ties; in addition to their shared heritage, Blanche had been married to Philip VI and Charles of Navarre had married Jeanne, the daughter of John II, in 1351. Because he was the son-in-law of John II and the brother-in-law of Charles V, Charles of Navarre would not be severely punished for his transgressions, but rather would be forgiven repeatedly. Blanche's other brother, Philip, count of Longueville, was Charles's lieutenant; his title appeared in documents as "gouverneur des terres de roi de Navarre en France et en Normandie."[89] He married Yolande of Flanders in 1353.

Blanche was constantly involved in Charles's conflicts, often using her special position as dowager queen to help him. It is difficult to fully characterize Blanche's role in her brother's struggles with John II and Charles V because the major source for these conflicts is contemporary chronicles. The authors of these histories rarely conveyed the activities of a woman, and when they were described, they were typically portrayed as acting only in the roles that were expected for a queen, such as mediator between warring factions. For this reason, most of Blanche's appearances in the historical records in this period are as a mediator between King John II and Charles of Navarre. But it is not necessarily an inaccurate portrait; scholars have noted that queens might embrace the role of a mediator as an avenue for exercising power at the late medieval court, and it is likely that Blanche perceived the advantages of the role.[90]

---

88   The conflicts between Charles of Navarre and the French kings are part of the history of the Hundred Years War. For documents relating to Charles and Blanche specifically, see Sécousse, *Mémoires*, and by the same author, *Recueil de pièces servant de preuves aux mémoires sur les troubles excités en France par Charles II, dit le Mauvais, roi de Navarre et comte d'Évreux* (Paris, 1775).

89   Lesort, "La Reine Blanche dans le Vexin et le Pays de Bray" (1954), p. 11, n. 5, citing Paris, Bibliothèque nationale, MS fr. 26005.

90   Lois Honeycutt, "Intercession and the High Medieval Queen: The Esther Topos," in *Power of the Weak: Studies on Medieval Women*, ed. Jennifer Carpenter and Sally-Beth McLean (Urbana, IL, 1995), pp. 126–46, and John Carmi Parsons, "The Queen's Intercession in Thirteenth-Century England," in *Power of the Weak*, pp. 147–77.

THE LIFE AND PATRONAGE OF BLANCHE OF NAVARRE
53

The first of Blanche's many interventions on behalf of her brother took place in 1354, when Blanche and Jeanne of Evreux requested a pardon of Charles for the assassination of the king's favorite, Charles of Spain. The intervention was commemorated in a manuscript image in the *Grandes chroniques* of Charles V painted two decades after the event (Fig. 1.15).[91] The two queens are depicted at the pardon ceremony of March 1354, standing behind Charles of Navarre as he kneels before the French king John II. From the perspective of more than twenty years later, the emphasis on the queens' intervention was surely intended to deflect readers' curiosity about why Charles had ever been pardoned in the first place, when this infraction was the first of many committed by the king of Navarre. Indeed, the queens were called upon to plead Charles's case several times again in the next few years, when the king of Navarre was accused of masterminding a number of plots to overthrow John II.[92] The most acute crisis among these was the rebellion in Paris led by Étienne Marcel in 1357–58; Charles allied himself with Marcel because he believed himself to be the most genealogically appropriate alternative to the Valois kings. Jeanne of Evreux and Blanche of Navarre were in Paris negotiating between Charles of Navarre and the dauphin Charles, who was regent for John II, a hostage in England since the disastrous battle of Poitiers in 1356.[93]

Blanche's intervention on her brother's behalf may also have been occasionally much more partisan than neutral. In August 1358, Navarrais forces took control of the town and château of Melun, Blanche's dower property southeast of Paris on the Seine, a crucial point for control of traffic on the river.[94] Blanche was present at the fall of the city and for the subsequent siege by the dauphin Charles, but her precise role is less clear – did she invite the troops into the city and deceive the townspeople with assurances that their stay was only temporary, according to one account, or was she an unwilling host, according to

---

91   On this manuscript, MS fr. 2813, and other illuminated *Grandes chroniques* manuscripts, see Anne D. Hedeman, *The Royal Image: Illustrations of the* Grandes chroniques de France, *1274–1422* (Berkeley, 1991).

92   The letters from the dowager queens to Charles of Navarre are published in Sécousse, *Recueil de pièces servant de preuves*, pp. 565–66, 569–70, 573–74.

93   For the negotiations of Jeanne and Blanche in this period, see Sécousse, *Mémoires*, pp. 195, 262, 276.

94   Melun was one of Blanche's dower properties. In March 1350, Philip VI had given her a dower largely similar to the dower of the recently deceased queen Jeanne of Burgundy, near Paris. For analysis of Blanche's dower, see Lesort, "La Reine Blanche" (1948), 35–67; and Lesort, "La Reine Blanche" (1954), 9–88.

FIGURE 1.15 *Pardon of Charles II, king of Navarre,* Grandes chroniques, *1375–80.* PARIS, BIBLIOTHÈQUE NATIONALE DE FRANCE, MS FR. 2813, FOL. 395R. PHOTO CREDIT: BIBLIOTHÈQUE NATIONALE DE FRANCE.

THE LIFE AND PATRONAGE OF BLANCHE OF NAVARRE

another?[95] The conflict at Melun ended in the summer of 1359, when the dauphin and Charles of Navarre agreed to a treaty. Blanche signed a separate agreement to return Melun to the crown in exchange for the châteaux and towns of Vernon, Vernonnet, and Pontoise, the château of Neaufles (which Blanche would make her major residence in the last few decades of her life), Gisors with the exception of the town and the château, Neufchâtel, and Gournay.[96] One negotiator on behalf of the Navarrais faction was Regnault de Braquemont, a knight who was still in Blanche's service at the time her will was written in 1396.[97]

Blanche was at Bernay in Normandy with Jeanne, the wife of Charles of Navarre, from December 1359 to July 1361, interrupted by at least one seventeen-day stay in Paris, accompanied by the same queen.[98] In 1363, Blanche's brother Philip fell ill in Vernon and died; a chronicler relayed that Blanche was greatly grieved at his death.[99] That her grief was worth mentioning is intended to be a testament to the reputation of her brother – the chronicler praises him as a 'bon chevalier' – as well as evidence that Blanche's devotion to her brothers and to their cause and the Navarrais party was clearly recognized. Blanche arranged for Philip's burial at the cathedral of Evreux, but declined, via a letter from her confessor, to serve as the executor of his will; the letter, written by Pierre Basin, establishes an early appearance in Blanche's service of the confessor who would still be serving her in this role 30 years later.[100]

In the spring of 1364, Blanche was again swept up in her brother's conflicts, as Charles launched another campaign in France. The dauphin's forces sacked the Navarrais stronghold of Mantes in April 1364; Blanche lost a number of valuable possessions there, among them a crown, two silver reliquaries, and a piece of coral.[101] At Vernon in mid-April, she negotiated a peace agreement

---

95   For the accounts of Blanche's participation in the fall of Melun, see Sécousse, *Mémoires*, pp. 322–23, and the letters published in Sécousse, *Recueil de pièces servant de preuves*, pp. 88–89, 102–3, 117, 122.

96   Lesort, "La Reine Blanche" (1954), pp. 10–11.

97   Sécousse, *Mémoires*, p. 123.

98   Lesort, "La Reine Blanche" (1954), p. 11, citing Paris, Bibliothèque nationale, MS fr. 26004, p. 1229.

99   *Chronique des quatre premiers Valois*, ed. S. Luce (Paris, 1862), pp. 132–33.

100   For the burial arrangements, *Chronique des quatre premiers Valois*, p. 133, and for the letter of Pierre Basin, see Michelle Bubenicek, *Quand les femmes gouvernent: droit et politique au XIVe siècle: Yolande de Flandre* (Paris, 2002), p. 218, nn. 75 and 76, citing Archives départementales du Nord, B. 454.

101   *Catalogue des livres et documents historiques du cabinet de M. de Courcelles* (Paris, 1834), p. 16.

with the dauphin to avoid a siege of Vernon by his army. To avoid future instances of her châteaux being used to house her brother's forces, she agreed to accept captains loyal to the French king to administer her properties.[102] In the spring of 1365, Blanche of Navarre and Jeanne of Evreux negotiated another peace treaty between Charles V and Charles of Navarre.[103]

The Dowager Queen at Home and at Court

Blanche was at the French court for the baptism of the king's daughter in June 1366, for whom she served as godmother with Jeanne of Evreux and Margaret, countess of Artois.[104] In August 1366, Charles V gave permission for Blanche to use 500 livres parisis on foundations for the care of her husband's soul.[105] The recipient of part of the funds was Saint-Denis, as an August 1372 document indicates that 200 of the 500 livres had already been spent to endow two chaplaincies there.[106] The date of August 1372 for the second document suggests that the remaining amount, 300 livres, was also intended for Saint-Denis, as Blanche had endowed the chapel there only two months earlier.

On 16 July 1370, Blanche's daughter Jeanne was engaged in Paris to John, duke of Girona, heir of the king of Aragon; the tragic outcome of this engagement was described in the introduction above.[107] Charles V gave the young princess at least one book as a wedding gift, detailed in one of his inventories as "a breviary with an embroidered binding with the arms of France and Aragon, which was returned after the death of Jeanne de France …"[108] The book was returned to Charles presumably because it was his wedding gift to the princess, though it is also possible that it was not yet finished when the

---

102　The Treaty of Vernon is British Library Add. Ch. 23; for analysis of the treaty, see Roland Delachenal, *Histoire de Charles V*, 5 vols. (Paris, 1909–31), 3:543–55, and Jonathan Sumption, *The Hundred Years War II: Trial by Fire* (Philadelphia, 1999), p. 507.

103　*Mandements et actes divers de Charles V*, ed. Léopold Delisle (Paris, 1874), pp. 104–11.

104　*Chronique des règnes de Jean II et Charles V*, ed. Roland Delachenal, 2 vols. (Paris, 1917–20), 2:20–21.

105　*Mandements de Charles V*, p. 167.

106　*Mandements de Charles V*, pp. 473–74.

107　The marriage was arranged on 16 July 1370 at the Hôtel Saint-Pol, in the presence of King Charles V and two knights from Aragon; *Chronique des règnes de Jean II et de Charles V*, 2:143.

108　Léopold Delisle, *Recherches sur la librairie de Charles V*, 3 vols. (Paris, 1907), 2:27–28. For books as typical wedding gifts, see Brigitte Buettner, "Women and the Circulation of Books," *Journal of the Early Book Society* 4 (2001), 9–31, especially pp. 16–19.

THE LIFE AND PATRONAGE OF BLANCHE OF NAVARRE

princess died. It is not clear why it was still associated with Jeanne's name in Charles's collection, but probably the unusual combination of France and Aragon merited an explanation of how the book had come into the king's possession. In the spring of 1371, probably about the same time he commissioned the breviary for Jeanne of France, he had another book rebound as a gift to Charles of Navarre, a sign of a reconciliation between them.[109] The practice of rebinding books before giving them away, here for Charles of Navarre in the silk fabric camaca from the Holy Land, was a way of repurposing a book as a special gift (it is analyzed in chap. 3).

After the death of her daughter, Blanche began to plan in earnest for the final resting place of her daughter's body and her own, though, as noted above, she had likely intended to request burial in the chapel of Saint Hippolyte at Saint-Denis as early as 1350, after her husband's death on this saint's feast day.[110] Charles v paid for the transport of her daughter's body home, for her funeral at Saint-Denis, and for the commission of the tomb at Saint-Denis; an act of 4 November 1371 signed in Paris indicated that he agreed to do so.[111] That he paid for the tomb made Charles v the 'patron' of the work, in the traditional sense of the word, though he was presumably not in any meaningful way involved in the choice of objects that were to go in the chapel. In this instance, Blanche was a 'maker' of the tomb and the chapel in the way that Therese Martin has described (see introduction above).[112]

Our knowledge about Blanche of Navarre's activities at the French court drops off precipitously after 1371, after the death of her daughter, the death of Jeanne of Evreux (in March 1371), and after her brother ceased to be a significant threat to Charles v. We depend on fragmentary household records to see her presence in Paris and in Neaufles and the administration of her lands. She was present at the funeral of the queen of France, Jeanne of Bourbon, in 1378, as well as at the October 1380 meeting to determine the regency of the French

---

109   "Pour une alne et demi quartier de camocas d'oultre mer, delivrée de nostre commandement à messire Michiel, nostre chapellain, pour faire une couverture et une chemise à un breviaire que nous envirasme à nostre très chier et amé frère le roy de Navarre, le xvie jour d'avril [M ccc lxxi]"; *Mandements de Charles v*, p. 400, no. 779.

110   Damien Berné, "L'action mémorielle des princesses capétiennes à Saint-Denis au xive siècle," *Histoire de l'art* 63 (Oct. 2008), 39–40.

111   This agreement is published in Léon de Laborde, *Musée des Archives (de l'Empire) nationales, Actes importants de l'histoire de France* (Paris, 1867), pp. 224–25.

112   Therese Martin, "Exceptions and Assumptions: Women in Medieval Art History," in *Reassessing the Roles of Women as 'Makers' of Medieval Art and Architecture*, ed. Therese Martin, 2 vols. (Leiden, 2012), pp. 1–33.

58   CHAPTER 1

kingdom after the death of Charles V when his son was still a minor.[113] She also
continued to commission works of art, such as stained-glass windows for the
cathedral of Evreux, dated by Françoise Gatouillat to 1388–90.[114]

A typical study of a medieval patron would end here, with what we know
about the subject through official histories and archival documentation. But
for Blanche it is possible to turn to a more personal document, her will, written
over two days in 1396 with a codicil added in 1398. These testaments fill out
Blanche's narrative because we can see from their details where she lived, with
whom she lived, her broader familial and social ties, and what she prioritized
for her remembrance after death. The testament is not exempt from the biases
of historical documentation noted throughout this chapter; testaments have
their own conventions and typical formulations that dictate the wishes of the
deceased. Indeed, as will be discussed in chapter 2, Blanche's testament is different enough from other testaments in its strategies that it stands in a category
all its own, as much sentimental autobiography as legal document.

The will mentioned several people that have been already named in the
historical records discussed thus far, such as Regnault de Braquemont, who is
called by Blanche in the will an 'amé et féal chevalier et conseiller,' and Pierre
de Basin, her confessor. These two men were joined by Oudart le Gendre (in
the will he is 'Oudart de Venderez'), Thibaut Roussel, and Estienne Joffroy (in
the will 'Estienne Gieuffron'), three of the will's executors, at the transfer of the
nail relic to the Carmelites in 1398.[115] We would know, therefore, about their service to Blanche regardless of the serendipitous survival of the will, but there are
dozens of other members of Blanche's household who are otherwise unmentioned in historical documentation, especially the women, about whom we
learn a great deal. To one, Jeanne de Rouières, a damoiselle, or lady-in-waiting,
she left a suit of clothing and four books: the breviary used by her daughter, a
book with advice on living and dying well, a *Miracles de Notre-Dame*, and a book
on surgery.[116] These bequests are analyzed in the third chapter. The last bequest
listed was a house, worth about 200 francs. We know the value of the house

---

113   *Chronique de Jean II et de Charles V*, 2:278–82, 385, n. 2.

114   See Françoise Gatouillat, "La Vierge de Blanche de Navarre et quelques vitraux inédits de
        la cathédrale d'Évreux," in *Pierre, lumière, couleur: études d'histoire de l'art du Moyen Âge
        en l'honneur d'Anne Prache*, ed. Fabienne Joubert and Dany Sandron (Paris, 1999), pp. 309–
        25. This commission was also discussed in *Paris 1400: les arts sous Charles VI* (Paris, 2004),
        p. 327.

115   For the later history of the family of Oudart de Venderez, see Dominique Hervier, *Pierre le
        Gendre et son inventaire après décès: une famille parisienne à l'aube de la Renaissance: étude
        historique et méthodologique* (Paris, 1977).

116   Delisle 276–80.

FIGURE 1.16 *Château of Blanche of Navarre, Neaufles.* PHOTO CREDIT: MARGUERITE KEANE.

because if Jeanne did not want the house, Blanche agreed to compensate her for this amount.[117] The gifts to Jeanne de Rouières demonstrate another model for understanding the collection and dissemination of objects by Blanche, as they radiate outward from the most personal to the most public, from a suit of clothing that Blanche had worn, to her books, and finally, to a house. This trajectory is an indication of how Blanche valued her gifts to the members of her household, and these kinds of strategies will be analyzed in the next chapter. This bequest tells us not only the identity of Jeanne de Rouières, but also about the transfer of books between women (who educated children, a role Blanche commemorates with the book with which her daughter had learned), and Blanche's desire to set up an independent household for a beloved servant through the gift of a house, with the generous provision that Jeanne could decide not to choose the house and be given money instead.

Blanche owned several residences, but the two where she primarily lived in the last decades of her life were at Neaufles, near Gisors, and in Paris. In the will she wrote that she expected her death to occur at one of these two places. Only the tower of the château at Neaufles survives today (Fig. 1.16). Built in the twelfth century, the tower had three floors, with a diameter of about forty feet and walls more than six feet thick; it was in its current fragmentary state by

---

117 Delisle 281.

1610.[118] In the early 18th century, Félibien described Blanche's house in Paris as one on the rue de la Tixanderie, between the rue du Coq and the rue des Deux Portes.[119] This would mean that her local parish was Saint-Jean-en-Grève, accounting for her wish that she be taken to this church if she died in Paris.[120] This house eventually went to Pierre of Navarre; three years after Pierre's death in 1412, a house described as in the rue Vieille Tixanderie and left to him by Queen Blanche of Navarre was sold.[121]

From this discussion of historical documents, I shift in the next chapter to an analysis of the will as a literary document. Blanche's life story as told in the present chapter is based on chronicles and documentary evidence, whereas the will is in the queen's own words (as much as we can assume); there we see her life and her household not from the perspective of documentary glimpses or of the monks at Saint-Denis, or as related to the activities of the Hundred Years War, but from her own viewpoint.

---

118   Lesort, "La Reine Blanche" (1948) p. 47.

119   Michel Félibien, *Histoire de la ville de Paris*, 2 vols. (Paris, 1725), 1:662.

120   Delisle 7.

121   Testament de Pierre de Navarre, Comte de Mortain, on the website Testaments enregistrés au Parlement de Paris sous le règne de Charles VI, <http://corpus.enc.sorbonne.fr/testaments>, citing: Accords des 22 décembre 1413, 14 décembre 1414, et 2 mai 1415, Arch. nat., X^{1C}, 106, 108, 109.

CHAPTER 2

The Testament: Legal Document and Sentimental Autobiography

This chapter treats the testament of Blanche of Navarre as part of the genre of testamentary writing of the second half of the 14th century. Each testament has a subject: the person who is disposing of possessions; for this reason, it can serve as a kind of autobiography. In this regard, Blanche portrays herself in two roles in the testament, as a mother and as a mediator,[1] both duties expected of the ideal 14th-century queen. Blanche was thereby celebrating an identity that had given her access to power at the French court, as well as an identity that connected her to queens past, like Jeanne of Evreux. This presentation of her identity and the detail she layered into her bequests, together with the emotions expressed in them, were intended to increase the efficacy of the testament, its ultimate goal being the promotion of Blanche's memory and prayer for her soul.

We know of three testamentary documents for Blanche of Navarre: a will and a codicil of 1396, and a codicil of 1398.[2] There were almost certainly earlier wills made by Blanche that these final wills superceded; her aunt Jeanne of Evreux was known to have drawn up wills in 1326 and 1349, but only her final

---

1 In my dissertation, I first explored the idea that Blanche's role as a mediator in the political life of the French court could also be evident in her 'mediating' of objects in her testament: "Remembering Louis IX as a Family Saint: A Study of the Images of Saint Louis Created for Jeanne, Blanche, and Marie of Navarre" (Ph.D. diss, University of California, Santa Barbara, 2002), pp. 90–118.

2 The original does not survive; a contemporary copy of the 1396 testament, the 1396 codicil, and the September 1398 codicil is Pau, Archives départementales des Pyrénées-Atlantiques, E512. It was published by Léopold Delisle, "Testament de Blanche de Navarre, reine de France," *Mémoires de la Société de l'histoire de Paris et de l'Ile de France* 12 (1885), 1–64. There was perhaps a codicil of October 1398; it was described as a testament by Hippolyte Sauvage, "Documents relatifs à la donation du comte-pairie de Mortain à Pierre de Navarre par Charles VI," *Mélanges de la Société de l'histoire de Normandie* 5 (1898), p. 226. I am grateful to Elizabeth A.R. Brown for this reference. See also Michel Georges Dubosc, *Inventaire–sommaire des Archives départementales de la Manche antérieures à 1790* (Saint-Lo, 1865), p. 41 for a reference to one of Blanche's documents listed as part of series A 213. Series A of the archive was destroyed in 1944.

© KONINKLIJKE BRILL NV, LEIDEN, 2016 | DOI 10.1163/9789004318830_004

62   CHAPTER 2

testaments, from 1366/67 and 1370, survive.[3] The survival of Blanche's will is serendipitous, a result of it having been copied soon after her death, for her nephew Charles III, king of Navarre (Fig. 2.1).[4] This copy was catalogued in the Archives des Basses-Pyrénées (today the Archives départementales des Pyrénées-Atlantiques) in the second half of the nineteenth century; it seems likely to have been part of the archive of the kings of Navarre previously conserved in the château of Pau.[5] The language is French; the use of the vernacular was typical for French royal wills in the second half of the 14th century.[6] The copy is written on paper.[7] Because it is a copy, the document is not signed but only describes the signatures, such as that on the September 1398 codicil: "et signé en marge: Par la royne, presens l'evesque de Senlis, frère Pierre Basin, confesseur, le sire de Braquemont, maistre Estienne Gieuffron et maistre Oudart de Venderez, et moy: T. Roussel."

The 1396 testament was written in Paris on two days in March 1396, the first document on 18 March and the first codicil on 20 March, and signed 'par la royne' by two of the queen's secretaries, Thibaut Roussel and Jean Menart. It was written in the first person (the first person plural 'nostre' is used throughout), and indeed Blanche should be considered the author of the testament even if she did not take pen to paper. The lengthy bequests with personal details – my husband loved this diamond a lot and it was given to him by his sister, the book was one with which my daughter learned to read – make it clear that Blanche's personal memories and wishes for each bequest were recorded by the men who were writing the documents. Shona Kelly Wray and Roisin Cossar have cautioned against a straightforward reading of the bequests of the will as the desires of the testator, however, noting that the scribes and

---

3   Elizabeth A.R. Brown, "The Testamentary Strategies of Jeanne d'Évreux: The Endowment of Saint-Denis in 1343," in *Magistra Doctissima: Essays in Honor of Bonnie Wheeler*, ed. Dorsey Armstrong, Ann W. Astell, and Howell Chickering (Kalamazoo, MI, 2013), pp. 217–47.

4   Delisle identified the document as an approximately contemporary copy, "Testament," p. 1. The outside edge of the testament is addressed: "Au roy de Navarre." An original, if it was once kept with the other royal wills, does not survive in the Trésor des Chartes in Paris.

5   *Inventaire-sommaire des Archives départementales antérieures à 1790: Basses-Pyrénées*, ed. Paul Raymond, 6 vols. (Paris, 1863–79), vol. 4, *Titres de Navarre*.

6   The 1347 and 1350 wills of Philip VI are also in French, as are the 1366/67 and 1370 wills of Jeanne d'Evreux.

7   Paper had become increasingly popular in the 14th century in France as a cheaper alternative to parchment. For data on the cost of paper relative to parchment, see Carlo Bozzolo and Ezio Ornato, *Pour une histoire du livre manuscrit au Moyen Âge: trois essais de codicologie quantitative* (Paris, 1980). For the use of paper in late medieval Brittany, see Diane Booton, *Manuscripts, Market, and the Transition to Print in Late Medieval Brittany* (Farnham, Surrey, UK, 2010).

THE TESTAMENT: LEGAL DOCUMENT AND SENTIMENTAL AUTOBIOGRAPHY 63

FIGURE 2.1 *Testament of Blanche of Navarre, c. 1398.* ARCHIVES DÉPARTEMENTALES DES PYRÉNÉES-ATLANTIQUES, PAU, E 525. PHOTO CREDIT: MARGUERITE KEANE.

64 CHAPTER 2

others present at the writing of the will might well have greatly influenced the wording and outcome of the bequests.[8]

The first testament, written on 18 March 1396, outlined Blanche's plans for her funeral, the burial, and the money and gifts that should be given to churches. The objects that were given away on this day were vestments, paintings, sculpture, and reliquaries, those that would be appropriate for churches, in a more public than personal devotional context. It was on this first day therefore that Blanche took care of the corporate commemoration of her memory and care for her soul. On the second day, 20 March, Blanche's executors composed the list of funds and objects that were to be given away to individuals (with the exception of the nail reliquary for the Carmelites, which was the only object given to a church on the second day, and a bequest of funds to the abbey of Noe for an anniversary Mass). In this individual commemoration of Blanche's memory, transmitted by the books, reliquaries and other *joyaux*, room hangings, and household textiles, the communities of her life come into view. These included the members of her household, her family, and the larger community at the royal court in Paris. The second codicil was added two and a half years later, on 10 September 1398, at the queen's residence at Neaufles; it was required because Blanche had partially executed the first will already. She wrote about her affection for her servants and the events of the day in which she gave them the funds promised in the will:

> Item, en la grant maladie que nous eusmes ou mois de mars mil CCC IIII^xx et seze, nous, pour l'affeccion et grant amour que nous avons eue et avons touz jours à nos serviteurs, considerans les longs, bons et agréables services que ceulx que lors avions nous avoient faiz continuelment, les feismes tous venir devant nous en les merciant de leurs diz services, leur criant mercy et pardon des poines et travaulx que nous leur avions faiz, ce que ilz ous pardonnèrent moult charitablement, la leur mercy, en nous recommandant en leurs bonnes prieres. Et en après ordenasmes leur estre paié en deniers comptans, que nous feismes bailler de noz coffres, les lez en deniers que à un chascun d'eulx avions faiz en nostre dit premier codicille, et des sommes qui leur furent paiées est faitte mencion cy en après, et par ce deschargie en avons nostre execucion. Et neantmoins, d'abondant, par ce present codicille, donnons et laissons encore à noz serviteurs presentement, pour et en remuneracion de leurs bon services,

---

8 Shona Kelly Wray and Roisin Cossar, "Wills as Primary Sources," in *Understanding Medieval Primary Sources: Using Historical Sources to Discover Medieval Europe*, ed. Joel T. Rosenthal (New York, 2012), pp. 59–71.

THE TESTAMENT: LEGAL DOCUMENT AND SENTIMENTAL AUTOBIOGRAPHY   65

que depuis ilz nous ont continuelment faiz et feront encores, se Dieu plaist, les lez qui ensuyvent, c'est assavoir:[9]

[Item, in the great sickness that I had in the month of March 1396 [ancien style, so March 1397], I, for the affection and great love that I have and have always had for my servants, considering the long, good, and pleasant service that they have done continuously, had them come before me, thanking them for their service, asking for their mercy and their forgiveness for the pains and work I had caused them, they pardoned me most charitably, in their mercy, and recommended me in their prayers. And after I ordered that they be paid in money, that I had delivered from my coffers, the money that each had been set out in the first codicil, and the sums that they were paid is made mention after, and by this discharged the execution. Nevertheless, furthermore, by this present codicil I give and leave still to my present servants, for remuneration of their good service that they continually and still give to me, as God please, that which follows, to wit:]

Blanche ensured that at least this part of the will would be executed the way that she wished by doing so in her lifetime, echoing what had been done by Jeanne of Evreux with her own testaments.[10] When Blanche survived this illness of March 1397, the 10 September 1398 codicil was necessary to acknowledge what had been already given away and what new money was to be offered to each household member. She also had several new possessions in 1398 for which a recipient had to be named, among them a set of textile hangings decorated with the letter B and another with lilies of the Virgin Mary, and a relic of Saint Bartholomew. The 1398 codicil was signed by Roussel again, who described the others who were also present: the bishop of Senlis; Pierre Basin, the queen's confessor; the sire of Braquemont; Estienne Gieuffron; and Oudart de Venderez. Regnault de Braquemont, Oudart de Venderez, and Pierre Basin are also mentioned in the first will and codicil, as is the bishop of Senlis, Jean Dieudonné. Blanche died less than a month after this codicil was signed, in the first week of October 1398.

Blanche's dower properties reverted to the king, so these are not part of the testament, but she did give away properties that she had purchased herself (such as the house given to Jeanne de Rouières discussed in chap. 1), as well as objects like jewelry, books, or textiles that in testament terminology are called

---

9   Delisle 411.
10   Brown, "The Testamentary Strategies of Jeanne d'Évreux," pp. 217–47.

'movables.' It is not surprising that Blanche, as a dowager queen with a great deal of property, would write a testament, but this was not the case for most women in the late Middle Ages. In her analysis of 550 medieval wills in which at least one movable was given away, Kristen Burkholder determined that only 16.5 percent of wills were made by women, and almost all were widows.[11] That Blanche's daughter predeceased her made it much more likely that her testament would be detailed, with a long discussion of her possessions. If her daughter Jeanne had still been alive in 1396, Blanche perhaps would have left the bulk of her possessions to her and as a result left them undescribed in the testament. In her 1371 will, Jeanne of Evreux left three books to individuals and all the rest to her daughter; the books that were given to her daughter were not described.[12]

As a legal document with a certain number of conventions, much of the content of Blanche's testament is typical of the testaments written by her contemporaries. In the analysis that follows, I compare Blanche's testament with those written by her husband Philip VI in 1347 and 1350, and the two made for his first wife, Queen Jeanne of Burgundy, of 1329 and 1336.[13] These testaments long predate Blanche's testament, but Philip VI and Jeanne of Burgundy would have likely served as models for how Blanche might disseminate her own possessions. Blanche cited the ownership or provenance of Jeanne of Burgundy for five items in her testament.[14] Another testamentary exemplar was Blanche's aunt Jeanne of Evreux, who made a number of testaments in her life; Elizabeth A.R. Brown has argued that this queen was particularly attuned to the ben-

---

11   Kristen Burkholder, "Threads Bared: Dress and Textiles in Late Medieval English Wills," in *Medieval Clothing and Textiles*, vol. 1, ed. Robin Netherton and Gale Owen-Crocker (Woodbridge, UK, 2005), pp. 133–53, esp. 133–37.

12   For this queen's book collection and this bequest, see Joan Holladay, "Fourteenth-century French Queens as Collectors and Readers of Books: Jeanne d'Evreux and Her Contemporaries," *Journal of Medieval History* 32 (2006), 69–100. In her 1329 will, Jeanne of Burgundy requested that all of her books be given to her daughter Marie; Murielle Gaude-Ferragu, "Les dernières volontés de la reine de France. Les deux testaments de Jeanne de Bourgogne, femme de Philippe VI de Valois (1329, 1336)," *Annuaire-Bulletin de la Société de l'histoire de France, année 2007* (2009), p. 44. For evidence of the dissemination of books more widely, beyond the children of the testator, see Joel T. Rosenthal, "Aristocratic Cultural Patronage and Book Bequests, 1350–1500," *Bulletin of the John Rylands University Library of Manchester* 64 (1982), 522–48.

13   For the will of Jeanne of Burgundy, see Gaude-Ferragu, "Les dernières volontés de la reine de France," pp. 23–66.

14   Delisle 192, 195, 200, 204, and 211. Delisle 205, a crown, was also associated with Jeanne of Burgundy, but this seems to be an error on the part of the scribe; see the discussion in chapter 5 below.

efit of testaments for control over her memory.[15] I consider the testamentary acts of Jeanne of Evreux throughout this book, but especially important is the record of the execution of Jeanne's will in 1372, because it lists so many of her possessions.

Finally, there are three testaments that are particularly illuminating for comparison to the testament of Blanche of Navarre because they were made by members of her family within five years of the writing of her testament. The analysis that follows will consider the ways in which Blanche's bequests both parallel and diverge from their practices. The first is the May 1392 testament of the daughter of Jeanne of Evreux, Blanche, duchess of Orléans; the controversy over this duchess's nail reliquary was discussed above.[16] The second was created in 1401 by Jeanne, viscountess of Rohan, a younger sister of Blanche of Navarre.[17] The last was written in 1399 by Blanche's cousin, Louis of Evreux, count of Étampes.[18] Blanche of Orléans was born in 1328, the daughter of Jeanne of Evreux and Charles IV. She was married to Philip, duke of Orléans, the son of Blanche's husband Philip VI, in 1345. Blanche exchanged a number of gifts in her lifetime with Blanche of Orléans (see below). The latter Blanche died in 1393 and was buried in her mother's chapel at Saint-Denis. As noted in the previous chapter, Blanche's sister Jeanne was probably born in 1342, and lived with Blanche, probably until her marriage before 1377 to John, viscount of Rohan. She died in 1403. Louis of Evreux, born in 1336, was Blanche's cousin, the son of her father's brother Charles (and therefore also a nephew of Jeanne of Evreux; the significance of this relationship for a gift will be considered in chap. 5). He was a longtime companion and advisor of King Charles V. He died in 1400 of an attack of apoplexy at a dinner with the duke of Berry at the hôtel

---

15 Brown, "The Testamentary Strategies of Jeanne d'Évreux," pp. 217–47.

16 For this project I use Blanche's testament of 21 May 1392 and codicil of January 1393, published by Gaston Vignat, "Testament de Blanche, duchesse d'Orléans," *Mémoires de la Sociéte archéologique de l'Orléanais* 9 (1866), 115–44. Blanche died in February 1392, before Easter, so February 1393; P. Anselme, *Histoire généalogique et chronologique de la maison royale de France*, 9 vols. (Paris, 1726–33), 1:675. For the testament of Blanche of Orléans, see also Elizabeth A.R. Brown, "The Parlement de Paris and the Welfare of the Dead," in *Le parlement en sa cour. Études en l'honneur du Professeur Jean Hilaire*, ed. Olivier Descamps, Françoise Hildesheimer, and Monique Morgat-Bonnet (Paris, 2012), pp. 47–73.

17 The will of Jeanne of Rohan was published by Pierre-Hyacinthe Morice, "Testament de Jeanne de Navarre, vicomtesse de Rohan," in *Mémoires pour servir de preuves à l'histoire ecclésiastique et civile de Bretagne*, 3 vols. (Paris, 1742–46), 2:716–22.

18 The will of Louis of Étampes was published by Jacques Lescournay, "Testament de Louys, comte d'Estampes," *Mémoires de la ville de Dourdan* (Paris, 1624), pp. 103–11.

du Nesle.[19] He, too, was buried at Saint-Denis.[20] Like Blanche of Navarre and Blanche of Orléans, Louis of Evreux had no living children on whom to settle his possessions.

At the outset of all of these wills, the testators stated their soundness of mind and body, gave declarations about religious faith, and supplied instructions for the executors. The testator's wishes for his or her burial followed. Blanche's instructions for her funeral and burial (discussed in the previous chapter) were extensive. In their great detail, the directives are comparable to the 1392 testament of her cousin Blanche of Orléans and the 1401 testament of her sister Jeanne of Rohan, both of whom also left exhaustive instructions for funerary commemoration.[21]

The instructions for burial were typically followed by the testator's gifts to religious houses; these gifts would ensure that Masses would be said for the soul of the deceased. Most of the churches and religious institutions that were recipients of Blanche's generosity were in Paris or near to this city in her current or former dower lands (Fig. 2.2). The obligation she must have felt to distribute funds and objects to the churches in her lands is expressed explicitly in one of the bequests of the will, in which she says that the churches of Vernon, Evreux, and Melun are or were at one time part of her dower.[22] Blanche, following the examples of so many of her fellow royal testators, among them Jeanne of Evreux and Blanche of Orléans, also gave precious gifts in addition to money to religious foundations, including statues, reliquaries, paintings, and vest-

---

19   *Chronique du Religieux de Saint-Denys, contenant le règne de Charles VI, de 1380 à 1422*, ed. L. Bellaguet, 6 vols. (Paris, 1839–52), 2:751

20   For the epitaphs of Louis of Evreux and his wife, Jeanne de Brienne (d. 1389), see Michel Félibien, *Histoire de l'Abbaye royale de saint Denys en France* (Paris, 1706), pp. 559–60.

21   Blanche's wishes for her funeral and burial are in Vignat, "Testament de Blanche, duchesse d'Orléans," pp. 117–20; for Jeanne's intentions for her funeral, see Morice, "Testament de Jeanne de Navarre, vicomtesse de Rohan," 2:716–22.

22   The phrase from the will is "que nous avons longuement tenuz en douaire"; Delisle 529. Evreux was actually a part of her brother Charles's lands; Melun was given to Blanche in March 1350 as part of her original dower by Philip VI. After the rebellions of Charles of Navarre in which Blanche aided her brother by giving him access to Melun, it was taken from her. In 1359, Charles V, still regent, gave Blanche, in exchange for Melun, the châtellenies, châteaux, and towns of Vernon, Vernonnet, and Pontoise, the château of Neaufles near Gisors, all of the vicomté of Gisors, with the exception of the town and the château, Neufchâtel and Gournay; Denis-François Sécousse, *Mémoires pour servir à l'histoire de Charles II, roi de Navarre et comte d'Évreux, surnommé le Mauvais* (Paris, 1758), 1:398. For the typical patterns of distribution of funds for the salvation of the soul, see Wray and Cossar, *Wills as Primary Sources*, pp. 66–68.

THE TESTAMENT: LEGAL DOCUMENT AND SENTIMENTAL AUTOBIOGRAPHY   69

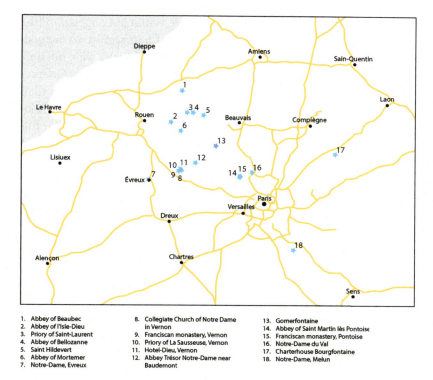

1. Abbey of Beaubec
2. Abbey of l'Isle-Dieu
3. Priory of Saint-Laurent
4. Abbey of Bellozanne
5. Saint Hildevert
6. Abbey of Mortemer
7. Notre-Dame, Evreux
8. Collegiate Church of Notre Dame in Vernon
9. Franciscan monastery, Vernon
10. Priory of La Sausseuse, Vernon
11. Hotel-Dieu, Vernon
12. Abbey Trésor Notre-Dame near Baudemont
13. Gomerfontaine
14. Abbey of Saint Martin lès Pontoise
15. Franciscan monastery, Pontoise
16. Notre-Dame du Val
17. Charterhouse Bourgfontaine
18. Notre-Dame, Melun

FIGURE 2.2   *Map of the churches and other religious foundations in France (outside Paris) given bequests of devotional objects or vestments in the testament of Blanche of Navarre (not all sites are extant).*

ments.[23] The gifts of these objects permitted Blanche's memory to be retained and celebrated by their continued use in the church (see chaps. 3–6).

Once she had settled the corporate commemoration of her soul at churches and other religious foundations, Blanche could turn to individuals, and she resembles these other 14th-century testators both in the kinds of objects she gave away and in her strategies for bequeathing them. For example, in her 1329 will, Jeanne of Burgundy left her great crown to her son, John, while she left four other crowns, six circlets, and six golden cups, as well as all of her books, to her daughter Marie.[24] The 1372 execution of the will of Jeanne of Evreux indicates that she left most of her books to her daughter, Blanche, with three exceptions, one book that was given to the French king Charles V, another,

---

23   Some were given during her life and others at death; for these gifts, Elizabeth A.R. Brown, "Testamentary Strategies of Jeanne d'Evreux," pp. 217–47, and "Jeanne d'Évreux: ses testaments et leur exécution," *Le Moyen Âge* 119 (2013), 57–83.

24   Gaude-Ferragu, "Les dernières volontés de la reine de France," p. 44.

described as a 'beau livre,' left to Jeanne of Navarre, a nun at Longchamp (the sister of Blanche of Navarre), and the third, a book of hours, given to her god-daughter, Jeanne de Harcourt.[25] The recipients of her generosity were not only those with elevated social status; Jeanne of Burgundy and Blanche of Orléans, like Blanche of Navarre, gave funds to dozens of people who worked in their households, naming each person. This practice makes it possible to trace, for example, a cook who worked first for Blanche of Orléans who moved after this princess's death in 1393 to work in the household of Blanche of Navarre.[26] Blanche of Navarre's bequests of clothing also follow the practice of the testaments of Jeanne of Burgundy, Philip VI, Blanche of Orléans, and Jeanne of Rohan, all of whom left their clothing to members of their households.[27] These bequests to individuals are analyzed by material in greater detail in the chapters that follow.

Although much is typical in Blanche's will, it has garnered so much scholarly attention because much is also unusual.[28] The long provenance that is often given for her objects is one such strikingly unusual element. Though other testators, like Blanche of Orléans or Louis of Étampes, might name one or two prior owners for one or two possessions, Blanche did this for many of her objects, and extended the provenance history of two of her possessions, her books of Saint Louis, back more than 100 years to the hands of the saint

---

25 For analysis of these bequests, see Holladay, "Fourteenth-century French Queens," pp. 69–71 and 88–89.

26 Blanche of Navarre notes in her will his name, Belin, his occupation as cook, and his previous service in the household of Blanche of Orléans; Delisle 377 and 476. This man also appears in the will of Blanche of Orléans; there he is called Bolin, her cook, and she gives him 12 livres parisis. Blanche of Orléans also left money to a 'femme Bolin,' probably the wife of this Bolin, who is not named in the later will of Blanche of Navarre; Vignat, "Testament de Blanche, duchesse d'Orléans," pp. 135–36.

27 The will of Philip VI is Paris, Archives nationales J 406, no. 33 (testament of 23 May 1347) and no. 34 (testament of 2 July 1350). For the bequests of clothing in the will of Blanche of Orléans, see Vignat, "Testament de Blanche, duchesse d'Orléans," pp. 133–34. For the clothing bequests in the will of Jeanne of Burgundy, see Gaude-Ferragu, "Les dernières volontés de la reine de France," pp. 46 and 59.

28 Blanche's testaments have been valuable for scholars seeking data about book ownership and reading habits; this scholarship will be discussed in chapter 3. See, among others, Keith Busby, *Codex and Context: Reading Old French Verse Narrative in Manuscript*, 2 vols. (New York, 2002); Richard H. Rouse and Mary A. Rouse, *Manuscripts and Their Makers: Commercial Book Producers in Medieval Paris, 1200–1500*, 2 vols. (Turnhout, 2000); and Karen Green, "What were the Ladies in the *City of Ladies* reading? The Libraries of Christine de Pizan's Contemporaries," *Medievalia et Humanistica* 36 (2011), 76–100.

THE TESTAMENT: LEGAL DOCUMENT AND SENTIMENTAL AUTOBIOGRAPHY 71

himself.[29] Another eccentricity of Blanche's will is its description of affection, directed not only toward people or institutions, which is relatively common in testamentary discourse, but also toward objects.[30] This emotion was explicit at least once, in the diamond that Philip VI loved a lot (discussed in the introduction), and occasionally implied, for example, with respect to the diamond ring she said that this same king wore on his finger.[31] Blanche also disseminated her objects to members of the French court much more widely than did her contemporaries. In contrast, Blanche of Orléans gave only a handful of her possessions to the dukes and duchesses at the French court, and Jeanne of Rohan gave nothing at all to these individuals.[32] Blanche's desire to give at least something to her assorted noble relations at the French court was not a *pro forma* choice but a meaningful one, related to her role as the mother of the court who bestows a gift on everyone. I have argued in a past publication that the detail in Blanche's bequests resulted from a desire to ensure the authenticity of her objects, one of which, the nail reliquary, had been challenged.[33] Here, I expand this argument, linking it to the roles of mother and mediator, and sug-

---

29   For example, Blanche of Orléans notes that a small reliquary in her collection was previously owned by the duke of Berry; Vignat, "Testament de Blanche, duchesse d'Orléans," p. 122. Louis of Étampes indicated that a book of hours had been owned by Marie of Brabant and a 'queen Jeanne' before it came into his possession; Lescournay, "Testament de Louys, comte d'Estampes," p. 107. For the practice of listing the prior owners of books in English testaments, see Rosenthal, "Aristocratic Cultural Patronage and Book Bequests," pp. 522–48. For analysis of prior owners listed in the bequests of the 1377 will of Marie of Saint-Pol, see Sean Field, "Marie of Saint-Pol and Her Books," *The English Historical Review* 125, no. 513 (2010), 1–24.

30   For example, in her 1343 act that gifted reliquaries to the abbey church of Saint-Denis, Jeanne called her husband Charles IV 'treschier' and 'tres ame' and also noted the 'vraie affection' that the abbot of Saint-Denis and the monks had for her deceased husband; Brown, "The Testamentary Strategies of Jeanne d'Évreux," pp. 219, 227–32. For the medieval contexts of the citation of emotion, see Barbara Rosenwein, "Thinking Historically about Medieval Emotions," *History Compass* 8, no. 8 (2010), 828–42.

31   The diamond that was loved a lot is Delisle 199, and the diamond ring is Delisle 206. The 1372 execution of the testament of Jeanne of Evreux described a small diamond with a family history that she gave to Blanche of Navarre that she said was worn on her brother's hand. This bequest is analyzed in chapter 5.

32   Blanche of Orléans gave objects only to Blanche of Navarre, the duke and duchess of Berry, the duke and duchess of Burgundy, Louis, duke of Touraine (future duke of Orléans), Louis, count of Étampes, and Charles de Trie, count of Dammartin; Vignat, "Testament de Blanche, duchesse d'Orléans," pp. 131–32.

33   Marguerite Keane, "Most Beautiful and Next Best: Value in the Collection of a Medieval Queen," *Journal of Medieval History* 34 (December 2008), 360–73.

72   CHAPTER 2

gesting that the association of the objects in Blanche's will with love and affection was a strategy to ensure her memory.[34]

Another genre to consider when setting Blanche's testamentary bequests in context are inventories; though quite different from wills in their motivation and the way that they privilege information, they provide valuable information about collections. The 14th-century inventories relevant for this study are those of the French royal collection during the reigns of Charles V and Charles VI, the inventories made for John, duke of Berry, and those done for Philip, duke of Burgundy, and his wife Margaret of Flanders, as well as the inventory made in the context of the execution of the will of Jeanne of Evreux in 1372, discussed above.[35] The 1399 inventory of the English royal treasure under Richard II also provides comparative material; the similarities of these two courts and the intermarriage among their families means that many of the observations that hold true for Blanche's testament can be applied to English and broader European testamentary writing.[36] The 1358 inventory of the English queen Isabella and the 1377 testament of the noblewoman Marie of Saint-Pol, in addition to the testaments and inventories cited above, will serve to set Blanche's book collecting in context in the next chapter.

---

34   For the question of whether emotion was attached to testamentary wishes for objects in the early 17th century, see Lena Cowen Orlin, "Empty Vessels," in *Everyday Objects: Medieval and Early Modern Material Culture and Its Meanings*, ed. Tara Hamling and Catherine Richardson (Farnham, Surrey, UK, 2010), pp. 299–308.

35   Here I include only comprehensive inventories; for inventories limited by medium, consult the relevant chapter of this book. *L'inventaire du trésor du dauphin futur Charles V (1363): les débuts d'un grand collectionneur*, ed. Danielle Gaborit-Chopin (Nogent-le-Roi, 1996); Jules Labarte, *Inventaire du mobilier de Charles V, roi de France* (Paris, 1979); Philippe Henwood, *Les collections du trésor royal sous le règne de Charles VI (1380–1422), l'inventaire de 1400* (Paris, 2004). For John of Berry, see Jules Guiffrey, *Inventaires de Jean, duc de Berry (1401–1416)*, 2 vols. (Paris, 1894–96). For Philip of Burgundy, see Chrétien-César-Auguste Dehaisnes, *Documents et extraits concernant l'histoire de l'art dans la Flandre, l'Artois, et le Hainaut avant le XV siècle, 1374–1401* (Lille, 1886); and Bernard Prost and Henri Prost, *Inventaires mobiliers et extraits des comptes des ducs de Bourgogne de la Maison de Valois (1363–1477)*, 2 vols. (Paris, 1902–8). For a study of the 1328 testament and inventory of Clémence of Hungary, see Mariah Proctor-Tiffany, "Lost and Found: Visualizing a Medieval Queen's Destroyed Objects," in *Queenship in the Mediterranean: Negotiating the Role of the Queen in the Medieval and Early Modern Eras*, ed. Elena Woodacre (New York, 2013), pp. 73–96, and "Transported as a Rare Object of Distinction: The Gift-giving of Clémence of Hungary, Queen of France," *Journal of Medieval History* 41, no. 2 (2015), 208–28.

36   Jenny Stratford, *Richard II and the English Royal Treasure* (Woodbridge, UK, 2012), p. 87.

There are some caveats that apply to the study of wills.[37] Blanche's testament mentions only the possessions that she had at the end of her life. This tells us what she valued most – some of the objects had been in her possession more than forty years – but it does not give a full picture of her collection. The handful of objects that she owned in 1398 that she did not yet have in 1396 – the two sets of room hangings, and a relic of Saint Bartholomew, among others – indicate that her collection was dynamic; she actively sought new possessions. She also gave items away; she had to change two bequests in 1398, a breviary and a set of room hangings that were no longer in her possession. These were either damaged or more likely given away in the intervening two years. With all of the media, books, reliquaries, jewelry, and textiles, we cannot judge the evidence that is absent, those things that were given away during her life before this will was written. If she had bestowed money, relics, or other gifts comprehensively before her death, that person or foundation would not be mentioned in the will. The chapel of Saint Hippolyte, surely the most important foundation of her life – her final resting place as well as that of her daughter – merited only a single mention in the will in the section where she said where she wanted to be buried, because she had endowed it and furnished it with works of art during her lifetime.[38]

There are also a number of complications with using written descriptions to analyze objects. Blanche described her objects relatively extensively, so it is possible to determine their general appearance but little else. This problem is particularly acute in the case of books (see chap. 3). In the case of reliquaries and jewelry, marvelous small objects that were held in the hand, it is difficult to imagine their materiality. Descriptions do not give a work's tactile qualities; these can only be imagined from the text in comparison with extant works. The descriptions are also not necessarily comprehensive or well suited to art historical analysis. The writer of a will and an art historian do not have the same interest in the object; the former wants to be sure to elucidate the distinguishing features of each object so that it is clear which one is referred to once it is time to dispose of the objects, whereas the latter is interested in the circumstances of the commission, why the materials were chosen, why a particular form was selected, and how the patron might have used the objects. Because Blanche did not name artists in her will or talk very much about the

---

37   For some caveats of the use of wills as evidence, see Clive Burgess, "Late Medieval Wills and Pious Convention: Testamentary Evidence Reconsidered," in *Profit, Piety, and the Professions in Later Medieval England*, ed. Michael Hicks (Gloucester, 1990), pp. 14–33.

38   She mentions the chapel only in the context of where her body should be placed; Delisle 5.

circumstances of her commissions, rarely including the cost of materials, for example, I will not analyze the production of the objects. The kind of information we have from the will and other descriptions of her objects is about reception – how Blanche perceived them, where she kept them, what they might have meant to her.

The categories of household, court, and family did not necessarily have the same meaning in the Middle Ages as they do today. In this book, the term 'family' refers to Blanche's siblings and their children; her 'household' is defined as the constellation of individuals who served her in some capacity; and 'royal court' encompasses those individuals around the French king and queen, Charles VI and Isabeau of Bavaria, and the dukes and duchesses and other nobles who were associated with the French royal family. These categories are permeable and not necessarily exclusive. The members of Blanche's household might be as close to her as a sister or daughter. For example, Blanche gave money to a Marion, daughter of Thevenin le Grant, to support a future marriage. Blanche noted that Marion had been nourished or raised "en nostre chambre entour noz femmes," or in her house around the women of her household.[39] Blanche mentioned this emotional attachment to justify her interest in Marion's marriage; Marion was like a daughter to her in that she sought to assist the young woman in starting a new life after marriage.

At her death, Michel Pintoin said that Blanche's character was exemplary; she was beloved 'like a mother.'[40] In her testament, Blanche, who had served as a stepmother and grandmother to three subsequent kings – John II, Charles V, and Charles VI – celebrated this role. She called the members of the royal court in the will her sons and daughters, using 'filz' and 'fille' for someone like John, the duke of Berry and his wife, Jeanne. In her presentation as a mother in the will, Blanche both recognized the obligations that the role entailed and expected the devotion to which a mother was entitled. For example, she supported her godchildren, giving money and crowns to goddaughters to provide for their new lives after marriage, and to a godson, money for his education. She gave money and clothing to a lady-in-waiting, Marguerite de Vymont, "who I recently married," an indication that she felt responsible for her financial well-being.[41] Mothers in the Middle Ages provided moral guidance, and

---

39   Delisle 505.

40   *Chronique du Religieux de Saint-Denys*, 2:659.

41   Delisle 292.

Blanche did so with the gifts of didactic and devotional books to her heirs; these bequests will be analyzed in the next chapter.[42]

In her lifetime she had been a peacemaker between the French kings John II and Charles V and her brother Charles, king of Navarre. Now, in the bequests of the will, she was the connection beween the present and the past. When she gave two objects once owned by Philip VI and worn on his body to his great-grandson, Charles VI, it was the legacy of Philip VI that she possessed and that she passed on to the present king. She also served as a mediator between her Capetian ancestors and the reigning Valois, giving Philip, duke of Burgundy, a book that had been owned by her great-grandmother, daughter of Saint Louis and Capetian duchess of Burgundy. If her career as an intercessor in the 1350s and 1360s had afforded her access to the king and the ability to wield influence at the French court, her intercessory role in the 1390s was now to provide for her salvation. The mother and the mediator would serve to remind her recipients that she was the ideal queen, and the power she would derive from that would be to have them remember her in their prayers and assist in the salvation of her soul.

Blanche's desire to obligate her heirs to her also speaks to the insecurity inherent in testamentary discourse. A testament is a wish for a series of things to happen, and indeed, as Elizabeth A.R. Brown has shown, French royal testaments were occasionally executed only partially or not at all.[43] The instructions in the testament represent Blanche's desire for control of the dissemination of her objects and, ultimately, her memory. If the testament of Blanche of Navarre tells us what she wanted to have happen, it also tells us what she wanted to avoid: heirs who did not remember properly the person who had given them

---

42 For studies of the role of mother as educators, see Susan Groag Bell, "Medieval Women Book Owners: Arbiters of Lay Piety and Ambassadors of Culture," in *Women and Power in the Middle Ages*, ed. Mary Erler and Maryanne Kowaleski (Athens, GA, 1988), pp. 149–87; Pamela Sheingorn, "'The Wise Mother': The Image of St. Anne Teaching the Virgin Mary," *Gesta* 32 (1993), 69–80; and Michael Clanchy, "Did Mothers Teach Their Children to Read?" in *Motherhood, Religion, and Society in Medieval Europe, 400–1400: Essays presented to Henrietta Leyser*, ed. Conrad Leyser and Lesley Smith (Farnham, Surrey, UK, 2011), pp. 129–53.

43 Elizabeth A.R. Brown, "La mort, les testaments et les fondations de Jeanne de Navarre, reine de France (1273–1305)," in *Une histoire pour un royaume (XIIe-XVe siècle). Actes du colloque Corpus Regni en hommage à Colette Beaune*, ed. A.H. Allirot, M. Gaude-Ferragu, et al. (Paris, 2010), pp. 124–41, 508–10; and Brown, "The King's Conundrum: Endowing Queens and Loyal Servants, Ensuring Salvation, and Protecting the Patrimony in Fourteenth-century France," in *Attitudes to the Future in the Middle Ages*, ed. John Burrow and Ian Wei (Woodbridge, UK, 2000), pp. 115–65.

an object or gave it away without citing the previous owner and therefore forgot the person for whom they were meant to pray. Blanche's interest in presenting herself as a mother, obligating those around her, as well as a mediator, an important link between generations, together with the exhaustive detail and the emotion of bequests, all contributed to her presentation of herself as the ideal queen. But they were also meant to hedge against and compensate for the unexpected and the ungrateful, for all that could potentially go awry in the execution of her testament.

CHAPTER 3

Books as Evidence to Perpetuate Memory

The number of books in Blanche's collection, forty-two, is the largest number of a single type of object mentioned in her testament.[1] Blanche's relationship to her books is revealed by the bequests in her will. Her books were a sign of her piety, learnedness, genealogical heritage, and relationship with her close relatives like her daughter Jeanne and her aunt Jeanne of Evreux, as well as evidence of a community of readers in her household. In her gifting practices she is typical of many late medieval female book owners, a cohort studied by Susan Groag Bell, who was among the first to foreground the importance of gender in the interpretation of medieval ownership of books.[2] Groag Bell argued that female book owners helped to advance the development of both vernacular literature and lay piety in the late Middle Ages; she noted in particular the important function of books for women who used them to teach their children. My study of Blanche's use and dissemination of books also considers the importance of gender. Blanche gave more books to women than to men, she described her books for women differently, and with her bequests she commemorated the special role of women as educators.

Studies of other 14th-century book owners have described these patterns of book ownership in individual collections. The books of Jeanne of Evreux are

---

1 The will lists forty-two books with one breviary in two volumes, so in total forty-three volumes. Many of her books also contained more than one work in a single volume. Blanche's book collection has been mined by scholars for its evidence for understanding the literary interests of medieval women; see, for example, Karen Green, "What Were the Ladies in the *City of Ladies* Reading? The Libraries of Christine de Pizan's Contemporaries," *Medievalia et Humanistica* 36 (2011), 76–100. The collection of Blanche of Navarre was also analyzed by Keith Busby in his study of the material implications of French manuscripts; *Codex and Context: Reading Old French Verse Narrative in Manuscript*, 2 vols. (New York, 2002), 2:657–58. Brigitte Buettner used Blanche's will as evidence for her reconsideration of medieval patronage models for women in "Women and the Circulation of Books," *Journal of the Early Book Society* 4 (2001), 9–31, expanding this argument in "Le système des objets dans le testament de Blanche de Navarre," *CLIO. Histoire, Femmes et sociétés* 19 (2004), 37–62. Richard H. Rouse and Mary A. Rouse traced the history of the *Somme le roi* of Philip the Fair in part with Blanche's provenance in *Manuscripts and Their Makers: Commercial Book Producers in Medieval Paris, 1200–1500*, 2 vols. (Turnhout, 2000), 1:151–52.

2 Susan Groag Bell, "Medieval Women Book Owners: Arbiters of Lay Piety and Ambassadors of Culture," in *Women and Power in the Middle Ages*, ed. Mary Erler and Maryanne Kowaleski (Athens, GA, 1988), pp. 149–87.

© KONINKLIJKE BRILL NV, LEIDEN, 2016 | DOI 10.1163/9789004318830_005

particularly important for understanding Blanche's book ownership; the two women had close family ties, and Blanche owned a number of books that she associated with the older queen.[3] The book collection of Isabelle of France (1295–1358), queen of England, also provides context for Blanche's book ownership. In addition to seeking books that were intended to educate the young, Isabelle also acquired devotional and didactic volumes with themes appropriate to rulership. Anne Rudloff Stanton has argued that this queen made a connection between books and the shaping of character, an idea that can be extended to the book bequests of Blanche of Navarre.[4] The 1377 testament of Marie of Saint-Pol, countess of Pembroke (c. 1304–1377), reveals this patron's relationships with religious houses and individuals that she marked with the gifts of books.[5] Comparison with the collections of these three women as well as with other wills and inventories from the 14th century – among them those created for Charles V, John of Berry, and Philip of Burgundy – further highlights the typical and the idiosyncratic in Blanche's collection.[6] The scale

---

3 The book collection of Jeanne of Evreux has been studied by Joan Holladay, "Fourteenth-century French Queens as Collectors and Readers of Books: Jeanne d'Evreux and Her Contemporaries," *Journal of Medieval History* 32 (2006), 69–100.

4 Anne Rudloff Stanton, "Isabelle of France and Her Manuscripts, 1308–1358," in *Capetian Women*, ed. Kathleen Nolan (New York, 2003), pp. 225–52.

5 For Marie of Saint-Pol's book ownership, see Sean Field, "Marie of Saint-Pol and Her Books," *The English Historical Review* 125, no. 513 (2010), 1–24; Richard Rouse and Mary Rouse, "Marie de St-Pol and Cambridge University Library, MS Dd.5.5," in *The Cambridge Illuminations: The Conference Papers*, ed. Stella Panayatova (London, 2007), pp. 187–91, and their larger study of book patronage by the counts of Saint-Pol, "French Literature and the Counts of Saint-Pol, ca. 1178–1377," *Viator* 41, no. 1 (2010), 101–40.

6 For the book ownership of these individuals, see the following studies: for Charles V, Léopold Delisle, *Recherches sur la librairie de Charles V*, 3 vols. (Paris, 1907), and by the same author, *Notice de douze livres royaux* (Paris, 1902). Of particular interest is the Europeana Regia website that has reconstructed the king's book collection with links to extant digitized books: <http://www.europeanaregia.eu/en/historical-collections/library-charles-v-family>. On the collections of Philip of Burgundy and Margaret of Flanders, see Muriel Hughes, "The Library of Philip the Bold and Margaret of Flanders, First Valois Duke and Duchess of Burgundy," *Journal of Medieval History* 4 (1978), 145–88, and Patrick de Winter, *La bibliothèque de Philippe le Hardi, duc de Bourgogne (1364–1404)* (Paris, 1985). For this couple's books, see also the exhibition catalogue *Art from the Court of Burgundy: Patronage of Philip the Bold and John the Fearless, 1364–1419* (Cleveland, 2004). The inventories of John of Berry have been studied by Millard Meiss, *French Painting in the Time of Jean de Berry: The Late Fourteenth Century and the Patronage of the Duke*, 2 vols. (New York, 1967), and more recently by Timothy Husband, *The Art of Illumination: The Limbourg Brothers and the Belles Heures of Jean de France, Duc de Berry* (New York, 2008). For Isabeau of Bavaria, see Auguste Vallet de Viriville, *La bibliothèque d'Isabeau de Bavière, femme de Charles VI, roi de France* (Paris, 1858).

BOOKS AS EVIDENCE TO PERPETUATE MEMORY

of the collections of Charles v, who had more than nine hundred books, John of Berry, about three hundred, and Philip of Burgundy, about two hundred, requires some caution with regard to comparison, as noted below. In contrast, individual women's collections numbered in the dozens rather than the hundreds: for example, Jeanne of Evreux had between fifty-two and fifty-four documented books, while Isabelle, queen of England, left thirty-four manuscripts in her testament and eleven more books have been associated with her.[7] Blanche's book collection is typical of the collections of these women, with some variation in the kinds of titles owned by each. What is different is the evidence available for Blanche's collection, a testament with reminiscences about each book that offers a trove of information about how she interacted with her books. The inventories of Jeanne of Evreux and Isabelle of England and the testament of Marie of Saint-Pol, though valuable for their lists of titles and recipients of books, do not have the same richness as Blanche's testamentary discussion of her books.

Looking at one kind of book, the breviary, helps to elucidate the interest of Blanche's book collection overall. Blanche had six breviaries, ranging in date of production from the 12th to the 14th century.[8] Probably these books ranged from quite lavish to very simple, but there is only limited information about them because Blanche or her executors prioritized relatively few aspects of the books' content and appearance in bequests. Blanche's most valuable breviary had been owned by Saint Louis, another that Blanche described as her 'best' had belonged to Jeanne of Burgundy, first wife of Philip vi. A third, perhaps more modest, had come to Blanche after the death of her sister Jeanne, a nun at Longchamp; the fourth was the breviary from which Blanche's daughter Jeanne had learned when she was young. A breviary in two volumes that had been owned by Jeanne of Evreux was given to Valentina Visconti, duchess of Orléans. And finally, Blanche gave her niece Marie of Navarre a breviary that had a binding decorated with Annunciation and Crucifixion images.

In these six breviary bequests, the strategies and insights of Blanche's will with regard to her book ownership come into focus: her breviaries could be educational and edifying, to teach a child to read; they were books freighted

---

7 For these quantities, see Holladay, "Fourteenth-century French Queens," p. 89, and Stanton, "Isabelle of France and Her Manuscripts," p. 227.

8 Six breviaries are mentioned in the will. She may have had more books that are not mentioned in the will, but it seems unlikely considering her practice of disseminating her books widely among her heirs. In a will in which she leaves books to queens, duchesses, ladies-in-waiting, and chambermaids, it seems unlikely that she would have missed an opportunity to infuse meaning into one of her possessions for an heir.

with family heritage and royal models, from distant ancestors, like Saint Louis, and more recent ones, like Jeanne of Evreux. The gift of the breviary of Saint Louis could also trace lines between family members past and present, uniting generations. In addition, it reveals another strategy of the testament: to paper over disagreements, as Blanche omitted from the bequest crucial information that she must have known about the breviary's past ownership, probably because it had been controversial. Books could pass easily between the châteaux of the queen and a convent in Paris. One of Blanche's breviaries had previously belonged to her sister in the convent of Longchamp;[9] it was rebound for its new owner and transformed into a 'presentation copy.' A breviary could be used to mark an important transition in life, such as the wedding of Blanche's niece Marie. And finally, of Blanche's six breviaries, five were given to women, and this practice of gifting more books to women than to men holds up for the will overall.

The function of these books clearly went beyond their utility for daily prayer, as even the most devout medieval owner did not need six breviaries. Joan Holladay has suggested that duplicates in the book collection of Jeanne of Evreux might have been a result of the queen's appreciation for the varied illumination or bindings of books, or a need to have more than one copy of a text to distribute among multiple residences.[10] If these aesthetic or pragmatic factors motivated Blanche in her acquisition of breviaries, they are unmentioned in the will, because Blanche was motivated in the testaments to give value to the books for her heirs. This value mostly inhered in the role of her breviaries as carriers of family identity, but occasionally a decorated binding might be highlighted, as in the breviary given to Marie of Navarre. Finally, the details of the book bequests consistently present Blanche in the role that she desired for herself in the composition of the will, that of a mother. For example, though there were likely several reasons why she kept the breviary from which her daughter had learned as a child, at least one would have been because it signified her daughter's acquisition of religious knowledge and celebrated Blanche's role as a mother in educating her child.

---

9   Sean Field analyzed this passage of books between nuns and laywomen in "Marie of Saint-Pol and Her Books," pp. 1–24.

10   Holladay, "Fourteenth-century French Queens," pp. 84–85. Holladay notes that Clémence of Hungary, the wife of Louis x, also had duplicates. Clémence had five breviaries, for example. Brigitte Buettner discusses the ways in which medieval manuscripts might be appreciated for multiple reasons above and beyond their content in "Profane Illuminations, Secular Illusions: Manuscripts in Late Medieval Courtly Society," *Art Bulletin* 64, no. 1 (March 1992), 75–90.

BOOKS AS EVIDENCE TO PERPETUATE MEMORY

As with the study of all the objects in Blanche's collection, analysis of her book collection is affected by the way we know about it, mostly through the sentimental and transactional accounts of the will and its codicils. That our knowledge of her collection would be almost nonexistent without the wills shows the value of this kind of evidence for the history of medieval women. Blanche had a range of books at the end of her life, in a collection numbering forty-two items, among them the six breviaries discussed above, two missals, four psalters, two books of hours, two copies of the *Somme le roi*, and other devotional books in French and Latin, as well as at least one book perhaps intended for entertainment, described as having 'pluseurs romans.' Beyond the comments in the bequests, such as 'this one has good information,' or 'this one teaches about sinning,' the will does not convey in very great detail how often Blanche read her books or why she might have chosen one over another for use.[11] The transactional evidence of a will skews the analysis of books toward material qualities; the books are treated like objects, similar in that respect to reliquaries or textiles for which appearance and provenance can be analyzed much better than use or production.

Books in Blanche's collection ranged from some of the most valuable books of her day to volumes modest enough to give to the women who worked in her household. As with her other bequests, the books mentioned earlier in the will tended to be the more valuable. One of the first books given away was the breviary of Saint Louis that had been returned to him on crusade, a 'book relic' of enormous prestige.[12] One of the last, much less important, was a book on surgery that was given to a woman who worked as a healer, Symmonete.[13] Its placement at the end of the book bequests and its recipient suggest not only that it was a modest volume, but also pointed to its utility: Symmonete would use this book, presumably in her capacity as someone who cared for the sick.[14] Blanche's most valuable books are characterized by their lack of use; even if one imagined that Blanche might pray from Saint Louis's breviary, we know that she did not use all her books. She described a gift to the duke of Berry of a

---

11   As noted by Holladay for the collection of Jeanne of Evreux; "Fourteenth-century French Queens," pp. 70–71.

12   For another contact relic of Saint Louis, his clothing, see Anne-Hélène Allirot, "Longchamp and Lourcine: The Role of Female Abbeys in the Construction of Capetian Memory (Late Thirteenth Century to Mid-Fourteenth Century)," in *Memory and Commemoration in Medieval Culture*, ed. Elma Brenner, Meredith Cohen, and Mary Franklin-Brown (Farnham, Surrey, UK, 2013), pp. 243–60.

13   Delisle 427.

14   For analysis of this bequest, see Monica Green, "Books as a Source of Medical Education for Women in the Middle Ages," *Dynamis* 20 (2000), 331–69, especially p. 336.

book of hours, and then gave away another book of hours later in the will that she indicated was her next-most-valuable book of hours and the one she prayed from each day, an indication that she did not regularly use the book of hours that she gave to the duke of Berry.[15]

Blanche's collection of books was weighted toward the devotional and didactic. Only a handful (such as the book containing *romans* or a book of medicine) were not part of devotional practice or explicitly intended to be morally edifying. This is in part because we know about most of her books only through the will; she owned books throughout her life that were not recorded in her testamentary documents.[16] Blanche likely owned a *Dame à la licorne* (Paris, Bibliothèque nationale, MS fr. 12562), commissioned around the time of her marriage in 1350.[17] She also almost certainly had one or more copies of the missal she had translated into French (one of which may be mentioned in the will, a missal in French given to a woman called the dame de Fontenay).[18] In comparison to the volumes found in the collections of her contemporaries, analyzed below, one might conclude that Blanche was less interested in books like a *Romance of the Panther* (owned by Jeanne of Evreux, purchased by her from the sale of books belonging to Queen Clémence of Hungary) or the *Roman de Renart*, purchased by the French king John II in exile in England in

---

15 Delisle 230.

16 In her analysis of late 15th-century book ownership, Carol Meale considered the question of how the impulse to make a testament might have affected the books listed in it, noting that religious books were probably considered to serve a commemorative function particularly well; "'... alle the bokes that I haue of latyn, englisch, and frensch': Laywomen and Their Books in Late Medieval England," in *Women and Literature in Britain, 1150–1500*, ed. Carol Meale (Cambridge, 1993), pp. 128–58. For patterns of bequests of religious literature in wills, see Anne M. Dutton, "Passing the Book: Testamentary Transmission of Religious Literature to and by Women in England, 1350–1500," in *Women, the Book and the Godly: Selected Proceedings of the St. Hilda's Conference, 1993*, ed. Lesley Smith and Jane Taylor (Woodbridge, UK, 1995), pp. 41–54.

17 For the attribution to Blanche's ownership, see Anthime Fourrier, "La destinataire de 'La Dame a la Licorne,'" in *Mélanges de langue et de literature médiévales offerts à Pierre Le Gentil* (Paris, 1973), pp. 265–76, and for analysis of the manuscript more generally, Jane H.M. Taylor, "Le Roman de la Dame a la Lycorne et du Biau Chevalier au Lion: Text, Image, Rubric," *French Studies* 51 (January 1997), 1–18.

18 For the missal translated into French, Delisle cites a 1404 inventory of the Burgundian duke Philip the Bold in which a missal translated from Latin to French by the queen Blanche is mentioned; "Testament de Blanche de Navarre, reine de France," *Mémoires de la Société de l'histoire de Paris et de l'Ile de France* 12 (1885), 3. The missal given to the dame de Fontenay is Delisle 250.

BOOKS AS EVIDENCE TO PERPETUATE MEMORY

1360.[19] But it is clear that the will does not give a complete picture of her collection. For one, if she were interested in the *Dame à la licorne*, she surely had others like it. Though it seems unlikely that in this detailed and loquacious will she would leave out many of her books, the will is itself a document of memory, and Blanche wanted to be prayed for and to be remembered as part of spiritual life, so that may be why nondevotional or didactic books are less frequently mentioned. The 1377 testament of Marie of Saint-Pol, countess of Pembroke, likewise listed only liturgical and devotional books, but there is other evidence that she owned a vernacular romance of the crusader Godefroy de Bouillon prior to 1373.[20] Blanche's testament tells us only about the books she wanted to keep or happened to keep until her death; it does not tell us about the books she gave away during her life.[21]

Blanche's most valuable books by any measure were the two that had belonged to Saint Louis. These books had special significance because they had been owned by a saint – they were contact relics. Both books appear very early in the 1396 will in which Blanche gave away her possessions to individuals, another sign of their status among her belongings. The first of these was the breviary that had been miraculously returned to the king on crusade and the second the psalter with which the saint had learned as a child. Louis's breviary had been returned to him on crusade by a Saracen, according to his biographer Guillaume de Chartres.[22] As the story of Louis's devotion to his breviary evolved in the first few decades after his death, an angel became the one who had returned the breviary, transforming the return of the book into a miraculous event. The story emphasized the king's devotion to his daily prayers and the necessity of the book in his life.

The story of the miraculous return of the breviary and its representation were popular at the French court; images of it appear in many cycles of the saint's life. This scene was included in two books created for Blanche's family members: in the *Hours of Jeanne of Evreux* (Fig. 3.1), and in a book of hours

---

19   For this acquisition by Jeanne of Evreux, and others from the sale of Clémence's books, see Holladay, "Fourteenth-century French Queens," pp. 83–86. John II's purchase of the *Roman de Renart* is analyzed in Busby, *Codex and Context*, pp. 645–46.

20   Field, "Marie of Saint-Pol and Her Books," pp. 14–15.

21   Though, as Keith Busby points out, there were also many more books in Latin than in the vernacular: "The possession of a vernacular manuscript of a secular narrative was a relatively rare phenomenon compared with the universality of religious and didactic material in Latin"; *Codex and Context*, p. 638.

22   For the historical source of the story and its development, see Larry S. Crist, "The Breviary of Saint Louis: The Development of a Legendary Miracle," *Journal of the Warburg and Courtauld Institutes* 28 (1965), 319–23.

FIGURE 3.1 *Miraculous return of the breviary of Saint Louis,* Hours of Jeanne of Evreux, c. 1325–28. THE METROPOLITAN MUSEUM OF ART, NEW YORK, THE CLOISTERS COLLECTION, 1954 (54.1.2), FOLS. 154V-155R. PHOTO CREDIT: METROPOLITAN MUSEUM OF ART.

painted for Blanche's sister, Marie, known as the *Hours of Marie of Navarre* (Fig. 3.2). In each case, Louis's devotion to his precious book served as a model for the owner of the book of hours. Blanche did not have to settle for an image of the book; she had the book itself, a contact relic of her esteemed ancestor and a physical sign of the efficacy of prayer. In the will Blanche left the breviary to her nephew, Charles III, who had inherited the kingdom of Navarre at his father's death in 1387. She wrote:

> Item nous laissons à nostre très chier et très amé neveu le roy de Navarre le breviaire qui fu monseigneur le roy saint Loys de France, lequel l'ange lui apporta en la chartre quant il fu pris des ennemis de la foy, et fu monseigneur le roy Phelippe, son filz ainsné, qui mourust en Arragon, mary de madame la royne Marie, nostre besaiole, et le lui donna en sa vie. Et depuis est venu de hoir en hoir de la ligniée monseigneur saint Loys. Et le

BOOKS AS EVIDENCE TO PERPETUATE MEMORY 85

FIGURE 3.2 *Miraculous return of the breviary of Saint Louis,* Hours of Marie of Navarre, *c. 1340.*
BIBLIOTECA NAZIONALE MARCIANA, VENICE, MS LAT. I.104/12640, FOL. 178V.
PHOTO CREDIT: BIBLIOTECA NAZIONALE MARCIANA.

nous donna nostre frère le roy de Navarre, son père. Et pour reverence et la sainteté de monseigneur saint Loys, et que par grace il est venu de la ligne de nous, et depuis que nous eusmes le dit breviaire promeismes à nostre dit frère que il retourneroit en nostre ligne, nous voulons et ordonnons que à nostre dit neveu il demeure, et desormais ensuivament à ses successeurs, senz estre aucunement estrange, et les requerons que ilz le facent tousjours garder comme precieux et noble jouel de venu de noz anccesseurs, et qu'il ne parte point de la lignie.[23]

[I leave to my ... nephew the king of Navarre the breviary that the king Saint Louis had brought to him by an angel when he was imprisoned by the enemies of the faith, and it belonged to the king Philip, his eldest son, who died in Aragon, and he gave it to his wife Marie, my grandmother, while he was still living. And then it came heir by heir through the line of Saint Louis, to my brother, the king of Navarre, his father (of the present king of Navarre), who gave it to me. And for reverence and the holiness of Saint Louis, and that by grace it comes from my family line, and since I promised my brother that the breviary would be returned in my line, I want that it should remain with this nephew, and follow to his successors, without being estranged, and I wish that they should always keep it as a precious and noble gift coming from my ancestors, and that it will never leave the family line.]

Blanche traced the provenance of the book from the king's eldest son to Marie of Brabant, his wife, and then heir by heir to Charles of Navarre, Blanche's brother. Notably absent in the provenance is the name of each owner between Marie of Brabant and Charles of Navarre. In this will in which Blanche carefully detailed the chain of provenance of so many of her objects, 'heir by heir' seems unusually vague. Blanche's mother Jeanne had lived with Marie of Brabant as a child, so this was one potential route for the book's passage to Charles of Navarre, who would then have inherited it from his mother. But if this were the ownership history of the book, Blanche did not know it or she surely would have included it. It is hard to imagine that Charles did not tell her precisely from whom he had acquired the book when he gave it to her. Blanche may have been deliberately vague because Charles of Navarre had come by it through means that were best left undescribed in the will, if it had been in the context of one of his many feuds with the French kings, or if his acquisition had

---

23   Delisle 196.

been contested. The bequests of Blanche's testament might efface an awkward history as well as they could highlight an illustrious one.

Charles III himself was a bibliophile, as can be seen by a lavishly decorated book of hours owned by him that he acquired on a visit to Paris in 1404.[24] He may have wanted Louis's book for its fame as a book as well as its value as a relic. Blanche's insistence that the book was promised to her brother's son suggests that someone else might have had his or her eye on it, perhaps the duke of Berry, a notoriously acquisitive collector. The book does not seem to have been identified with Saint Louis or Blanche in the 1412 inventory of Charles III.[25] But a 1461 inventory of a grandson of Charles III, Carlos, prince of Viana, noted a breviary of Saint Louis in the prince's collection that may be the book described in Blanche's will.[26]

Blanche also gave Charles III three other gifts, grouped together in one bequest that followed that of the breviary of Saint Louis:

> Et aussi lui laissons un fermail d'or ront, où il a un gros saphir un milieu; et autour du fermail a rubis, perles et dyamans, lequel fu beau frère messire Phelippe de Navarre, que Diex absoille; et avecques ce nostre livre des Croniques de France; et nostre chambre broudée à lyons, des armes de France, de Bourgongne et d'Evreux toute entière.[27]

> [And also I leave him a round gold brooch which has a sapphire at the center, and around the brooch there are rubies, pearls, and diamonds, which belonged to my brother Philip of Navarre; and with this my book of

---

24 It is now in the collection of the Cleveland Museum of Art and known as the Hours of Charles the Noble; William Wixom, "The Hours of Charles the Noble," *Bulletin of the Cleveland Museum of Art* 52 (1965), 50–83, and Stephen N. Fliegel, "The Hours of Charles the Noble," in *Sacred Gifts and Worldly Treasures: Medieval Masterworks from the Cleveland Museum of Art*, ed. Holger Klein (Cleveland, 2007), p. 217.

25 María Narbona Cárceles notes that this book is not mentioned in the 1412 will of Charles III; "La 'Discreción Hermosa': Blanca de Navarra, reina de Francia. Una dama al servicio de su linaje," in *La dama en la corte bajomedieval*, ed. Martí Aurell et al. (Pamplona, 2001), p. 88.

26 Delisle, *Douze livres royaux*, p. 56, published the wording of the inventory: "Item un hun stoig de cuyro, que es en la dita casa, es lo breviari de sant Luis ab cuberta de brocat et dos tancados d'or y registre"; see also the inventory list in *Inventaire-sommaire des Archives départementales antérieures à 1790: Basses-Pyrénées*, ed. Paul Raymond, 6 vols. (Paris, 1863–79), 4:149.

27 Delisle 197.

88   CHAPTER 3

> the *Chroniques de France*, and my room hangings embroidered with lions
> and the arms of France, Burgundy, and Evreux.]

The items in this bequest are linked by their ties to family and to kingship –
Philip of Navarre was the uncle of the king, the administrator of the Navarrais
lands in France, and the esteemed 'bon chevalier' who Blanche had mourned
so greatly in 1363 that it merited mention by a chronicler. The gold brooch with
a sapphire was a valuable item because of the expense of its gems, but it may
have had an apotropaic significance in addition since sapphires were associated with protective qualities in the Middle Ages. A lapidary of the second
quarter of the 14th century advised that the sapphire, among its other beneficial effects, would protect from imprisonment.[28] (The qualities imputed to
precious stones are analyzed in greater depth in chap. 5.)

The second book that Blanche left to Charles was the *Chroniques de France*,
a history of his French royal ancestors, a reminder of his descent from the
Capetian kings, and a history of kings and their great deeds for someone who
was himself a king. The third gift, heraldic room hangings, are a visual expression of a book like the chronicle of the kings of France, with its lions – associated
with kingship – and its heraldry of France, Burgundy, and Evreux. That the
arms of Navarre are lacking make it unlikely that Blanche herself commissioned this set, but the absence of the arms of Navarre clearly did not disqualify
the use of the room hangings for the king of Navarre. It is possible that these
are the arms used by Blanche's mother Jeanne after her marriage to Philip of
Evreux in 1318 but before she became queen of Navarre in 1328. The French
royal and dynastic significance of the breviary of Saint Louis was comple-
mented with this trio of French royal gifts – a book, room hangings, and a
sapphire brooch that had belonged to an uncle.

Blanche owned a second Saint Louis book relic, the psalter from which he
had learned in his childhood. This psalter was one of several at the French
court in the second half of the 14th century that were attributed to the ownership of the saint. Jeanne of Evreux gave one to Charles V in 1369, two years
before her death; it is known today as the Psalter of Saint Louis (Paris, Bibliothèque nationale, MS lat. 10525).[29] A second psalter of Saint Louis owned by

---

28   The lapidary is Oxford, Bodleian Library, Douce 291, published in Joan Evans, *English
      Medieval Lapidaries* (London, 1933; repr. 1960), pp. 16–37.

29   It was described in the 1380 inventory of Charles V: "Item ung autre psaultier mendre, qui
      fut aussi monseigneur saint Loys, très bien escript et noblement enluminé, et a grant
      quantité d'ystoires au commancemen de dit livre, et se commence ou second fueillet *vas
      figuli*. Ouquel a deux petiz fermouers d'or plaz, l'un esmaillé de France, et l'autre d'Evreux,

BOOKS AS EVIDENCE TO PERPETUATE MEMORY

Charles V and kept at his château at Vincennes is today known as the Ingeborg Psalter (Chantilly, Musée Condé, MS 1695).[30] Both of these books, as well as Blanche's book, were associated with the ownership of Saint Louis by an inscription. This kind of captioning of the book drastically improved its odds of being cherished and therefore of surviving.[31] These inscriptions demonstrate an interest in authenticity and assert the relic status of the books; in this way they are similar to the provenance lists in the will of Blanche of Navarre.

Blanche left her psalter of Saint Louis to Philip, duke of Burgundy, brother of Charles V and uncle of the current king. Certainly it was given to the duke, as a psalter with an inscription described as "c'est le psaultier MS Saint Loys, ouquel il aprit en son enfance," was documented in a 1420 inventory of the duke's collection.[32] A 12th-century English psalter today in Leiden has been identified with this book because of its inscription: "Cist psaultiers fuit mon seigneur saint loys qui fu roys de france. Duquel il aprint en lenfance" (Fig. 3.3).[33] Léopold Delisle suggested that this book was first owned by Louis VIII who had acquired it during his stay in England and then gave it to his wife, Blanche of Castile, who taught her son with it.[34] Blanche wrote about the book's provenance in her bequest:

> Item nous laissons à nostre très chier fils le duc de Bourgongne le psaltier où monseigneur saint Loys aprint: et fu à madame la grant duchesse Agnès, duchesse de Bourgongne, sa fille; et depuis la duchesse Agnès vint à nostre dicte dame la royne Jehanne de Bourgongne, sa fille; et en après

---

a une pippe ou il a ung très gros ballay et quatre très grosses perles"; Delisle, *Douze livres royaux*, p. 14. For analysis of this book and its bequest see Holladay, "Fourteenth-century French Queens," pp. 76–81.

30   For the ownership by Charles V of the Ingeborg Psalter, see Delisle, *Douze livres royaux*, p. 14.

31   The inscription in Jeanne of Evreux's psalter reads: "Cest psautier fu saint Loys. Et le donna la royne Jehanne d'Evreux au roy Charles, filz du roy Jehan, l'an de nostre Seigneur mil troys cens soissante e nuef"; Delisle, *Recherches*, 1:175. The inscription in the Ingeborg Psalter is: "Ce psaultier fu saint Loys"; Delisle, *Douze livres royaux*, p. 14. For the implications more broadly of inscribing ownership on works of art, see Gail Feigenbaum, "Manifest Provenance," in *Provenance: An Alternate History of Art*, ed. Gail Feigenbaum and Inge Reist (Los Angeles, 2012), pp. 6–28.

32   Léon de Laborde, *Les ducs de Bourgogne*, 2 vols. (Paris, 1849–51), 2:266, no. 4255.

33   This inscription must date before 1420, as it was described with this inscription in the duke's inventory of that date, and it must postdate the canonization of Louis in 1297; it was therefore added to the book when it was in the possession of Agnes of Burgundy, Jeanne of Burgundy, Blanche of Navarre, or soon after Blanche's death.

34   Delisle, *Douze livres royaux*, p. 24.

FIGURE 3.3 Psalter of Saint Louis, *c. 1200*. LEIDEN UNIVERSITY LIBRARY, BPL 76A, FOL. 30V. PHOTO CREDIT: LEIDEN UNIVERSITY LIBRARY.

à nostre dit seigneur et espoux, qui le nous donna, e nous tesmongna, et aussi firent les femmes de la dicte madame la royne qu'il nous bailla que c'estoit icellui vraiement. Si desirons qu'il soit à la ligne. Et pour ce prions à nostre dit filz que il le vueille garder et faire tenir à ses successeurs et en sa ligne, pour l'amour de ceulx dont il est venu.[35]

---

35 Delisle 200. In *Douze livres royaux*, pp. 19–26, Delisle gives a slightly different version of the bequest in Blanche's will, in this line, "et nous tesmongna (et aussi firent les femmes

BOOKS AS EVIDENCE TO PERPETUATE MEMORY

[I leave to my very dear son, the duke of Burgundy, the psalter with which Saint Louis learned to read; and it belonged to the duchess Agnes, duchess of Burgundy, his daughter; and from the duchess Agnes it came to the queen Jeanne of Burgundy, her daughter; and after to my spouse, who gave it to me, and he affirmed (that it was truly the same psalter) and it was also attested by the ladies of the queen that it was given to me and it was truly this psalter. And I wish that it should be in the family line. And I pray that my son will keep it and hold it for his successors and in this line, for love of those from whom it has come.]

The book had an unassailable provenance dating back to Agnes of Burgundy, the saint's daughter, and the mother of the first wife of Philip VI. At the death of Jeanne, it had passed to Philip. Despite this clear chain of ownership, the bequest is worded defensively. Blanche thought it necessary to note that Philip VI had affirmed that it was Saint Louis's psalter, and the women who had served the queen had done so as well. If Philip had attested it, it is not clear why it was necessary for the women who had worked for Jeanne to do so too, unless someone had challenged its authenticity. The inscription, if it dates from the ownership of Blanche of Navarre, would have been another way for the queen to verify the identity of the book.

Blanche was acting as a mediator with the gift of the psalter of Saint Louis to the duke of Burgundy. The question of the succession to the duchy of Burgundy had caused a rift between the French king John II and Charles of Navarre, Blanche's brother, 30 years before this bequest was written.[36] In 1361, the last direct Capetian duke of Burgundy, Philip of Rouvres, had died without an heir. Charles of Navarre claimed the duchy through his descent from Margaret of Burgundy, his grandmother, and King John II based his claim on his descent from his mother Jeanne of Burgundy, Margaret's younger sister. Although his mother was the younger sister of Margaret, John had additional support for his case because he had married Jeanne of Boulogne, the widowed duchess of Burgundy and mother of Philip of Rouvres, and therefore he had served as stepfather to the last duke. John II was eventually successful in his claim, and in 1362 he awarded the duchy to his youngest son, Philip. By giving

---

de la dicte madame la royne qui l[e] bailla) que c'estoit icellui vraiement," writing: "Je suis porté à croire que le texte original devait porter 'les femmes de la dicte madame, qui le nous baillèrent.'"

36   For the Burgundian succession crisis, see Joseph Calmette, *The Golden Age of Burgundy: The Magnificent Dukes and Their Courts*, trans. Doreen Weightman (New York, 1963; repr. London, 2001).

Philip this book and describing its descent, from the saint to Agnes of Burgundy and then to Jeanne of Burgundy (Philip's grandmother), Blanche reminded him of the Burgundian history that was carried with the book.

That a book had been used by someone in their childhood education offered additional significance to a provenance. In 1407, Louis II, duke of Anjou and king of Naples, gave John, duke of Berry, the book of hours with which John II (his father) had learned to read.[37] Blanche herself gave to one of her ladies-in-waiting, Jeanne de Rouières, the book with which Blanche's daughter had learned to read:

> Avecques le breviare qui fu Jehanne de France, nostre fille, où elle aprint, que elle a en sa garde.[38]

> [With the breviary that belonged to Jeanne of France, my daughter, where she learned, that she has in her possession.]

The significance of the book with which someone learned to read was associated probably with the acquisition of religious knowledge. Mothers were usually charged with the education of their children, as in the image of Blanche of Castile overseeing her son Saint Louis's education by a monk in the *Hours of Jeanne of Navarre* (Fig. 3.4). Blanche may have owned the *Hours of Jeanne of Navarre*, as I suggest below. If indeed Blanche owned this book, it was an instance in which she owned a painted image of a book that was in her collection, similar to her possession of the breviary miraculously returned to Saint Louis on crusade pictured in the book of her aunt Jeanne. Though neither gift mentioned here, the gift of the book from Louis of Anjou to the duke of Berry nor the gift of the book from which Blanche's daughter had learned to read, is intended specifically for mothers, as far as we know, books from childhood may show a kind of care for the religious education of the person to whom they are given and a celebration of the piety of the person who had used it. Another bequest linked to this idea is a book that Blanche gave to her cousin, Louis, count of Étampes:

> Et aussi nostre livre où sont les euvangiles des quatre euvangelistes, et pluseurs sermons en françois, qui fu à l mère de monseigneur saint Loys de France.[39]

---

37 Jules Guiffrey, *Inventaires de Jean, duc de Berry (1401–1416)*, 2 vols. (Paris, 1894–96), 1: 257.
38 Delisle 280.
39 Delisle 238.

[My book that has the four Gospels and many sermons in French, which belonged to the mother of Saint Louis of France.]

That Blanche of Navarre calls Blanche of Castile 'the mother of Saint Louis,' rather than using her name, may imply – or intend to imply – for Louis of Étampes, that the saint's mother had used it in her son's religious education. Though it may simply have been shorthand (it was not Blanche of Castile's name or her status as queen of France that was particularly important in later history, but her role as mother of the saint), it is possible that in this case the educational value of the book was what was meant to be emphasized.

Blanche paired another book related to Saint Louis with a relic to explicitly emphasize the book's educational value. She left to the Hôtel Dieu of Vernon a relic of a finger of Saint Louis accompanied by a book of the life of Saint Louis:

> Item nous laissons à l'ostel Dieu de Vernon un reliquiaire d'argent que deux anges tiennent, là où il y a une jointe de monseigneur saint Loys de France, et avecques ce un livre de la vie monseigneur saint Loys de France qui est en françoys, pour lire aux dames quant elles veilleront à l'ostel, pour avoir memoire de saint Loys de qui ilz sont fondez.[40]

> [I leave to the Hôtel Dieu of Vernon a silver reliquary held by two angels which contains a joint of Saint Louis of France and with this a book of the Life of Saint Louis which is in French, for these women to read when they come to the Hôtel Dieu, to remember Saint Louis who founded it.]

In this bequest the book gave an explanatory text for the reliquary; it functioned as a sort of extended caption for the reliquary. Blanche was presented in this bequest as an educator who advised the women of the Hôtel Dieu not simply to venerate the relic of Saint Louis but to read the book to understand how Saint Louis might serve as a model for behavior.

The books discussed thus far derived their prestige ultimately from their ownership by Saint Louis or an association with him. But Blanche also gave away many books with a provenance that while not saintly, was still stellar, such as those books owned by a trio of queens – her mother Jeanne of Navarre, her aunt Jeanne of Evreux, and her great-aunt and her husband's first wife, Jeanne of Burgundy. Blanche thought that the provenance of these women would give value to the books for her heirs – there would not have been any point in mentioning them otherwise. It is clear why someone would have

---

40   Delisle 35.

wanted a book owned by Saint Louis, but the value imputed to a book by an ancestor queen is more difficult to determine and also likely much more varied; it may have depended on the reputation of the queen for piety or her example as a patron of authors, or it could be as simple as knowledge that this person had owned beautiful and aesthetically pleasing books. Family ties are another important factor, as two books that were owned by the mother of Blanche of Navarre were given to her sisters, clearly a reference to the maternal relationship. But a third book owned by Jeanne of Navarre was given to John, duke of Berry, who had not known this queen and who would have had no such affectionate response to her name. The citation of the earlier queens might also have been prescriptive, particularly for some of the younger female heirs, like Isabeau of Bavaria, who had never known Jeanne of Burgundy, though Blanche cited this queen's ownership in the book she gave her. Perhaps Blanche hoped that the younger queen would find an exemplar in her long-deceased predecessor; it goes without saying that such a prescriptive bequest was no guarantee that Isabeau perceived the gift in the same way.

Blanche owned three books that had previously been in her mother's collection. She gave one to the duke of Berry, and two others to her sisters. To the duke of Berry, Blanche left her mother's book of hours:

> Item nous laissons à nostre très chier filz le duc de Berry, nos plus belles heures, que nostre très chiere dame et mère, que Dieux pardoint, nous lessa à son trespassement.[41]

> [I leave to ... the duke of Berry my most beautiful book of hours that my ... mother ... left to me at her death.]

John did not know Jeanne of Navarre, who had died when he was still a child, and as noted above, the value of the book could therefore not have been personal. Its description as 'most beautiful,' an aesthetic assessment, suggests that the value of the book for the duke of Berry was artistic.[42] The book dated from at least the middle of the 14th century, so that the duke may also have esteemed it as a product of mid-14th-century artists and wanted to add such a book to his collection.

---

41 Delisle 198.
42 Keith Busby has suggested that the books borrowed by the duke of Berry from the Louvre indicate that he was someone more interested perhaps in illumination than in text; *Codex and Context*, pp. 664–65.

BOOKS AS EVIDENCE TO PERPETUATE MEMORY

Though this was her mother's 'most beautiful' book of hours, it may seem a modest gift in comparison to the psalter of Saint Louis that had been given to the duke of Burgundy, the brother of the duke of Berry. But it is unlikely that Blanche would have slighted the duke of Berry, a well-known collector of books and other objects (his collection of gems is discussed in chap. 5). Therefore, the book must have been remarkable for this reason alone – the person to whom it was given; furthermore, Blanche called it her 'most beautiful' book of hours and she had kept it since her mother's death in 1349. There is one candidate for this book that survives, the only book of hours that we know belonged to Jeanne of Navarre, the *Hours of Jeanne of Navarre* (Fig. 3.4). A lavishly illustrated book, it was painted for Jeanne in the 1330s by Jean le Noir and other artists. For this book to be the one left to the duke of Berry, it would require that Jeanne had left it to Blanche and not one of her other children, and that of Blanche's books of hours (she had at least two, perhaps three, if a book called 'a book of prayers and devotions' is a book of hours), Blanche considered it her most beautiful.

The other books that had been previously owned by Blanche's mother were given to her sisters. To Agnes, countess of Foix, Blanche gave two books, one of which had been their mother's:

> Et aussi nostre livre de l'enseignement du *Mirouer des dames*, lequel est couvert de veluau, et a les fermoirs d'argent.[43]

> Et un psaltier qui fu nostre très chiere dame et mère, que Dieux absoille; et y a sept paires de heures et pluseurs oroisons.[44]

> [And also my book of teaching of the *Mirouer des dames*, which is covered in velvet, and has silver clasps.

> And a psalter which belonged to our mother, and there are seven pairs of hours and many prayers in it.]

Agnes had married Gaston Fébus, count of Foix, in 1349.[45] This marriage had collapsed in 1362 with her repudiation by her husband (caused at least partially

---

43   Delisle 222.

44   Delisle 223.

45   On this couple, see Pierre Tucoo-Chala, "L'histoire tragique d'un couple au XIVe siècle: Agnès de Navarre et Gaston Fébus," *Homenaje a José Maria Lacarra de Miguel* 2 (Pam-

FIGURE 3.4 *Education of Saint Louis,* Hours of Jeanne of Navarre, c. 1330–40. PARIS, BIBLIOTHÈQUE NATIONALE DE FRANCE, MS NOUV. ACQ. LAT. 3145, FOL. 85V. PHOTO CREDIT: BIBLIOTHÈQUE NATIONALE DE FRANCE.

by the non-payment of her dowry).[46] The *Miroir des dames* was a French translation of the *Speculum dominarum*, a manual of correct behavior for women written for Jeanne of Navarre (1285–1305), the wife of Philip the Fair, meant specifically for royal women.[47] Jeanne of Evreux may also have owned a copy,

---

plona, 1986), 741–54, as well as Sophie Lagabrielle, "Agnès de Navarre: l'amour des beaux objets," in *Gaston Fébus: Prince Soleil, 1331–1391* (Paris, 2011), pp. 52–67.

46   For this crisis, see Elena Woodacre, *The Queens Regnant of Navarre: Succession, Politics, and Partnership, 1274–1512* (New York, 2013), pp. 83–84.

47   On this text, see the essays in *Virtue Ethics for Women, 1250–1500*, ed. Karen Green and

BOOKS AS EVIDENCE TO PERPETUATE MEMORY 97

as one owned by Valentina Visconti had Jeanne's arms and may once have been in her collection.[48] This book of the *Miroir des dames* was purchased by or given to Blanche of Navarre as a guide for her own behavior, and Blanche thought it would be equally useful for her sister. The second book was a psalter owned by their mother that had the canonical hours as well as many other prayers in it; the limited description of this book does not tell us what it was like beyond that it was likely not as lavishly decorated as the 'plus belles' book given to the duke of Berry, but it does indicate that occasionally the sole value of a book for a recipient could be who had owned it.

Blanche's youngest sister Jeanne, viscountess of Rohan, was also given two books, one of which had been owned by their mother:

Et aussi nostre livre du pelerinage du monde, où il y a plusieurs oroisons, et est cellui qui parle après la mort.

Et noz heures de Nostre Dame, où nous disons touz les jours noz heures, qui furent madame nostre mère, que Diex absoille, qui sont les meilleurs que nous aions, après celles que nous lessons à nostre dit filz de Berry.[49]

[And also my book of the *Pèlerinage du monde*, where there are many prayers, and those which are said after death.

And my hours of the Virgin, which I use for my daily prayers, which belonged to my mother, which is the best that I have after that which I left to the duke of Berry.]

Karen Green has identified this *Pèlerinage du monde* with the *Pèlerinage de vie humaine* of Guillaume de Degulleville.[50] Blanche owned a second work by the same author, the *Pèlerinage du Jésus Christ*, which she gave to her niece, Marie

---

Constant Mews (Heidelberg, 2011), including Rina Lahav, "A Mirror of Queenship: The *Speculum Dominarum* and the Demands of Justice," pp. 31–44; Constant Mews, "The *Speculum Dominarum* (*Miroir des dames*) and Transformations of the Literature of Instruction for Women in the Early Fourteenth Century," pp. 13–30; Janice Pinder, "A Lady's Guide to Salvation: The *Miroir des dames* Compilation," pp. 45–52; and Karen Green, "From *Le miroir des dames* to *Le livre des trois vertus*, pp. 99–114. For the occasional confusion between the *Miroir des dames*, a French translation of the *Speculum dominarum*, and the *Miroir aux dames*, an allegorical poem by Wautriquet de Couvin, see Holladay, "Fourteenth-Century French queens," p. 82, n. 24.

48   Holladay, "Fourteenth-century French queens," p. 82, n. 24.
49   Delisle 229, 230.
50   Green, "What Were the Ladies in the *City of Ladies* Reading?" p. 96, n. 20.

of Navarre, discussed further below.[51] These books were intended to be a guide to the reader, a pilgrim on a journey toward salvation. The second bequest is the book that had been owned by her mother, an hours of the Virgin that Blanche used daily.[52] This bequest reveals that Blanche had books that were not used, as she did not pray daily from the 'most beautiful' book of hours that she gave to the duke of Berry. The one she used every day was a pleasing book, because it was her next-best book of hours, so whatever the qualities of the 'most beautiful' book that made it not appropriate for everyday use, they must have been significantly greater – in degree of illumination, in the size of the book, or in a lavish binding – which made it impractical or unwise to use every day. Blanche had kept these three books – the most beautiful book of hours, the next-best book of hours, and the psalter – for nearly 50 years, since her mother's death, and they are evidence of the value of such a maternal connection in a book collection.

Another queen associated with Blanche of Navarre's books was Jeanne of Burgundy, Blanche's great-aunt and her husband's first wife. A great patron of books, she had commissioned translations from Jean de Vignay of the *Miroir historial* of Vincent Beauvais and the *Golden Legend* by Jacobus da Voragine, among others.[53] Blanche associated four of her books with the older queen's ownership: the psalter of Saint Louis (discussed above), a didactic book beginning *Audi fili Israel*, a breviary, and a book of Josafas and Barlaam.

Blanche gave the book beginning *Audi fili Israel*, in which, Blanche noted, 'there is a lot of good information,' to the French queen Isabeau of Bavaria.[54] This volume has been identified by Richard Rouse and Mary Rouse as a *Legiloque* collection, after the title of the first work; there are three extant manuscripts of this collection from the first half of the 14th century.[55] Blanche's citation of Jeanne of Burgundy in the gift to Isabeau of Bavaria placed Isabeau as third in the line of queens who had owned this book, linking her to her predecessors and flattering her as a bibliophile.[56] But there is also an element of mentorship

---

51   Delisle 236.

52   Neither of these books is attested clearly in the 1401 testament of Jeanne of Rohan. She left two books of hours in her testament, but the description is not sufficient to know if either of these books was the book of hours left to her by Blanche; Pierre-Hyacinthe Morice, "Testament de Jeanne de Navarre, vicomtesse de Rohan," *Mémoires pour servir de preuves à l'histoire ecclésiastique et civile de Bretagne*, 3 vols. (Paris, 1742–46), 2:720.

53   Green, "What Were the Ladies in the *City of Ladies* Reading?" p. 80, and Murielle Gaude-Ferragu, "Les dernières volontés de la reine de France. Les deux testaments de Jeanne de Bourgogne, femme de Philippe VI de Valois (1329, 1336)," *Annuaire-Bulletin de la Sociéte de l'histoire de France, année 2007* (2009), 23–66.

54   Delisle 195.

55   "French Literature and the Counts of Saint-Pol," pp. 122–29.

56   For this queen's library, see Vallet de Viriville, *La bibliothèque d'Isabeau de Bavière*.

BOOKS AS EVIDENCE TO PERPETUATE MEMORY

here. The book is bequeathed with an acknowledgement that there is good information in it, appropriate for queens like Jeanne of Burgundy, Blanche of Navarre, and now Isabeau. This is also an indication that she expected Isabeau to use the book, in this way much more like Symmonete the healer than the owners of the revered books of Saint Louis, Charles III of Navarre, and the duke of Burgundy.

To the widow of Louis, duke of Anjou, Marie of Blois (1345–1404), also known as the queen of Sicily, Blanche left another book from Jeanne of Burgundy:

> Item nous laissons à nostre très chiere fille la royne de Sezille nostre breviare le milleur, qui fu a la dicte madame la royne Jehanne de Bourgongne.[57]

> [I leave to the queen of Sicily my best breviary, which belonged to the queen Jeanne of Burgundy.]

Blanche's 'best' breviary was the one returned to Saint Louis by an angel. By calling this one her best is an indication that it had been elevated beyond the status of a book to become a relic. She did not count it among her breviaries. That she gave Marie her 'best' breviary is an indication that the two had an affectionate or at least a close relationship. They were of the same generation – Marie was fourteen years younger than Blanche, and lived six years longer. Christine de Pizan grouped Blanche and Marie together with Jeanne of Evreux and Blanche of Orléans as examples of royal female virtue.[58] At least one of the books in Marie's collection survives, a *Pèlerinage de vie humaine* (Heidelberg, Pal. Lat. 1969), also by Guillaume Degulleville, the author of two of Blanche's volumes.[59] The mention of Jeanne of Burgundy here for Marie was a citation of a renowned bibliophile, and it must have been in some way a beautiful book to have been designated by Blanche as her 'best' breviary.

Another such bibliophile was Marie of Valois (1344–1404), duchess of Bar, the sister of Charles V and another patron of authors. She was named as the dedicatee of the *Roman de Mélusine* by Jean d'Arras along with her brother, John, duke of Berry.[60] Blanche left her:

---

57   Delisle 204.

58   Christine de Pizan, *The Book of the City of Ladies*, trans. Rosalind Brown-Grant (London, 1999), book 1, chap. 13.

59   Green, "What Were the Ladies in the *City of Ladies* Reading?" p. 81, citing Anne-Marie Legaré, "La reception du *Pèlerinage de Vie humaine* de Guillaume de Digulleville dans le milieu angevin d'après les sources et les manuscrits conserves," in *Religion et mentalités au Moyen Âge: mélanges en l'honneur d'Hervé Martin*, ed. Sophie Cassagnes-Brouquet et al. (Rennes 2003), pp. 543–52.

60   On Mélusine, see the essays in *Melusine of Lusignan: Founding Fiction in Late Medieval France*, ed. Donald Maddox and Sara Sturm-Maddox (Athens, GA, 1996).

> Item à nostre très chiere fille la duchesse de Bar, le livre du lignage de
> Nostre Dame et de ses suers; et est au commancement du dit livre la
> louenge de saint Jehan l'euvangeliste.[61]

> [the book of the genealogy of the Virgin Mary and her sisters and at the
> beginning of this book is the praise of Saint John the Evangelist.]

Though Blanche is not specific about how she viewed this book or why she
gave it to Marie of Valois, these gifts are invaluable for bringing to light a book
community, the men and women of her generation who appreciated books –
the siblings of Charles V, John of Berry, Marie of Valois, and Philip of Burgundy,
and Charles's sisters-in-law, Marie of Blois (married to his brother Louis of
Anjou), and in the bequest below, Margaret of Flanders, the wife of Philip of
Burgundy.

The fourth book in Blanche's collection that had been previously owned by
Jeanne of Burgundy was given to Margaret of Flanders (1350–1405), duchess of
Burgundy. Blanche gave her a set of paternoster beads that had belonged to
Jeanne of Evreux, and

> aussi le livre de Josafas et Balaham et de pluseurs autres choses, et est
> armoié de France et de Bourgongne; et fu à madame la royne Jehanne de
> Bourgongne.[62]

> [also my book of Josafas and Barlaam and many other things, and it has
> the arms of France and of Burgundy, and it belonged to the queen Jeanne
> of Burgundy.]

The book of Barlaam and Josephat was a story about early Christian martyrs
perhaps based on the life of the Buddha. Like the *Legiloque* texts above for
Isabeau of Bavaria, this volume contained not just this story but had 'many
other things' that might have endeared it to Margaret of Burgundy. But primarily Blanche thought that the bequest would be appropriate for this duchess
because of the book's prior owner. It had been owned by a descendant of
the Capetian dukes of Burgundy, Jeanne, and it would be given to the current duchess of Burgundy, connecting generations of book owners through a
shared heritage, as the gift of the psalter of Saint Louis had done for Margaret's
husband Philip.[63] Margaret of Flanders was perhaps known as a bibliophile; in

---

61   Delisle 214.

62   Delisle 211.

63   For the book collection of Margaret and her husband, see Hughes, "The Library of Philip
      the Bold and Margaret of Flanders," pp. 145–88.

BOOKS AS EVIDENCE TO PERPETUATE MEMORY

her 1392 testament, Blanche of Orléans gave the duchess of Burgundy a book about the Crusades, the story of Godfrey de Bouillon in the Holy Land.[64]

The third in the trio of queens who supplied a prestigious provenance in Blanche's will was Jeanne of Evreux; Blanche also had two books that had belonged to her. The first was given to Valentina Visconti (c. 1368–1408), the duchess of Orléans, married to Louis of Orléans, younger brother of Charles VI, in 1389. To her she gave:

> Et un livre d'oroisons et devocions qui fu à noz très chieres dames la royne Marie et la ditte madame la royne Jehanne d'Evreux; et le nous donna la duchesse d'Orliens, sa fille, derreniere trespassée; et se commance après le kalendrier *Gloria in excelsis Deo*.[65]

> [a book of prayers and devotions that had belonged to the queen Marie and to the queen Jeanne of Evreux, and the duchess of Orléans her daughter, recently deceased, gave it to me, and it begins after the calendar *Gloria in excelsis Deo*.]

The identity of this 'queen Marie' is elusive; it most likely refers to Marie of Brabant, but Marie of Luxembourg, the second wife of Charles IV, is also a possibility.[66] In this bequest, Blanche gave a book to the duchess of Orléans that had previously been owned by another duchess of Orléans, continuing a practice seen throughout the will, as in the gift to the duchess of Burgundy above.

---

64 Gaston Vignat, "Testament de Blanche, duchesse d'Orléans," *Mémoires de la Sociéte archéologique de l'Orléanais* 9 (1866), 131. All the others listed with the duchess of Burgundy in this testament were given stones – the duke of Berry got a ruby, the duchess of Berry, a diamond, the duke of Burgundy, a 'beau' ruby, followed by a diamond for the duke of Touraine, and a statuette of Saint John the Baptist to the count of Étampes. This book was the only book given by Blanche of Orléans to this group of heirs at the French court. She does say it was a 'beau' livre, so perhaps its lavish decoration made it an appropriate gift, but it seems also to signal the interest of the duchess of Burgundy in books rather than in gems.

65 Delisle 213.

66 Joan Holladay has argued convincingly that this Queen Marie is Marie of Brabant; "Fourteenth-century French Queens," p. 87, n. 50. This book may be described in the will of Blanche of Orléans. Her bequest to Blanche of Navarre reads: "She leaves to the queen Blanche, her breviary from which she says her hours, a small book of prayers that belonged to the queen Jeanne her mother"; Vignat, "Testament de Blanche, duchesse d'Orléans," p. 131.

102   CHAPTER 3

In the 1398 codicil, Blanche changed her mind about this breviary; she replaced it with a two-volume breviary that had also once belonged to Jeanne of Evreux.

> Premierement, pour et en lieu du livre d'oroisons et devocions que nous lessions en nostre dit premier codicille à nostre tres chiere fille la duchesse d'Orleans, lequel fu à noz très chieres dames la royne Marie et la royne Jehanne, nous voulons et ordenons que notre ditte fille ait nostre breviaire à l'usage de Romme, qui est en deux volumes, qui fu ma ditte dame la royne Jehanne.[67]

> [In place of the book of prayers and devotions that I left in the first codicil to the dear duchess of Orléans, which had belonged to the queen Marie and the queen Jeanne, I want and order that the aforementioned daughter should receive my breviary of the use of Rome, which is in two volumes, which had belonged to Queen Jeanne.]

No indication is given of why she changed her mind about this bequest or what had happened to the breviary that belonged to the queens Marie and Jeanne of Evreux described in the 1396 will. There is also no account given of how she obtained the new two-volume breviary, not mentioned in the 1396 will. If she came into possession of this breviary between 1396 and 1398, it would demonstrate that she continued to acquire books to the end of her life.[68] A two-volume breviary with the arms of France attested in a 1408 inventory done after the death of Valentina might be this bequest.[69]

The books in Blanche's collection with prior female owners that she thought important enough to note were not always queens. Two were nuns, albeit both princesses, at the convent of Longchamp: Jeanne, her sister, and Blanche, a

---

67   Delisle 405.

68   Alternately, it is possible that she lost track of the volumes in her collection. Had she dictated the will from memory, without the book at hand (indeed, it is hard to imagine that all the possessions listed in the will were at her home in Paris where the will was dictated), it is reasonable to assume that she misremembered what the book was. Might she have realized that the breviary she asserted to have been owned by a queen Marie and Jeanne of Evreux was actually not the book she was thinking of at all, but rather a two-volume breviary owned by Jeanne of Evreux? It would explain the substitution and the absence of a fate for the breviary of Queen Marie and Queen Jeanne. Against this interpretation is the evidence of the wording of the bequest about the book: "and it begins after the calendar *Gloria in excelsis Deo*" is very specific information for a book that neither she nor her executors had at hand.

69   For the breviaries listed in the 1408 inventory of Valentina Visconti, see Pierre Champion, *La librairie de Charles d'Orléans* (Paris, 1910), pp. lxxi-lxii, cited by Green, "What Were the Ladies in the *City of Ladies* Reading?" p. 82, p. 97, n. 32.

BOOKS AS EVIDENCE TO PERPETUATE MEMORY   103

daughter of Philip v. The first of these books, a breviary owned by her sister, Jeanne, was given to her niece, Jeanne (1370–1437), a daughter of Charles II. Jeanne was married to the duke of Brittany in 1386. Widowed in 1399, she married Henry IV, king of England, in 1403. Blanche wrote:

> Item à nostre très chiere niece la duchesse de Bretaigne, nostre breviaire, qui fu nostre seur madame Jehanne de Navarre, de Longchamp, lequel nous avons fait estoffer.[70]

> [To ... the duchess of Brittany, my breviary which belonged to my sister Jeanne de Navarre, of Longchamp, which I have had rebound.]

Blanche may have been given this book by her sister while she was alive or inherited the book at her sister's death in 1382.[71] We know of at least one other book in Jeanne's collection at Longchamp, the 'beau livre' given to her by Jeanne of Evreux at her death. Notable in this bequest is that Blanche had the book rebound and then deemed it necessary to indicate to the duchess of Brittany that she had done so. The motivation for rebinding may be simply that the binding was old or damaged, or she may have wanted to add a new coat of arms to the book; this was done by Jeanne of Evreux for two books in her collection.[72] The rebinding perhaps permitted Blanche to repurpose the gift with additional symbolic significance, by adding the duchess's coat of arms, for example, or using a lavish textile that increased the value of the book for its recipient, turning it into a kind of presentation copy.

Regardless of the reason for rebinding the book, Blanche thought it important to convey that she had done so; this information both helped her executors find the book in her collection and perhaps instilled additional value in the gift for the duchess of Brittany. In 1371, the French king Charles v had a new binding made for a book for Blanche's brother, Charles (discussed in chap. 2), repurposing a book that he owned already to celebrate his rapprochement with Charles of Navarre.[73] Another instance of rebinding comes from the book

---

70   Delisle 218.

71   Her death date is recorded on the epitaph of her tomb from Longchamp: "Cy gist très noble dame de claire mémoire, madame Jehanne de Navarre, soeur mineuse en l'eglise de céans, fille du roi de Navarre qui trépassa en Grenade pour la foi de Notre-Seigneur Jésus-Christ, et trépassa la dite Jehanne l'an de grâce M.CCC.LXXXII le IIIme jour de juillet"; transcribed in Henri-Gaston Duchesne, *Histoire de l'Abbaye de Longchamp* (Paris, 1905), p. 139.

72   Holladay, "Fourteenth-century French queens," p. 91, citing Delisle, *Recherches*, 1:175 and 2, no. 164.

73   Gilly Wraight, "Books: Covers," in *Encyclopedia of Dress and Textiles in the British Isles, c. 450–1450*, ed. Gale R. Owen-Crocker, Elizabeth Coatsworth, and Maria Hayward (Leiden,

104   CHAPTER 3

collection of John of Berry, who redecorated the book with which his father had learned to read, probably an early 14th-century book, if not older, with new fittings of gold and gems as well as a new sleeve in which to carry it.[74]

Because the impulse of the will is to describe the materials of the book, Blanche's will offered considerable evidence about book bindings. Blanche had at least one book with a figural binding; she left to another niece, Marie of Navarre, a breviary that had a purple satin cover embroidered with gold and pearls, with an Annunciation on one side and a Crucifixion on the other. There was not a prior female owner, as with so many of the bequests before and after it; rather, Blanche indicated that she purchased it in Paris:

> Et aussi un breviare à l'usage de Romme, qui fu achaté à Paris, et est la couverture brodée sur satarin ynde à or et à perles, et est d'un costé l'adnunciacion, et d'autre cruxifis.[75]

> [And also a breviary for use of Rome, which was bought in Paris, and which has a purple satin cover embroidered with gold and with pearls, and has on one side the Annunciation and on the other the Crucifixion.]

That Blanche offered the information that she had purchased the book, in this case in Paris, is unusual for the bequests of her will, and suggests that there were special circumstances surrounding this bequest. Marie of Navarre married Alfonso of Aragon in 1396; it seems likely that Blanche purchased the book as a gift for this wedding.[76] The citation of the purchase of the book then might refer to its personalization for Marie with heraldic devices.

Blanche gave Marie another book, discussed above, that included, among other texts, a guide to behavior known as the *Pèlerinage du Jésus Christ*:

> Et aussi un rommant qui au commancement parle du pelerinage de Jhesu Crist, et pluseurs autres bons enseignemens.[77]

> [And also a book which at the beginning has the *Pèlerinage du Jésus Christ*, and much other good information.]

In the bequest of the *Pèlerinage du Jésus Christ* she noted that the book had 'much other good information,' in addition to the moral guide offered by the

---

2012), p. 88. For the book given to Charles of Navarre by Charles V, see *Mandements et actes divers de Charles V*, ed. Léopold Delisle (Paris, 1874), p. 400, no. 779.

74   Guiffrey, *Inventaires de Jean, duc de Berry*, 1:257.

75   Delisle 233.

76   For this marriage, see Woodacre, *Queens Regnant of Navarre*, p. 83.

77   Delisle 236.

stories. This kind of additional commentary places Blanche in the role of the older educator, advising her niece about the content of the book and its value, especially appropriate for a new bride. This practice is also seen in the testament of Jeanne of Evreux, who gave a book of hours with the life of Saint Catherine to her goddaughter; it was one of only three books that she cited by title and gave to an heir other than her daughter. Her mention of Jeanne de Harcourt as her goddaughter suggests that she intended a special care for her spiritual education with the gift of the book.[78] What is also notable about Blanche's gift of two books to Marie of Navarre is that she combined two different sources for the books; one was purchased new, and the other was from her own collection, because Blanche could attest that it had good information. Blanche gave two other gifts to Marie of Navarre in the will, a hat with pearls and a set of bedsheets that will be discussed in chapter 6.

Another book textile was described in a gift to the duchess of Berry, a book previously owned by the daughter of Philip V, Blanche (1313–1358), a nun at Longchamp:

> Et aussi un livre où est le psaltier et oroisons, qui se commance *Beatus vir*, et la premiere oroison de saint Elysael, lequel est couvert d'un changant, et fu madame Blanche de Longchamp.[79]

> [And also a book which has a psalter and prayers that begins *Beatus vir*, and the first prayer of Saint Elysael, which is covered with 'un changant,' and it belonged to Blanche of Longchamp.]

The term 'un changant' probably refers to a textile whose color changed with light. The duchess of Berry in 1396 was Jeanne of Auvergne (1378–1424); married since 1389 to John, duke of Berry, she was eighteen in 1396. She does not have any of the connections to Blanche at Longchamp that commemorated earlier bequests in the will: Blanche and Jeanne did not share a name, a status, or close family ties. They were, however, both bibliophiles. One of Blanche's books was a breviary decorated by the well-known artist Jean Pucelle (Rome, Bib. Apostolica, MS Urb. Lat. 603).[80] It is possible that Blanche at Longchamp

---

78   Holladay, "Fourteenth-century French queens," pp. 88–89.

79   Delisle 209.

80   The manuscript is discussed by Joan Holladay, "Jean Pucelle and His Patrons," in *Jean Pucelle: Innovation and Collaboration in Manuscript Painting*, ed. Kyunghee Pyun and Anna Russakoff (Turnhout, 2013), pp. 18–19. See also Kathleen Morand, *Jean Pucelle* (Oxford, 1962), pp. 47–48, no. 13. For the books in Blanche's collection, see Allirot, "Longchamp and Lourcine," p. 254, n. 55.

was known as a connoisseur of books and Jeanne would have been flattered by a book from her collection.

Bequests to men have been infrequently mentioned thus far because Blanche gave many fewer books to men. Blanche's female book recipients outnumber male recipients twenty-two to ten. To these twenty-two women she gave twenty-nine books, and to the ten men, twelve books (one of her books went to an institution, the Hôtel Dieu of Vernon). The books given away earlier in the will to men, to Charles III of Navarre, to Philip, duke of Burgundy, and to John, duke of Berry, were a chronicle, a psalter, and a book of hours, and the five that will be discussed below were a chronicle, a moralized hunting book, two books on governing, and a *Somme le roi*, a book on virtues and vices. To take one example, she owned only two chronicles – one of France and one of the Holy Land (a *Chronique d'Outre-Mer*), and these were given to Charles III of Navarre and Pierre of Navarre, his brother.[81] Is this a sign that Blanche thought historical chronicles were suited to her male heirs more so than to her female heirs? Gendered book ownership is borne out by the work of other scholars, such as that of Alison Stones, who noted that portraits of women in books *c.* 1300 appear most often in vernacular and devotional books, whereas those of men occur most often in books for liturgy, law, and government.[82] But the numbers are discouragingly small – only two chronicles, only two books on governing; to determine that Blanche was using gender as a determinant of who would receive a particular book would be easier to ascertain if she owned more books like these.

To Louis, duke of Bourbon (1337–1410), brother of Jeanne de Bourbon, the wife of Charles V, an older statesman, Blanche gave a book on governing:

Et aussi nostre livre du gouvernement des princes selon theologie, et y a dedens le livre des eschaz et d'autres choses.[83]

[my book of *Government of Princes* according to theology, and in it there is a book of chess and other things.]

Louis of Bourbon served as an advisor to his nephew, Charles VI; this gift of a guide for good governing was an acknowledgement of this role, combined with the *Jeu des échecs*, a treatise on politics and the game of chess.[84] Blanche owned

---

81 Delisle 225.

82 Alison Stones, "Some Portraits of Women in Their Books, Late Thirteenth-Early Fourteenth Century," in *Livres et lectures de femmes en Europe entre Moyen Âge et Renaissance*, ed. Anne-Marie Legaré (Turnhout, 2007), pp. 3–27.

83 Delisle 207.

84 On this text, see Jenny Adams, *Power Play: The Literature and Politics of Chess in the Late Middle Ages* (Philadelphia, 2006).

BOOKS AS EVIDENCE TO PERPETUATE MEMORY

a second such book, which she gave to Robert Cresserel, a monk, probably a Franciscan, in her household. In this bequest, Blanche described the book as "gouvernement des princes par Gilles l'Augustin"; a French translation of *De regimine principum* by Gilles of Rome.[85] This text on governing wisely was owned widely at the French court; among others, it was included in the collections of Jeanne of Evreux, Charles V, John of Berry, and Margaret of Flanders, duchess of Burgundy.[86]

A related gift was the book of the *Somme le roi* left to the brother of Charles VI, Louis, duke of Orléans. Louis, like his uncle, assisted in guiding the country's affairs during his brother's bouts of insanity.[87] Blanche wrote:

> Item, nous laissons à nostre très chier filz le duc d'Orléans nostre bon livre de la Somme le roy, que fu au roy Phelippe le Bel, et est bien enluminé.[88]

> [I leave to ... the duke of Orléans my good book of the *Somme le roi*, which belonged to the king Philip the Fair, and is well illuminated.]

The *Somme le roi*, a book that taught virtues and vices and had been compiled for one of Louis's ancestors, Philip III, was an appropriate gift for his descendant who was ruling as de facto king.[89] This *Somme le roi* described in Blanche's will, illuminated for the son of Philip III, Philip the Fair, is likely British Library Add. 54180 (Fig. 3.5).[90] It might be assumed that the wording 'my good book' referred to the book's decoration, as at the end of the bequest it is called 'well illuminated,' but this designation seems redundant. It is possible that it referred to the quality of the parchment or the condition of the book (about 100 years old in 1396). The designation 'my good book' also likely distinguished it from a second copy of the *Somme le roi* that Blanche left to one of the women of her household. If Blanche perceived her chronicles and her book on government to be appropriate for men, she did not apply the same filter to the *Somme le roi*, as her copies were given to both a male and a female heir.

---

85   Delisle 315. For history and ownership of this text, see Noëlle-Laetitia Perret, *Les traductions françaises du "De regimine principum" de Gilles de Rome: parcours matériel, culturel et intellectuel d'un discours sur l'éducation* (Leiden, 2011).

86   For the *Government of Princes* in 14th-century French royal collections, see Perret, *Les traductions françaises*, pp. 130–59.

87   For this period, see Richard Famiglietti, *Royal Intrigue: Crisis at the Court of Charles VI, 1392–1420* (New York, 1986).

88   Delisle 202.

89   Édith Brayer and Anne-Françoise Leurquin-Labie, *La somme le roi, par frère Laurent* (Paris, 2008).

90   Rouse and Rouse, *Manuscripts and Their Makers*, 1:150–53.

FIGURE 3.5 *Humility and Pride, a sinner and a hypocrite*, La Somme le roi *of Philip the Fair, c. 1295.* LONDON, BRITISH LIBRARY, ADD. MS 54180, FOL. 97V. PHOTO CREDIT: BRITISH LIBRARY.

BOOKS AS EVIDENCE TO PERPETUATE MEMORY

The last of the books intended for Blanche's male heirs was given to a nephew, Charles of Rohan, son of her sister Jeanne of Rohan:

> Et le livre du deduit des chiens et oyseaux que fist messire Gasse de la Buyne, jadiz chapellain des trois roys.[91]

> [And the book *Roman des déduis* by Gasse de la Buyne, formerly chaplain of three kings.]

The *Roman des déduis* of Gace de la Buigne was a hunting book composed at the behest of the French king John II for his son Philip, duke of Burgundy.[92] Though ostensibly about a courtly pastime, it had larger moral themes and was intended as a guide for princely behavior.

Following the gift of the *Roman des déduis* to Charles of Rohan were a series of book gifts to noblewomen, likely companions of Blanche in Paris or at Neaufles. These women, the dames de Fontenay, Gisors, and la Mote, are named only by their titles; these, as well as the place they appear in the hierarchy of the will, are an indication that they were part of the lesser nobility. Blanche noted that one of them, the dame de Fontenay, lived with her. The dame de Fontenay was given a missal in French, discussed above.[93] To the dame de Gisors, Blanche gave a psalter with the arms of France and Champagne, and to the dame de la Mote a book of Sydrac, an encyclopedia in the form of questions and answers.[94] Though the coat of arms on the book given to the dame de Gisors might have permitted Blanche to identify the previous owner, she does not indicate who it was.

Another community of female readers comes into view with the next few gifts of books in the will; they are given to the women in Blanche's household who lived with her and served as companions, called by her 'damoiselles.'[95] She gave their names: Jeanne la Besaine, Jeanne de Rouières, Jeanne du Mesnil, Marguerite de Vymont, Margot le Grant, and the last, recently in Blanche's ser-

---

91 Delisle 242.

92 Elizabeth Eva Leach, *Sung Birds: Music, Nature, and Poetry in the Later Middle Ages* (Ithaca, NY, 2007), pp. 206–10. John II had one in his collection as well; Holladay, "Fourteenth-century French Queens," p. 94.

93 Delisle 250. In the 1398 codicil, Blanche left money to Bélote, the lady-in-waiting of the dame de Fontenay; Delisle 496.

94 Delisle 251 and 256. For the many extant copies of the book of Sydrac and bibliography, see the ARLIMA site for the text: <http://www.arlima.net/qt/sidrac_livre_de.html>.

95 Maria Narbona Cárceles, "Ladies-in-waiting," in *Women and Gender in Medieval Europe, an Encyclopedia*, ed. Margaret Schaus (New York, 2006), pp. 447–48.

vice, called only Agnote. The term 'damoiselle' might designate an unmarried noblewoman in service to the lady of a household, though at least two of Blanche's damoiselles, Marguerite de Vymont and Margot le Grant, were married, both recently, according to the will. They were certainly literate, as is clear by Blanche's gifts of books to them, and one, Jeanne de Rouières, who was bequeathed the book with which Blanche's daughter learned to read, may have served as a teacher in the household. These gifts of books attest a culture of reading and using books in Blanche's homes. For the books to the women of her household Blanche never mentioned a prestigious prior owner (with the exception of the book that her daughter had used to learn to read, though the citation of her daughter there is probably not intended to assert a prestigious provenance). The value of these books was not dynastic or genealogical.

As with the members of French court listed before them in the will, the ladies-in-waiting seem to be ranked, as the first gift was given to a woman described as 'nostre premiere damoiselle,' Jeanne la Besaine.[96] Blanche gave her a book that had a set of 'pluseurs romans,' perhaps for entertainment, though Blanche was not more specific on the topic (and for this bequest it seems impossible for her executors to know which book was meant, without the intervention of Jeanne la Besaine, who presumably knew which book Blanche intended).[97] Along with this book, she gave her four hundred francs, a suit of clothing, a set of blue room hangings, a coffer, rings, and other things of her bedchamber that were not spoken for.[98]

The next lady-in-waiting mentioned in the will, Jeanne de Rouières, was much more interested in books; she was given four. One was described as teaching how to 'live and die well,' a *Miracles de Notre-Dame*, one of Blanche's two books on surgery, and finally the book from which her daughter Jeanne had learned (Blanche noted that Jeanne de Rouières already had this book in her possession).[99] Their close relationship is further exemplified by the gift of a house, discussed in chapter 1, and its furnishings, including bedclothes, towels, bowls, plates, and ewers.[100] She also left her a suit of clothing and room hangings of green toile, as well as wheat and wine from her supplies.[101] If Jeanne decided she did not want to live in the house, she was to be given the two hundred francs that Blanche paid for it, and the house then sold. A mea-

---

96   Delisle 273.
97   Delisle 274.
98   Delisle 273, 275.
99   Delisle 276–79.
100   Delisle 282.
101   Delisle 283–85.

BOOKS AS EVIDENCE TO PERPETUATE MEMORY

sure of her affection may be that Jeanne would not be expected to sell the house herself; she is given the option of refusing the house and taking the funds instead, leaving the sale of the house to Blanche's executors. These gifts are evidence of Blanche's care, both spiritual and material, for Jeanne de Rouières.

Blanche's second copy of the *Somme le roi*, mentioned above, was given to another lady- in-waiting, Jeanne du Mesnil, a book, as Blanche wrote, "where there are remedies against sinning."[102] She did not seem to think it would be confused with the *Somme le roi* that was given to the duke of Orléans; indeed, the differences between the two bequests are telling, and for this reason, it is worth juxtaposing the two bequests (though one has already been discussed). The first bequest reads:

> Item, nous laissons à nostre très chier filz le duc d'Orléans nostre bon livre de la Somme le roy, que fu au roy Phelippe le Bel, et est bien enluminé.[103]

> [I leave to ... the duke of Orléans my good book of the *Somme le roi*, which belonged to the king Philip the Fair, and is well illuminated.]

And the second bequest, to Jeanne du Mesnil:

> Et aussi le livre de la Somme le Roy, où sont les remèdes contre les pechiez.[104]

> [And also the book of the *Somme le roi*, where there are remedies against sinning.]

In the earlier bequest, she did not tell the duke of Orléans what the book was about, as she did for Jeanne du Mesnil; rather, she told him (or her executors) what it looked like ('well-illuminated') and who had previously owned it (Philip the Fair). These differences indicate how the books would have been valued: by the duke, for the ownership of Philip the Fair and the quality of the illumination; whereas Blanche thought it was important to tell the female companion in her household how the book would help her morally, how it should be used, reiterating the difference noted at the beginning of the chapter between books as material objects and books that might be used.

---

102   Delisle 274, 291.
103   Delisle 202.
104   Delisle 291.

Three more ladies-in-waiting, Marguerite de Vymont, Margot le Grant, and Agnote were also given books. Marguerite received *Le trésor de l'âme*; Blanche noted that it "speaks of the seven mortal sins and other examples and remedies against the same and of many other things, and it is covered in green leather."[105] To Margot, married to Robert le Grant, she gave "the book of Psalterion de x cordes, de Anticlaudien, the lives of many saints, and many other good things."[106] Agnote, new in her service, received "a book which teaches 'la vie devote,' and contains the testament of maistre Jean de Meun, and many sermons."[107]

Blanche gave books to two more young women for whom she served as a mentor and educator, one of her goddaughters and the daughter of one of her executors. Her goddaughter Blanche, daughter of Jean le Porchier, was given:

> Et aussi un gros livre des Miracles Nostre Dame abregiées en prose, couvert de cuir rouge; et y a pluseurs bonnes choses, c'est assavoir de sainte Baudeur, de sainte Elysabel, de saint Gile et la Voie d'enfer et de paradis.[108]

> [And also a large book of the Miracles of Our Lady abbreviated in prose, covered with red leather; and there are many good things, to wit of Saint Baudeur, of Saint Elysabel, of Saint Gile and the Road to hell and paradise.]

Striking here is the description of the content of the book, like the detailed description given in the bequests to Blanche's damoiselles; the younger Blanche would not just be given the book, but should be advised about its edifying content. Blanche gave to Jeanette Sante, daughter of her executor Oudart de Venderez, a *Ci nous dit*, a moralized encyclopedia whose chapters offered lessons about spirituality and virtue.[109] The last gift of a book to a female heir was the book on surgery given to Symmonete, discussed at the beginning of the chapter.

The gifts to Blanche's damoiselles offer some insight into the great disparity in numbers between male and female book heirs named in Blanche's will. As noted above, twenty-two women received twenty-nine books, whereas the ten

---

105   Delisle 293.

106   Delisle 297.

107   Delisle 299.

108   Delisle 288.

109   Delisle 307; Christian Heck, *Le* Ci Nous Dit *et le manuscrit de Chantilly: l'image médiéval et la culture des laics au XIVe siècle. Les enluminures du manuscript de Chantilly* (Turnhout, 2012), pp. 15–21.

BOOKS AS EVIDENCE TO PERPETUATE MEMORY 113

male book recipients were given only twelve books. The five women called damoiselles in Blanche's will received nine books. Though there were noblemen in her household, knights, someone like Regnault de Braquemont, or three more knights mentioned in the will – Jean de Richebourc, Desrée de Longroy, and Mahieu de Pontmolain – were not given books.[110] All were given money (as were Blanche's damoiselles, who were given money in addition to their books), and Regnault de Braquemont was also given a horse, one of Blanche's best that he might pick out after her funeral.[111] The disparity in gifting between this group of male and female heirs strongly skewed the total number of books given to women; for this community, Blanche deemed books more appropriate for women than for men.

The last bequests analyzed in this chapter, though not the last of the will, are those books that were given to Blanche's confessor, Pierre Basin. His bequests appear just after those given to the dame de la Mote and immediately before the first objects given to Blanche's servants, a sign of his place in the will's hierarchy: below the noblewoman but above any other member of the household. Blanche gave him two books as well as a sculpted reliquary of Saint Catherine, a painting of the Annunciation of the Virgin and the Crucifixion, a set of red serge room hangings, vestments, a chalice and textiles for an altar, and five hundred francs.[112] These gifts are analyzed in the following chapters. The first of the books was a volume with a *Vie des pères* and the *Dialogue* of Saint Gringoire and his *Pastoral*.[113] The second book was included in the bequest with the chalice and altar textiles; it was a missal that Pierre Basin had used to say Mass in Blanche's house and chapel, and she wished him to use it wherever he lived after her death, remembering her soul particularly with these Masses.[114] This bequest exemplifies Blanche's strategies for commemoration, as it was a physical object, a missal, that would prompt Pierre Basin to pray for her for as long as he was alive. In 1377, Marie of Saint-Pol gave to her confessor 'my little breviary' that the queen had given to her.[115] The provenance of the queen suggests that this was an important book for Marie, and she honored her confessor by giving it to him and marking her activity of prayer that he had guided.

---

110   Delisle 266–69.
111   Delisle 266.
112   Delisle 258–64.
113   Delisle 259.
114   Delisle 263.
115   The queen noted here was probably the English queen Isabelle, according to Sean Field, "Marie of Saint-Pol and Her Books," pp. 9–10.

114   CHAPTER 3

Pierre Basin recognized Blanche's strategies of commemorating her book
ownership because he did the same after her death. A book owned by him
survives in the British Library today (Additional MS 20697).[116] Though it was
never owned by Blanche of Navarre, this book is evidence of an interest in her
household in claiming books, in creating a relationship between the reader
and the book, with the past and present, with an inscription. The inscription
appears in a volume that included the *Jeu des échecs*, a guide to behavior written using the game of chess, another moral treatise called the *Beau traité de
sainte abbaye*, and a French translation of Bonaventure's *Lignum vitae*.[117] It
reads:

> This book belongs to Brother Pierre Basin, which he had written at
> Neauphe [Neaufles], while he was living there with the queen Blanche,
> whose God has her soul.[118]

That Pierre Basin sought to inscribe the book this way suggests that he wanted
to make reference to a book community in Blanche's household – he referred
to the point at which he had the book made, when he was living with Blanche.
He adopted Blanche's strategy in the will of establishing object histories for
books tied to her; in this case the prestigious association for Pierre Basin was
the queen herself.

Blanche's practices are typical of those for 14th-century book owners, as
seen by the analysis above. She had about as many books as did other women
of her station, and she gave them away in the same kinds of ways as did all
the women cited above: to celebrate family ties, to give advice, to convey
moral lessons and models for behavior, to emphasize queenly status, and to
mark an occasion. As noted in the introduction to this chapter, her testament
is crucially different from the evidence that we have for other women's book
ownership, however, because of the unusual level of detail Blanche included
in her bequests. She used the provenance of books, and also the formula of *filz*
and *fille*, to present herself as a mother and to mediate between family members. Ultimately, what is most striking in the book bequests of Blanche's will

---

116   Paul Meyer, "Notice sur le ms. du Musée britannique add. 20697," *Bulletin de la Société des
       anciens textes français* 18 (1892), 94, and Jacques de Cessoles, *Le jeu des eschaz moralisé:
       traduction de Jean Ferron (1347)* (Paris, 1999), pp. 15–16.

117   It is not clear if the three texts were already bound together at the time of Pierre Basin's
       ownership. But the French translation of the *Lignum vitae* begins on a verso of the "traitie
       qui parle," which would suggest that it was written at the same time.

118   The inscription is in Latin: "Iste liber pertinet fratri Petro Basin, quem fecit scribi Neau-
       phe, dum erat ibi residens cum domina regina Blancha, cujus deus habeat animam."

is her assumption of authority. She owned these books, all of them valuable, some because they were relics of a saint, some because they had been handed down to her by earlier queens and carried the memory of these women, some because of their aesthetic value, and some for their content, full of 'good information.' It was her hand that disseminated this value to her heirs, a hand that carried the queenly authority of both a mother and a mediator.

CHAPTER 4

Reliquaries, Altarpieces, and Paintings

If books were considered appropriate for testamentary memory, reliquaries might be thought even more efficacious, not only prompting the prayers of the relics' recipients but also identifying Blanche with devotion to particular saints. The heir of one of Blanche's reliquaries would both remember Blanche in his or her prayers and request the intercession of the saint whose body parts were enshrined in the reliquary. Books were used alongside reliquaries in Blanche's devotions. The reading of a book of hours with a painted image of the Virgin Mary would have been inflected by the presence in her space for prayer of a statue of the Virgin Mary holding a crystal fleur-de-lis containing a relic of her milk, while her silver statuette of Saint John the Baptist on the altar in her home surely reminded her of the alabaster statue of the saint that she had supplied for the chapel she founded at Saint-Denis. Blanche herself created these connections in her testament with the gift of both the *Vie de Saint Louis* and the reliquary of the saint to the Hôtel Dieu of Vernon, discussed in the previous chapter. In this chapter, I examine how Blanche used devotional items in her household, her ensemble of reliquaries and other objects functioning in what Henk van Os has called "an intimate theatre of spirituality."[1]

The pattern of gifting reliquaries in the testament differs, however, from that of books. Blanche left nearly all her books to individuals (with the exception of the *Vie de Saint Louis* that went to the Hôtel Dieu), but most of her reliquaries were given to churches or religious foundations. Of her twenty-eight reliquaries, eighteen were given to or commissioned for religious foundations

---

1 Henk van Os, *The Art of Devotion in the Late Middle Ages in Europe, 1300–1500* (Princeton, 1994), p. 99. The literature on medieval art and devotion is enormous, but, in short, in addition to the citations of scholarly literature in the footnotes of each chapter, as well as the Henk van Os publication cited here, the essays in the edited collection *Push Me, Pull You* also offer insights for the study of 'devotional interactivity'; see Sarah Blick and Laura Gelfand, eds., *Push Me, Pull You*, vol. 1, *Imaginative and Emotional Interaction in Late Medieval and Renaissance Art*, and vol. 2, *Physical and Spatial Interaction in Late Medieval and Renaissance Art* (Leiden, 2011). For one example of the interaction of the viewer with diptychs, see Alfred Acres, "The Middle of Diptychs," in *Push Me, Pull You*, 1:595–621. For women specifically, see Fabrice Rey, "Princely Piety: The Devotions of the Duchesses Margaret of Flanders and Margaret of Bavaria (1369–1423)," in *Art from the Court of Burgundy: Patronage of Philip the Bold and John the Fearless, 1364–1419* (Cleveland, 2004), pp. 81–83.

© KONINKLIJKE BRILL NV, LEIDEN, 2016 | DOI 10.1163/9789004318830_006

while only ten went to individuals.[2] Metalwork objects were described and valued differently from books. The provenances seen in the previous chapter for Blanche's books are lacking for the reliquaries that she gave to churches; only once did Blanche indicate a prior owner for a reliquary given to a church, and that was for the nail reliquary given to the Carmelites with its contested history. Of the ten reliquaries that went to individuals, she gave a provenance of one or two prior owners for six, and did not indicate any prior ownership for four. Rather than concluding that reliquaries did not carry family memory as readily as books might have, I suggest that it was the recipients of the reliquaries who required less information from Blanche about provenance, because Blanche perceived institutions to be less interested in prestigious family histories. It is probably also true that the value of silver and gold reliquaries did not have to be motivated for the recipient quite as clearly or in the same way that a book's value had to be described.

The question of how to divide the quantity of material in Blanche's testament for analysis is particularly vexed in the case of metalwork. A single chapter that considered all Blanche's *joyaux*, all her sculptural reliquaries and statues, the diptychs, rings, crowns, brooches, and prayer beads, would be unmanageably long and complex. For this reason, I have divided the analysis of Blanche's *joyaux* into two sections: in this chapter, I focus on the objects that were employed as part of Blanche's devotional practice at home, pairing the analysis of her reliquaries that were freestanding or suspended in her devotional space with items that were used in concert with *joyaux*, such as her paintings and an altarpiece. The next chapter considers the reliquaries that were meant to be worn on the body: the reliquary belt of Philip VI, the brooch for displaying relics owned by this same king, and two reliquary brooches, along with Blanche's rings, loose gems, crowns, and prayer beads.

Analysis of the devotional context of a medieval household depends on three interrelated historiographical traditions. The first is the study of reliquaries, a field that has benefited recently from a number of publications that have elucidated the history, iconography, use, and various contexts of these precious containers that were meant to bring heaven to earth.[3] The second encompasses

---

2   The silver statuette of Saint John the Baptist that Blanche put on her altar in her chapel and that she bequeathed to the abbey of Beaubec is not included here because Blanche did not say if it had relics. If it did, it would bring the number of her reliquaries to 29. The bequest is Delisle 30.

3   Among these publications are the recent *Treasures of Heaven: Saints, Relics, and Devotion in Medieval Europe*, ed. Martina Bagnoli *et al.* (Baltimore, 2010), and the edited collection that was the result of a conference associated with the exhibition: *Matter of Faith: An Interdisciplinary Study of Relics and Relic Veneration in the Medieval Period*, ed. James Robinson, Lloyd de Beer,

methods to study material culture, which is also particularly important for the study of reliquaries. As Caroline Walker Bynum has noted, matter was crucially important for reliquaries because the material itself signified meaning, rather than simply being used to create the illusion of an object.[4] Though the methodology of material culture offers a great deal more than just an assessment of materials, an important part of this historiography is an elucidation of the various meanings of the materials used for reliquaries, and recent publications have considered the meaning medieval viewers may have attached to materials such as rock crystal or amethyst.[5] Finally, the scholarly literature on domestic devotional environments – chapels and other spaces for prayer in the medieval household – provides a context and comparative material for Blanche's use of reliquaries and other devotional items.[6] As was the case for the books already discussed, the devotional items mentioned in the testament were only those she possessed at the end of her life; we know that she gave away at least one

---

and Anna Harnden (London, 2014), as well as Cynthia Hahn, *Strange Beauty: Issues in the Making and Meaning of Reliquaries, 400-circa 1204* (University Park, PA, 2012), and Henk van Os, *The Way to Heaven: Relic Veneration in the Middle Ages* (Amsterdam, 2000).

4   Caroline Walker Bynum, *Christian Materiality: An Essay on Religion in Late Medieval Europe* (New York, 2011), p. 35. For an assessment of the importance of the study of material culture for medieval religious practices, see also Beth Williamson, "Material Culture and Medieval Christianity," in *The Oxford Handbook of Medieval Christianity* (Oxford, 2014), pp. 60–75.

5   For an overview of how reliquaries signified their precious contents, see Hahn, *Strange Beauty*; Martina Bagnoli, "The Stuff of Heaven: Materials and Craftsmanship in Medieval Reliquaries," in *Treasures of Heaven*, pp. 137–47; and Brigitte Buettner, "From Bones to Stones – Reflections on Jeweled Reliquaries," in *Reliquiare im Mittelalter*, ed. Bruno Reudenbach and Gia Toussaint (Berlin, 2005), pp. 44–59. Two studies of the meanings of rock crystal in reliquaries are Genevra Kornbluth, "Active Optics: Carolingian Rock Crystal on Medieval Reliquaries," *Different Visions: A Journal of New Perspectives on Medieval Art* 4 (Jan. 2014), 1–36, and Stefania Gerevini, "Christus crystallus: Rock Crystal, Theology and Materiality in the Medieval West," in *Matter of Faith*, pp. 92–99. For an interpretation of amethyst in a reliquary, see James Robinson, "From Altar to Amulet: Relics, Portability, and Devotion," in *Treasures of Heaven*, pp. 111–15.

6   An influential study of a noblewoman's domestic devotional life was published by C.A.J. Armstrong, "The Piety of Cicely, Duchess of York: A Study in Late Medieval Culture," in *England, France, and Burgundy in the Fifteenth Century* (London, 1983), pp. 135–56. See also two publications by Jennifer Kolpacoff Deane: "Medieval Domestic Devotion," *History Compass* 11, no. 1 (2013), 65–76, and "Pious Domesticities," in *The Oxford Handbook of Women and Gender in Medieval Europe*, ed. Judith Bennett and Ruth Mazo Karras (Oxford, 2013), pp. 262–78; also Diana Webb, "Domestic Space and Devotion," in *Defining the Holy: Sacred Space in Medieval and Early Modern Europe*, ed. Andrew Spicer and Sarah Hamilton (Aldershot, UK, 2005), pp. 27–47.

RELIQUARIES, ALTARPIECES, AND PAINTINGS 119

reliquary during her life and there were surely many more.[7] The consideration of the devotional context of Blanche's household that follows is, therefore, a view only of what it was at the end of her life.

Devotional Spaces within the Household

Blanche had several spaces for devotion in her household that are described in the testament, among them a chapel and at least two more spaces for individual prayer, called *clotets*; a *clotet* was an enclosure made of fabric or wood that framed a private space for prayer.[8] I consider these spaces in greater detail below, but it is important to note first a caution about terminology. Blanche's household should not be considered 'private' in the modern sense; as other scholars have noted, modern distinctions between private and public, as well as individual versus community devotion, were blurred in the medieval household.[9] Blanche's household had a chapel and dozens of inhabitants, and though in my analysis I consider primarily Blanche's relationship with and reaction to devotional works because they are recorded in her testament, it also should be assumed that these works had a much larger audience in her household.

---

7 For example, she gave her cousin Blanche of Orléans a reliquary of Saint Agnes, noted in the 1392 will of this duchess: "*Item*, à son très cher cousin, Monseigneur le Duc de Dompmartin, son reliquiaire de Sainte-Agnès dernierrement donné à la ditte Dame par la Royne Blanche"; Gaston Vignat, "Testament de Blanche, duchesse d'Orléans," *Mémoires de la Sociéte archéologique de l'Orléanais* 9 (1866), 131–32. She also had a reliquary of a finger of Saint Denis that was left to her by Jeanne of Evreux in her testament; if it was indeed delivered to Blanche, she did not still own it in 1396; Constant Leber, "Le compte de l'execution du testament," in *Collection des meilleurs dissertations, notices et traits particuliers relatives à l'histoire de France*, 20 vols. (Paris, 1838), 19:152.

8 Eugène Viollet-le-Duc, *Dictionnaire raisonné de l'architecture française du XIe au XVIe siècle*, 9 vols. (Paris, 1858–68), 7:208; Victor Gay, "Clotet," *Glossaire archéologique du Moyen Âge et de la Renaissance*, 2 vols. (Paris, 1882–1928), 1:398. The English term for *clotet* is 'closet,' in the sense of a small freestanding enclosure, not a space set into a wall as in the modern definition of a closet. For the sake of clarity, however, I retain the French term. For a detailed study of the prayer closet in the 14th century, see Lisa Monnas, "The Furnishings of Royal Closets and the Use of Small Devotional Images in the Reign of Richard II: The Setting of the Wilton Diptych Reconsidered," *Fourteenth-century England* 3 (2004), 185–206.

9 For discussion of these categories, see Sarah Rees-Jones, "Public and Private Space and Gender in Medieval Europe," in *The Oxford Handbook of Women and Gender in Medieval Europe*, pp. 246–61, and Deane, "Pious Domesticities," pp. 263–64.

Blanche's confessor, Pierre Basin, was first among the other viewers and users of her devotional works; as her confessor he celebrated Mass in her chapel and advised her devotions. The existence of the chapel is noted in the testament in the description of an altarpiece that was left to the cathedral of Evreux:

> Item nous laissons à l'eglise Nostre Dame d'Evreux noz grans tableaux de la nativité Nostre Seigneur, que nous avons acoustumé à mettre sur le grant autel de nostre chapelle à Noel et aux bonnes festes ...[10]

> [... my large *tableaux* of the birth of the Lord, that I am accustomed to putting on the great altar of my chapel at Christmas and on important feast days ...]

The material of this altarpiece is not indicated. The Nativity scenes may have been painted on wood or they may have been sculpted, for example, in ivory, alabaster, or marble. The bequest indicates that the altar in her chapel could be decorated specifically for Christmas with an altarpiece of the Nativity; devotional works rotated in her chapel depending on the religious calendar and were placed elsewhere when not in use. Blanche also put a statuette of Saint John the Baptist on this altar occasionally, describing it in the testament:

> ... un ymage d'argent de monseigneur saint Jehan Baptiste, que nous avons acoustumé de mettre sur nostre grant autel aux festes.[11]

> [... a silver statuette of Saint John the Baptist that I am accustomed to put on my great altar on feast days.]

Blanche's chapel also had the expected paraphernalia for the celebration of the Mass; the other goods were described in a bequest to Pierre Basin:

> Et avecques ce un calice d'argent doré, un corporalier et les corporaux, six touailles d'autel plaines et une touaille parée, et le messel où lui et les autres frères chantent messe en nostre hostel et chapelle, afin que il puisse estre pourveu de ce qui appartient à dire et celebrer sa messe ou

---

10   Delisle 38.
11   Delisle 30.

RELIQUARIES, ALTARPIECES, AND PAINTINGS

lieu où il demourra après nostre mort, et que il y vueille en especial avoir pour recommandée l'ame de nous.[12]

[And with this a silver-gilt chalice, a corporalier (a box for storing corporals) and the corporals (linen cloths on which the Host and chalice are placed for Mass), six plain altar towels and one decorated towel, and the missal that he and the other brothers use to say Mass in my house and chapel, so that he can say Mass in the place that he stays after my death, and that he will remember me especially.]

In addition to this fixed space for worship, Blanche had other sites where she kept reliquaries and prayed, and she probably moved her reliquaries from space to space within her house as appropriate for her devotional purposes, taking them with her when she traveled between residences. Four reliquaries were kept in her *clotet*, a small enclosed area in her living quarters; one is described as in the small *clotet* near the bed, a storage area even closer to Blanche's person and therefore even more intimate.

Several such enclosures might be present in a household; in her testaments Blanche mentioned a *clotet*, a small *clotet*, and a small *clotet* near the bed.[13] She does not indicate the material of these *clotets*, but Jeanne of Evreux had a *clotet* for relics made of cloth-of-gold.[14] The use of cloth-of-gold suggests the creation of a place of honor; it framed a space with a rich material that expressed the value of those objects contained within it. The *clotet* was also a more private space of devotion than the chapel; it was necessitated, presumably, by the number of people who were in Blanche's household, affording her a place of retreat for prayer.[15] Representations of prayer *clotets* are relatively

---

12   Delisle 263.

13   It is not clear if these are three separate spaces or if the small *clotet* and the small *clotet* near the bed are meant to be understood as the same space; she describes different objects that were associated with each of these *clotets*, however, suggesting that they were discrete spaces.

14   It was described in the 1372 execution of her will, as "un drap d'or de Chipre pour le clotet a mettre reliques"; Leber, "Le compte de l'execution du testament," p. 157. The term 'or de cipre' means "metallic gold thread wrapped around a core of silk or membrane"; Jenny Stratford, *Richard II and the English Royal Treasure* (Woodbridge, UK, 2012), p. 59.

15   For the spaces designed for privacy for the French king Charles V in the Louvre, see Mary Whiteley, "Royal and Ducal Palaces in France in the Fourteenth and Fifteenth Centuries. Interior, Ceremony and Function," in *Architecture et vie sociale. L'organisation intérieure des grandes demeures à la fin du Moyen Âge et à la Renaissance, Actes du colloque tenu à Tours du 6 au 10 juin 1988*, ed. Jean Guillaume (Paris, 1994), pp. 47–63.

common in donor images in books of hours; the draped textiles of the *clotet* serve visually as a kind of shorthand to indicate the activity of prayer in these books. Two appear in the images of the duke and duchess of Berry kneeling in prayer in an early 15th-century manuscript, the *Belles Heures*, in which textile curtains suspended from rods enclose the prayer of each (Figs. 4.1, 4.2).[16] That the space is meant for an individual is emphasized in each illumination by the person with the mace who pulls back the curtain, revealing that the kneeling worshiper is alone, in a private space. In the image of the duke of Berry, the face of the attendant is hidden, reiterating the privacy of the duke's prayer.

Devotional images – objects that could be set on a surface as well as those that hung from the curtains – were displayed in the *clotet*. The suspension of a devotional diptych in a *clotet* can be seen in a mid-15th-century manuscript image of the duke of Burgundy, Philip the Good, attending Mass (Fig. 4.3).[17] Although this image postdates Blanche's life by several decades, it may show how objects were suspended in her *clotet*. Blanche does not say if any of her three *clotets* were in her chapel in her château at Neaufles – at least one was near her bed – nor does she mention if she heard Mass in the *clotets*. Just described as 'in my *clotet*' were a reliquary with a bell tower containing the relics of the companions of Saint Maurice and the 11,000 Virgins, a small silver reliquary with relics of the leg of Saint Loup and that of Saint Leonard, a small silver reliquary of Saint John the Baptist, a small pendant cross, and a gold reliquary containing a nail from the Crucifixion.[18] The only object in her 'small *clotet*' was a reliquary of Saint Lawrence.[19] Another object was a cross 'to hang in a *clotet*,' but Blanche is not specific about whether that is where she displayed it in her household.[20] In the small *clotet* designated as 'near my bed' were a statuette of Saint Catherine, a small reliquary of Saint Louis of Toulouse, and a painted diptych with the Crucifixion and the Annunciation to the Virgin. Also significant is that two of these objects used in the small *clotet* near the bed, the statuette of Saint Catherine and the painted diptych, were given in the

---

16   For analysis of these images, see Timothy Husband, *The Art of Illumination: The Limbourg Brothers and the* Belles Heures *of Jean de France, Duc de Berry* (New York, 2008), pp. 148–51, and Stephen Perkinson, *The Likeness of the King: A Prehistory of Portraiture in Late Medieval France* (Chicago, 2009), pp. 263–68.

17   Monnas, "The Furnishings of Royal Closets," p. 197. The manuscript image is Jean Miélot, Treatise on the *Oraison Dominicale*, Brussels, Bibliothèque royale de Belgique, MS 9092, fol. 9r.

18   Delisle 27, 31, 37, 244, 395.

19   Delisle 32.

20   Delisle 194.

FIGURE 4.1 *John, duke of Berry, at prayer,* Belles Heures, *1405–1408/1409, fol. 91r.* THE METROPOLITAN MUSEUM OF ART, NEW YORK, THE CLOISTERS COLLECTION, 1954 (54.1.1). PHOTO CREDIT: METROPOLITAN MUSEUM OF ART.

FIGURE 4.2 *Jeanne of Auvergne, duchess of Berry, at prayer,* Belles Heures, *1405–1408/1409, fol. 91v, detail.* THE METROPOLITAN MUSEUM OF ART, NEW YORK, THE CLOISTERS COLLECTION, 1954 (54.1.1). PHOTO CREDIT: METROPOLITAN MUSEUM OF ART.

will to Pierre Basin, her confessor, associating her confessor with her most private devotions.

Two factors suggest that Blanche's prayer *clotets* were more permanent installations than temporary structures. First, she expected the location of some of the objects in the *clotets* to remain fixed, such as the statuette of Saint Catherine, or else she would not have instructed her executors that that is where they could be found. Second, she does not bequeath the *clotets* to anyone; in a will where she gives away textiles as minor as altar towels, it would seem likely that the *clotets*, if fabric, would also have been bequeathed. It is

RELIQUARIES, ALTARPIECES, AND PAINTINGS 125

FIGURE 4.3 *Philip the Good attending Mass, from Jean Miélot,* Traité sur l'oraison dominicale, *after 1457.* BRUSSELS, BIBLIOTHÈQUE ROYALE DE BELGIQUE, MS 9092, FOL. 9R. PHOTO CREDIT: BIBLIOTHÈQUE ROYALE DE BELGIQUE.

possible that the *clotets* matched the sets of textiles for rooms, and so should be considered part of the eight *chambres* that she gives away (discussed in chap. 6). Alternately, the *clotets* might have been part of the sets of liturgical textiles, or *chapelles*, that Blanche left to churches in her testament; these are treated in the sixth chapter. Finally, it is also possible that the *clotets* were considered part of the furniture of the house, like a table or chairs, and might be sold at the execution of the will rather than given away. Blanche's display of her collection of devotional objects in her *clotets* also suggests that these *clotets* served the function that Pierre Mariaux has called "furniture for conservation," a self-conscious distribution of a set of objects according to criteria set by the collector – in this case, Blanche's devotional preferences.[21]

Blanche had three paintings that also would have served as part of her devotional practice (four if the altarpiece of the Nativity discussed above was painted and not sculptural). One was the diptych depicting the Annunciation and Crucifixion that was given to Pierre Basin and considered above. The other two were given to noblewomen in her circle. One was small, round, and depicted heaven and hell: "Et unz petiz tableaux rons pains, que nous donna nostre fille la duchesse d'Orléans, où est pain[t] paradiz et enfer."[22] This painting was given to Blanche by her cousin Blanche, duchess of Orléans, and Blanche bequeathed it to the dame de la Mote. A second did not have its subject matter described, just that it was a painting on wood that had belonged to the dame de Bailleul: "Et uns tableaux de bois pains qui furent à la dame de Bailleul."[23] The other gifts to the dame de Fontenay included money, a missal in French, and clothing, while the additional gifts to the dame de la Mote, besides the small round painting, were money, clothing, and a book, Blanche's *Roman de Sidrac*. That Blanche owned so few paintings is an indication that she prioritized metalwork reliquary sculpture over paintings in her devotional practice.

Reliquaries

As I turn to the detailed analysis of Blanche's reliquaries, one example will serve to introduce and elucidate her relationship to relics and reliquaries. In the codicil to her will written in 1398, just before her fatal illness in October, Blanche commissioned a reliquary of Saint Bartholomew for her relic of the saint. The relic, probably procured in the recent past because she did not mention it in the 1396 will, was likely an acquisition related to her illness described in the 1398 codicil as a 'grant maladie,' as Saint Bartholomew was associated with healing in the Middle Ages.[24] The bequest reads:

---

21 Pierre Mariaux, "Collecting (and Display)," in *A Companion to Medieval Art: Romanesque and Gothic in Northern Europe*, ed. Conrad Rudolph (Oxford, 2006), p. 218 and p. 226, n. 21. On relic display, see also Hahn, *Strange Beauty*, pp. 199–208.

22 Delisle 257.

23 Delisle 249.

24 Saint Bartholomew was associated particularly with diseases of the skin because the manner of his martyrdom was flaying; David Herlihy, "Tuscan Names, 1200–1530," in *Women, Family and Society in Medieval Europe, Historical Essays, 1978–1991* (Providence, RI, 1995), pp. 330–52, for Saint Bartholomew, p. 350. In January 1328, King Charles IV, who was

RELIQUARIES, ALTARPIECES, AND PAINTINGS

Item nous faisons faire un reliquiaire de saint Barthelemy, pour le garnir d'une jointe d'un de ses doiz que nous avons, et le donner par devocion à aucune eglise de saint Berthelemy. Si voulons que, ou cas que en nostre vivant n'en aurions ordené, que noz diz executeurs le baillent et delivrent de par nous à l'eglise de Saint Berthelemy devant le palais de Paris, ou cas que il n'y en auroit point, ou autre part où ilz verront que bon sera à faire.[25]

[I want to have made a reliquary of Saint Bartholomew, to contain a joint of one of his fingers that I have, and give it to any church of Saint Bartholomew. I want, in the case that it has not been realized while I am still alive, that my executors take and deliver it to the church of Saint Bartholomew near the royal palace in Paris, in the case that it will not be there, or somewhere else if they see that it would be good to do.]

In this commission Blanche gave no instructions for what the reliquary should look like or what it should be made of, simply that it should be created. Perhaps there was a typical reliquary of Saint Bartholomew that the goldsmith would follow as a model, or the artist was given freedom to do as he wished. The most important thing for Blanche, it seems, was what the finger relic would signify – it would be placed inside a receptacle that identified its contents and signified value and preciousness, and all of this would be done in her memory and for her salvation, and in gratitude to the saint who had apparently intervened in her recent recovery. It was to go to a church of Saint Bartholomew that would value it all the more highly because it was a relic of the patron saint, and therefore the worshipers would be more likely to remember Blanche. To be remembered when the gift was to a church that might deposit the reliquary with dozens of other such gifts, she had to give it a special value; the association with Saint Bartholomew's relics for a church of Saint Bartholomew was just such an added value.

This reliquary exemplifies Blanche's relic collection and her practices of enclosing these relics and distributing them. The relic of Saint Bartholomew was loose, not part of a reliquary; she redeployed it in her memory by having it

---

ill and had only a few weeks to live, ordered a reliquary for the head of Saint Bartholomew at an abbey dedicated to Saint Bartholomew at Joyenval; Barbara Drake Boehm, "Le mécénat de Jeanne d'Évreux," in *1300 ... l'art au temps de Philippe le Bel. Actes du colloque international, Galeries nationales du Grand Palais, 24 et 25 juin 1998*, ed. Danielle Gaborit-Chopin and François Avril, with Marie-Cécile Bardos (Paris, 2001), p. 17.

25   Delisle 530.

enclosed in a reliquary and giving it to this church.[26] The church, in Paris, was likely to be visited by friends and family members, but even the strangers who visited would remember Blanche. These relics and their reliquaries that were meant for personal devotion in her lifetime served as agents of her memory after her death. Reliquaries make material something that is intangible, a wish for the saint's intervention and the glories of heaven. With their gold, silver, and gems, they beautify decayed body parts of saints and scraps of other contact relics. Blanche's reliquary collection is notable for its variety, in materials, form, and subject matter; the unique qualities of each work would have created a marvelous visual display and contributed to an evocative devotional practice. Materials included silver, silver-gilt, gold, rock crystal, and precious gems, and there were a variety of types, from architectural and single figure statues, to handheld reliquaries and pendant crosses.

Blanche bequeathed twenty-eight reliquaries: twenty-four were described in the 1396 will and codicil, and then four more reliquaries were ordered just before the queen died in 1398. Eighteen in total were given to churches, and the balance, ten reliquaries, went to individuals. Blanche's reliquary collection is typical of devotional practice in 14th-century France in its inclusion of such popular saints as Catherine, whose miracle-working relics were in Rouen, and Margaret, beloved patron saint of childbirth. John the Baptist was also a local saint; a relic of his head, of which Blanche claimed to have a part, was relatively close by at Amiens cathedral. Blanche's collection also included relics from two important French royal dynastic saints, Saint Louis of France and Saint Louis of Toulouse; sculpted figures of this pair also appeared on Blanche's tomb at Saint-Denis. Jeanne of Evreux likely had about the same number of reliquaries as did Blanche; at least twenty were described in the 1372 execution of Jeanne's will.[27] A caveat for this comparative evidence, however, is that it was not as easy to count reliquaries as it was to enumerate books in the medieval inventory because reliquaries were mixed in with other *joyaux* and the relics themselves not always evident to those making the inventory, so Jeanne of Evreux may have had more than were recorded. The 1401 testament of Blanche's sister, Jeanne of Rohan, noted only three reliquaries: a silver-gilt Virgin holding a relic of her milk in her hand, a silver-gilt reliquary of Saint

---

26 By 'loose' I mean that it had not yet been placed in a reliquary, but the relic itself would have been wrapped; Martina Bagnoli, "Dressing the Relics: Some Thoughts on the Custom of Relic Wrapping in Medieval Christianity," in *Matter of Faith*, pp. 100–109.

27 Leber, "Le compte de l'execution du testament," 19:120–69.

RELIQUARIES, ALTARPIECES, AND PAINTINGS

John, and a gold brooch with the relics of Saint Michael; all three were left to monasteries.[28]

It seems that Blanche meant for churches to have the kinds of objects that churches use for public display: statuettes, crosses with bases, and architectural reliquaries. The reliquaries given to churches were nearly all silver, silver-gilt, and crystal, and included materials like alabaster.[29] The one gold reliquary, the Crucifixion nail reliquary discussed in the first chapter, had special circumstances that mandated it be given to a church; it is not typical in this sense. No reliquary for a church was described as including precious stones. It is not Blanche's habit of description to omit precious gems – she describes sapphires, diamonds, pearls, and rubies on the reliquaries for her individual heirs. It seems that her reliquaries for churches did not have precious stones. When she described the material, it was silver or silver-gilt. Silver weighs less than gold, so larger objects, which were already more likely to be given to public venues like a church, were for practical reasons more likely to be silver or silver-gilt.

Ten reliquaries were given to individuals. These were gold and included precious stones, and several were wearable, such as a belt and a brooch. None of the reliquaries given to an individual were architectural as far as we can tell from the descriptions. Striking in the descriptions are details that make the reliquaries remarkable, such as a sapphire in the shape of a stag (likely representing Christ) or a heart-shaped sapphire. Many precious stones were described, such as diamonds and rubies, and several of the reliquaries were set with cameos. Though it is possible that she neglected to describe these unusual elements for the church gifts, it seems that those reliquaries were not remarkable in this way – she would not have had any reason to omit this information. Blanche treasured her personal reliquaries for the precious stones, hearts, stags, and cameos, and she thought her heirs would appreciate them for those reasons, too. It is clear that personal value was added to relics by using materials like gold and precious stones such as sapphires, as well as rare objects like cameos.[30] With reference to the collection of John, duke of Berry, Timothy Husband noted that gold and gems could more easily be con-

---

28   Pierre-Hyacinthe Morice, "Testament de Jeanne de Navarre, vicomtesse de Rohan," in *Mémoires pour servir de preuves à l'histoire ecclésiastique et civile de Bretagne*, 3 vols. (Paris, 1742–46), 2:719.

29   Of the eighteen reliquaries given to churches, fifteen were silver or gilded silver, one was gold, and two had no material indicated. Of the ten reliquaries given to individuals, six were described as gold, and four had no indication of material.

30   For analysis of such materials on reliquaries, see Buettner, "From Bones to Stones – Reflections on Jeweled Reliquaries," pp. 44–59, and Bagnoli, "The Stuff of Heaven: Materials and Craftsmanship in Medieval Reliquaries," pp. 137–47.

130   CHAPTER 4

verted to cash than objects made of other materials, such as those of silver-gilt.[31] Reliquaries made of gold and gems were for this reason more likely to be prized, though Blanche also surely hoped her heirs would not have her golden reliquaries converted in this way.

One crucial mode of description of all the reliquaries, those given to churches and to individuals, involved seeing. Blanche described clearly where all the relics could be found in the reliquary: for one, the True Cross was behind the crystal; for another, the relics of the 11,000 Virgins were under a round crystal; and for a third, there were relics underneath a crucifix. This kind of information was not for her executors, who have enough information from the rest of the description to identity each reliquary, but rather it represented what the reliquary crucially signified: the relic itself, which should be in some way seen. Martina Bagnoli has argued that there is a 'shift to visuality' in the thirteenth century, that reliquaries began to reveal relics rather than simply symbolize them with precious materials.[32] Another mechanism of viewing is represented by reliquaries that open, such as the reliquary belt of Philip VI or the gold cross given to Isabeau of Bavaria. This insistence on pointing out the location of the relics is an indication that the materials of the reliquary were actually obscuring the relic; Blanche needed to reassure her heirs that the relics were indeed contained in each reliquary.

The first bequest of a reliquary in the will was a gift of a statue of the Virgin Mary to the abbey of Bourgfontaine:

> Item nous laissons aux diz religieux de Borfontaine un grant ymaige d'argent de Nostre Dame qui tient en sa main un poy de cristal, duquel ist une fleur de liz, et y a dedenz du let Nostre Dame; et ou pié de l'ymaige a de pluseurs reliques.[33]

> [To the monks of Bourgfontaine a large silver statue of Our Lady who holds in her hand a small piece of crystal, which has a fleur-de-lis, and inside the milk of the Virgin Mary, and at the foot of the statue are many relics.]

---

31   Husband, *The Art of Illumination*, p. 19.
32   Bagnoli, "The Stuff of Heaven: Materials and Craftsmanship in Medieval Reliquaries," p. 142.
33   Delisle 21.

RELIQUARIES, ALTARPIECES, AND PAINTINGS

Philip VI was a major patron of this church, as was his father, Charles of Valois, and as previously mentioned, Philip's heart was buried there.[34] Sheila Bonde and Clark Maines have demonstrated that there was a structure added to the east end of the church of Bourgfontaine, and that this structure, what they have called a 'retro-choir,' was probably meant for the heart tomb of Philip VI. Blanche's reliquary may have been meant to be placed in this retro-choir, though Blanche does not specify this use. It is similar in its description to the Virgin statue given to Saint-Denis by Jeanne of Evreux, known as the Virgin of Jeanne of Evreux and dating to the second quarter of the 14th century (Fig. 4.4).[35] The Virgin of Jeanne of Evreux is silver-gilt instead of silver, but like Blanche's statue, the Virgin holds a crystal and silver-gilt fleur-de-lis which contained relics. The milk of the Virgin was contained in the crystal fleur-de-lis of both reliquary statues. If Blanche's statue had narrative scenes in enamel around its base, as does the Virgin of Jeanne of Evreux, she does not mention them. But the scale of Jeanne's statue, 69.85 centimeters, suggests what Blanche may have meant by 'large' when she described a large silver statue.

Three more statues of the Virgin Mary were commissioned by Blanche in the will, to be given to the churches of Evreux, Vernon, and Melun, long held in Blanche's dower territory, as she informed the reader of the will.[36] It is from this reliquary bequest that we have the single surviving copy of one of Blanche's reliquaries: a reproduction from the collegiate church of Vernon in Normandy that was made for Millin's catalogue of French antiquities in the late 18th century (Fig. 4.5).[37] The Vernon reliquary is likely identical to the one described in the will:

---

34   Sheila Bonde and Clark Maines, "The Heart of the Matter: Valois Patronage of the Charterhouse at Bourgfontaine," in *Patronage: Power & Agency in Medieval Art*, ed. Colum Hourihane (Princeton, 2013), pp. 77–98. Another source on the church is André Moreau-Néret, "Philippe VI de Valois et la Chartreuse de Bourgfontaine où son coeur fut déposé," *Mémoires de la Fédération des Sociétés d'histoire et d'archéologie de L'Aisne* 13 (1967), 149–63. There was a painting at Bourgfontaine showing Charles of Valois, Philip VI, and Saint Louis of Toulouse (now lost). Paris, BNF Estampes, Gaignières, Costumes Oa 11, fol. 30r; for analysis of this painting, see Bonde and Maines, "The Heart of the Matter," pp. 95–97.

35   For this sculpture, see *Le trésor de Saint-Denis*, ed. Daniel Alcouffe (Paris, 1991), pp. 246–51, no. 51, and *L'art au temps des rois maudits. Philippe le Bel et ses fils, 1285–1328* (Paris, 1998), pp. 231–33, no. 152.

36   Delisle 529.

37   I am grateful to Brigitte Buettner, who first told me of the existence of this reproduction, which she thought she had seen in Havard. It is in Aubin-Louis Millin, *Antiquités nationales, ou Recueil des monumens pour servir à l'histoire générale et particulière de l'Empire françois*, 5 vols. (Paris, 1791), vol. 3; the image is on the page in between pages 18 and 19, and is reproduced in Henry Havard, *Histoire de l'orfèvrerie française* (Paris, 1896), p. 221. Havard

FIGURE 4.4 *Virgin and Child reliquary statue, 1324–39, donated to Saint-Denis by Jeanne of Evreux in 1339.* PARIS, LOUVRE, MR 342, MR 419.
PHOTO CREDIT: MUSÉE DU LOUVRE.

RELIQUARIES, ALTARPIECES, AND PAINTINGS

Reliquaire dit de la reine Blanche
à l'église collégiale de Vernon.
(D'après une gravure des *Antiquités nationales* de Millin.)

FIGURE 4.5 *Reliquary commissioned by Blanche of Navarre for the church of Vernon, after 1396.* HENRY HAVARD, HISTOIRE DE L'ORFÈVRERIE FRANÇAISE (PARIS, 1896), P. 251 (AFTER AN ENGRAVING BY AUBIN-LOUIS MILLIN, ANTIQUITÉS NATIONALES, VOL. 3 [1791]). PHOTO CREDIT: MARGUERITE KEANE.

Item, pour la singuliere et especial devocion que nous avons aux eglises de Nostre Dame de Evreux, de Nostre Dame de Vernon et de Nostre Dame de Meleun, que nous avons longuement tenuz en douaire, nous avons ordonné estre fait trois ymages de Nostre Dame et de une royne à genoulx, assis sur un entablement, de six ou de sept mars d'argent doré chascune,

---

suggested that the reliquary was given to Vernon on the occasion of the transport of Blanche's heart to the church. A request for her heart to be buried at Vernon is not mentioned in Blanche's will. The reliquary was removed from the church in Vernon in 1792; Edmond Meyer, *Histoire de la ville de Vernon et de son ancien chatellenie*, 2 vols. (Les Andelis, 1876), 2:269–70, 279.

pour les donner aux dittes trois eglises, et les garnir des reliques que nous avons de Nostre Dame. Si voulons que, ou cas que en nostre vivant ne seroient par nous baillées aux dittes eglises, que noz diz executeurs les facent faire à noz armes et bien garnir des dittes reliques, et de leur envoier et delivrer de par nous pour perpetuel memore de nous.[38]

[For the special devotion I have for the churches of Notre-Dame in Evreux, Vernon, and Melun, that I have long held in my dower, I order to be made three images of the Virgin Mary with a kneeling queen, on a platform, of six or seven marks of gilded silver each, to give to these three churches, and to contain the relics I have of the Virgin Mary. And I wish that in the case that they are not delivered by me in my life, that my executors make them with my arms and with the aforementioned relics and deliver them on my behalf for my perpetual memory.]

As with the relic of Saint Bartholomew discussed above, Blanche already owned these relics, and she commissioned the reliquary to act as an external signifier of them and to cause them to be identified with her. To make the identification eternal, she added her heraldic device to the reliquary. The materiality of the work – the use of silver to create a representation of the queen in the act of prayer that would endure eternally – plays a crucial role in such elaboration and deployment of relics as a part of a project of memory.[39] The weight of the silver was given presumably to ensure that the reliquary was sufficiently lavish as a representation of its contents and its dedicator.

Single statue reliquaries with relics held in their hands are relatively common in Blanche's collection; they include statues of saints, such as Saint Didier and Saint Louis of Toulouse, or, alternately, statues of angels holding relics, such as an angel with the relics of Saint Christopher and angels holding the relic of Saint Louis. The motivation behind the decision to depict the saint with his or her relics or an angel holding the box of relics is lost to us; it is the kind of information that the will does not convey. Did the goldsmith choose the subject matter, or did the patron? Was there a generally accepted iconography for particular saints? An example of an angel presenting relics is the gift to the abbey of Mortemer of a silver-gilt angel who held a reliquary containing

---

38   Delisle 529.

39   For the associations of silver as a material in the Middle Ages, see Herbert Kessler, "The Eloquence of Silver: More on the Allegorization of Matter," in L'allégorie dans l'art du Moyen Âge. Formes et fonctions. Héritages, créations, mutations, ed. Christian Heck (Turnhout, 2011), pp. 49–64.

RELIQUARIES, ALTARPIECES, AND PAINTINGS

relics of Saint Christopher and "many other saints."[40] The abbey of Mortemer, founded in the 12th century, was a Cistercian monastery in Lyons-la-Forêt and part of Blanche of Navarre's dower. To the abbey of Saint Martin in Pontoise, Blanche gave "a silver statuette of Saint Didier, where there are relics."[41] If a statue of Saint Didier was appropriate for his relics, why, in the case of the Saint Christopher reliquary, does an angel hold the reliquary and not an image of the saint himself? It was perhaps because there were a number of relics mixed together in the case of the Saint Christopher relic, so a Saint Christopher statue would not have properly represented the contents of the reliquary box. And for the image of Saint Didier, and any image of a saint, a statue might also stand in for a very small relic – it would enlarge its importance, in a way that an angel holding a box would not.

Blanche gave a reliquary statuette of Saint Catherine to her confessor of many years, Pierre Basin. She kept this statuette in her *clotet* near her bed, discussed above; it was therefore a personal gift for her confessor:

> Une ymage de sainte Katherine, où il a des reliques, qui est en nostre petit clotet lez nostre lit.[42]

> [A statuette of Saint Catherine, where there are relics, which is in my small *clotet* near my bed.]

Blanche was generous to her confessor. With this bequest she gave him five hundred francs, vestments, room hangings, chapel goods, and a book (discussed in the previous chapter), as well as a diptych of the Annunciation and the Crucifixion. The cult of Saint Catherine was particularly popular in the Middle Ages in northern France, a result of the fame and efficacy of the saint's relics at the monastery of La Trinité-du-Mont in Rouen.[43] Blanche's aunt Jeanne of Evreux was also devoted to the saint and gave to the monastery a crystal reliquary of the saint with herself and Charles IV kneeling.[44] The *Belles Heures* of John, duke of Berry, made *c.* 1408, included an unusual cycle of the

---

40 Delisle 25.

41 Delisle 28.

42 Delisle 260.

43 The development of the cult in Normandy is traced by Jacqueline Jenkins and Katherine J. Lewis, "Introduction," in *Saint Katherine of Alexandria: Texts and Contexts in Western Medieval Europe*, ed. Jacqueline Jenkins and Katherine J. Lewis (Turnhout, 2003), pp. 1–18.

44 Boehm, "Le mécénat de Jeanne d'Évreux," pp. 21–22.

saint's life with scenes drawn from the Golden Legend.[45] Saint Catherine was highly educated and talented rhetorically, and in the Middle Ages was associated with the acquisition of knowledge. Timothy Husband has argued that the cycle of her life in John of Berry's *Belles Heures* was particularly focused on her intellectual life.[46] The first image in the cycle shows Saint Catherine at work in her study (Fig. 4.6). Blanche would have seen Saint Catherine as a model for her own practice of educating herself, her child, and the people in her household with learning and books.[47] This gift of the statuette of Saint Catherine to Pierre Basin, then, commemorates Blanche's interest in education and perhaps Pierre Basin's role, as her confessor, in directing her study and participating in discussion with her.

In addition to her single-figure metal reliquaries, Blanche had a reliquary that might be described as a narrative reliquary, in which several metal figures acted out the saint's martyrdom. She gave this reliquary of Saint Lawrence to the Cistercian priory of Saint Laurent in Lyons-la-Forêt:

> Item à l'eglise de la prieuré Saint Laurens en Lyon un reliquiaire de saint Laurens, qui est en nostre petit clotet, où il a un greil et saint Laurens dessus, et deux hommes d'argent qui atisent et souflent le feu, et y a de pluseurs autres reliques.[48]

> [To the priory of Saint Lawrence in Lyons, a reliquary of Saint Lawrence, which is in my small *clotet*, where there is a grid with Saint Lawrence on it, and two men of silver who stoke the fire, and in which there are many other relics.]

Though Blanche did not describe the material, it was probably silver or silver-gilt, like most of the reliquaries she gave to churches; in addition, the difficulty of casting such a complicated scene – the two men stoking the fire – would seem to mandate the use of a lighter and sturdier metal, silver or silver-gilt

---

45   Martha Easton, "Uncovering the Meanings of Nudity in the *Belles Heures* of Jean, Duke of Berry," in *The Meanings of Nudity in Medieval Art*, ed. Sherry Lindquist (Farnham, Surrey, UK, 2012), pp. 149–82.

46   Husband notes that it omits two otherwise important events from Catherine's life, the Vision of the Virgin and the Mystical Marriage; Husband, *The Art of Illumination*, p. 94.

47   For this image of Saint Catherine as a model for learning and devotion for medieval women, see Jenkins and Lewis, "Introduction," in *Saint Katherine of Alexandria*, pp. 11–12, and Anke Bernau, "A Christian *Corpus*: Virginity, Violence, and Knowledge in the Life of Saint Katherine of Alexandria," in *Saint Katherine of Alexandria*, pp. 109–30.

48   Delisle 32.

RELIQUARIES, ALTARPIECES, AND PAINTINGS

FIGURE 4.6 *Saint Catherine in her study*, Belles Heures, *1405–1408/1409, fol. 15r. Ink, tempera, and gold leaf on vellum; 9 3/8 × 6 5/8 in. (23.8 × 16.8 cm).* THE METROPOLITAN MUSEUM OF ART, NEW YORK, THE CLOISTERS COLLECTION, 1954 (54.1.1). PHOTO CREDIT: METROPOLITAN MUSEUM OF ART.

FIGURE 4.7 *Reliquary of Saint Lawrence, c. 1300.* PARIS, LOUVRE. PHOTO CREDIT: MUSÉE DU LOUVRE/DANIEL ARNAUDET.

rather than gold. The description of the reliquary is similar to a surviving reliquary for one of the fingers of Saint Lawrence today in the Louvre (Fig. 4.7). This small reliquary is dated *c.* 1300, and in its enactment of the martyrdom it is similar to Blanche's reliquary, though it lacks the two men attested in her version. This kind of narrative reliquary would have delighted Blanche in a different way from the devotional effect of a single figural statue or an angel holding a box, and this variety of form in her reliquary collection is one of its most striking features.

Architectural reliquaries – those in the form of buildings – make up another type in Blanche's collection; three of these, each with a tower, were given as gifts to churches.[49] Considered 'images of churches' according to Eric Palazzo, architectural reliquaries may have helped to create a devotional space in her household.[50] The first tower was set on a foot of silver and contained the relics of Saint Valentine; it went to the abbey of l'Isle-Dieu, a Premonstratensian monastery on an island in the river Andelle.[51] Another tower reliquary, this time specifically described as a bell tower, was given to the Cistercian abbey of Notre-Dame du Val:

---

49 Many scholars have analyzed such reliquaries, among them: Éric Palazzo, "Relics, Liturgical Space, and the Theology of the Church," in *Treasures of Heaven*, pp. 99–110; van Os, *The Way to Heaven*; and Arnold Angenendt, "Relics and Their Veneration," in *Treasures of Heaven*, pp. 19–28.

50 Palazzo, "Relics, Liturgical Space, and the Theology of the Church," pp. 98–109.

51 Delisle 26.

RELIQUARIES, ALTARPIECES, AND PAINTINGS 139

> Et si laissons à la ditte abbaye une chasse d'argent à clochier qui est en nostre dit clotet; et y a pluseurs reliques; par especial, desoubz le cruxefiz qui y est entaillé d'alebastre, sur une pierre vermeille, a des reliques des compaignons monseigneur saint Morice; et en l'autre partie, qui est entaillée semblablement, a des reliques des xi[iii] vierges.[52]

> [I leave to the aforementioned abbey a silver reliquary box with a bell tower that is in my *clotet*; and there are many relics in it, especially under the crucifix which is cut in alabaster, on a red stone, there are the relics of the companions of Saint Maurice, and in the other part, which is cut similarly, it has the relics of the 11,000 Virgins.]

This description is difficult to interpret because it is hard to imagine how this red and white crucifix related to a silver reliquary box with a bell tower. But the white alabaster Crucifixion on a red stone, likely carnelian, gives some insight into how the reliquary might have figured into Blanche's devotional practice. The alabaster would have reminded Blanche of the flesh and humanity of Christ on the cross, and the Eucharist. The red stone below, also resonant with Eucharistic symbolism, would have signified the blood of the Passion. Mariah Proctor-Tiffany has argued that the relics of the 11,000 Virgins may have been associated with royal women in France.[53] She notes that a reliquary of the Virgins was given by Clémence of Hungary, the wife of the French king Louis X, to Jeanne of Burgundy, the first wife of Philip VI; and reliquaries of the Virgins were also owned by Mahaut of Artois (who purchased them from the French queen Marie of Brabant), as well as Isabella of England, the wife of Edward II.

The third architectural reliquary, a silver one with relics of Saints Margaret, Catherine, and Christine, was bequeathed to the Cistercian convent of Gomerfontaine near Gisors. The bequest reads:

---

52 Delisle 27. Danielle Gaborit-Chopin hypothesized that the Saint Elizabeth of Hungary reliquary at The Cloisters originally included a bell tower; "The Reliquary of Elizabeth of Hungary at The Cloisters," in *The Cloisters: Studies in Honor of the Fiftieth Anniversary*, ed. Elizabeth Parker (New York, 1992), pp. 327–54, especially p. 337. She also makes reference to the Morgan Library's Virgin and Child reliquary, which had a bell tower.

53 Mariah Proctor-Tiffany, "Transported as a Rare Object of Distinction: The Gift-giving of Clémence of Hungary, Queen of France," *Journal of Medieval History* 41, no. 2 (2015), 225–27. For relics of the 11,000 Virgins, see also Joan Holladay, "Relics, Reliquaries, and Religious Women: Visualizing the Holy Virgins of Cologne," *Studies in Iconography* 18 (1997), 67–118.

CHAPTER 4

Item à l'eglise de Gomefontaine un petit reliquiaire d'argent, où il a trois tresteaux à deux tourelles aux deux coustez, et en la grant tour a de l'uile saintte Katherine, et aux tourelles a des reliques de saintte Crestine et de saintte Marguerite.[54]

[To the church of Gomerfontaine, a small silver reliquary where there are three trestles with two turrets on two sides, and in the large tower [is] the oil of Saint Catherine and in the turrets there are relics of Saint Christine and Saint Margaret.]

This description elucidated the way in which the relics signify in architectural reliquaries. The different towers are meant to differentiate the saints' relics – each saint gets her own tower. These three saints signify differently as a combination than they do singly, presumably, and this is why three separate reliquaries were not created. It is not clear whether Blanche acquired the three relics separately and then had the reliquary commissioned, or if it was a gift to her, but at some point a patron thought these three saints' relics would be appropriate together. The large tower described in the center presumably reflected the relative importance of the oil of Saint Catherine in relationship to the relics of Saints Christine and Margaret, but it is also possible that the oil was contained in a larger vial and that was why it was in the center, and it is not relative importance that gives Saint Catherine the largest vessel in the triple reliquary.

A number of reliquaries may have been small enough to hold in the hand. To the church of Sausseuse, in Vernon, Blanche left another reliquary of the 11,000 Virgins:

Item à l'eglise de Sausseusse lez Vernon un petit reliquiaire où il a des reliques des onze milles vierges dessoubz un cristal qui est ront, et environ a de pleusors autres reliques, et au doz du reliquiaire a enchiselé un ymage de saintte Margarite.[55]

[I leave to the church of Sausseuse near Vernon a small reliquary where there are relics of the 11,000 Virgins under a round crystal, and around it there are many other relics, and on the back of the reliquary is incised an image of Saint Margaret.]

---

54   Delisle 33.
55   Delisle 34.

RELIQUARIES, ALTARPIECES, AND PAINTINGS

Rock crystal, or quartz, is found throughout Blanche's collection of reliquaries. It was often used for reliquaries because, as Ronald Lightbown has noted, "it combined preciousness with transparency."[56] In Blanche's collection it is used for its translucency and for its function of magnification, to offer a transparent, enlarging lens through which the relic might be seen, as well as a more general sign of a precious and extraordinary material.[57] Stefania Gerevini has argued that rock crystal, because it seemed to be both solid and liquid, also functioned as a 'visual substitute' for the beholder for transmutations of matter that were otherwise difficult to understand, such as the Incarnation or the materiality of angels.[58]

Might this small reliquary have been a birth talisman? Saint Margaret, patron saint of childbirth, was a popular saint in the late Middle Ages. Jeanne of Evreux owned a number of objects associated with her; there was also a relic of the birth girdle of Saint Margaret at Saint-Germain-des-Prés in Paris.[59] James Robinson has argued that the reliquary of the Holy Thorn today in the British Museum from the mid-14th century was likely such a birth talisman.[60] Though Saint Margaret does not appear on that reliquary, he associates the amethyst stone on the reliquary with childbirth. But Saint Margaret was popular not only with women; Charles V had several images of the saint in 1363, among them a statuette with relics, a statuette showing Margaret emerging from the dragon's belly, and a small reliquary with an enamel image of Saint Margaret on one side and an amethyst on the other.[61]

Not surprisingly, Blanche celebrated the relics of the French dynastic saints Louis of France and Louis of Toulouse, as did so many other members of her family. Blanche had two book relics of Saint Louis as well as a reliquary that she

---

56   Ronald Lightbown, *Medieval European Jewellery, with a Catalogue of the Collection in the Victoria & Albert Museum* (London, 1992), p. 47.

57   Genevra Kornbluth has noted that rock crystal can also magnify whatever it covers; "Active Optics: Carolingian Rock Crystal on Medieval Reliquaries," p. 15. Stefania Gerevini argues that its strength and durability compared to glass made it appropriate for revealing but at the same time protecting relics; "Christus Crystallus: Rock Crystal, Theology and Materiality in the Medieval West," p. 93.

58   Gerevini, "Christus Crystallus: Rock Crystal, Theology and Materiality in the Medieval West," p. 94.

59   For Jeanne's Saint Margaret relics and objects, see Barbara Drake Boehm, "Jeanne d'Évreux, Queen of France," in *The Hours of Jeanne d'Evreux. Acc. No. 54.I.2 The Metropolitan Museum of Art, The Cloisters Collection, New York: Commentary* (Lucerne, 2000), p. 59.

60   Robinson, "From Altar to Amulet: Relics, Portability, and Devotion," pp. 111–15.

61   *L'inventaire du trésor du dauphin futur Charles V (1363): les débuts d'un grand collectionneur*, ed. Danielle Gaborit-Chopin (Nogent-le-Roi, 1996), nos. 173 bis, 174, 641, 672, and 681.

142

gave to the Hôtel Dieu of Vernon with a biography of the saint. Though these were discussed in the third chapter, the bequest is considered here in the context of other reliquaries. The bequest was given a thematic significance:

> Item nous laissons à l'ostel Dieu de Vernon un reliquiaire d'argent que deux anges tiennent, là où il y a une jointe de monseigneur saint Loys de France, et avecques ce un livre de la vie monseigneur saint Loys de France qui est en françoys, pour lire aux dames quant elles veilleront à l'ostel, pour avoir memoire de saint Loys de qui ilz sont fondez.[62]

> [I leave to the Hôtel Dieu of Vernon a silver reliquary held by two angels which contains a joint of Saint Louis of France and with this a book of the Life of Saint Louis which is in French, for these women to read when they come to the Hôtel Dieu, to remember Louis who founded it.]

The reliquary was of particular value to those at the Hôtel Dieu in Vernon, as it was part of the body of their founder, and they would therefore treasure it more highly. This reliquary also reminds the viewer of Blanche's role as a mother and a mediator; she cared for the inhabitants of the Hôtel Dieu with this gift and transmitted to them the relic of this saint that she owned physically, but also in a symbolic sense, because he was her ancestor. Another finger joint of Saint Louis was owned by Blanche of Navarre's cousin, also named Blanche, a nun at Longchamp (a book owned by her was discussed in the previous chapter). The nun Blanche was the daughter of Philip V, and therefore also a descendant of Saint Louis; she had a figural reliquary made for the convent for her relic of the saint. The reliquary was a silver-gilt statue of the saint holding a crystal containing the joint; it included a kneeling figure of Blanche as well as the heraldic devices of France and Burgundy.[63] It is striking how similar this reliquary produced by a nun for her convent is to the reliquaries of Blanche of Navarre, particularly the Virgin and Child statues produced for Evreux, Melun, and Vernon.

---

62 Delisle 35.

63 Anne-Hélène Allirot notes that these are the arms of Blanche of Longchamp's mother, Jeanne of Burgundy (the county of Burgundy, not the duchy), and clearly a heraldic device also used by Blanche herself; Allirot, "Longchamp and Lourcine: The Role of Female Abbeys in the Construction of Capetian Memory (Late Thirteenth Century to Mid-Fourteenth Century)," in *Memory and Commemoration in Medieval Culture*, ed. Elma Brenner, Meredith Cohen, and Mary Franklin-Brown (Farnham, Surrey, UK, 2013), p. 250, n. 35.

RELIQUARIES, ALTARPIECES, AND PAINTINGS

Blanche of Navarre owned two reliquaries of Saint Louis of Toulouse; appropriately, one of them was given to the Franciscans, the order to which Saint Louis belonged.

> Item nous laissons aux frères meneurs de Vernon un ymaige de saint Loys de Marseille, dont son mantel est paint des armes de Sezille, et tient en sa main un reliquiaire où il a dedens de ses reliques.[64]

> [I leave to the Franciscans of Vernon a statuette of Saint Louis of Marseille whose cloak is painted with the arms of Sicily and who holds in his hand a reliquary with relics inside.]

The arms of Sicily identify this figure as Louis of Toulouse, the dynastic saint of the Angevin rulers of Naples; he was also a dynastic saint for Blanche, and she included a sculpted figure of him on her tomb. As the relic of a Franciscan saint, the monks would value this object more highly than a relic of another saint. As with the relic of Saint Louis of France, Blanche bequeathed something that would be of particular value to its recipient, who would then be more likely to remember Blanche with the object. Clémence of Hungary bequeathed a reliquary sculpture of Saint Louis of Toulouse to Blanche's husband, Philip VI, in her 1328 testament; the sculpture is described in her will as an image of Saint Louis in the manner of a bishop: "nostre image de Monsieur Sainct Looys, fait en la maniere d'evesque qui tient son doit ..."[65] Though the description does not preclude it having been the same Louis of Toulouse reliquary owned by her late husband, it is hard to imagine that Blanche would have passed up the opportunity to note her husband's prior ownership of it.

But Saint Louis of Toulouse is not always used in a strategic or dynastic way, as Blanche had another Louis of Toulouse reliquary not used to promote her family ties even though it was evidently dear to her, as she kept it in the small *clotet* near her bed. This reliquary was given to Marguerite, dame de Préaux, the wife of Jacques de Bourbon.[66] Marguerite had long been in court circles; she had first been married to Jean, sire de la Rivière, a chamberlain of Charles

---

64   Delisle 36.

65   Proctor-Tiffany, "Transported as a Rare Object of Distinction," p. 227, n. 66, citing Jean P. Moret de Bourchenu, "Testament de Clémence de Hongrie reyne de France, seconde femme de Louis Hutin," in *Histoire de Dauphiné et des princes qui ont porté le nom de dauphins*, 2 vols. (Geneva, 1722), 2:217–21.

66   P. Anselme, *Histoire généalogique et chronologique de la maison royale de France*, 9 vols. (Paris, 1726–33), 2:127.

144   CHAPTER 4

v, who died in 1365. She was therefore the sister-in-law of Bureau de la Rivière, her husband's younger brother, the powerful adviser to Charles v and Charles VI. She remarried eventually to Jacques, sire of Préaux.[67] Blanche clearly viewed her with great affection as she gave Marguerite several intimate gifts, in terms of their history, use, and where they were kept in Blanche's household. She was given a gold paternoster that belonged to Blanche's daughter (the second of two paternosters belonging to Jeanne that Blanche had at her death), a small cross that hung in Blanche's *clotet*, and bedclothes, all of which are discussed in the following chapters.[68] The reliquary bequest reads:

> Et aussi le petit reliquiaire de saint Loys de Marseille qui est en nostre petit clotet lez nostre lit.[69]

> [And also a small reliquary of Saint Louis of Marseille which is in my small *clotet* near my bed.]

The particular value that is given to this relic is that Blanche says she kept it near her bed, near to her person. The dame de Préaux surely knew the esteem Blanche had for this relic, and Blanche transfers this sentiment to her friend with the gift.

As noted above, Blanche's reliquary gifts to churches are strikingly different in their material, form, and description from the reliquaries she left to individual heirs. The reliquaries for churches tended to be silver or silver-gilt, whereas those to individuals were more likely to be gold and include precious gems. One way to illustrate this divide between her reliquary heirs is by analysis of Blanche's True Cross reliquaries. She owned three: one was given to the abbey of Bellozanne near Gournay-en-Bray, and the other two went to individual heirs, the first to the queen of France, Isabeau of Bavaria, and the second to her niece, Jeanne, duchess of Brittany and future queen of England. For the True Cross reliquary that she gave to the abbey of Bellozanne (in Bremontier-Merval, now destroyed), Blanche described the material:

> Item à l'abbaye de Belosanne ... une croix dont le pié est d'argent et la croix de cristal, et y a derriere de la vraye croix Nostre Seigneur.[70]

---

67   *Mémoires et notes de Auguste Le Prévost pour servir à l'histoire du département de l'Eure*, ed. Léopold Delisle and Louis Passy, 3 vols. (Evreux, 1862–69), 2:8.

68   Delisle 243, 244, 245.

69   Delisle 246.

70   Delisle 29.

RELIQUARIES, ALTARPIECES, AND PAINTINGS

[To the abbey of Bellozanne ... a cross of which the foot is silver and the cross is crystal, and behind which is the True Cross of Our Lord.]

This was not the first time Blanche had supported Bellozanne, as would be expected (as the churches in the will were presumably all churches she had supported in her lifetime); a record from 1384 indicates that Blanche had given forty francs to the monks of the church for construction.[71] Stefania Gerevini has noted the association of rock crystal with the Resurrection, citing Richard of St. Victor, who wrote that Christ was like a crystal because he shone brightly, "gleaming with immortality," as he rose from the dead.[72] Though it is difficult to reconstruct the precise content of Blanche's devotions, when using this cross she would have recognized the sacrifice signified by the cross and the sliver of wood contained inside it, and perhaps also perceived the crystal material as signifying, in addition to beauty and preciousness, redemption and the Resurrection.

The crystal and silver cross reliquary for Bellozanne is strikingly different from the one Blanche gave to the French queen, Isabeau of Bavaria:

Item nous laissons à nostre très chiere fille la royne de France une croix d'or à pendre à un clotet, où il y a cinq balais, quatre saphirs et neuf perles, laquelle se euvre, et y a dedens de la vraie croix.[73]

[a golden cross to hang in a *clotet* where there are five balas-rubies, four sapphires and nine pearls, which opens, and inside is found some of the True Cross.]

As the queen, Isabeau was the most elevated of Blanche's female heirs, and was given a gift to match her station, a lavish cross laden with gems. Each stone might have had a particular meaning to Isabeau (the blue sapphire might have signified heaven; the red ruby, the Passion of Christ), but in an ensemble like this they also point in general to the Heavenly Jerusalem and demonstrate preciousness and high value.[74] The mention of the *clotet* showed how the pendant

---

71 Léon Mirot, "Paiements et quittances de travaux exécutés sous le règne de Charles VI (1380–1422)," *Bibliothèque de l'École des Chartes* 81 (1920), 183–304, this entry on p. 195.

72 Gerevini, "Christus Crystallus: Rock Crystal, Theology and Materiality in the Medieval West," p. 94.

73 Delisle 194.

74 Brigitte Buettner, in "From Bones to Stones," p. 50, has pointed out that a stone might have had multiple associations, with saints, or a value, or with Christ, depending on its context;

reliquary was displayed or used; it was not meant to be hung on the body, but displayed in a *clotet*, probably with other reliquaries. Likely this function is mentioned because it meant that the pendant cross was larger than one that would hang on the body, and therefore easier for her executors to distinguish from other objects. Blanche did leave another gemmed cross that hung in her *clotet* to the dame de Préaux, discussed above in connection with the Saint Louis of Toulouse reliquary:

> Avecques une petite croix qui pent en nostre clotet, où il y a ou milieu un camahieu, et autour quatre saphirs, huit perles assez grosses et pluseurs menues.[75]

> [a small cross that hangs in my *clotet*, where there is in the middle a cameo and around four sapphires, eight pearls rather large and many small.]

Like the Louis of Toulouse reliquary, this gemmed cross was an item kept close to Blanche; the use of the adjective 'small' suggests that it was smaller than the one given to Isabeau, though still decorated with its cameo, sapphires, and pearls.

The second True Cross reliquary does not seem to have been in the form of a cross, or at least Blanche does not describe it in that way. To the duchess of Brittany, Jeanne, the daughter of her brother Charles, Blanche left a family breviary, discussed in chapter 3, and a precious reliquary with relics from the Sainte-Chapelle:

> Et aussi un reliquiaire d'or, que le roy qui à present est nous donna, où il a de la vraie croix Nostre Seigneur, de son sang et du let Nostre Dame, que le roy print en la sainte chapelle du palais à Paris.[76]

> [And also a reliquary of gold, that the present king gave to me, which has a piece of the True Cross, Christ's blood and milk of the Virgin, that the king took from the Sainte-Chapelle in Paris.]

---

she notes that on the jeweled crosses, "the typology of the gems inserted in the center is almost endless."

75   Delisle 244.
76   Delisle 219.

FIGURE 4.8 *Reliquary of the Trinity, c. 1400. H. 44.5 cm, enamel on gold ronde-bosse (relief work), enriched with precious stones and pearls.* PARIS, LOUVRE, MR 552.

148 CHAPTER 4

This reliquary was a gift from Charles VI; Blanche mentioned this surely not only to show the provenance of the gift but also to attest the authenticity of the relics: they had come from the Sainte-Chapelle as an ensemble. This marker of authenticity and the identification of the relics held within the reliquary seem to have been more important than a description of what the reliquary looked like: the only indication of its appearance is that it was gold. We know of one gold reliquary that belonged to Jeanne and survives today, the elaborate reliquary in the Louvre known as the Trinity reliquary (Fig. 4.8.[77] She gave it to her son, John, duke of Brittany, in 1412. Though it is not the reliquary described in Blanche's will, it does serve as an example of the lavish and extraordinary reliquary gifts at the French and English courts *c.* 1400, and the overall luminous effect of the pearls, gems, and gilding that would have been part of many of Blanche's reliquaries.

Finally, two reliquaries, likely small, were given to the duchesses of Bar and Brabant, both of whom would treasure these reliquaries in the same way that Blanche had, for their precious materials and holy contents. Both reliquaries had inlaid cameos. Cameos, engraved stones from classical antiquity, were highly valued in the Middle Ages, and might be imitated by medieval artists.[78] They were a typical addition for reliquaries, functioning in the same way as the precious stones that exemplified the value of the reliquary and its contents. Blanche's contemporaries owned many. Three surviving examples were originally set into the reliquary of Saint Benoit that the duke of Berry gave to Saint-Denis in 1393.[79] Cameos significantly enhanced reliquaries, through their figural scenes, their preciousness and rarity, and their perceived status as ancient objects (whether or not the stone was indeed a medieval cameo). To Marie of Valois, duchess of Bar and sister of Charles V, Blanche gave:

> Et aussy un reliquiaire, lequel est garny des cheveux Nostre Dame; et par derriere a un camahieu; et y a pluseurs bonnes reliques.[80]

> [And also a reliquary which has the hair of Our Lady and behind it has a cameo; and there are many good relics.]

And to Jeanne, duchess of Brabant (1322–1406), Blanche left a possession of her daughter Jeanne's, a gold reliquary given to her by the king Charles V:

---

77   *Les fastes du gothique, le siècle de Charles V* (Paris, 1981), p. 262.

78   For cameos, see Daniel Alcouffe, "Camées et vases pierres dures," in *Fastes du gothique*, pp. 204–19; and Ronald Lightbown, "Cameos, Gems, Nomenclature, Sources and Value," in *Medieval European Jewellery*, pp. 23–32.

79   Husband, *The Art of Illumination*, p. 18.

80   Delisle 215.

RELIQUARIES, ALTARPIECES, AND PAINTINGS

Et aussy unz tableaux d'or, où il a par dehors deux camahieux aux deux costez, et par dessus deux mains qui tiennent un dyamant; et en chascun tableau a reliques; et le donna le roy Charles à Jehanne de France, nostre fille.[81]

[And also a *tableaux d'or*, which has outside two cameos on both sides, and above two hands which hold a diamond; and each *tableau* has relics, and it was given by the king Charles to my daughter Jeanne de France.]

Tableaux are folding diptychs or triptychs; Lightbown has noted that there was a fashion for miniaturizing these *tableaux* in the late 14th century to form pendants and adding cameos to them, but it is not clear if this *tableau* is intended to be a pendant.[82] That the cameos are on 'both sides' suggests that it was a diptych that could be opened to reveal the relics. The relationship between the diptych and the hands holding a diamond is less clear; the diamond likely represented strength and reflected the significance of strength of faith or tied into the context of the relics contained within. Though Blanche's bequests do not indicate the subject matter of the cameos, presumably the figural scenes on these stones reflected in some way the stories of the saints' relics behind them.

It is more difficult to determine the value Blanche assigned to a reliquary than to calculate the value of a book because Blanche did not give reliquaries as widely as books in her testament and she described them differently. In the analysis of books, we know that the *Somme le roi* given to Louis, duke of Orléans, was more valuable than that given to Jeanne du Mesnil, her damoiselle, because Blanche says so: the one for Louis of Orléans was previously owned by Philip the Fair and it was well-illuminated. This kind of differentiation is more difficult to do for reliquaries. Blanche did not describe the provenance for most of her reliquaries, as noted above, probably because she understood that churches and religious foundations would not value a family memory for an object in the same way that an individual would. Of the balance of her reliquaries that were given to individuals, only two of the ten persons were not royal or descended from kings, the dame de Préaux and Pierre Basin. A different kind of value inheres in the gifts to these two, however, because both were given reliquaries that Blanche kept in the small *clotet* near her bed: a reliquary of Saint Louis of Toulouse for the dame de Préaux and a statuette of Saint Catherine with her relics for Pierre Basin. These reliquaries were surely not more lavishly decorated or economically valuable than the golden container of the relics of the Sainte-Chapelle that Charles VI had given Blanche or the gemmed reliquary cross that Blanche gave to Isabeau of Bavaria. Blanche

---

81   Delisle 217.

82   Lightbown, *Medieval European Jewellery*, p. 25.

assigned a different kind of value to them, one that inhered in their placement in the household, in proximity to Blanche's person; this kind of value will be explored further in the next chapter.

When Blanche's reliquaries are considered together, as they would have been displayed in her household in various combinations on particular days, depending on the whim or needs of the owner and the demands of the religious calendar, they are most striking for their richness and their variety. This great variety in Blanche's collection indicates that reliquaries signified differently, via scale, materials, or iconography, or by where they were placed in her household and how she interacted with them. Her dissemination of these reliquaries to her heirs, though unfortunately lacking the explanatory notes that she gave to books, like "this one has good information," does supply hints as to how she expected her objects to be appreciated by her heirs. She made deliberate distinctions between gold, silver, and silver-gilt. With one exception, when she described the material, she left silver and silver-gilt reliquaries to the churches, and reliquaries made of gold and precious stones to individuals. Her motivation was to exponentially increase the benefit these saints had accorded to her in her life, in the 'spiritual theatre' of her household, by distributing their relics to others, all of whom would perpetuate Blanche's memory.

CHAPTER 5

Wearable Reliquaries, Metalwork, and Gems

Among Blanche's metalwork objects or *joyaux* for personal adornment – those that were worn on the body or held in the hand – are rings, brooches, crowns, prayer beads, and loose gemstones. Blanche would not necessarily have distinguished these *joyaux* from the objects in her collection discussed in the previous chapter, especially those *joyaux* specifically intended to display relics. But these wearable *joyaux* raise questions about personal identity in relation to value and status. Objects worn on the body are a sign of the self, especially the small metalwork objects like the ones in Blanche's will that were significant enough to her to keep until the end of her life. I will analyze her crowns, reliquary brooches, prayer beads, and loose gemstones together in this chapter not because they are similar to each other in function in the way that the books and reliquaries were, but because as a result of their display on the body and their common use of metalwork and gems, they created a personal efficacy related to status and identity. In this analysis, however, I give careful attention to the differences in the use and reception of these objects: a crown worn for a wedding and a reliquary belt intended for battle share characteristics but also differ in fundamental ways.

If Blanche prioritized the importance of sight for her reliquaries, noting specifically where the relics could be found in each one, with the objects in this chapter it was proximity to the body, or touch, that was important. Blanche would have touched and held the other objects in various ways, of course.[1] Indeed, touch was significant for at least two of her books; Blanche traced the provenance of the books of Saint Louis back to the hands of the saint himself because part of the value of these books was that they were contact relics of this saint. But wearable *joyaux* could also protect the body, and the contact

---

1 For examples of touch for medieval devotional practice, see Jacqueline Jung, "The Tactile and the Visionary: Notes on the Place of Sculpture in the Medieval Religious Imagination," in *Looking Beyond: Visions, Dreams, and Insights in Medieval Art and History*, ed. Colum Hourihane (Princeton, 2010), pp. 203–40; Corine Schleif, "St. Hedwig's Personal Ivory Madonna: Women's Agency and the Powers of Possessing Portable Figures," in *The Four Modes of Seeing: Approaches to Medieval Imagery in Honor of Madeline Harrison Caviness*, ed. Evelyn Staudinger Lane, Elizabeth Carson Pastan, and Ellen M. Shortell (Farnham, Surrey, UK, 2009), pp. 382–403; and Alexa Sand, "*Materia Meditandi*: Haptic Perception and Some Parisian Ivories of the Virgin and Child ca. 1300," *Different Visions: A Journal of New Perspectives on Medieval Art* 4 (2014), 1–28.

© KONINKLIJKE BRILL NV, LEIDEN, 2016 | DOI 10.1163/9789004318830_007

itself was crucially important, as James Robinson has argued; he noted that pendants and rings occasionally had an open back intended to facilitate contact of a gemstone with the skin.[2] In the analysis that follows, I show how and why Blanche's reliquaries that were worn on the body – her belt, brooches, and pendant, as well as her loose gemstones – were considered efficacious and protective.

The description of the *joyaux* in this chapter introduces a new element in Blanche's testament, the expression of emotion. Although (as noted above in chap. 2) the expression of love and faithfulness toward family and a request of reciprocity of such emotion are typical in testamentary discourse, in one of Blanche's bequests the emotion of love was unusually attached to an object, the diamond that Philip VI loved a lot. Another bequest of a sapphire in the shape of a heart was given 'with great love,' a sentiment emphasized by the heart iconography of the object itself, discussed below. In the bequests there is also occasionally an additional citation of proximity to the body and the association of value with this proximity, such as a diamond ring worn on the finger or a reliquary brooch worn every day, suggesting an emotional affinity for a particular object on the part of the owner. This kind of value was implicitly expressed with other media in the testament, such as the book of hours that had been owned by the mother of Blanche of Navarre that Blanche prayed from each day; she left this book to her sister, surely because her sister would value it more highly since it had belonged to their mother. The emotion, protective qualities, and guidance that were carried with the gifts of wearable *joyaux* also returns to the theme of Blanche's roles as mother and mediator in the testament; she presents herself in these gifts as both a benefactor of her heirs and a conduit of family history for the *joyaux*.

Most of what we know about Blanche's metalwork comes from her testament and scattered records from her lifetime that mention her jewelry. The limited quantities described in her will – one belt, one seal-ring, three brooches, one reliquary that was likely a pendant, five crowns, four paternosters, three loose diamonds, and three gem finger rings – suggest that these are the most-valued objects retained from a lifetime of collecting objects; we should expect that Blanche owned many more objects than are described here. Of the twenty objects meant for personal adornment mentioned in the will, she had owned thirteen for at least twenty-five years. A golden reliquary belt, a seal-ring, a diamond ring, a loose diamond, and two brooches had all come to her at the death

---

2   James Robinson, "From Altar to Amulet: Relics, Portability, and Devotion," in *Treasures of Heaven: Saints, Relics, and Devotion in Medieval Europe*, ed. Martina Bagnoli et al. (Baltimore, 2010), p. 114.

WEARABLE RELIQUARIES, METALWORK, AND GEMS

of Philip VI in 1350. Several objects – a crown, a ruby ring, two paternosters, a brooch, a reliquary pendant, and a diamond – had been in her possession since the deaths in 1371 of her daughter Jeanne and of her aunt Jeanne of Evreux.

The Reliquary Belt of Philip VI

The first bequest of a metalwork object for an individual was a reliquary belt for the French king Charles VI. The bequest raises a number of important themes that will recur throughout Blanche's patronage of *joyaux*: an interest in the visual display of status, the importance of proximity to the body to determine value, and the creation of an apparatus of value around an object that previously might not have been seen as important or have carried this value without Blanche's instructions. The bequest reads:

> Premierement nous laissons à nostre très chier et très amé sires et filz le roy de France une sainture de bisete d'or trait à losenges de perles aux armes de France à ys d'or, qui se euvrent, et y a pluseurs bonnes reliques; laquelle sainture nostre très chiere dame madame la royne Jehanne de Bourgongne fist faire pour nostre très chier seigneur et espoux le roy Phelippe, que Diex absoille, pour porter sur lui quant il aloit en guerre.[3]

> [First I leave to my very dear and beloved sire and son the king of France a belt of gold braid with lozenges decorated with pearls and the fleur-de-lis of France, and these lozenges open, and inside there are many relics; this belt my very dear lady madame the queen Jeanne of Burgundy had made for my very dear lord and spouse the king Philip, may God pardon him, to wear into battle.]

The fleur-de-lis, precious materials, and the prestigious provenance from Philip VI made this belt an appropriate gift for his royal progeny Charles VI.

Belts from the Middle Ages survive today in very small numbers, despite their medieval ubiquity for both everyday and ceremonial dress. The belt described in Blanche's will was more lavish than a leather or textile belt that might be worn daily; its gold material and pearls made it an expensive product appropriate for a royal heir and for ceremonial purposes.[4] Such belts made

---

3 Delisle 192.

4 For belts, see Ronald Lightbown, "Girdles and Belts," in *Medieval European Jewellery, with a Catalogue of the Collection in the Victoria & Albert Museum* (London, 1992), pp. 306–41.

of gold or silver, or an expensive textile like cloth-of-gold or silk, are widely represented in medieval inventories. The coronation belt of Jeanne of Evreux was made of rubies, emeralds, and pearls.[5] Blanche's sister Marie, wife of Peter IV of Aragon, had a coronation belt in the second quarter of the 14th century with thirty-two rubies, sixty-four emeralds, and thirty-one clusters of pearls.[6] The French king Charles V owned many belts; one particularly lavish example was decorated with rubies, diamonds, sapphires, and pearls. Among the many belts of his wife, Jeanne of Bourbon, one made of gold and silk was decorated with pearls.[7] If belts were ubiquitous in the medieval inventory, a belt that carried relics was not; this gift to Charles VI is unique among the testaments and inventories used for comparison in this project. It is possible that others existed, but their additional function as reliquaries was effaced in inventories; to a secretary intent upon cataloguing a long list of objects, a belt with lozenges that opened may simply have been a belt. It was not unlike a coronation belt in its use of fleur-de-lis, however, and these fleur-de-lis reinforced its purpose as a French royal dynastic sign. Heraldic devices were very common on belts, which seem to have been perceived as an appropriate site for expression of familial identity.[8]

In comparison to these belts, Blanche's reliquary belt of Philip VI was relatively modest, decorated only with pearls. But it was not intended to be just a visual display of wealth or status, as it also carried relics. Belts might be used to suspend objects carried on the person, such as a purse, and these purses might contain relics or efficacious gemstones. Belts could also be protective; the French king Charles V owned a belt made of lion's skin that was associated with vigor and strength.[9] The belt is similar in function to the pendant reliquaries in Blanche's collection – metalwork meant to contain relics for display on the body – and such metal talismans were not unusual in medieval jewelry. Some medieval ring brooches also carried inscriptions that indicated they had a protective function: Charles V had a ring brooch with the names of

---

5 Anatole de Montaiglon, "Joyaux et pierreries données au couvent des Grands Carmes de la place Maubert à Paris par la reine Jeanne d'Évreux en 1349 et 1361," *Archives de l'art français*, 2nd ser. (1861), 448–53.

6 Lightbown, *Medieval European Jewellery*, p. 323.

7 For the belts of Charles V and Jeanne of Bourbon, see Jules Labarte, *Inventaire du mobilier de Charles V, roi de France* (Paris, 1979), pp. 30–31.

8 Lightbown, "Girdles and Belts," pp. 332–33.

9 Joan Evans, *Magical Jewels of the Middle Ages and of the Renaissance, particularly in England* (Oxford, 1922), p. 119; Joan Evans, *A History of Jewellery, 1100–1870* (Mineola, N.Y., 1953; rev. ed. 1970), p. 49, citing Albertus Magnus, *De virtutibus animalium*, for the association of the lion with protective qualities.

WEARABLE RELIQUARIES, METALWORK, AND GEMS   155

the Three Kings that protected against illness, especially the "falling sickness," or epilepsy.[10]

Because the belt was meant to be worn in battle, an endeavor in which the king would be acting in a role expected for his office, this belt was surely also associated with kingly regalia. It is for this reason a more significant gift invested with more symbolism than another wearable metal reliquary. The gift of the belt from Jeanne to Philip VI, from wife to husband, may express the protective function of the belt. Michael Camille has argued that a gift of a belt from a woman to a man had an especially efficacious protective power; it is possible that Blanche thought Charles VI would perceive this gift from a wife to a husband in the same way.[11] Katherine French has compared gifts of belts to the legend of the Virgin's girdle dropped from heaven to convince the doubting apostle Thomas; a gift of a belt in this context might be understood as offering the strength of faith to the recipient.[12]

Its placement as the first bequest and its recipient would suggest that Blanche perceived this belt to be among her most valuable possessions. She had kept it for nearly fifty years, though presumably she would not have worn it herself, with its associations of kingship and apotropaic function for the battlefield. In order to give the belt value for Charles VI, Blanche had to reinvest it with kingly significance, and she does so by noting that it had personal significance to Philip VI: a talisman from a wife to a husband, worn by the king. Though Blanche was married to Philip VI for less than a year, her marriage to him defined her status and privileges as a dowager queen, and this importance is reflected in his prominent status in the will. He connected her to his successor kings, John II, Charles V, and Charles VI. By giving her this belt and his other metalwork objects, Philip VI bestowed influence on Blanche because these items were portable and they gave Blanche a kind of gifting agency. If the belt was given to Charles VI, as seems likely, as Blanche's will was indeed executed (her posssesions are recorded in the inventories of three of her heirs), it does not seem to be recorded in any of the king's inventories. Several belts

---

10   Labarte, *Inventaire du mobilier de Charles V*, p. 94. For the protection of the Three Kings against epilepsy and other illness, see Evans, *Magical Jewels of the Middle Ages and of the Renaissance*, pp. 125–26, and Eamon Duffy, *The Stripping of the Altars: Traditional Religion in England, 1400–1580* (New Haven, 2005), pp. 216–17.

11   According to Camille's argument, the girdle given to Sir Gawain in the poem *Sir Gawain and the Green Knight* "binds him within the circle of female control," and a girdle or a bracelet might be "associated with women's semi-magical protective power"; Michael Camille, *The Medieval Art of Love* (New York, 1998), p. 63.

12   Katherine L. French, "Genders and Material Culture," *The Oxford Handbook of Women and Gender in Medieval Europe* (Oxford, 2013), pp. 197–212, for this comment, p. 201.

were new in the inventories in 1400, the moment at which a cataloguer would have captured the belt given by Blanche, but none of these belts is described in a way that is similar to the reliquary belt of Philip VI (for example, though some have fleur-de-lis, these do not also have pearls).[13]

Reliquary Brooches

Blanche had three metalwork and gemstone brooches. One given to Charles III, king of Navarre, discussed in chapter 3 above, had a large sapphire at the center surrounded by rubies, pearls, and diamonds. A second brooch also had a sapphire at the center, but the stone created the body of a hart and the brooch also contained relics. Blanche's third brooch was intended to suspend relics; she does not mention any gems that decorated it. Brooches were one of the most popular items of medieval jewelry; that Blanche mentioned only three in her testament suggests that much of her collection of jewelry had been dispersed during her lifetime.[14] Brooches were functional as well as decorative – they could be used to fasten clothing or objects like a purse to clothing, and like belts, they might also be used to suspend purses with relics or stones that might have a talismanic protective effect.[15] To Philip of Burgundy, Blanche gave a brooch owned by Philip VI:

> Et lui laissons un fermail d'or que mon dit seigneur et espoux atachoit à sa poitrine, et y pendoit ses reliques chascun jour. Et lui prions que, pour l'amour de mon dit seigneur, qui fu son parrain, et de nous aussi, il le vueille garder durant sa vie.[16]

> [And I leave him a gold brooch that my aforementioned lord and spouse (Philip VI) attached to his chest and hung his relics on there each day.

---

13 For the gold belts in the collection of Charles VI, see Philippe Henwood, *Les collections du trésor royal sous le règne de Charles VI (1380–1422). L'inventaire de 1400* (Paris, 2004), nos. 529–40 and 1658–61.

14 Marian Campbell calls the brooch the "dominant type of medieval jewel," in *Medieval Jewellery in Europe, 1100–1500* (London, 2009), p. 36. The 1363 inventory of Charles V lists more than two dozen brooches; for a list, see the index of *L'inventaire du trésor du dauphin futur Charles V (1363): les débuts d'un grand collectionneur*, ed. Danielle Gaborit-Chopin (Nogent-le-Roi, 1996), p. 135.

15 Lightbown, *Medieval European Jewellery*, 138.

16 Delisle 201.

WEARABLE RELIQUARIES, METALWORK, AND GEMS   157

And I pray that, for love of my lord, who was his godfather, and also of me,
he will keep it during his life.]

Blanche noted that Philip VI was the godfather of the duke of Burgundy presumably because this relationship was significant to the duke and Blanche
commemorated it by giving him this brooch. Unlike the reliquary belt, brooches
meant to display relics were relatively common; Charles V had four, two of
which are described as having the names of the Three Kings, exemplifying the
protective function of these brooches.[17] The purses that were suspended from
such a brooch held relics or stones believed to have particular spiritual or protective value.[18] If the brooch of Philip VI had an inscription or other decoration,
Blanche does not give it, suggesting that there may be a great deal of information about what the works looked like that is missing from the will. It seems
that this brooch was valuable for Blanche because Philip VI wore it each day
and because he was the godfather of the duke of Burgundy, rather than for its
physical characteristics.

The reliquary brooch with a hart, or stag, made out of a sapphire, was given
to Blanche's cousin, Louis of Evreux, count of Étampes (1336–1400; the testament of this Louis was discussed in chap. 2). Added to this gift was another
reliquary that was probably a pendant; it had a sapphire in the shape of a heart.
Both reliquaries had been previously owned by Jeanne of Evreux, who was also
close to Louis, as he was her nephew, the son of her brother Charles.[19] Blanche's
first bequest to him reads:

> Item à nostre très chier cousin le conte d'Estampes, un fermail d'or à une
> chaenne d'or, lequel fait reliquiaire et fermail, ouquel a un cerf ou milieu,
> dont le corps est d'un saphir, et autour a trois rubys, trois dyamans, treze
> perles et six esmeraudes, et dedens pluseurs bonnes reliques; et le nous
> donna madame la royne Jehanne.[20]

> [to my very dear cousin the count of Étampes, a brooch with a chain of
> gold, which makes a reliquary and circle, which has a hart in the middle,

---

17   Labarte, *Inventaire du mobilier de Charles V*, pp. 89–90.
18   Listed in the inventory of Charles V after the brooches for hanging purses are the items for
      the purses: such as a reliquary for the tooth of Saint George and a stone described as "a
      small head of a black snake, called the Lapis Albazahar," meant to protect against poison;
      Labarte, *Inventaire du mobilier de Charles V*, p. 90.
19   P. Anselme, *Histoire généalogique et chronologique de la maison royale de France*, 9 vols.
      (Paris, 1726–33), 1:140.
20   Delisle 237.

of which the body is a sapphire, and around are three rubies, three diamonds, thirteen pearls, and six emeralds, and inside there are many relics; and it was given to me by the queen Jeanne.]

The hart, or stag, represented Christ; in Psalm 42 the stag seeks the water as the faithful seek Christ.[21] The hart was also associated with rulership; it signified "prudence in war without rashness."[22] This gift is mentioned several years later in Louis's will: "... to Marguerite d'Alençon, his niece, a reliquary in the shape of a deer, decorated with stones, pearls, and relics, which belonged to the queen Blanche and who left it to him in her testament ..."[23] This association of Blanche with the reliquary in the testament of Louis of Étampes is evidence that Blanche was at least occasionally successful in her attempt to attach her memory to her possessions.

Following the gift of the hart reliquary was a book with the Gospels and many sermons in French that belonged to the mother of Saint Louis of France; this book was discussed in chapter 3.[24] The mother of Saint Louis was Blanche of Castile; I suggested above that this book had an educational value for Louis of Étampes, as a book used by the mother of the saint for his education. It may also have been connected in some other way with the two reliquaries between which it appeared. Both were related to the Passion of Christ; it is possible the Gospel book was intended by Blanche to create a thematic relationship. She gave the count of Étampes another reliquary just after the book:

Et avecques [ce] un petit reliquiaire, où il y a un saphir en maniere d'un cuer, et le tiennent deux mains; et au dessus a un petit ruby d'Oriant entre deux perles; et dedens a de l'esponge Nostre Seigneur et du chief monseigneur saint Jehan Baptiste; lequel nostre ditte dame et tante madame la royne Jehanne nous donna par grant amour.[25]

[And with this a little reliquary, where there is a sapphire in the manner of a heart, and two hands holding it, and above a little Oriental ruby

---

21 Gertrude Grace Sill, *A Handbook of Symbols in Christian Art* (New York, 1975; repr. 1996), p. 21.

22 Lightbown, *Medieval European Jewellery*, pp. 165–66.

23 "Item à Madamoiselle Marguerite d'Alençon sa niece un reliquaire d'or en façon d'un cerf garny de pierreries, perles et reliques, que feu Madame la Royne Blanche luy a laissié par son testament ..."; Jacques Lescournay, "Testament de Louys, comte d'Estampes," in *Mémoires de la ville de Dourdan* (Paris, 1624), 107–8.

24 Delisle 238.

25 Delisle 239.

between two pearls, and inside some of the sponge of Our Lord and of the head of John the Baptist; which our lady and aunt the queen Jeanne gave us with great love.]

It seems likely that this was a pendant reliquary, because of its similarities to a pendant reliquary owned by Charles v that had a heart-shaped ruby supported by two hands, with an emerald and two pearls.[26] Another heart-shaped reliquary owned by his son, Charles vi, was also a pendant.[27] Like modern heart-shaped jewelry, the symbol of the heart in the Middle Ages signified the self and emotions of love and affection, particularly in this context of the two hands holding the sapphire; these hands were likely clasped.[28] Blanche's heart-shaped sapphire reliquary was a gift of Jeanne of Evreux to her, 'with great love,' and its form carried that affection, as well as the protection offered by the relics contained in the heart. John the Baptist would have been identified with Jeanne of Evreux through her name (she was named for him), and this association would have been part of the meaning of the gift. Precious stones like the sapphire and the ruby express the value of the relics; the red ruby may also have made reference to the Passion of Christ and expressed the significance of the sponge relic contained within. Blanche told Louis that Jeanne of Evreux had given this reliquary to her 'with great love' presumably because this affection would have been meaningful to him.

Heirloom Diamonds

Blanche had three items that she described simply as diamonds; these might have been loose stones or mounted in a setting perhaps too simple to be worth describing. Loose stones might be collected to be set into a larger piece, as often the customer of a medieval jeweler was expected to supply the gems for a piece.[29] But Blanche had owned these particular stones for many years. Clearly they were not simply spare stones; each had a special meaning for Blanche that she wished to convey to the recipient. All three were diamonds.

---

26   Lightbown, *Medieval European Jewellery*, p. 227.

27   Lightbown, *Medieval European Jewellery*, p. 227.

28   For a number of clasped-hand brooches and heart-shaped stones, see Lightbown, *Medieval European Jewellery*, pp. 183–85. Hearts and heart-shaped symbols in art are also analyzed by Camille, *The Medieval Art of Love*, pp. 111–17.

29   Lightbown, *Medieval European Jewellery*, p. 33.

160 CHAPTER 5

One, given to her nephew, Pierre of Navarre, had a long family history. In the bequests she gave him room hangings, a copy of a *Chronique d'Outre-Mer*, and:

> Et avecques ce un dyamant qui fu feu monseigneur le conte d'Evreux, nostre ayeul, que nous lessa ma dicte dame la royne Jehanne à son trespassement. Et lui prions que le dit dyamant il vueille garder toute sa vie pour l'amour de nostre dit seigneur et de nous.[30]

> [And with this a diamond which belonged to the count of Evreux, my grandfather, that the lady the queen Jeanne left to me at her death. And I pray that he will keep this diamond all his life for love of my lord (the count of Evreux) and me.]

Louis, count of Evreux (1275–1319), the brother of Philip the Fair, was the Capetian great-grandfather of Pierre of Navarre, a sign of his royal heritage. This provenance also indicates that the diamond had already been passed through the family for at least eighty years. Significant additional information about this diamond can be gleaned from the execution of the will of Jeanne of Evreux. It indicated that the diamond was 'small,' that it was owned by her brother, Philip, king of Navarre before it came to her, and it had been owned by their father:[31]

> Un petit dyamant que le roi de Navarre frère de ma dite dame li avoit pieca donne, le quel il portoit tousjours sur luy pour ce quil avoit esté a leur pere que Diex absoille: baillé aux gens de ma dicte dame par quittance.[32]

> [A small diamond that the king of Navarre, brother of my lady had long ago given to her, which he wore every day on him for it had belonged to their father ...]

This diamond may have been mounted in a ring. The 1372 execution of Jeanne of Evreux's will indicated that Blanche was left 'a gold ring with a diamond,' listing it after a gold eagle holding a joint of Saint Denis.[33] In the instructions

---

30   Delisle 226.

31   Constant Leber, "Le compte de l'execution du testament," in *Collection des meilleurs dissertations, notices et traits particuliers relatives à l'histoire de France*, 20 vols. (Paris, 1838), 19:166; see also Lightbown, *Medieval European Jewellery*, p. 33.

32   Leber, "Le compte de l'execution du testament," p. 166.

33   Leber, "Le compte de l'execution du testament," p. 152.

WEARABLE RELIQUARIES, METALWORK, AND GEMS   161

that followed for the disposition of Jeanne's goods, listed after the gold eagle with the joint of Saint Denis was the small diamond of Louis of Evreux, but this time a ring is not mentioned; simply a 'small diamond' is noted. This case is a reminder that we cannot assume that a citation of a diamond meant necessarily that it was a loose stone. Blanche did not give the provenance of her father in her own bequest although she surely knew that her father had owned it. Finally, that the execution of the will of Jeanne of Evreux indicates such specific information about this diamond – "he wore [it] every day on him for it had belonged to their father" – suggests that the wording came from her 1371 testament. Those who were cataloguing her possessions for dissemination probably would not have known the history of the diamond; almost certainly they were repeating information that they had seen elsewhere. It suggests that the 1371 testament of Jeanne of Evreux may have been a model for the provenances and emotion cited in Blanche's testament.

What did diamonds signify to Blanche? Loose stones would seem to have had a more significant personal meaning than a single stone among many set into a reliquary. A group of many stones might have signified the Heavenly Jerusalem, or preciousness and value. But a single diamond carried on the person must have conveyed some significant power inherent in that stone. We depend on medieval lapidaries, or lists of stones, for our interpretation of these gems, such as the lapidary of Marbode of Rennes from c. 1100 or the *Lapidary of King Philip* from the late 13th century.[34] Blanche's encyclopedia known as the *Roman de Sidrac* also had discussion of the properties of stones.[35] As a particularly hard stone, diamonds were associated with strength or courage.[36] The difficulty with using lapidaries, as has been noted by other scholars, is that we cannot be sure the meanings associated with stones were those for the viewer at this particular time.[37] Blanche conveys in the testament only how she valued the diamond, for its family history and for its age. The citation of an individual for this bequest, Louis of Evreux, may indicate that this stone,

---

34   On lapidaries, see Joan Evans, *English Medieval Lapidaries* (London, 1933; repr. 1960).

35   Françoise Féry-Hue, "*Sidrac* et les pierres précieuses," *Revue d'histoire des textes* 28 (1998), 93–181, and Féry-Hue, "*Sidrac* et les pierres précieuses: complément," *Revue d'histoire des textes* 30 (2000), 315–21.

36   Campbell, *Medieval Jewellery in Europe, 1100–1500*, p. 33.

37   Campbell, *Medieval Jewellery in Europe, 1100–1500*, p. 33, and Brigitte Buettner, "From Bones to Stones – Reflections on Jeweled Reliquaries," in *Reliquiare im Mittelalter*, ed. Bruno Reudenbach and Gia Toussaint (Berlin, 2005), pp. 50–51. James Robinson considers the the multiple associations of an amethyst set into a reliquary in "From Altar to Amulet: Relics, Portability, and Devotion," pp. 111–13.

162   CHAPTER 5

known to have belonged to him, was believed to have been particularly efficacious.

The other two gems mentioned in Blanche's will, also both diamonds, were given to John, duke of Berry, and Louis, duke of Orléans, the brother of Charles VI. To the duke of Berry, Blanche left her most beautiful book of hours, previously owned by her mother, and:

> Et un petit dyamant, lequel nostre dit seigneur et espoux portoit sur lui, et l'amoit moult, et le lui donna la bonne contesse de Henaut, sa suer. Et prions à nostre dit filz que pour amour de nous il le vueille garder.[38]

> [And a little diamond, which my lord and spouse (Philip VI) wore on him, and he loved it greatly and it was given to him by the good countess of Hainault, his sister. And I pray that my aforementioned son for love of me will keep it.]

Remarkable in this bequest of a diamond is Blanche's assertion that Philip 'loved it greatly,' and, like the diamond given to Pierre of Navarre, it was a diamond considered to be a family heirloom. This countess of Hainault was Jeanne of Valois (c. 1294–1342), a sister of Philip VI.[39] Her daughter, Philippa of Hainault, was married to the English king Edward III. Jeanne played an important role in negotiations between Philip VI and Edward III in 1340.

The duke of Berry was an avid collector of stones; he was famous for his interest in gems.[40] Notoriously acquisitive, he may have already expressed a desire to own this stone of Blanche's. Some of the jewels in the duke's remarkable collection were famous enough to have names, such as the Diamond of Saint Louis and the Diamond of Chartres.[41] The countess of Hainault had been dead eight years before Blanche married Philip VI; but the story that the

---

38   Delisle 199.

39   For Jeanne of Valois, see Anneke Mulder-Bakker, "Jeanne of Valois: The Power of a Consort," in *Capetian Women*, ed. Kathleen Nolan (New York, 2003), pp. 253–69.

40   Jules Guiffrey, *Inventaires de Jean, duc de Berry (1401–1416)*, 2 vols. (Paris, 1894–96), vol. 1 for the collection of precious stones of Jean de Berry; among many sources on the duke of Berry as a collector are the biographical essay by Timothy Husband, "Jean de France, duc de Berry," in *The Art of Illumination: The Limbourg Brothers and the Belles Heures of Jean de France, Duc de Berry* (New York, 2010), pp. 10–31, and an article by Michael Camille on the duke's collecting impulse, "'For our Devotion and Pleasure': The Sexual Objects of Jean, Duc de Berry," in *Other Objects of Desire: Collectors and Collecting Queerly*, ed. Michael Camille and Adrian Rifkin (Oxford, 2001), pp. 7–32.

41   Lightbown, *Medieval European Jewellery*, p. 37.

WEARABLE RELIQUARIES, METALWORK, AND GEMS   163

diamond had been given to him by his sister was significant enough to an understanding of this diamond that Blanche remembered it and attached it to the object for the benefit of the duke of Berry sixty-six years after the countess's death. That it was a significant diamond, though 'small,' is also evidenced by the duke of Berry's already extensive collection; that Blanche would give him this one even though he had many others suggests that it had great value, and almost certainly not limited to a monetary value. Its value is difficult to determine with only the limited information given by Blanche – it is possible that it was rare in some way or believed to carry a particular spiritual power. It is also possible that the protective quality that accompanied belts that were gifts from women also applied to gemstones. The countess of Hainault was a prolific patron of the goldsmiths of Paris. In 1323, she purchased chaplets, coronals, brooches, girdles, and precious stones for the weddings of her daughters, for them to wear and to give away as gifts.[42] The citation of the countess of Hainault in this gift might be an indication of the prestige of Jeanne of Valois as a collector of stones.

Blanche gave the diamond additional value in this bequest by saying that Philip VI 'loved it greatly.' There are instances of sentiment elsewhere in the will, directed toward people and expressed by objects. The heart-shaped sapphire reliquary given to the count of Étampes exemplified the emotion of love with its heart shape, and Blanche said that Jeanne had given it to her with great love. But this is the first time an emotion is described specifically as directed toward an object. The difficulty with analyzing love directed toward an object is that it is not clear precisely what is intended; is it the same as the modern notion of pleasure that derives from a material object that causes someone to love it? Barbara Rosenwein has shown the multiple meanings of the term 'amour' in medieval France; when used for a ruler, for example, it might signify political loyalty.[43] Elsewhere in Blanche's testament the verb 'love' was used in the sense of familial love, as when she indicated that Jeanne of Evreux gave her the sapphire and ruby reliquary, or as in this bequest, that the duke of Berry should keep the diamond for love of Blanche. In one instance, the obliging of love with a gift is corporate: Blanche expected that the Carmelites of Paris would keep the nail reliquary for love of Blanche, Blanche of Orléans, and Jeanne of Evreux. And finally, Blanche professed in her last codicil of 1398 a love for her servants, attesting that she is giving them money as a result of the "affection and great love that I have and have always had for my servants, con-

---

42   Lightbown, *Medieval European Jewellery*, pp. 57–58.
43   Barbara Rosenwein, "Thinking Historically about Medieval Emotions," *History Compass* 8, no. 8 (2010), 828–42.

164   CHAPTER 5

sidering the long, good, and pleasant service that they have done continuously
..."[44] These are all emotions of love directed toward and expected from people,
all close to Blanche. The love of the diamond derived at least in part, it seems,
from the fact that it had come from Philip's sister.

To Louis, the duke of Orléans, the brother of Charles VI, she left a copy of the
Somme le roi (analyzed in chap. 2) and another diamond:

> Et aussi un dyamant plat, que le roy nous donna aux noces de madame
> Katherine de France, sa suer.[45]

> [And also a flat diamond that the king gave me at the marriage of madame
> Catherine of France, his sister.]

A 'flat diamond' was a table-cut diamond, a new fashion in the 14th century for
the cutting of diamonds.[46] The wedding referenced in the bequest was between
Catherine (1378–1388) and the son of the duke of Berry, John, in 1386. This
bequest illustrates the practice of distributing gifts to guests at weddings.[47]
Blanche may have identified this diamond as the one she received at this wedding to ensure the authenticity of the object; if Louis of Orléans had seen the
diamond or knew the occasion, he would have known the size and appearance
of the stone.

Several gemstones were certainly set in finger rings, including a diamond,
ruby, and emerald. The diamond finger ring had also been worn, according to
Blanche, by Philip VI:

> Item à nostre très chier et très amé neveu le duc de Bourbon, un anel à
> dyamant, qui fu nostre dit seigneur et espoux, et le portoit en son doy.[48]

> [I leave to my very dear and beloved nephew the duke of Bourbon a dia-
> mond ring which belonged to my aforementioned lord and husband
> (Philip VI) and he wore it on his finger.]

Louis of Bourbon (1337–1410) was the brother of the queen of Charles V, Jeanne
of Bourbon, and an uncle of the reigning king Charles VI. The other two finger

---

44   Delisle 411.
45   Delisle 203.
46   Evans, *A History of Jewellery, 1100–1870*, p. 48.
47   Lightbown, *Medieval European Jewellery*, p. 38.
48   Delisle 206.

WEARABLE RELIQUARIES, METALWORK, AND GEMS

rings were bequeathed to other members of the French court, to Jeanne of Auvergne, the young duchess of Berry, and to Valentina Visconti, duchess of Orléans. Perhaps significant is that these two noblewomen are the spouses of the two men to whom Blanche gave loose diamonds. The bequests read:

> Item à nostre très chiere fille la duchesse de Berry un annel ruby, lequel nostre dit seigneur et espoux nous donna, et depuis le donnasmes à nostre très chiere dame madame la royne Jehanne d'Evreux, que Diex absoille, qui le lessa à Jehanne de France nostre fille.[49]

> [To my very dear daughter the duchess of Berry a ruby ring that my aforementioned lord and spouse (Philip VI) gave to me, and since I gave it to my very dear lady madame the queen Jeanne of Evreux, who left it to Jeanne of France my daughter.]

This ring was mentioned in the 1372 execution of Jeanne's will, with the same provenance:

> a ring and an Oriental ruby that belonged to the king Philip her father, that the queen Blanche gave to my lady [Jeanne d'Evreux] ...[50]

Blanche gave another ring to Valentina Visconti, the duchess of Orléans, herself known for her lavish trousseau full of gems brought from Milan for her 1389 wedding:[51]

> Item à nostre très chiere fille la duchesse d'Orleans, une esmeraude en un annel, que nous donna nostre filz de Berry.[52]

---

49   Delisle 208.

50   Leber, "Le compte de l'execution du testament," p. 167; Jeanne of France is not explicitly indicated (it says simply "A Madame ... de France"), but Philip VI was her father and the other details of the bequest mean it could not be anyone else. The bequest says: "un annel et un rubis d'Oriant qui fut le roy Philippe son pere que Diex absoille, que Mad. la royne Blanche donna a ma dicte dame ..." It is not clear why the construction is 'a ring and an Oriental ruby' rather than 'a ring *with* an Oriental ruby'; Blanche described it simply as a ruby ring.

51   For Valentina's inventory, see Jules Camus, *La venue en France de Valentine Visconti, duchesse d'Orléans, et l'inventaire de ses joyaux apportés de Lombardie* (Turin, 1898).

52   Delisle 212.

[To my very dear daughter the duchess of Orléans, an emerald in a ring that was given to me by my son (the duke) of Berry.]

These bequests and those of the three diamonds illustrate the constant transfer of gems and other objects typical of the manic gift-giving practices at the French court. The ruby ring given to the duchess of Berry was transferred from Philip VI to Blanche, from Blanche to Jeanne of Evreux, then from Jeanne of Evreux to Blanche's daughter. This repeated exchange of a single gem is not unusual; in the 1392 will of Blanche of Orléans, she left to the duke of Berry her 'good ruby,' which had belonged to her husband, the duke of Orléans, which he had given to her.[53] To the duchess of Berry, she gave a diamond that the duke of Burgundy had given her, and to the duke of Burgundy, a 'beautiful ruby' that the king had given her. Finally, to the duke of Touraine, she left her 'good pointed diamond' that the duke of Burgundy had given her. The citation of the previous owner seems superfluous for an executor who presumably would not have difficulty locating each gem even if the provenance were missing. It is clear that the prior ownership of a gem gave it an additional value; the provenance commemorated the exchanges that took place in the vibrant culture of gift-giving and reciprocity at the Valois court.[54] Brigitte Buettner has noted that the gift practices of the Valois in the early 15th century continued despite occasional feuds and animosity among those receiving the gifts; according to this argument, we might read the citations of prior owners for the objects in the wills of Blanche of Navarre and Blanche of Orléans as a hope for familial harmony and connection rather than its expression.[55]

Heirloom Paternoster Beads

Another item worn or suspended on the body or held in the hand and made of precious materials was the paternoster, or rosary; Blanche owned four, three that were gold and one less expensive version in silver-gilt. The paternoster developed as an aid for counting the number of times the Lord's Prayer (or 'Our Father'/*pater noster*) was to be said.[56] Blanche's paternosters were family

---

53　Gaston Vignat, "Testament de Blanche, duchesse d'Orléans," *Mémoires de la Sociéte archéologique de l'Orléanais* 9 (1866), 131.

54　Brigitte Buettner, "Past Presents: New Year's Gifts at the Valois Courts c. 1400," *Art Bulletin* 83, no. 4 (Dec. 2001), 598–625.

55　Buettner, "Past Presents: New Year's Gifts at the Valois Courts c. 1400," p. 602.

56　For paternosters, see Lightbown, *Medieval European Jewellery*, pp. 342–54.

WEARABLE RELIQUARIES, METALWORK, AND GEMS

heirlooms, and at least one bore a sign of heraldic identity, the arms of France. The first was a gift to the duchess of Burgundy:

> Item à nostre très chiere fille la duchesse de Bourgongne, unes patenostres à perles, à saigneaux de rubyz et saphirs, et une esmeraude ou milieu, et y en a un cent, que nostre ditte dame madame la royne Jehanne d'Evreux lessa à nostre ditte fille.[57]

> [To my very dear daughter the duchess of Burgundy, a paternoster with pearls, with marker beads of rubies and sapphires, and an emerald in the middle, and there are one hundred of them (pearls), that the queen Jeanne d'Evreux left to my daughter.]

This was an extraordinarily lavish object; the beads of the paternoster were pearls, one hundred in number, with the marker beads in between the decades made of rubies and sapphires. This paternoster is mentioned, together with the ruby ring analyzed above, in the 1372 execution of Jeanne's will:

> un annel et un rubis d'Oriant qui fut le roy Philippe son pere que Diex absoille, que Mad. la royne Blanche donna a ma dicte dame et unes patenostre de perles dont les signaux sont de balays et de saphirs: baille comme dessus.[58]

> [a ring and an Oriental ruby that belonged to the king Philip her father, that the queen Blanche gave to the aforementioned lady and paternoster of pearls of which the marker beads are balas rubies and sapphires: take as above.]

Jeanne of Evreux died in March 1371 and Blanche's daughter, Jeanne, in September 1371; this paternoster was likely among the possessions of Jeanne of France that reverted to her mother after death. These objects illustrate the use of precious stones as part of devotion; they were not just suspended on the body, but their pearls, rubies, and sapphires were passed one by one through the fingers in the more active performance of prayer. The protective or efficacious qualities of these stones in brooches or rings applied to their use in

---

57   Delisle 210.
58   See note 50 above.

168 CHAPTER 5

rosaries as well; Katherine French has described the various apotropaic associations of rosary beads, such as coral for fertility and amber for childbirth.[59]

A second paternoster demonstrated the significance of such personal objects for the display of familial identity; it was given to Jeanne, duchess of Brabant (1322–1406):

> Item à nostre très chiere cousin[e] la duchesse de Breban unes patenostres d'or à saigneaux d'or esmaillez aux armes de France; et y a un ruby ou milieu.[60]

> [To my very dear cousin the duchess of Brabant, a gold paternoster with gold marker beads enameled with the arms of France; and there is a ruby in the middle.]

This paternoster was perhaps commissioned by Blanche herself because she did not identify a prior provenance. Jeanne was the daughter of John III of Brabant and Marie of Evreux, the older sister of Jeanne of Evreux and Blanche's father. The duchess of Brabant was therefore Blanche's cousin and entitled to the arms of France through her great-grandfather, Philip III.

Then, to Marguerite, dame de Préaux, whose reliquary gift was discussed in the previous chapter, she gave another paternoster:

> Item à nostre très chiere cousine la dame de Preaulx, unes patenostres d'or en façon de baton creux coppé, et en y a un cent, et les saigneaux d'or parmy, où il y a un poy d'esmail, qui furent à Jehanne de France, nostre fille.[61]

> [To my very dear cousin the lady of Préaux, a gold paternoster in the manner of a small hollow stick and there (are) one hundred (beads?), and gold marker beads, where there is a bit of enamel, which belonged to Jeanne my daughter.]

This is the second paternoster that Blanche saved that had belonged to her daughter; though its materials are still valuable, they seem to be less so than those on the set for the duchess of Brabant, with its ruby and its gold beads enameled with the arms of France. And finally, to the dame de Gisors, Blanche gave a paternoster that was an additional step down in terms of value of the metalwork and stones: "And one of my best silver-gilt paternosters which they

---

59 French, "Genders and Material Culture," p. 201.
60 Delisle 216.
61 Delisle 243.

WEARABLE RELIQUARIES, METALWORK, AND GEMS   169

will find in my coffers."[62] This bequest indicates that she had several silver-gilt paternosters and where she kept them. How the executors were to determine which of these silver-gilt paternosters was her 'best' is not clear; perhaps the dame de Gisors would be permitted to choose.

The Queen's Crowns and Sealing Ring

I shift for the last part of this chapter away from reliquaries, brooches, pater-nosters, and rings intended for personal adornment, spiritual efficacy, or religious devotion, to metalwork adornment that was intended to show status, such as a signet ring and a series of crowns given to goddaughters. There is some overlap between these functions, for example, the king's reliquary belt, which had both religious resonance and status significance; and the crowns were laden with the same rubies, emeralds, and pearls that were found in the rings and brooches already discussed. From Philip VI, Blanche had received another item associated with regalia and official status, a signet or seal-ring that had previously been owned by Charles IV, the last Capetian king before the accession of the Valois Philip VI in 1328. Blanche left it to Charles VI:

> un signet que portoit mon dit seigneur, lequel nous portons continuel-ment sur nous, et fu au roy Charles père de nostre très chiere fille la duchesse d'Orléans, que Diex pardoint, qui en usoit, et aussi fist mon dit seigneur après lui, et nous aussi en nostre vivant.[63]

> [a signet ring worn by Philip VI, which I wear continuously on me, and it belonged to the king Charles father of my dear daughter the duchess of Orléans, who used it, and also by my spouse after him, and I also wore it in my lifetime.]

The seal had been used by her husband and by his Capetian predecessor, Charles IV. Blanche herself had used the seal during her lifetime; presumably it was in her capacity as widow of Philip VI and dowager queen that she was enti-tled to this seal.[64] As one of only two gifts from Blanche to Charles VI, it must have had significant value as a sign of royal identity and a relic of the king's

---

62   Delisle 252.

63   Delisle 193.

64   In correspondence of October 2007, Brigitte Bedos-Rezak suggested that this seal may have been applied to transient documents dealing with the private administration of the royal household; I am grateful to her for discussing the seal with me. For the seals used by Charles IV and Philip VI, see Martine Dalas, *Corpus des sceaux français au Moyen Âge: les sceaux des rois et de regence* (Paris, 1991), pp. 181–200.

170   CHAPTER 5

ancestors. Like the reliquary belt and the small diamond, its value inhered in that the king wore it on his body. Like the reliquary belt, this signet ring, if it was indeed given to Charles VI, is not recorded in his collection.[65]

Blanche owned five crowns that are mentioned in the will. She had at least three crowns on deposit at the cathedral in Rouen, in a box that also contained 4,000 francs, a sign of the close relationship between metalwork and cash as assets.[66] Other archival records attest to additional crowns in her possession; in 1364, Charles V reimbursed Blanche for the loss of objects taken during the sack of Mantes, and among these was a crown decorated with rubies, emeralds, and the arms of France.[67] Crowns were a visual sign of status: they could signify queenship, as the one that Blanche ordered for Notre-Dame if her body was to be laid out there after her death, and they might also display the change in status associated with marriage, a significant function of these objects in Blanche's will. All five crowns mentioned in the will were given to women, and all were Blanche's goddaughters. Four were given the crown as they were about to be married or in anticipation of it, and it seems likely that the fifth crown, for Isabelle of France, the daughter of Charles VI, was also associated with her wedding.[68] The gifts of the crowns were associated with Blanche's role as godmother; the gift commemorated this change in status and Blanche's responsibility for sponsoring it.

Any analysis of medieval crowns must struggle with definitions of terms in medieval wills and inventories. Without the surviving object, we cannot be certain what Blanche meant when she used a particular term, and there are three different terms used in the will for what seems to be the same kind of object, a gold head ornament. To Isabelle of France, daughter of Charles VI, Blanche gave an object described as a 'chapeau d'or.' To two of her goddaughters, Blanchete le Grant and Blanchete de Vymont, she gave a 'chapel d'or,' the first worth seventy-two francs and the second forty-six francs. The last two crowns that she gave away to her goddaughters are described as a 'couronne d'or' and then a 'petite couronne d'or.' The differences between the 'chapeau d'or' and

---

65   The signet rings listed were all in his collection prior to 1396; Henwood, *Les collections du trésor royal*, pp. 120–21, 171.

66   Vincent Tabbagh, *Gens d'église, gens de pouvoir: France, XIIIe-XVe siècle* (Dijon, 2006), p. 188.

67   The crown is described in a letter written by Blanche: "un chapel d'or, sur demi-jonc; des armes de France à 8 losanges pleines de grosses perles; 8 assiettes de pierreries, en chacune assiette 7 rubis et 1 emeraude"; *Catalogue des livres et documents historiques du cabinet de M. de Courcelles* (Paris, 1834), p. 16.

68   Lightbown notes that it was a standard wedding gift; for this discussion and several examples, see *Medieval European Jewellery*, pp. 121–31.

the 'couronne d'or' that caused the writer of the will to use different terms to describe them are not indicated. It is not a question of value; the most significant difference in value would have been between the 'chapeau d'or' given to Isabelle, a royal heir, and the 'chapel d'or' worth only seventy-two francs that went to her goddaughter, but these crowns are not significantly differentiated in terminology. The differentiation between these objects is in their descriptions, but Blanche gave little additional information about elements like fleurons or the number of stones which might tell us how lavish or large a crown was. At the most basic, they were metal head ornaments, occasionally set with gems. For clarity, I will use the term 'crown' with an understanding of that term as potentially encompassing both simple and complex objects, from a relatively unadorned garland to a more elaborate crown with fleurons.

Not mentioned in the testament is Blanche's own crown or her other regalia, which she may never have owned since she was not crowned before her husband's death. Alternately, the crown lost in the 1364 sack of Mantes with the arms of France (described above) may have been considered the crown associated with her queenship, even if she were never crowned in a ceremony. In 1349, Jeanne of Evreux had donated her royal regalia to the convent of the Carmelites in Paris. She gave them the gold crown, described as a 'couronne,' and a belt that she had worn at her coronation, as well as the gold fleur-de-lis that she had carried at her wedding and coronation, and insisted as part of the bequest that these objects be sold.[69] Jeanne's insistence that the objects be sold probably related to her desire to renounce these visible signs of queenship; it was a sign of her great piety that she wanted them to be sold for the benefit of a religious house.[70]

In her will Blanche made a provision for the purchase of a crown: if she died in Paris and her body was to be carried to Notre-Dame, she left 260 francs for a crown and cloth-of-gold to be purchased for the display of her body.[71] She did not make the same provision for Saint-Denis, where she was to be taken, bypassing Notre-Dame, if she died at her château at Neaufles. This suggests that she expected to use a crown for the display of her body that was already at

---

69   Montaiglon, "Joyaux et pierreries données au couvent des Grands Carmes," pp. 448–53.

70   Lisa Victoria Ciresi has analyzed the divesting of regalia by kings before death in "Of Offerings and Kings: The Shrine of the Three Kings in Cologne and the Aachen Karlsschrein and Marienschrein in Coronation Ritual," in *Reliquiare im Mittelalter*, ed. Bruno Reudenbach and Gia Toussaint (Berlin, 2005), pp. 165–83. She suggests that kings donated regalia to the church as a way of demonstrating humility. Jeanne of Evreux's donation of her regalia was likewise a way of showing that she did not want or need physical signs of power and would give them for the benefit of the church.

71   Delisle 15.

the abbey, but this can only be speculation. Notre-Dame was an important enough site for royal identity that Blanche did not want to be viewed there after death without a crown; she did not make the same provision for a crown for Saint-Jean-en-Grève, for example. This provision in the will is an indication that goldsmiths would have had crowns ready to be sold, as there would have been only a few days' notice between her death and the arrival of her body at Notre-Dame. It seems likely that the crown that would have been made for Notre-Dame was more expensive than the cloth-of-gold, but even dividing them evenly, 130 francs for each, would mean that Blanche's funerary crown was about double or triple the expense of the crowns she gave to her goddaughters. The purchase of a crown was not necessary in the end, as Blanche died at her château at Neaufles and was presumably taken directly to Saint-Denis, as she had wished, and not to Notre-Dame in Paris.

Blanche's collection of crowns, numbering five (possibly eight, if the ones at Rouen cathedral are in addition to those described in her will), was relatively small considering her status and long life. By comparison, Jeanne of Evreux's 1372 postmortem execution of her testament included fourteen crowns: a couronne d'or, three small coronnettes d'or, and ten objects identified with a form of the word 'chapel.'[72] The inventory made in 1380 of the collection of Charles V and Jeanne de Bourbon lists eight crowns for the king, eight for the queen, and more than two dozen others.[73]

The first crown mentioned in Blanche's will went to Isabelle of France, the daughter of Charles VI:

> Item à nostre très chiere fille madame Ysabel de France, nostre fillole, un chapeau d'or pierrerie, que nostre très chiere dame la royne Jehanne de Bourgongne donna à Jehanne de France, nostre fille, que Diex absoille, qui fu sa fillole, ainsi que est nostre ditte fillole la dicte madame Ysabel.[74]

> [I leave to my very dear daughter madame Isabelle of France, my goddaughter, a crown with stones that my very dear lady the queen Jeanne of Burgundy gave to Jeanne of France, my daughter, may God pardon her, who was her goddaughter, equally as my goddaughter is the aforementioned madame Isabelle.]

---

72   Leber, "Le compte de l'execution du testament," pp. 122–25.

73   Evans, *A History of Jewellery*, p. 55.

74   Delisle 205.

WEARABLE RELIQUARIES, METALWORK, AND GEMS

Blanche commemorated a relationship between women in this bequest: Isabelle was her goddaughter, so the gift that had been given to Blanche's own daughter by her godmother should be, in parallel, bequeathed to Isabelle.

The French queen known as Jeanne of Burgundy and mentioned elsewhere in the will was the first wife of Philip VI, but Jeanne died in 1349 and could not have left this crown to Blanche's daughter and indeed could not have been her godmother. Blanche's executors may have made a mistake in the provenance of this crown, but it is difficult to imagine such an error when Blanche was commemorating a relationship as significant as a godmother. There are two candidates for this queen Jeanne. The first is Jeanne of Evreux, Blanche's aunt and her close friend; if Jeanne is intended here, the use of Burgundy is straightforwardly an error, as Jeanne of Evreux had no titles of Burgundy. It is also possible that this queen Jeanne is the second wife of the king John II. She was heir to the counties of Auvergne and Boulogne, and had been married to the duke of Burgundy, Philip, until his death in 1346. She then married the French king John in February 1350, only a few weeks after Blanche was married to Philip VI. This Jeanne might well have been known to Blanche as 'Jeanne of Burgundy,' or alternately, as 'Jeanne of Boulogne,' with Burgundy mistakenly substituted for Boulogne in the bequest. These two queens, sharing an office and married within months of each other, were close enough to merit one being named as the godmother for the other's child.

This practice of commemorating the relationship of godmother and goddaughter is expanded upon in the next mention of a goddaughter in the will. It comes more than 100 bequests later, clearly to a person of lesser social status than Isabelle of France. Blanche gave to Blanchete, her goddaughter, the daughter of Robert le Grant, her butler, sixty francs and a crown, both intended for 'advancement of her marriage':[75]

> Item à Blanchete, nostre fillole, fille de Robert le Grant, nostre eschanson, un chapel d'or pesant V onces V esterlins, à X assiettes à VIII perles en l'assiette, et X rubis que esmeraudes, assis entre II petis; et nous cousta LXXII frans.[76]

> [To Blanchete, my goddaughter, daughter of Robert le Grant, my butler, a gold crown weighing five ounces five esterlins, with ten plates with eight pearls in each plate, and ten rubies, with emeralds between two little (rubies), and it cost me seventy two francs.]

---

75 Delisle 301.
76 Delisle 300.

174   CHAPTER 5

Godchildren were often named for their godmothers, as is the case with this Blanchete and the three that follow, all who were given a diminutive of their godmother Blanche's name.[77] The crown for Blanchete is here associated explicitly with a marriage. It is likely that the crown given to Isabelle of France was also associated with a marriage because Isabelle was married in 1396, the year of the will. And indeed, the crown may have been given to Blanche's daughter Jeanne originally for her own marriage. Jeanne of Boulogne died in 1360, so the crown would have been given well in advance of her marriage, if indeed that was the occasion for the gift.

Isabelle of France received many crowns on the occasion of her wedding, more than a dozen lavish gold head ornaments with fleurons and laden with precious stones.[78] Blanche only briefly described her gift of a crown, which is odd because she described the crowns below in great detail, including weight and gems. So it must have been very different from the other crowns; it must have been clearly a royal crown appropriate for Isabelle of France. The value she gave to it was familial; it was a gift from a godmother, and this seems to have been more important than a list of precious stones or a specific monetary value.

Three more goddaughters and crowns are then named in the will. In the gift to Blanchete, daughter of Marguerite de Vymont, Blanche gave sixty francs and said that the money and the crown were meant to enable her marriage:

> Item à Blanchete, nostre fillole, fille de Marguerite de Vimont, nostre damoiselle, un chapel d'or pesant V onces dix esterlins, à X assietes à piegnes de perles, en chascune assiete VI perles, et ou milieu un petit ruby ou une esmeraude, et IX que rubys que esmeraudes entre deux petis, et est de pierrerie d'Alexandrie, et nous cousta XLVI frans.[79]

> [To Blanchete, my goddaughter, daughter of Marguerite de Vimont, my damoiselle, a gold crown weighing five ounces ten esterlins, with ten plates with pearls, in each plate six pearls, and in the middle a small ruby or an emerald, and nine rubies as well as emeralds between two small, and it is precious stonework of Alexandria, and it cost me forty-six francs.]

In contrast to the cost of the crown for the daughters of Blanche's 'damoiselle' and butler, the price of the crown purchased by Charles V for his queen Jeanne

---

77   Nicholas Orme, *Medieval Children* (New Haven, 2001), pp. 36–37.

78   The crowns are described in Lightbown, *Medieval European Jewellery*, pp. 69–70.

79   Delisle 302.

of Bourbon in 1377 was 2,318 francs for the jewels alone. Blanche's gifts were thus modest, not on par with the lavish spending at the French court.[80] Unusual in the will is the indication of costs, for one seventy-two francs and for the other forty-six francs. Although the amount spent on metalwork and gems can be another way of describing the crowns,[81] it is likely that Blanche expected her heirs to sell them; therefore, it was important that the monetary value be clearly associated with them. Their cost was therefore related to a financial obligation that she had to her goddaughters. It should be noted Blanche did not neglect her one godson mentioned in the will. He did not receive a crown, but rather money:

> Item à Blanchart, nostre fillol, filz de Blanche, nostre fillole, dame de Troussy, quatre vinz frans pour le faire aprandre à l'escole.[82]

> [To Blanchart, my godson, son of Blanche, my goddaughter, dame de Troussy, eighty francs for learning in school.]

Money for his education was deemed appropriate for launching him, as the gifts of crowns would do for Blanche's goddaughters.

The next two bequests to goddaughters of crowns were not objects that Blanche purchased specifically as gifts, but objects that she used in her household. In both cases the term used in the will has shifted from 'chapeau' or 'chapel d'or' to 'couronne,' though there is not evidence in the bequest itself to identify the reason for the change:

> Item à Blanchete, nostre fillole, fille de maistre Jehan de Poupaincourt, une petite couronne d'or de pierrerie d'Alexandrie, que nous feismes pieça achater pour prester à faire les noces de noz serviteurs et amis.[83]

> [To Blanchete, my goddaughter, daughter of master Jehan de Poupaincourt, a small gold crown of Alexandrian precious stonework that I bought to lend to the weddings of my servants and friends.]

---

80   Lightbown, *Medieval European Jewellery*, p. 35.
81   I am grateful to Genevra Kornbluth for this observation, offered in response to a conference paper in Kalamazoo in May 2013.
82   Delisle 304.
83   Delisle 305.

The description of the use of the crown tells us that crowns could be borrowed for a wedding; indeed, Blanche purchased this crown specifically for this purpose.

And the last bequest of a crown:

> Item à Blanche, nostre fillole, fille du sire d'Aumont, une couronne d'or de pierrerie d'Alexandrie et d'autre pierrerie; et y a grans fleurons et petis florons de saphirs. Et la prestons à noz femmes quant elle sont mariées en nostre presence.[84]

> [To Blanche, my goddaughter, daughter of the sire of Aumont, a gold crown of Alexandrian stonework and other stonework, and where there are large fleurons and small fleurons of sapphire. And I lend it to my women when they are married in my presence.]

Blanche had a crown meant for the women of her household that was differentiated from the other she lent out, an indication of how an object might commemorate different relationships even within one household.

This gift was a symbolic way to note that the goddaughter was passing from the protection of her godmother as she became a married woman. Blanche's description of a practice that seems to have been routine suggests that she wanted to commemorate it. Other evidence of this practice comes from the 1401 testament of Blanche's sister Jeanne of Rohan, who left to a 'petite Marie' one hundred livres to help with her marriage and with this 'a small crown of silver,' linking explicitly the crown and the funds for her marriage.[85] Blanche's testament is different from that of her sister, however, in that she foregrounds the role of the godmother. She said in the first bequest of a crown to Isabelle of France that the crown had come from her daughter Jeanne who had been given it by her godmother, the queen Jeanne, and equally was Isabelle the goddaughter of Blanche. This was a self-conscious celebration of what godmothers did: a crown had been given several decades before to Blanche's daughter by her godmother, a queen Jeanne. Blanche would cite this gift as she gave away the crown again, to her goddaughter Isabelle, who was herself a daughter of a king of France, from Blanche, who like the queen Jeanne, was a queen of France.

---

84 Delisle 306.

85 Jeanne does not indicate if this Marie was a goddaughter; Pierre-Hyacinthe Morice, "Testament de Jeanne de Navarre, vicomtesse de Rohan," in *Mémoires pour servir de preuves à l'histoire ecclésiastique et civile de Bretagne*, 3 vols. (Paris, 1742–46), 2:720.

WEARABLE RELIQUARIES, METALWORK, AND GEMS 177

Blanche was conscious of the utility of objects for inscribing a history and for standing in for relationships.

Blanche's care for her godchildren was a typical practice, seen, for example, in the gift of a book from Jeanne of Evreux to her goddaughter, Jeanne de Harcourt (discussed in chap. 2), and the gift to Philip, the duke of Burgundy, of a brooch for suspending relics once owned by his godfather Philip VI (considered above). These other instances also demonstrate that you could care for a godchild not only monetarily but spiritually with a book or a brooch for relics. These gifts of crowns are also part of the larger construction of identity in the testament, as Blanche presented herself as a mother in her gifts to the king and queen and the dukes and duchesses of the French court, with her gifts of books and reliquaries; she also cared for her godchildren with gifts of funds and of crowns that were easily converted to money. The connection between Blanche's name and those of her godson, Blanchart, and goddaughters, all called Blanche or Blanchete, is also a practice that Blanche celebrates for her objects in the testament. She gave the duke of Burgundy a psalter of Saint Louis that was once owned by a duchess of Burgundy, and left to the current duchess of Orléans a book that had been owned by a deceased duchess of Orléans. It is unlikely that these lineages were accidental; Blanche clearly saw them as a way for past ancestors to care for those in the present, mediated through her person.

A theme of this chapter has been efficacy, with a reliquary belt that could protect in a battle, a reliquary from which relics could be suspended to protect the owner from illness, precious stones that might provide the strength of faith to the bearer, a heart-shaped sapphire given with great love, and paternosters for performance of prayer themselves made of precious stones like rubies and diamonds. Crowns that signified the change in status from single to married were also efficacious in Blanche's rendering; she gave the cost of each because she expected them to be sold to benefit the new couple. This narrative of protection and assistance offered by wearable *joyaux* replicates that which was offered by the books with family provenances as well as good information in the third chapter and the devotional items displayed in Blanche's household from chapter 4, though with the *joyaux* the reciprocity of love given and expected from the testamentary bequests was more explicit.

CHAPTER 6

Textiles: Vestments, Wall Hangings, and Clothing

Considering the textiles in this last chapter acknowledges Blanche's ordering of her gifts of objects in the testament, which follows a ranking by social status. The first gifts went to the king and queen, and the last to the chambermaids in her household. Most of the liturgical textiles were given to churches and therefore disposed of early in the testament, together with the silver and silver-gilt reliquaries, but most of the remaining textiles appear relatively late in the list of objects. Thus, Blanche's textiles bracket the other possessions given away in the testament. Her personal and household textiles – another set of liturgical textiles, her room hangings, clothing, bedding, and kitchen textiles – were given to her sisters, nieces (including one great-niece), nephews, and members of her household. None went to the members of the French court who figure so prominently in the gifts of books, jewelry, and reliquaries. It seems that domestic household textiles were meant to commemorate a closer relationship, a familial relationship, more so than gifts of jewels or reliquaries. Notably these relationships could also be commemorated with books, as discussed above, as so many of Blanche's books were given to women in her service. Nevertheless, domestic textiles might have been perceived as more appropriate gifts for a close family or household member, and less appropriate for a wider social circle.

The historiography of textiles intersects with the domestic devotional environments considered above in chapter 4, as the chapel and devotional *clotets* in Blanche's homes would have been decorated with her liturgical and devotional textiles (in addition to her altar textiles, she had one embroidered devotional image of the Virgin Mary, discussed below). She gave away four sets of liturgical textiles to churches, a typical practice for medieval women as a way for them to participate in the life of the church.[1] In what follows, I suggest

---

1 For this practice, see Katherine French, "'I leave my best gown as a vestment': Women's Spiritual Interests in the Late Medieval English Parish," *Magistra* 4, no. 1 (1998), 57–77, and by the same author, *The Good Women of the Parish: Gender and Religion after the Black Death* (Philadelphia, 2008), esp. chap. 1, "'My Wedding Gown to Make a Vestment': Housekeeping and Churchkeeping," pp. 17–49, as well as Nicola A. Lowe, "Women's Devotional Bequests of Textiles in the Late Medieval English Parish Church, ca. 1350–1550," *Gender & History* 22, no. 2 (August 2010), 407–29. I am grateful to Laura Gathagan for her discussion with me of the repurposing of vestments from women's clothing and her insights based on her own research on Mathilda of Flanders.

© KONINKLIJKE BRILL NV, LEIDEN, 2016 | DOI 10.1163/9789004318830_008

TEXTILES: VESTMENTS, WALL HANGINGS, AND CLOTHING 179

that Blanche may have transformed her own clothing into altar textiles, a practice also attested in the testament of her sister, Jeanne of Rohan. In addition to being textiles specifically made for a devotional space, Blanche's room hangings would have created a sense of liturgical and seasonal time, and would have helped to differentiate between everyday and special occasions. Blanche had a set of gray room hangings, probably intended for Lent, and green hangings with foliage for other times of the year. When she was first widowed, she had black room hangings to signify her mourning. One set of room textiles was described in the will as the one she hung when her friends came to see her; they were green and decorated with circles containing her heraldic device. This marker of identity through textiles extended to the clothing of Blanche's servants; she provided their livery during their lifetime and asked that it be worn in her memory after her death.

The present study of Blanche's textiles depends on the scholarly literature devoted to the people, customs, spaces, and decoration of the medieval household.[2] Scrutiny of Blanche's household is more limited than what would be possible for the kings of France or the dukes of Berry or Burgundy because Blanche's château at Neaufles survives only in ruins and her house in Paris not at all. But from the evidence of Blanche's textiles at the end of her life, it is possible to suggest some ideas about how she perceived and interacted with these textiles and how they were part of her construction of identity and the perpetuation of her memory. Like so many other gifts in the will, such as the book from which Blanche's daughter learned to read or the crowns for goddaughters, Blanche's textiles commemorated significant life events like mourning, child-

---

2 An important study of the medieval household in the context of court culture is Malcolm Vale, *The Princely Court: Medieval Courts and Culture in North-West Europe, 1270–1380* (Oxford, 2001). See also Christopher Woolgar, *The Great Household in Late Medieval England* (New Haven, 1999); P.J.P. Goldberg and Maryanne Kowaleski, "Introduction. Medieval Domesticity: Home, Housing and Household," in *Medieval Domesticity: Home, Housing and Household in Medieval England*, ed. Maryanne Kowaleski and P.J.P Goldberg (Cambridge, 2008), pp. 1–13; and Mary Whiteley, "Royal and Ducal Palaces in France in the Fourteenth and Fifteenth Centuries. Interior, Ceremony and Function," in *Architecture et vie sociale. L'organisation intérieure des grandes demeures à la fin du Moyen Âge et à la Renaissance, Actes du colloque tenu à Tours du 6 au 10 juin 1988*, ed. Jean Guillaume (Paris, 1994), pp. 47–63. See also Alain Salamagne, "Le Louvre de Charles v," in *Le palais et son décor au temps de Jean de Berry* (Tours, 2010), pp. 73–138, and the essays by various scholars on the residences of the dukes of Burgundy in *Art from the Court of Burgundy: Patronage of Philip the Bold and John the Fearless, 1364–1419* (Cleveland, 2004), pp. 137–63. For an overview of the royal and noble textile inventories in this period, see Frédérique Lachaud, "Les textiles dans les comptes des hôtels royaux et nobiliaires (France et Angleterre, XIIe-XVe siècle)," *Bibliothèque de l'École des Chartes* 164 (2006), 71–96.

180   CHAPTER 6

birth, or weddings by bestowing gifts that commemorated women's roles as
pious benefactors, teachers, mothers, and godmothers.

The analysis of Blanche's textile collection begins with the bequest of a set of
bedsheets. This gift exemplifies the queen's strategy of commemoration in the
will, as the sheets would have had little significance if they had been included
in a list of textiles in an inventory. Only because Blanche wrote about them can
we fully appreciate their function, and like so many other objects in her collection, these were given to a family member for whom Blanche believed they
would have a particular resonance. The set of sheets was one of three items
that Blanche left to her niece Jeanne, daughter of Charles II of Navarre, duchess of Brittany and future queen of England. Blanche was also generous to her
brother's other children: she left gifts in the will to his sons Charles and Pierre
and to his daughter, Marie.[3] Many of Blanche's textile gifts were bestowed on
these nieces and nephews; as noted above, she restricted her household textile
gifts to sisters, nieces, and nephews, and to those in her household.

Blanche's niece, Jeanne of Navarre, the recipient of the bedsheets, was born
in 1368 and married to the duke of Brittany in 1386; she and her husband had
eight children.[4] Widowed in 1399, she married Henry IV, king of England, in
1403, and she died in England in 1437. Blanche left her two objects discussed in
previous chapters, a breviary that had belonged to Blanche's sister Jeanne who
was a nun at Longchamp (another Jeanne of Navarre), and a reliquary. In this
chapter I consider the third of her gifts, perhaps modest considering the value
of the first two gifts:

> Et avecques ce une paire de noz draps à lit deliez, des millieurs, à mettre
> à dames pour leurs gesines.[5]

> [And with this a pair of loose bedclothes, the best that I have, to put on
> women in labor.]

Loose bedclothes were one of the many textiles that made up the soft furnishings of the medieval bed.[6] The sheets, at least in a royal household like

---

3 The only child in this family who did not receive a bequest in Blanche's will was an Isabelle
   who was a nun at the convent of Santa Clara in Estella, Navarre.

4 Michael Jones, "Joan of Navarre," in *Oxford Dictionary of National Biography* (Oxford, 2004).

5 Delisle 220.

6 For my discussion of Blanche's bed textiles, I depend on the definitions and analysis of Frances
   Pritchard, "The Uses of Textiles, *c.* 1000–1500," in *The Cambridge History of Western Textiles*
   (Cambridge, 2003), pp. 363–64, and Penelope Eames, *Furniture in England, France and the
   Netherlands from the Twelfth to the Fifteenth Century* (London, 1977), pp. 73–93.

TEXTILES: VESTMENTS, WALL HANGINGS, AND CLOTHING 181

Blanche's, were most likely made of linen. They were typically listed in inventories in pairs.[7] Blanche owned four pairs; she left the other pairs to her sister, Jeanne of Rohan, to her niece, Marie of Navarre, and to a friend, Marguerite, dame de Préaux. The homogeneity in their social status – noblewomen – as well as their close family relationship to Blanche indicates that bedsheets were an appropriate gift for a wealthy female family member or companion. Four pairs was probably a typical number for a household like Blanche's; the duke of Berry, who collected all things on a larger scale, had a dozen pairs listed in a 1416 inventory.[8] The sheets in Blanche's will are listed separately from the rest of the textiles of the bed, which included canopies, curtains, coverlets, and cushions – these were presumably included in the *chambres* of Blanche's will, or a set of textiles for an entire room, discussed below.[9]

Blanche also left household beds with their furnishings to her ladies-in-waiting, an indication not only of the monetary value of all textiles in the Middle Ages but also of the additional personal value of beds. Blanche told these women that each should take the bed that they had used for sleeping; this bequest tells us that beds were something you could be entitled to take if a household was being dissolved:

> Item nous voulons et ordonnons que après nostre trespassement noz damoiselles aient les liz où ilz ont geu en nostre hostel tous garniz, et aussi que ilz aient leurs despens bien et honnestement pour eux en retourner là où ilz verront que bon sera à demourer pour eux, et que ilz y soient conduiz et menez à noz despens.[10]

> [I want and order that after my death my ladies-in-waiting have the beds, fully furnished, that they have slept on in my household, and also that they have their expenses (paid) well and honestly for them to return where they see fit to live, and that they be taken there at my expense.]

The pairing of the gift of the beds with the payment of the expenses of these women indicated that Blanche could take care of the women of her household

---

7   Pritchard, "The Uses of Textiles," p. 364.

8   Jules Guiffrey, *Inventaires de Jean, duc de Berry (1401–1416)*, 2 vols. (Paris, 1894–96), 2:248–49.

9   To translate the word *chambre* in Blanche's testament, I follow the definition of chamber used by Penelope Eames: "all the textiles to equip a chamber"; *Furniture in England, France and the Netherlands*, p. 80.

10   Delisle 174.

with both money and a bed. One member, Jeanne de Rouières, to whom she had also given the book with which her daughter learned to read, was looked after with a gift of two beds, their accoutrements, and additional household textiles:

> Item lui laissons pour son mesnage les choses qui ensuivent: c'est assavoir deux liz communs de nostre fourriere, deux paires de draps pour chascun, et deux couvertoirs de connins pour iceulx, avecques le lit où elle gist, que nous lui laissons en nostre grant testament, item six nappes, douze touailles des milleurs à prendre en l'office de la panneterie; deux douzaines d'escuelles d'estain, une douzaine de plas, deux quartes et deux aiguieres d'estain à prendre en la sausserie et eschançonnerie.[11]

> [I leave to her for her household the things that follow, to wit: two common beds, two sets of bedclothes for each, and two covers for them with the bed where she lies that I left in my great testament, six table linens, twelve towels the best to take from the office of the pantry, two dozen pewter bowls, a dozen plates, two quarts and two pewter ewers to take from the sauce kitchen and butler's kitchen.]

Jeanne de Rouières was also given in the will a house valued at about 200 francs; these beds, kitchen textiles, and pewter dishes would help her set up a new household.[12]

The importance of the bed to the household is an indication of how personal the gift of bedsheets to Jeanne of Brittany was; it was an affectionate gift that expressed a close family relationship and the care of an aunt for the well-being of a niece. But the bedsheets given to Jeanne were not typical sheets; these were sheets for childbirth. In this period an expectant mother might have such sheets and other objects made specifically for her confinement. An Italian inventory dated 1470 lists such items as "painted birth trays, a box containing birth charms, a birth mantle, two sets of embroidered birth sheets, two embroidered birth pillows, and a birthing chair."[13] Blanche does not indicate

---

11   Delisle 282.

12   The house bequest is Delisle 281.

13   Though Jacqueline Musacchio has noted that the large number in this inventory was probably not typical; *The Art and Ritual of Childbirth in Renaissance Italy* (New Haven, 1999), p. 13. For additional records of the furnishings for childbirth, see Victor Gay, "Gésine," in *Glossaire archéologique du Moyen Âge et de la Renaissance*, 2 vols. (Paris, 1882–1928), 1:772–75.

TEXTILES: VESTMENTS, WALL HANGINGS, AND CLOTHING

what about the sheets made them her 'best,' but this designation perhaps indicated that they had embroidery. This embroidery may have had an image appropriate for childbirth, such as that of Saint Margaret. There was certainly some physical property of the sheets that distinguished them from each other, however, because the subsequent three bequests of sheets in the will indicated 'my best,' or 'the best after which I have already given'; this distinction demonstrates that there was a standard of value that her heirs would have understood. The sheets were not a practical gift, as Jeanne, mother of seven children by 1396, surely had plenty of furnishings for childbirth.[14] It was meant to be a symbolic and affectionate gift.

That Blanche gave away in the will items as minor as kitchen towels informs us that nearly all of her textiles remained in her household till the end of her life. Gifted during her lifetime, though, were many other textiles of which we catch glimpses in the archival records, which suggest a much larger number in her collection than those listed in the will. She had five sets of liturgical textiles (these sets, called *chapelles*, might have included textiles to be worn by the priest as well as fabrics to adorn the altar), eight sets of room hangings, nine robes or sets of clothing, several pairs of bedsheets, and various other textiles, such as a hat with pearls, and embroidered book covers. As noted above, with the exception of the liturgical textiles, Blanche gave all these items to members of her household, to her sisters, or to her nieces and nephews.

Among the most lavish and elaborate of Blanche's textiles were the *chapelles,* the ones meant for liturgical and devotional settings. Five *chapelles* are described in the will, one black (material not noted), one black velvet set with three copes, one red velvet decorated with gold suns and squirrels, another yellow velvet with silver rosettes, and a set made of silk from Lucca with gold thread. Two additional sets of altar textiles and one vestment are also known to have belonged to Blanche: a chasuble that survives today in the treasury of the cathedral of Sens (discussed below) and two sets that were in the collection of the duke of Berry in 1402.[15] Since the latter are not mentioned in the will, Blanche must have given them to the duke of Berry as a gift while she was still alive; the first was red silk decorated with lions and griffins and the arms of France and Burgundy, and the second, purple velvet embroidered with images of the apostles and with Blanche's arms. These elaborate textiles were used in her household along with more modest surplices and amices, enough to give one at her death to each chaplain of her household, as well as corporal cloths and altar towels. Blanche's number of sets of liturgical textiles seems average;

---

14   Her last child, named Blanche, perhaps named after her great-aunt, was born in 1397.

15   Guiffrey, *Inventaires de Jean, duc de Berry*, 2:155–56.

184 CHAPTER 6

in comparison, Blanche of Orléans identified 12 such sets that she gave away to churches in her 1392 testament.[16]

To Blanche's confessor Pierre Basin went a number of gifts in recognition of his more than three decades of service to the queen. In addition to altar textiles, discussed below, he received Blanche's reliquary statuette of Saint Catherine, a book of the *Vie des pères*, a painting, a set of red serge room hangings, and the accoutrements of the altar: a chalice, the corporals (altar cloths), the corporalier or burse (box for the corporals), and altar towels, as well as the missal that Blanche said he used to say Mass in her house.[17] Blanche noted in the bequest that he needed these objects to say Mass in his new home. This gift parallels that of the beds in that Blanche gave Pierre Basin what he had used each day in her household; there is a sense of entitlement associated with this gift. But it is a more significant gift than the beds because each time he said Mass using these items, he would remember Blanche as part of his prayer, and she could ensure the perpetuation of her daily devotion by bequeathing these elements of it to her confessor.

Pierre Basin was assisted in his religious duties in Blanche's households by nine chaplains who are named in the will: Nicole de Rueil, Pierre Hesterel, Nicolas Moysy, a Dominican, and his companion, named Pierre; Aubery Gosset, Pierre Gautier, Pierre de Venise, Jehan Heudain, and Gieffroy Grioires. These men would have served various roles in Blanche's homes beyond their religious duties, such as writing letters or managing accounts.[18] There was also at least one 'clerk of the chapel,' Colin Baudin. In her will she gave her chaplains basic liturgical garments:

> Item nous voulons que chascun de nos chapellains de nostre chappelle que nous aurons en nostre hostel au jour de nostre trespassement ait un de noz surpeliz et une aumusse que ilz ont acoustumé de mettre en nostre ditte chappelle, selon l'adviz et ordonnance de noz executeurs.[19]

> [I want that each of the chaplains of my chapel that I have in my house on the day of my death to have one of my surplices and an amice that

---

16 Gaston Vignat, "Testament de Blanche, duchesse d'Orléans," *Mémoires de la Sociéte archéologique de l'Orléanais* 9 (1866), 124, 129–33.

17 For altar textiles, see Maria Hayward, "Liturgical Textiles: post-1100," in *Encyclopedia of Dress and Textiles in the British Isles, c. 450–1450*, ed. Gale R. Owen-Crocker, Elizabeth Coatsworth, and Maria Hayward (Leiden, 2012), pp. 333–37.

18 The duties of chaplains are described in Woolgar, *The Great Household in Late Medieval England*, pp. 176–78.

19 Delisle 170.

TEXTILES: VESTMENTS, WALL HANGINGS, AND CLOTHING

they are accustomed to wear in my chapel, according to the advice of my executors.]

The surplice was a plain vestment and the amice a square or rectangular cloth that was put over the head and then draped on the shoulders; they were not of great enough value that they were distributed by name individually, but valuable enough so that giving each man a set recognized his service and acknowledged that he may move on after Blanche's death to another household where he might wear these garments.[20] Seven of the men mentioned in the 1396 will were still in her service in 1398 and given additional gifts of money, an indication of the steady service offered by a large household like Blanche's.

Pierre Basin was given a lavish set of altar textiles made of a fabric that Blanche called "d'or de Luques," silk woven or embroidered with gold thread from the city of Lucca, famous for its textiles in the 14th century.[21]

Et aussi une chapelle de trois garnemens, c'est assavoir frontier, dossier, et chasuble d'or de Luques; et est l'orfrois de la ditte chapelle de broudure à champ d'or de noz armes et à papegaux.[22]

[And also a set of liturgical textiles of three pieces, the frontier, dossier, and chasuble of gold of Lucca, and the orphreys of this set are embroidered with field of gold of my arms and with birds.[23]]

---

20   For the amice, see Elizabeth Coatsworth, "Amice," in *Encyclopedia of Dress and Textiles in the British Isles*, pp. 36–37.

21   For this definition of "Lucca gold," see Susan Mosher Stuard, *Gilding the Market: Luxury and Fashion in Fourteenth-century Italy* (Philadelphia, 2005), p. 156. For Lucca silk, see Anna Muthesius, "Silk in the Medieval World," in *The Cambridge History of Western Textiles*, pp. 325–54; and Lisa Monnas, "Cloth of Gold," in *Encyclopedia of Dress and Textiles in the British Isles*, pp. 132–33.

22   Delisle 262.

23   *Papegaux* can be translated as parrots, but probably the more generic 'bird' is intended rather than an accurate identification of a particular kind of bird. The subject of the second clause in this bequest is not clear; is it the *chapelle* or the *orfrois* that is the intended subject? Elsewhere in the will, the construction *et est* is used when Blanche wanted to carry over the subject from the first clause. If she intended to do that here, the sentence would read: "the chapelle is the orphrey of the aforementioned chapelle of embroidery." This infelicitous result makes it most likely that *orfrois*, or orphrey, is the intended subject here.

186   CHAPTER 6

This bequest demonstrates the importance of textiles in the creation of sacred space; these portable textiles created Blanche's worship space wherever she was staying. Two were meant to adorn the altar: the frontier, or frontal, was placed on the altar, while the dossier, or dossal, was suspended behind the altar to frame the space for Mass.[24] The chasuble was worn by Pierre Basin; the matching textiles created a unified devotional space shimmering with gold thread. Blanche's heraldic device on the textiles associated the liturgy with her personally, and this attaching of her identity and memory to the celebration of Mass would continue as long as the vestment existed.

It is possible to get a sense today of Blanche's liturgical textiles through a vestment that likely belonged to her that survives today in the treasury of the cathedral of Sens (Fig. 6.1). The vestment is a chasuble made of silk from Italy, probably Lucca, with a woven, golden brown pattern of birds, lions, deer, dragons, and griffins on a cream ground (Fig. 6.2).[25] The back of the vestment has two escutcheons embroidered with the arms of France, Evreux, and Navarre; almost certainly these indicate Blanche's commission, though it is also possible that the arms are those of her aunt, Jeanne of Evreux (Fig. 6.3).[26] The repeating pattern of the vestment with its paired animals, among them dragons and winged griffins, is an Italian imitation of Chinese patterns popular in the second half of the 14th century. These so-called tiny-pattern silks adopted

---

24   Hayward, "Liturgical Textiles: post-1100," p. 336.

25   Otto von Falke, *Kunstgeschichte der Seidenweberei*, 2 vols. (Berlin, 1913), 2:34–35, fig. 281. Von Falke calls it a damask silk. Though its pattern suggests that it was made in Lucca, Anne Wardwell has argued that we do not have sufficient evidence to localize Italian silks to specific weaving centers; "The Stylistic Development of 14th- and 15th-century Italian Silk Design," *Aachener Kunstblätter* 47 (1976–77), 177–226. Another source on the vestment is Eugène Chartraire, *Les tissus anciens du trésor de la cathédrale de Sens* (Paris, 1911), pp. 43–44. It was long associated with the early medieval Saint Loup himself, despite the chasuble's 14th-century production date. It was described in *Mercure de France* in 1729 as the chasuble of Saint Loup at the church of Brienon; "Extrait d'une lettre écrite d'Auxerre à M. de la R. le 1 octobre 1728, sur une nouvelle découverte de Médailles faite à cinq lieuës de cette ville" (Paris, 1729), p. 56. See also Charles de Linas, *Rapports sur les anciens vêtements sacerdotaux et les anciens tissus conservés en France* (Paris, 1860), pp. 25–26.

26   The heraldic devices on the vestment are identical to those used by Blanche, for example, on the opening initial of the document that recorded the founding of the chapel of Saint Hippolyte at Saint-Denis (see Fig. 1.1 above). It is less likely that it was Jeanne's arms; a surviving representation of Jeanne of Evreux's arms in the Coronation Book in Illinois was France impaled with Evreux, with Navarre not included; Anne D. Hedeman, "The Commemoration of Jeanne d'Evreux's Coronation in the *Ordo ad Consecrandum* at the University of Illinois," *Essays in Medieval Studies: Proceedings of the Illinois Medieval Association* 7 (1990), 13–28.

FIGURE 6.1   *Chasuble of Blanche of Navarre, second half of the 14th century.*
TREASURY OF THE CATHEDRAL OF SENS. PHOTO CREDIT:
MARGUERITE KEANE.

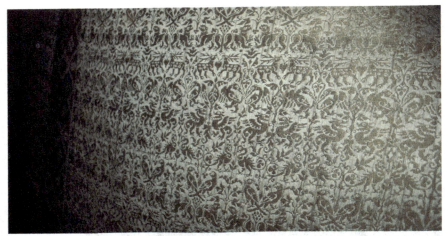

FIGURE 6.2 *Chasuble of Blanche of Navarre, detail.* PHOTO CREDIT: MARGUERITE KEANE.

FIGURE 6.3 *Chasuble of Blanche of Navarre, detail of the heraldic device.* PHOTO CREDIT: MARGUERITE KEANE.

TEXTILES: VESTMENTS, WALL HANGINGS, AND CLOTHING

an exotic iconography of fantastic animals from the East and imitated the densely populated visual effect of Chinese silks.[27] This expensive figured textile might have been appropriate for special days like Christmas, and accompanied something like Blanche's painting of the Nativity that she indicated she placed on the altar at Christmas. Prior to its arrival in Sens, the chasuble was in the collection of the church of Saint Loup at Brienon, in Burgundy, where it had been since at least the early 18th century.[28]

The rest of Blanche's liturigical textiles mentioned in the will were given to churches, to three that were or had once been in her lands, at Vernon, Gournay, and Melun, and the last much further afield, to the cathedral of Pamplona in Navarre. The church of Saint Hildevert at Gournay, in the Pays de Bray, near Blanche's home at Neaufles, received a set of black liturgical textiles with three copes.[29] The black color meant that the priests of this church would use these vestments in Masses or processions in honor of the dead; the priest wearing her cope was a way to ensure that Blanche would be remembered in such celebrations. Blanche had claimed a 'singular and special devotion' for Notre-Dame at Melun and Notre-Dame at Vernon when she gave them statues of herself kneeling with the Virgin Mary, and this special status was extended with gifts of altar textiles to each church. To Melun, she gave a yellow velvet set embroidered and studded with silver rosettes.[30] To Vernon, she gave a set of black textiles that Blanche indicated she had purchased from the archbishop of Sens.[31] Blanche also gave money to both churches for anniversary masses, and she left fifty francs for the building fund of Vernon. It is likely that she was continuing bequests to the church at Vernon during her life, as it is hard to imagine that she was not involved in some way in funding the extensive building program undertaken at this church in the 14th century.[32] These bequests reveal that Blanche had three ways of ensuring that she would have perpetual prayers for her salvation – through altar textiles, through contributing to the building fund of a church, and through anniversary masses.

---

27 For tiny pattern silks, see Anne Wardwell, "The Stylistic Development of 14th- and 15th-century Italian Silk Design," pp. 186–87.

28 It seems unlikely that Blanche gave it directly to this church because she had no other evident connection to Brienon, though it cannot be ruled out.

29 Delisle 24.

30 Delisle 40.

31 Delisle 22. Most likely it was Guillaume de Dormans, archbishop of Sens at the time the will was written in 1396; he was archbishop from 1390–1405.

32 For the building activity at the church in the 14th century, see Docteur Couton, "L'église Notre-Dame de Vernon," *Bulletin Amis monuments de rouennais* 11 (1911–12), 89–104.

Blanche gave to the church of Notre-Dame in Pamplona, where, she noted, her father's body was buried, a set of altar textiles of red velvet decorated with golden suns and squirrels.[33] Though golden suns might convey the glory of God's creation and in general create a lavish visual effect, the meaning of squirrels for a vestment is more perplexing. Squirrels were pets in the Middle Ages, often associated with women.[34] In 1387, the French queen Isabeau of Bavaria ordered a collar for her pet squirrel decorated with pearls and a gold buckle.[35] Philippa of Hainault wore a purple dress with embroidered squirrels for her churching, or first public appearance after the birth of her child in 1330.[36] Squirrel fur was a luxury material, and this association perhaps was attached to the representation of the squirrel on clothing.[37] And Blanche's gift was not unique; in 1361, an Englishwoman, Matilda Wight, left a silk cloth decorated with gilt squirrels to the church of Saint Mary de Wolnoth in London.[38]

The decoration of this vestment raises the possibility that it was made from another item of clothing, perhaps a set of clothes owned by Blanche. Clothing was often repurposed to make vestments, both for practical reasons – cloth was expensive – and for the symbolic significance of donating one's finery to a church. Blanche's predecessor, the queen Jeanne of Burgundy, gave to the abbey of Longchamp in Paris a red robe made of cloth-of-gold that was used to make vestments; Anne-Hélène Allirot has suggested that it may have been the queen's coronation robe.[39] In her 1401 testament, Blanche's sister Jeanne of Rohan left instructions that her sets of clothing, in colors of white, red, black,

---

33 Delisle 39.

34 Kathleen Walker-Meikle, *Medieval Pets* (Woodbridge, UK, 2012), p. 48.

35 Walker-Meikle, *Medieval Pets*, p. 52, citing Gay, *Glossaire archéologique*, 1:607

36 Maria Hayward, "Squirrel Robe of Queen Philippa," in *Encyclopedia of Dress and Textiles in the British Isles*, p. 543, and S.M. Newton, "Queen Philippa's Squirrel Suit," in *Documenta Textilia: Festschrift für Sigrid Müller-Christensen*, ed. M. Flury-Lemberg and K. Stolleis (Munich, 1981), pp. 342–48.

37 Maria Hayward, "Squirrel Fur," in *Encyclopedia of Dress and Textiles in the British Isles*, p. 542.

38 Kristen Burkholder, "Threads Bared: Dress and Textiles in English Wills," in *Medieval Clothing and Textiles*, vol. 1, ed. Robin Netherton and Gale Owen-Crocker (Woodbridge, UK, 2005), p. 147.

39 Anne-Hélène Allirot, "Longchamp and Lourcine: The Role of Female Abbeys in the Construction of Capetian Memory (Late Thirteenth Century to Mid-Fourteenth Century)," in *Memory and Commemoration in Medieval Culture*, ed. Elma Brenner, Meredith Cohen, and Mary Franklin-Brown (Farnham, Surrey, UK, 2013), p. 257. In her will of 1336, Jeanne asked that her silk robes be given to churches; the embroidered ones should be given to large churches and the plain silk to smaller churches; Murielle Gaude-Ferragu, "Les dernières volontés de la reine de France. Les deux testaments de Jeanne de Bourgogne,

TEXTILES: VESTMENTS, WALL HANGINGS, AND CLOTHING 191

and green, should be made into chasubles for churches.[40] If indeed the red velvet vestments embroidered with squirrels were repurposed women's clothing, the reuse functioned eternally as a sign of the gift and advertised to the viewer the piety of the woman who had donated it.

Blanche also had a textile image of the Virgin Mary that she gave to a local Cistercian convent dedicated to the Virgin Mary, near Baudemont, south of Gisors, founded in the early 13th century[41] (along with a reliquary of Saint Loup and Saint Leonard discussed in chap. 4):

> Item nous laissons à l'église du Trésor Nostre Dame lez Baudemont un ymage de Nostre Dame qui est de bordure, et un petit reliquiaire d'argent de nostre clotet, où il a reliques, où, dedens le cristal qui est ou milieu, a de la jambe saint Leu et de celle de saint Lienart, et y a dessus un cruxefiz.[42]

> [To the church of Trésor Notre Dame near Baudemont an embroidered image of the Virgin Mary, and a small silver reliquary from my *clotet* which has relics; the crystal in the middle has part of the leg of Saint Loup and that of Saint Leonard, and over it is a crucifix.]

The subject matter of the panel was an appropriate gift considering the dedication of the convent. The embroidered image seems to have been a single panel; it may have been similar to the framed embroidered image of the Virgin that was described in the wardrobe accounts of the English king Richard II. Lisa Monnas has suggested that this image may have been among those used in the king's *clotet* for his private devotions.[43] By donating it to a convent, Blanche may have intended that it should be added to a vestment.[44]

---

femme de Philippe VI de Valois (1329, 1336)," *Annuaire-Bulletin de la Sociéte de l'histoire de France, année 2007* (2009), 62–63.

40   Pierre-Hyacinthe Morice, "Testament de Jeanne de Navarre, vicomtesse de Rohan," in *Mémoires pour servir de preuves à l'histoire ecclésiastique et civile de Bretagne*, 3 vols. (Paris, 1742–46), 2:718–19.

41   For the records of this convent, see *Inventaire sommaire des Archives départementales antérieures à 1790, Orne: Archives ecclésiastiques. Série H (No 3352–4738)*, ed. Louis Duval, 4 vols. (Alençon, 1899), 3:300–321.

42   Delisle 31.

43   Lisa Monnas, "The Furnishings of Royal Closets and the Use of Small Devotional Images in the Reign of Richard II: The Setting of the Wilton Diptych Reconsidered," *Fourteenth-century England* 3 (2004), 199.

44   For example, as in the early 14th-century embroidered panel today in the British Museum with scenes from the life of the Virgin Mary that was meant to be attached to a vestment;

192   CHAPTER 6

The next bequest of textiles in the will, after the dissemination of the liturgical textiles, consisted of the bedsheets that were given to Jeanne, duchess of Brittany, Blanche's niece. As noted above, none of Blanche's remaining textiles – her room hangings, bedding, and clothing – was given to someone other than a sister, niece, nephew, companion, or household member. Nevertheless, there is some gradation of rank within these gifts. Eight *chambres* were mentioned in the 1396 will. Five were given to family members: two green sets, one with roses, one with purple and white leaves, both decorated with her arms; a gray set; a set with stripes or diamond pattern; and a red quilted set without armorials. Three sets made of more modest fabric, red serge, blue serge, and green toile, were given to Pierre Basin and two of her ladies-in-waiting.[45] In the 1398 codicil, she bequeathed two sets that she called newly made: one with lilies in pots with her arms, and another with her monogram of the letter B. It is only for her household heirs that she indicates the material of her room hangings, serge or wool; that she designates these specifically as serge indicates that her other room hangings were not serge, but the will gives no additional information on material. Though her collection seems varied and luxurious, it was in fact modest. In comparison, Charles V had 59 such sets described in an inventory.[46]

Ultimately, of all of the objects described in the testament, the room hangings probably express Blanche's personal identity most strongly: these include room hangings with the letter B and another set that she put up on the days when visitors came, which signified a public presentation of selfhood. The earliest set of room hangings that we know about for Blanche of Navarre was black, purchased on the occasion of the death of her husband and signifying a change in status, her widowhood.[47] Another somber set, described as 'encendrée,' or the color of ashes, was likely used during Lent; it was given to her sister, Agnes, countess of Foix. Indeed the absence of color in the textiles for the time after Blanche's widowhood and in her set for Lent is an indication of the importance of color for the textiles of everyday life.[48] Blanche had two sets that were green, a color associated with springtime in this period, that

---

London, British Museum, M&ME 1919, 3–5, 1.

45   Mark Chambers, "Serge," in *Encyclopedia of Dress and Textiles in the British Isles*, p. 503.

46   Lachaud, "Les textiles dans les comptes des hôtels royaux et nobiliaires," pp. 71–72.

47   Jules Viard, "Compte des obsèques de Philippe VI," in *Archives historiques, artistiques et littéraires* (Paris, 1890–91), vol. 2, pp. 49–53. See also Murielle Gaude-Ferragu, *D'or et cendres: la mort et les funérailles des princes dans le royaume de France au bas Moyen Âge* (Villeneuve-d'Ascq, 2005), p. 158.

48   Désirée Koslin has pointed out that the lack of color in the garments of religious who wore black, white, and gray signified their humility and rejection of worldly concerns; "Value-Added Stuffs and Shifts in Meaning: An Overview and Case Study of Medieval Tex-

TEXTILES: VESTMENTS, WALL HANGINGS, AND CLOTHING

were also decorated with foliage (one with roses, the other with purple and white leaves).[49] She shared this preference for green room hangings with the dukes of Burgundy, who preferred bright colors, especially red and green, for the decoration of their residences.[50]

Blanche's nephew, Charles of Rohan, was given the room hangings that Blanche used in her household when she had friends visit; they were green, with five circles that enclosed Blanche's arms, each surrounded by white and purple leaves.

> nostre chambre vert entiere, que l'en tent en nostre hotel quant noz amis viennent devers nous; et est à v compas, en chascun une losenge de noz armes qui est environnée d'un compas fueilleté de feuilles blanches et yndes.[51]

> [My complete set of green room hangings, the one that is put up in my house when my friends come before me, and it has five circles in each a lozenge of my arms that is surrounded by white and purple leaves.]

She gave her nephew a gold cup with this gift as well:

> un gobelet d'or couvert à ys gregoiz, armoiez des armes de nostre dicte dame et tante et des nostres.[52]

> [A gold cup covered with lilies, decorated with the arms of my aforementioned lady and aunt (Jeanne of Evreux, named two bequests prior) and mine.]

The term Blanche uses is *gobelet*, a tall drinking cup without a stem.[53] These two gifts were associated with familial identity, as both carried the arms of the

---

      tile Paradigms," in *Encountering Medieval Textiles and Dress: Objects, Texts, Images*, ed. Désirée Koslin and Janet Snyder (New York, 2002), pp. 235–49.

49   Lisa Monnas, "Some Medieval Colour Terms for Textiles," in *Medieval Clothing & Textiles* 10 (2014), ed. Robin Netherton and Gale R. Owen-Crocker, with Monica L. Wright, pp. 25–57, esp. p. 42.

50   Sophie Cassagnes-Brouquet, "Decor of the Ducal Residences," in *Art from the Court of Burgundy*, pp. 140–41.

51   Delisle 240.

52   Delisle 241.

53   The gobelet, or goblet, was a tall cup without a stem that might be placed on a stand to increase its magnificence; Ronald Lightbown, *Secular Goldsmiths' Work in Medieval*

family members of Charles of Rohan. They also commemorated Blanche's hospitality as the room hangings were used when Blanche hosted her friends; the cup may have been associated with display on such occasions as well. Blanche did not name other metal tableware with the exception of the pewter items given to Jeanne de Rouières, discussed above; if she did eventually retrieve the silver tableware pawned on her daughter's journey to Perpignan in 1371, she had long since given it away.

At least four of her sets of room hangings included her heraldic device, evidence of the importance of these textiles for personal identity. Though caveats apply – paintings are ideologically motivated and should be considered with care as reflections of actual objects – the Gaignières painting of the chapel decoration at Saint-Denis shows a heraldic tapestry hanging behind Blanche and gives a sense of what one of Blanche's hangings might have looked like (Fig. 1.10). Blanche had red quilted room hangings without armorials that she gave to her sister, Jeanne, viscountess of Rohan, as well as a panel of the same material that did have her armorials, with angels holding the arms of France and Navarre.[54] Also among her heraldic textiles were the room hangings given to her nephew, Charles III, king of Navarre, analyzed above in the third chapter in the context of the books and brooch that the king of Navarre also received. Notably, none of Blanche's room hangings seems to have been narrative. In comparison, the 1405 inventory of Margaret of Flanders, duchess of Burgundy, described 41 tapestries, all with religious, historical, chivalric, or allegorical subjects, among them Alexander the Great, heroes, knights, pastoral and biblical scenes.[55] Though Blanche may have perceived this kind of detailed discussion of subjects as not necessary for identifying the room hangings, or alternately, as not crucial to the perpetuation of her memory, which was the task of the testament, it seems unlikely that her textiles were much more detailed than what she conveys in the testament descriptions. By comparison, the testaments of Blanche of Orléans and Jeanne of Rohan also do not mention such narrative textiles.

A niece, Marie of Navarre, daughter of Blanche's brother Charles II, was given a set of green room hangings with roses, decorated with Blanche's arms, described as "nostre chambre vert entiere à rosiers armoiés de noz armes"[56] [my complete set of green room hangings with roses, decorated with my arms]. As noted in chapter 3, the items given to Marie of Navarre were likely intended

---

France (London, 1978), p. 22.

54   Delisle 227 and 228.

55   Fabrice Rey, "The Tapestry Collections," in *Art from the Court of Burgundy*, pp. 123–25.

56   Delisle 232.

TEXTILES: VESTMENTS, WALL HANGINGS, AND CLOTHING

as gifts for her wedding. Blanche's arms on the tapestries expressed the ancestry and identity of her niece, an appropriate gift to mark her transition to a new family; Charles V had a breviary with an embroidered binding with the arms of France and Aragon made for Blanche's daughter, Jeanne, on the occasion of her wedding (discussed in chap. 1). Marie was also given a hat, described as:

> un chapperon pendant à troches de perles, dyapré d'or sur un camocas noir. Et voulons que se le dit chapperon n'estoit fourré que on le face fourrer en letesses.[57]

> [a hat hanging with strings of pearls, diasper of gold on black camacas. And I want that this aforementioned hat, if it is to be lined in fur, only be lined with lettice.]

A *chaperon* was a hood with a cornet, or tube of cloth, attached to its crown.[58] This *chaperon* was made of black camaca, a silk fabric, patterned with gold thread.[59] The wording of the bequest suggests that the *chaperon* was not yet finished, as Blanche left instructions for its lining that she wished to be lettice, or the white fur of the snow weasel.[60] The singular quality of this gift – there are no other *chaperons* mentioned in the will, and this one seems also to have been unfinished – suggests that it had been ordered as a gift for her niece and was probably not a hat that Blanche had herself owned. It was indeed much more elaborate than any of Blanche's other clothing and not typical dress for a widow in the 14th century. The last of the gifts for Marie of Navarre were bedsheets, "une paire de noz milleurs draps deliez à lit" [a set of my best loose bedclothes].[61]

In the 1398 will, Blanche changed her mind about the red room hangings she had left to Jeanne of Rohan that were discussed above:

> Item, pour et en lieu de la chambre vermeille pourpointe senz armoierie, que nous lessions à nostre très chier seur madame Jehanne de Navarre,

---

57   Delisle 234.

58   Anne van Buren, *Illuminating Fashion: Dress in the Art of Medieval France and the Netherlands, 1325–1515* (New York, 2011), pp. 298–301.

59   Mark Chambers, Elizabeth Coatsworth, and Gale R. Owen-Crocker, "Camaca," in *Encyclopedia of Dress and Textiles in the British Isles*, pp. 108–9.

60   Maria Hayward, "Lettice," in *Encyclopedia of Dress and Textiles in the British Isles*, p. 324; Margaret Scott defines *lettice* as "a white fur, mimicking ermine"; *Medieval Dress and Fashion* (London, 2007), p. 80.

61   Delisle 235.

vicontesse de Rohan, nous lui laissons par ce present codicille nostre chambre toute entiere à pos à liz benoists passans dedens; et sont les pos armoiez de noz armes, laquelle nous avons nagaires fait faire. Et neant-moins voulons que elle ait les autres choses que nous lui laissons en nostre dit premier codicille, si comme en icellui est contenu.[62]

[For and in place of the red quilted set of room hangings without armori-als, that I left to the viscountess of Rohan, I leave to her in this present codicil my complete room hangings with sections with blessed lilies inside and the pots are decorated with my arms, which I have recently had done. And nevertheless I want her to have the things mentioned in the first codicil.]

The fate of the red set is not given; it was perhaps given away to someone else or damaged in the intervening two years. The blessed lilies in pots or vases on Blanche's new room hangings were a reference to the Virgin Mary; lilies in a vase often appear in images of the Annunciation in medieval art.[63] Jeanne Nuechterlein has noted the significance of the lilies in the vase of the Annunciation; in addition to having a sacred resonance, they also function simply as decoration for a room, surely a factor in Blanche's use of them for room textiles.[64] The lily might also have been associated with healing, perhaps appropriate for a room hanging newly made after Blanche's illness of 1396, though the specification of lilies in vases suggests that the Virgin Mary is the primary intended association.[65]

The second set of room hangings made in the last two years of her life Blanche left to her great-niece, Blanche of Navarre, daughter of Charles III, king of Navarre. This king had an older daughter, Jeanne, but Blanche of

---

62   Delisle 409.

63   Hans Memling painted an image at the end of the 15th century of a vase holding lilies and irises with the monogram of Christ; Zsombor Jékely, "Maiolica Jugs in Late Medieval Painting," in *The Dowry of Beatrice; Italian Maiolica Art and the Court of King Matthias*, ed. Gabriella Balla and Zsombor Jékely (Budapest, 2008), pp. 55–66. Jékely suggests that the vase of flowers in the painting might have been juxtaposed to a panel with a coat of arms, an effect similar to that of Blanche's textiles, though in the case of Blanche's room hang-ings, the coat of arms was on the vase itself.

64   Jeanne Nuechterlein, "The Domesticity of Sacred Space in the Fifteenth-Century Nether-lands," in *Defining the Holy: Sacred Space in Medieval and Early Modern Europe*, ed. Andrew Spicer and Sarah Hamilton (Aldershot, 2005), pp. 49–79, this comment p. 65.

65   Margaret Freeman, *The Unicorn Tapestries* (New York, 1976), pp. 149–51.

TEXTILES: VESTMENTS, WALL HANGINGS, AND CLOTHING

Navarre passed her over in favor of her younger sister; the reason for her choice becomes clear with the gift:

> Item nous laissons par ce present codicille à nostre très chiere niece madame Blanche de Navarre, fille de nostre neveu le roy de Navarre, nostre chambre entiere à B, armoiée de noz armes, laquelle nous avons nagaires fait faire toute neufve.[66]

> [I leave to my niece Blanche of Navarre, daughter of my nephew the king of Navarre, my room hangings with a B, decorated with my arms, which I have recently had made entirely new.]

The letter B on this set of room hangings was an emblem, an indicator of status or identity for visual display conveyed by colors, initials, or short phrases; emblems were increasingly popular in the second half of the 14th century at the French court.[67] Monograms like Blanche's letter B were popular for wall decorations; for example, at one of the residences of Margaret of Flanders, the château at Germolles, a room was painted with the letters *M* (for Margaret) interspersed with letters *P* (for her husband, Philip) on a light green ground.[68] Paintings of such textiles embroidered with monograms also occasionally appear in manuscript borders.[69] In this gift Blanche returned to a practice seen in her book bequests, where a book associated with a particular person or with particular heraldic devices, such as France and Burgundy, was then given to someone else with the same name or heraldic device; in this way, she recognized the shared identity. This younger Blanche of Navarre eventually inherited her father's throne when he died in 1425.[70]

The gift of the monogram textiles is one of the few in Blanche's testament for which we can see its reception by the heir. In 1401, Johan Caritat, the treasurer of the king of Navarre, paid a fee to the proprietors of a ship that had

---

66   Delisle 410.

67   Laurent Hablot, "The Use of Emblems by Philip the Bold and John the Fearless," in *Art from the Court of Burgundy*, pp. 81–83.

68   Margaret of Flanders engaged painters from 1388 to 1393 for Germolles; Michel Maerten, "The Germolles Château," in *Art from the Court of Burgundy*, pp. 146–47.

69   Margaret Goehring, "The Representation and Meaning of Luxurious Textiles in Late Medieval Franco-Flemish Manuscript Illumination," in *Weaving, Veiling and Dressing: Textiles and Their Metaphors in the Late Middle Ages*, ed. Barbara Baert and Kathryn Rudy (Turnhout, 2007), pp. 121–55.

70   For this Blanche, known as Blanca I of Navarre, see Elena Woodacre, *The Queens Regnant of Navarre: Succession, Politics, and Partnership, 1274–1512* (New York, 2013), pp. 77–107.

arrived from Cherbourg with the room hangings for the princess Blanche from Blanche, queen of France.[71] A second payment for additional room hangings (*ciertos paramentos de cambra*) and other things (*et otras cosas*) from the queen Blanche did not name the recipient.[72] Other textiles intended for the kingdom of Navarre were the red liturgical textiles with squirrels and suns for the cathedral at Pamplona, and the green room hangings with roses for Marie of Navarre, married in 1396.

The narrative in this chapter of Blanche's textiles has moved from the most to the least lavish, according to what we know from Blanche's descriptions, from a discussion of her household textiles, including altar textiles and room hangings, to now consider her clothing. She gave away her clothing only to the women of her household, from the dame de Fontenay, who, Blanche noted, lived with her, to Symmonete, a healer. In the will, Blanche noted nine long robes and three short.[73] The robe was a suit of clothes; it included a gown with a garment worn over it, a surcote or mantle.[74] The term might also be used for a single gown, though Blanche's long robes seem to have been sets, not single gowns.[75] For three of the bequests, Blanche called the garments a 'robe de nostre corps.'[76] Since she did not otherwise distinguish the robes from each other, it is possible that all of her clothes could be said to fall into this category.

---

71   Maria Narbona Cárceles, "La 'Discreción Hermosa': Blanca de Navarra," in *La dama en la corte bajomedieval* (Pamplona, 2001), pp. 91–92, citing Pamplona, Archivo General de Navarra, Reg. 263, p. 47v.

72   Cárceles, "La 'Discrecion Hermosa'," p. 92, citing Archivo General de Navarra Caj. 80, no. 8, XI.

73   This assumes that she means 'long robe' whenever she does not indicate whether it was long or short. The last robe given before the first short robe is described as 'long' as well. Margaret Scott has noted: "Around 1350 Gilles Li Muisis, Abbot of St. Martin of Tournai, said that women previously had three outfits – a best one for great feast days; a second one for ordinary feast days and Sundays; and a third for daily life"; *Medieval Dress and Fashion*, p. 80.

74   "Robe," Lexis of Cloth and Clothing Project, University of Manchester.

75   The first two bequests of long robes just use the term 'robe,' nos. 248 and 255, but the third bequest, no. 273, calls the robe 'entière,' or a complete set, the best after the one already given (i.e., no. 255), suggesting that they are the same type of object.

76   A 'robe de corps' was later used to describe a widow's clothing; Charles du Fresne du Cange, "Robe de corps," *Glossarium novum ad scriptores medii aevi* (Paris, 1766), vol. 4, p. 90. But against this definition here is that Jeanne of Burgundy, wife of Philip VI, never a widow, gave away a 'robe de mon cors' in her will of 1329; Gaude-Ferragu, "Les dernières volontés de la reine de France," p. 45.

TEXTILES: VESTMENTS, WALL HANGINGS, AND CLOTHING

A widow's clothing was likely a somber color, but the testament is silent on precisely the color or material of each set.[77]

The robes described in the will are likely similar to those in which Blanche is depicted on works of art. In the Saint-Denis charter initials (Figs. 1.1, 1.3) and tomb sculptures (Fig. 1.5), she wears the clothing typical of a widowed queen in the late 14th century: a mantle, a wimple, and a crown. Of the nine long robes in Blanche's will, two went to noblewomen (the dame de Fontenay and the dame de la Mote), six to damoiselles (Jeanne la Besaine, Jeanne de Rouières, Jeanne du Mesnil, Marguerite de Vymont, Margot le Grant, and Agnote), and the last to a goddaughter (Blanche, dame de Troussy).[78] Blanche did not give clothes to her sisters or nieces, and she did not give away her clothing outside of her immediate circle. Giving clothes to the members of the household was a typical practice: the French queens Clémence of Hungary and Jeanne of Burgundy both gave dresses to the women of their household, and Philip VI also gave his clothing to household members.[79] She does differentiate them by 'best' and 'next best' as she does so many of her possessions, so it was possible to have a preference for one over another. These differences in value were left to her female heirs to determine as they chose the dresses; Blanche does not establish a standard, though it seems likely to have been the fabric used. The varied status of the heirs – for example, two were noblewomen, while two others, Blanche de Troussy and Margot le Grant, had recently been married – suggests that the gowns were generic enough to be useful to any woman (or alternately, might be remade into something else). Blanche had three short robes in her possession that were given to her washerwoman, who was unnamed, to Symmonete, who cared for the sick, and to Gilette, a chambermaid.[80] Short robes were associated with labor, and indeed Blanche of Navarre gave all three of these short robes to women who worked in her household.[81]

---

77   For widow's clothing, see Scott, *Medieval Dress and Fashion*, pp. 112–13.

78   Delisle 248, 255, 273, 276, 287, 290, 292, 295, 298.

79   For Clémence, see Mariah Proctor-Tiffany, "Transported as a Rare Object of Distinction: The Gift-giving of Clémence of Hungary, Queen of France," *Journal of Medieval History* 41, no. 2 (2015), 211, n. 16; for Jeanne, Gaude-Ferragu, "Les dernières volontés de la reine de France," pp. 45–46, 59. Philip VI left 'robes' to the "sommeliers de nostre chambre et aus varles de noz garderobes"; Paris, Archives nationales J 406, no. 33 (the testament of 23 May 1347).

80   Delisle 311, 312, 313.

81   The distinction between short and long robes appeared first in the 1330s, when the English king Edward's expense account showed that he had been ordering both short and long suits. Stella Mary Newton argues that wearing the "dress of valets and artisans" was a

The last instance of textile use in Blanche's life was one that she carefully orchestrated so that her textiles would continue to signify her status and identity as they had done in her lifetime. She wrote:

> Et de noz obsèques, de l'atour de nostre corps, de draps d'or, d'enterrement et sepultre il nous plaist, voulons et ordonnons que ilz soient faiz honnestement, senz orgueil et vanité, selon le regart et bon adviz de noz executeurs; et que, se bonnement et honnorablement se puet faire, que nostre corps soit porté à visaige descouvert, vestue de veloux violet et mantel de mesmes; et que, par la discrecion de noz executeurs, soit advisé, selon le lieu de nostre trespas, soit à Neaufle ou vers Paris, où les processions et les amis assembleront, et ensivant quant à ce qui en fu fait pour nostre très chiere dame et tante madame la royne Jehanne, que Diex absoille.[82]

> [And for my funeral, I wish that they should put honestly without vanity according to the regard and good advice of my executors, cloth-of-gold around my body, for the funeral and burial; and that my body should be carried with uncovered visage if possible, clothed in purple velvet and mantel of the same, and that by the discretion of my executors, it be advised, according to the place of my death, be it at Neaufles or at Paris, where the procession and the friends will assemble, following that which was done for Jeanne my aunt, may God pardon her.]

Notably she left money for cloth-of-gold in the case that she was taken to Notre-Dame, but she did not do so for Saint-Denis.[83] This suggests that Saint-Denis already possessed the accoutrements for a funeral, both the crown and the cloth-of-gold. Blanche intended that the final textile associated with her before death should be the most valuable cloth-of-gold and that most royal of colors, purple, both signs of the importance of material and colors of textiles for personal identity.

---

gesture by the king; *Fashion in the Age of the Black Prince: A Study of the Years 1340–1365* (Woodbridge, UK, 1980), p. 15.

82 Delisle 8.

83 "To the college of Notre-Dame of Paris, in the case that my body is carried there after the funeral, and not otherwise, by the manner which is mentioned before, 260 francs to buy a crown and cloth-of-gold, with 40 francs to distribute to the maregliers and sonneurs who ring for me in this church, as it was done for my aunt"; Delisle 15.

Blanche's gifts of textiles in many ways exemplify the practices of gift dissemination seen throughout her testament. Though some of her textiles were given to churches and religious foundations, like her silver and silver-gilt reliquaries, to provide for the corporate commemoration of her soul, the rest went to individuals, and in this case, only her close family and household members, revealing the kind of values assigned to textiles in the late Middle Ages. Giving these textiles – her clothing and the furnishings of the bed on which her companions and servants had slept – was a way of taking care of close family and household members, just like the books with good information considered above. For some gifts, Blanche infused additional value, like the bedsheets for Jeanne of Brittany that were efficacious for childbirth or the monogrammed textiles for a great-niece who shared Blanche's name; these relatives would not have known Blanche as well as the women of her household, so it was a strategy for ensuring that they would value the gifts highly. In her gifts of textiles Blanche resembles the other royal testators considered in this book: Clémence of Hungary, Jeanne of Burgundy, and Philip VI in her gifts of clothing; and Blanche of Orléans and Jeanne of Rohan in her bequests of liturgical textiles. Through these gifts Blanche was participating in the stereotype of the pious royal benefactor, to further her memory and prompt prayers for her salvation.

Conclusions

From all the evidence of the testament, an image of the household of a medieval queen emerges. A dowager queen, Blanche of Navarre was concerned with maintaining her privileges and being remembered in the roles that had given her access to power: as mother and as mediator. She was a patron who commissioned works of art and served as a conduit for works of art. In her lifetime, these artworks met her spiritual and comfort needs, supplied devotional variety, permitted her to participate in the gift exchange so characteristic of the Valois court in the second half of the 14th century, and served to create an identity as a privileged and pious dowager queen. She is much a patron of her time – like Charles V, Jeanne of Evreux, and John of Berry – in that she celebrated the details of her objects; it is only through her celebration of these objects and their appearance that we can reconstruct so much of her collection. Her testament goes well beyond those of other patrons, however, in its interest in layers of detail. The descriptions were in part motivated, as I have argued above, by a kind of insecurity: about her status and whether she would be buried as she wished and remembered as she wanted; she also had an interest in increasing the value of her possessions for her heirs. The testament and its bequests were parallel to the strategies for memory deployed at places like Saint-Denis, or the Jacobins, or the churches where the priests would wear her vestments; Blanche had a prestigious family history and was intimately connected to the current members of the French court through her family ties and her status as a dowager queen. In concluding this study, which was intended as an overview of Blanche's collection, I note that there is still much more to say. Blanche's testament and the other testaments considered in this book are rich sources for the history of late medieval art, the history of women, and the history of devotional practice, among other areas. For example, here I elucidated the kinds of objects Blanche owned for devotion in her homes – reliquaries, paintings, liturgical textiles, and paternosters – but I did not consider in depth how these objects interacted to support her devotion.[1] How, for example, might the juxta-

---

1 For this idea I depend on Paul Binski's discussion of the entire image 'installation' of the late medieval parish church, how such images acted on viewers, and how they might have found them attractive or moving: "The English Parish Church and Its Art in the Later Middle Ages: A Review of the Problem," *Studies in Iconography* 20 (1999), 1–25.

CONCLUSIONS   203

position of an image of Saint Catherine and a diptych with the Annunciation and Crucifixion in a personal devotional *clotet* have meaning?[2]

This project has depended on recent scholarly studies of testaments, such as publication and analysis of the testaments of Jeanne of Evreux by Elizabeth A.R. Brown and Jeanne of Burgundy by Murielle Gaude-Ferragu, as well as the study of the testament and inventory of Clémence of Hungary by Mariah Proctor-Tiffany. But the objects owned by women like Jeanne of Burgundy, Blanche of Orléans, and Jeanne of Rohan that survive only in the description of testaments and inventories are still not well known in comparison to works for patrons that have actually survived, such as Jeanne of Evreux, Charles V, John of Berry, or Philip of Burgundy. All have had major exhibitions devoted to their patronage and collecting.[3] Because an exhibition curator depends on the assemblage of gorgeous objects to tell a story, the collection of Blanche of Navarre has not benefited from such attention; two marble sculptures, a couple of marble head fragments, a vestment, and two charters are not sufficient to build a compelling visual narrative. But when exhibitions motivate the production of scholarship, one result can be the neglect of women's collections because they are smaller and fewer objects survive.[4]

Further analysis of the testament of Blanche of Navarre and her contemporaries will depend at least in part on the capability of mastering the vast quantity of information contained in late medieval wills. Here the methods of digital humanities, the digitization and interpretation of information based on analysis of data, has been and will continue to be useful. Such studies of the data contained in testaments were valuable for this project, particularly those that noted gender or class differences in the dissemination of objects. Another

---

2   For analysis of devotional practice from the evidence of books owned by women, see Alexa Sand, *Vision, Devotion, and Self-representation in Late Medieval Art* (Cambridge, 2014).

3   For example, the exhibitions of the *Hours of Jeanne d'Evreux* and of the *Belles Heures* of the duke of Berry at the Metropolitan Museum of Art prompted considerable scholarly attention, published in the catalogues *The Hours of Jeanne d'Evreux. Acc. No. 54.I.2 The Metropolitan Museum of Art, The Cloisters Collection, New York: Commentary* (Lucerne, 2000), and *The Art of Illumination: The Limbourg Brothers and the* Belles Heures *of Jean de France, Duc de Berry* (New York, 2009), as well as scholarship inspired by the exhibition of these works published in other venues. Other recent exhibitions that considered Valois patronage are *Art from the Court of Burgundy: Patronage of Philip the Bold and John the Fearless, 1364–1419* (Cleveland, 2004), and *Paris 1400: les arts sous Charles VI* (Paris, 2004).

4   Indeed, Stephen Perkinson pointed out in his 2006 review of several exhibition catalogues, among them *Paris 1400* and *Art from the Court of Burgundy*, that they were "surprisingly silent on the question of female patronage"; Perkinson, "Courtly Splendor, Urban Markets: Some Recent Exhibition Catalogues," *Speculum* 81, no. 4 (Oct. 2006), 1150–57.

example of the benefit of the methods of digital humanities is the virtual reconstruction of the library of the French king Charles V and his family, with links to books that survive today in libraries, by the *Europeana Regia* project.[5]

Considerable obstacles to the productive use of digitized material remain, however. Two seem primary: first, the variation in terminology from one document to another, for example, as seen in this book in the diamond of Blanche of Navarre that might have been a loose diamond, except that the inventory of Jeanne of Evreux called it a diamond ring; and second, the tendency in digitization to flatten variation in sources. Testaments and inventories are different in the way that they assemble information, occasionally crucially different. In this project, where I have foregrounded Blanche's voice as an important part of her testament, an assessment of her collection without it – a list of objects that could be compared to other lists of objects – would strip it of a great deal of meaning. That said, the power of computing to look across dozens of collections at the same time for patterns is alluring. Might we find that particular saints were suited to the devotional collections of men or women, or across other more minor categories like women with the name of Blanche? In my study, I have come across hints of patterns, such as the hand and finger reliquaries of Saint Louis in the collections of French royal women; such patterns could be confirmed with more data. What such a sustained consideration of royal collections would also reveal is what is left out of collections. Blanche of Navarre does not seem to have owned a single ivory sculpture, if we can assume that the few objects for which a material is not named (three reliquaries, for example) were not made of ivory. Barbara Drake Boehm has noted that Jeanne of Evreux owned only two ivories, arguing that she did not prefer them, in contrast to the earlier patrons Mahaut of Artois and Clémence of Hungary who owned many.[6] Establishing such larger patterns of aesthetic preference or taste in ownership would be a benefit of greater digitization and study of late medieval testaments.

Another implication of the study of Blanche's testament and the objects contained within it is the importance of cross-cultural comparison. Blanche lived in and near Paris for nearly her entire life, but the collections of the kings of Navarre in their residence of Olite near Pamplona, that of her sister Agnes in Orthez in southern France, and of her youngest sister Jeanne, in Brittany, among others, would have been influential in Blanche's own collecting prac-

---

5 <http://www.europeanaregia.eu/en/historical-collections/library-charles-v-family>.
6 Barbara Drake Boehm, "Le mécénat de Jeanne d'Évreux," in *1300 ... L'art au temps de Philippe le Bel. Actes du colloque international, Galeries nationales du Grand Palais, 24 et 25 juin 1998*, ed. Danielle Gaborit-Chopin and François Avril, with Marie-Cécile Bardos (Paris, 2001), p. 24.

tices and in her dissemination of her possessions. Blanche herself signaled the importance of her farflung family ties by leaving so many of her possessions to family members in Navarre. Comparative study of such collections is affected by the limitations and expense of travel and scholarly research and the various languages in which archival records were written and can be accessed today. One example of the value of such an approach is the appreciation of the implications of the record of the room hangings that arrived in Pamplona from Cherbourg in 1401 for the princess Blanca of Navarre from Blanche, queen of France; study of such an object is richer with a depth of understanding of the artistic production of both the French and the Navarrese court.

Appendices: Gifts and Their Recipients

1 Gifts of Books

Description of the gifts of books, excerpted from the bequests, in the order listed in the will (followed by the number in Delisle's edition of the will)	Recipients
Vie de Saint Louis ["Item nous laissons à l'ostel Dieu de Vernon un reliquiaire d'argent que deux anges tiennent, là où il y a une jointe de monseigneur saint Loys de France, et avecques ce un livre de la vie monseigneur saint Loys de France qui est en françoys, pour lire aux dames quant elles veilleront à l'ostel, pour avoir memoire de saint Loys de qui ilz sont fondez."] (Delisle 35)	Hôtel-Dieu, Vernon
Book with good teachings, beginning "Audi fili Israel..."; had belonged to Jeanne of Burgundy ["Et avecques ce un de noz livres qui se commance *Audi fili Israel*, et y a pluseurs bons enseignemens, et fu à ma ditte dame la royne Jehanne de Bourgongne, et lui prions que elle le vueille garder sa vie durant pour amour de nous."] (Delisle 195)	Isabeau of Bavaria (c. 1370–1435)
Breviary of Saint Louis ["Item nous laissons à nostre très chier et très amé neveu le roy de Navarre le breviaire qui fu monseigneur le roy saint Loys de France, lequel l'ange lui apporta en la chartre quant il fu pris des ennemis de la foy, et fu monseigneur le roy Phelippe, son filz ainsné, qui mourust en Arragon, mary de madame la royne Marie, nostre besaiole, et le lui donna en sa vie. Et depuis est venu de hoir en hoir de la lignée monseigneur saint Loys. Et le nous donna nostre frère le roy de Navarre, son père. Et pour reverence et la sainteté de monseigneur saint Loys, et que par grace il est venu de la ligne de nous, et depuis que nous eusmes le dit breviaire promeismes à nostre dit frère que il retourneroit en nostre ligne, nous voulons et ordonnons que à nostre dit neveu il demeure, et desormais ensuivament à ses successeurs, senz estre aucunement estrange, et les requerons que ilz le facent tousjours garder comme precieux et noble jouel de venu de noz anccesseurs, et qu'il ne parte point de la lignie."] (Delisle 196)	Charles III, king of Navarre (1361–1425)

© KONINKLIJKE BRILL NV, LEIDEN, 2016 | DOI 10.1163/9789004318830_010

GIFTS AND THEIR RECIPIENTS

Description of the gifts of books, excerpted from the bequests, in the order listed in the will (followed by the number in Delisle's edition of the will)	Recipients
Chroniques de France ["nostre livre des Croniques de France"] (Delisle 197)	Charles III, king of Navarre (cont.)
Book of hours, her "most beautiful," had belonged to her mother ["Item nous laissons à nostre très chier filz le duc de Berry, noz plus belles heures, que nostre très chiere dame et mère, que Dieux pardoint, nous lessa à son trespassement."] (Delisle 198)	John, duke of Berry (1340–1416)
Psalter with which Saint Louis learned to read ["Item nous laissons à nostre très chier fils le duc de Bourgongne le psaltier où monseigneur saint Loys aprint: et fu à madame la grant duchesse Agnès, duchesse de Bourgongne, sa fille; et depuis la duchesse Agnès vint à nostre dicte dame la royne Jehanne de Bourgongne, sa fille; et en après à nostre dit seigneur et espoux, qu le nous donna, e nous tesmongna, et aussi firent les femmes de la dicte madame la royne qu'il nous bailla que c'estoit icellui vraiement. Si desirons qu'il soit à la ligne. Et pour ce prions à nostre dit filz que il le vueille garder et faire tenir à ses successeurs et en sa ligne, pour l'amour de ceulx dont il est venu."] (Delisle 200)	Philip, duke of Burgundy (1342–1404)
Somme le roi previously owned by Philip the Fair ["Item nous laissons à nostre très chier filz le duc d'Orleans nostre bon livre de la Somme le roy, qui fu au roy Phelippe le Bel, et est bien enluminé."] (Delisle 202)	Louis, duke of Orléans (1372–1407), brother of Charles VI
Breviary, her "best," had belonged to Jeanne of Burgundy ["Item nous laissons à nostre très chiere fille la royne de Sezille nostre breviare le milleur, qui fu a la dicte madame la royne Jehanne de Bourgongne."] (Delisle 204)	Marie of Blois (1345–1404), duchess of Anjou, known as the queen of Sicily
Book of the *Gouvernement des princes* with a *Livre des échecs* ["Et aussi nostre livre du gouvernement des princes selon theologie, et y a dedens le livre des eschaz et d'autres choses."] (Delisle 207)	Louis, duke of Bourbon (1337–1410), brother of Jeanne of Bourbon (wife of Charles V)
Psalter and prayerbook, had belonged to Blanche, nun at Longchamp ["Et aussi un livre où est le psaltier et oroisons, qui se commance *Beatus vir*, et la premiere oroison de	Jeanne of Auvergne, duchess of Berry (1378–1424)

Description of the gifts of books, excerpted from the bequests, in the order listed in the will (followed by the number in Delisle's edition of the will)	Recipients
saint Elysael, lequel est couvert d'un changant, et fu madame Blanche de Longchamp."] (Delisle 209)	Jeanne of Auvergne, duchess of Berry (cont.)
Book of *Barlaam et Josephat* and many other things, had the arms of France and Burgundy, owned by Jeanne of Burgundy ["Et aussi le livre de Josafas et Balaham et de pluseurs autres choses, et est armoié de France et de Bourgongne; et fu à madame la royne Jehanne de Bourgongne."] (Delisle 211)	Margaret of Flanders (1350–1405), duchess of Burgundy
In her 1396 will, Blanche left her a book of prayers and devotions, beginning after the calendar with *Gloria in Excelsis*, owned by the queens Marie and Jeanne. ["Et un livre d'oroisons et devocions qui fu à noz très chieres dames la royne Marie et la ditte madame la royne Jehanne d'Evreux; et le nous donna la duchesse d'Orliens, sa fille, derreniere trespassée; et se commance après le kalendrier *Gloria in excelsis Deo*."] (Delisle 213). In 1398, she substituted a breviary, use of Rome, 2 volumes, that had belonged to Jeanne of Evreux and "queen Marie." ["Premierement, pour et en lieu du livre d'oroisons et devocions que nous lessions en nostre dit premier codicille à nostre tres chiere fille la duchesse d'Orleans, lequel fu à noz très chieres dames la royne Marie et la royne Jehanne, nous voulons et ordenons que notre ditte fille ait nostre breviaire à l'usage de Romme, qui est en deux volumes, qui fu ma ditte dame la royne Jehanne."] (Delisle 405)	Valentina Visconti, duchess of Orléans (c. 1368–1408)
Book of the *Lignage du Notre-Dame* ["Item à nostre très chiere fille la duchesse de Bar, le livre du lignage de Nostre Dame et de ses suers; et est au commancement du dit livre la louenge de saint Jehan l'euvangeliste."] (Delisle 214)	Marie of Valois (1344–1404), duchess of Bar
Breviary, had belonged to her sister Jeanne at Longchamp ["Item à nostre très chiere niece la duchesse de Bretaigne, nostre breviaire, qui fu nostre seur madame Jehanne de Navarre, de Longchamp, lequel nous avons fait estoffer."] (Delisle 218)	Jeanne, duchess of Brittany (1370–1437), became queen of England in 1403

GIFTS AND THEIR RECIPIENTS

209

Description of the gifts of books, excerpted from the bequests, in the order listed in the will (followed by the number in Delisle's edition of the will)	Recipients
Miroir des dames ["Et aussi nostre livre de l'enseignement du Mirouer des dames, lequel est couvert de veluau, et a les fermoirs d'argent."] (Delisle 222) Psalter with seven pairs of hours, had belonged to her mother ["Et un psaltier qui fu nostre très chiere dame et mère, que Dieux absoille; et y a sept paires de heures et pluseurs oroisons."] (Delisle 223)	Agnes, countess of Foix (*c.* 1335–1397)
Chroniques d'outremer ["Et aussi nostre livre des Croniques d'oultre mer."] (Delisle 225)	Pierre of Navarre (1366–1412), her nephew
Book of the *Pèlerinage du monde* in which there are many prayers, and those which are said after death ["Et aussi nostre livre du pelerinage du monde, où il y a plusieurs oroisons, et est cellui qui parle après la mort."] (Delisle 229) Book of hours, the one she used every day, had belonged to her mother ["Et noz heures de Nostre Dame, où nous disons touz les jours noz heures, qui furent madame nostre mère, que Diex absoille, qui sont les meilleurs que nous aions, après celles que nous lessons à nostre dit filz de Berry."] (230)	Jeanne, viscountess of Rohan (d. 1403)
Breviary, use of Rome, purchased in Paris, binding embroidered with Annunciation and Crucifixion images ["Et aussi un breviare à l'usage de Romme, qui fu achaté à Paris, et est la couverture brodée sur satarin ynde à or et à perles, et est d'un costé l'adnunciacion, et d'autre le cruxifis."] (Delisle 233) Book of the *Pèlerinage de Jésus Christ* and much other good information ["Et aussi un rommant qui au commancement parle du pelerinage de Jhesu Crist, et pluseurs autres bons enseignemens."] (Delisle 236)	Marie of Navarre, her niece, daughter of Charles II
Book that has the four Gospels and many sermons in French, which belonged to the mother of Saint Louis of France ["Et aussi nostre livre où sont les euvangiles des quatre euvangelistes, et pluseurs sermons en françois, qui fu à l mère de monseigneur saint Loys de France."] (Delisle 238)	Louis, count of Étampes (1336–1400)

Description of the gifts of books, excerpted from the bequests, in the order listed in the will (followed by the number in Delisle's edition of the will)	Recipients
Le roman des deduis ["Et le livre du deduit des chiens et oyseaux que fist messire Gasse de la Buyne, jadiz chapellain des trois roys."] (Delisle 242)	Charles of Rohan, her nephew
Missal in French ["Et nostre messel escript en françois."] (Delisle 250)	Dame de Fontenay
Psalter with the arms of France and Champagne ["... un psaltier qui a les fermoirs l'un des armes de France et l'autre des armes de Champaigne; et en la fin du psaltier une oroison de saint Loys."] (Delisle 251)	Dame de Gisors
Roman de Sidrac ["Et nostre rommant de Sydrac."] (Delisle 256)	Dame de la Mote
Book with the *Vie des pères*, the *Dialogue de Saint Gringoire* and his *Pastoral* ["Item le livre où est la Vie des Pères, le dyalogue saint Gringoire et son Pastoral."] (Delisle 259) Missal that was used for Mass in her household [" ... le messel où lui et les autres frères chantent messe en nostre hostel et chapelle."] (Delisle 263)	Pierre Basin
Book that has many *romans* ["Et avecques ce lui laissons un livre où il y a pluseurs romans."] (Delisle 274)	Jeanne Besaine, a lady-in-waiting, her 'first' damoiselle
Book on living well and dying well ["Le livre qui aprent à bien vivre et bien morir."] (Delisle 277) *Les Miracles de Notre-Dame* ["Et pluseurs miracles de Nostre Dame."] (Delisle 278) One of Blanche's two books on surgery ["Et l'un de noz deux livres de cirurgie."] (Delisle 279) Breviary from which her daughter had learned ["Avecques le breviare qui fu Jehanne de France, nostre fille, où elle aprint, que elle a en sa garde."] (Delisle 280)	Jeanne de Rouières, a lady-in-waiting
Large book of the *Miracles de Notre-Dame* abbreviated in prose, covered with red leather; and there are many good things, to wit of Saint Baudeur, of Sainte Elysabel, of Saint	Blanche de Troussy, her goddaughter

GIFTS AND THEIR RECIPIENTS

Description of the gifts of books, excerpted from the bequests, in the order listed in the will (followed by the number in Delisle's edition of the will)	Recipients
Gile, and the Road to hell and paradise ["Et aussi un gros livre des Miracles Nostre Dame abregiées en prose, couvert de cuir rouge; et y a pluseurs bonnes choses, c'est assavoir de sainte Baudeur, de sainte Elysabel, de saint Gile et la Voie d'enfer et de paradis."] (Delisle 288)	Blanche de Troussy, her goddaughter (cont.)
Somme le roi ["Et aussi le livre de la Somme le Roy, où sont les remèdes contre les pechiez."] (Delisle 291)	Jeanne du Mesnil, a lady-in-waiting
And also the book called *Le trésor de l'âme*, and speaks of the seven mortal sins and other examples and remedies against the same and of many other things, and it is covered in green leather ["Et aussi le livre nommé le Tresor de l'ame, et parle des sept pechiez mortelx et d'aucuns examples et remèdes contre iceulx, et de pluseurs autres choses; et est couvert de cuir vert."] (Delisle 293)	Marguerite de Vymont, a lady-in-waiting
Book of *Psalterion de x cordes, Anticlaudien, Vie des Saints*, and other things ["Et le livre du Salterion de x cordes, de Anticlaudien, les vies de pluseurs sains, et moult d'autres bonnes choses."] (Delisle 297)	Margot, a lady-in-waiting
Book that teaches the devotional life and contains the testament of Jean de Meun and many sermons ["Et un livre qui enseigne la vie devote, et si contient le testament maistre Jehan de Meun, et pluseurs sermons."] (Delisle 299)	Agnote, a lady-in-waiting
A *Ci-nous dit* ["le livre de Si nous dit."] (Delisle 307) Another *Ci-nous dit* is mentioned in the 1398 codicil ["le livre de Si nous dit"], probably identical to the first. (Delisle 425)	Jeanette Sante, daughter of a household member (Oudart de Venderez)
Book of the *Gouvernement des princes* ["Et le livre du gouvernement des princes selon philosofie, et le fist frère Gille l'augustin."] (Delisle 315)	Robert de Cresserel, companion of her confessor
Book on surgery ["l'un de noz livres de cirurgie."] (Delisle 427)	Symonnete

212 APPENDICES

2 Gifts of Reliquaries, Altarpieces, and Paintings

Description of the gifts of reliquaries to religious foundations, excerpted from the bequests, in the order listed in the will (followed by the number in Delisle's edition of the will)	Recipient
To the monks of Bourgfontaine: a large silver image of Our Lady who holds in her hand a small piece of crystal, which has a fleur-de-lis, and inside the milk of the Virgin Mary, and at the foot of the image are many relics. ["Item nous laissons aux diz religieux de Borfontaine un grant ymaige d'argent de Nostre Dame qui tient en sa main un poy de cristal, duquel ist une fleur de liz, et y a dedenz du let Nostre Dame; et ou pié de l'ymaige a de pluseurs reliques."] (Delisle 21)	Abbey of Bourgfontaine
Silver-gilt angel holding relic of Saint Christopher and many other saints. ["Et si laissons à la ditte abbaye un ange d'argent doré qui tient un reliquiaire, où il a des reliques de saint Cristofle et de pluseurs autres sains."] (Delisle 25)	Abbey of Mortemer, near Lyons-la-Forêt
Small reliquary shaped like a tower with the relics of Saint Valentine, on a high foot of silver. ["Et si laissons à la ditte abbaye un petit reliquiaire en maniere d'une tournelle, où il a des reliques de saint Valentin; et est assiz sur un haut pié d'argent."] (Delisle 26)	Abbey of L'Isle-Dieu (Perruel)
Silver reliquary box with a bell tower that is in my *clotet*; and there are many relics in it, especially under the crucifix which is cut in alabaster on a red stone, there are the relics of the companions of Saint Maurice, and in the other part, which is cut similarly, it has the relics of the 11,000 Virgins. ["une chasse d'argent à clochier qui est en nostre dit clotet; et y a pluseurs reliques; par especial, desoubz le cruxefiz qui y est entaillée d'alebastre, sur une pierre vermeille, a des reliques des compaignons monseigneur saint Morice; et en l'autre partie, qui est entaillée semblablement, a des reliques des XIiii vierges."] (Delisle 27)	Abbey of Notre-Dame du Val, near Beaumont
Silver statuette of Saint Didier that has his relics. ["Et si laissons à la ditte abbaye un ymaige d'argent de monseigneur saint Didier, où il a de ses reliques."] (Delisle 28)	Abbey of Saint Martin, Pontoise

GIFTS AND THEIR RECIPIENTS

Description of the gifts of reliquaries to religious foundations, excerpted from the bequests, in the order listed in the will (followed by the number in Delisle's edition of the will)	Recipient
Cross of which the foot is silver and the cross is crystal, and behind which there is the True Cross. ["et aussi une croix dont le pié est d'argent et la croix de cristal, et y a derriere de la vraye croix Nostre Seigneur."] (Delisle 29)	Abbey of Bellozanne
Silver statuette of Saint John the Baptist that I am accustomed to put on my great altar on feast days [no relics are mentioned]. ["un ymage d'argent de monseigneur saint Jehan Baptiste, que nous avons acoustumé de mettre sur nostre grant autel aux festes."] (Delisle 30)	Abbey of Beaubec
Small silver reliquary from my *clotet* which has relics; the crystal in the middle has part of the leg of Saint Loup and that of Saint Leonard, and over it is a crucifix. ["petit reliquaire d'argent de nostre clotet, où il a des reliques, où, dedens le cristal qui est ou milieu, a de la jambe saint Leu et de celle de saint Lienart, et y a dessus un cruxefiz."] (Delisle 31)	Trésor Notre-Dame near Baudemont
Reliquary of Saint Lawrence, which is in my small *clotet*, where there is a grid with Saint Lawrence on it and two men of silver who stoke the fire, and [in which] there are many other relics. ["un reliquaire de saint Laurens, qui est en nostre petit clotet, où il a un greil et saint Laurens dessus, et deux hommes d'argent qui atisent et souflent le feu, et y a de pluseurs autres reliques."] (Delisle 32)	Priory of Saint Laurent
Small silver reliquary where there are three trestles with two turrets on two sides, and the large tower has the oil of Saint Catherine and in the turrets there are relics of Saint Christine and Saint Margaret. ["un petit reliquaire d'argent, où il a trois tresteaux à deux tourelles aux deux coustez, et en la grant tour a de l'uile saintte Katherine, et aux tourelles a des reliques de saintte Crestine et de saintte Marguerite."] (Delisle 33)	Church of Gomerfontaine (near Gisors)

Description of the gifts of reliquaries to religious foundations, excerpted from the bequests, in the order listed in the will (followed by the number in Delisle's edition of the will)	Recipient
Small reliquary where there are the relics of the 11,000 Virgins under a round crystal, and around it there are many other relics, and on the back of the reliquary is incised an image of Saint Margaret. ["un petit reliquaire où il a des reliques des onze mille vierges dessoubz un cristal qui est ront, et environ a de pluseurs autres reliques, et au doz du reliquiaire a enchiselé un ymage de saintte Margarite."] (Delisle 34)	Church of Sausseusse in Vernon
Silver reliquary held by two angels which contains a joint of Saint Louis of France and with this a book of the Life of Saint Louis which is in French, for these women to read when they come to the Hôtel Dieu, to remember Saint Louis who founded it. ["un reliquiaire d'argent que deux anges tiennent, là où il y a une jointe de monseigneur saint Loys de France, et avecques ce un livre de la vie monseigneur saint Loys de France qui est en françoys, pour lire aux dames quant elles veilleront à l'ostel, pour avoir memoire de saint Loys de qui ilz sont fondez."] (Delisle 35)	Hôtel-Dieu of Vernon
Statuette of Saint Louis of Marseille whose cloak is painted with the arms of Sicily and who holds in his hand a reliquary with relics inside. ["un ymaige de saint Loys de Marseille, dont son mantel est paint des armes de Sezille, et tient en sa main un reliquiaire où il a dedens de ses reliques."] (Delisle 36)	Franciscans of Vernon
Small silver statuette of Saint John the Baptist, which is one from my *clotets*, and he holds in his hands relics and a rather high engraving which has six squares and escutcheons, one of which is the arms of France and the other is my arms. ["un petit ymage d'argent de monseigneur saint Jehan Baptiste, qui est un de noz clotez, et tient entre ses mains de ses reliques, et est sur un entaillement assez hautelet, lequel entaillement est à six carrés et à six escussons, dont l'un est de France et l'autre de noz armes."] (Delisle 37)	Franciscans of Pontoise

GIFTS AND THEIR RECIPIENTS

Description of the gifts of reliquaries to religious foundations, excerpted from the bequests, in the order listed in the will (followed by the number in Delisle's edition of the will)	Recipient
Gold reliquary that hangs in my *clotet*, where there is a nail which was made of one of the nails of Our Lord, which the duchess of Orléans left me in her testament; it belonged to the queen Jeanne. And I wish and order that they keep it in their church perpetually for love of them and of me. ["Item nous laissons au couvent des frères du Carme de Paris un reliquiaire d'or qui pent en nostre clotet, où il y a un clouet qui fu fait d'un des cloux Nostre Seigneur, lequel nostre dicte fille la duchesse d'Orléans nous lessa en son testament; et fu a madame la royne Jehanne. Et voulons et ordonnons que ilz le gardent en leur dicte englise perpetuelment comme digne saintuaire et pour l'amour d'elles et de nous."] (Delisle 395) *Discussed in chapter 1.*	Carmelites of Paris
Commissioned: three sculpted reliquaries of the Virgin Mary with Blanche kneeling. ["Item, pour la singuliere et especial devocion que nous avons aux eglises de Nostre Dame de Evreux, de Nostre Dame de Vernon et de Nostre Dame de Meleun, que nous avons longuement tenuz en douaire, nous avons ordonné estre fait trois ymages de Nostre Dame et de une royne à genoulx, assis sur un entablement, de six ou de sept mars d'argent doré chascune, pour les donner aux dittes trois eglises, et les garnir des reliques que nous avons de Nostre Dame. Si voulons que, ou cas que en nostre vivant ne seroient par nous baillées aux dittes eglises, que noz diz executeurs les facent faire à noz armes et bien garnir des dittes reliques, et de leur envoier et delivrer de par nous pour perpetuel memore de nous."] (Delisle 529)	For the churches of Notre Dame in Vernon, Evreux, and Melun
Commisioned: reliquary of Saint Bartholomew. ["Item nous faisons faire un reliquiaire de saint Barthelemy, pour le garnir d'une jointe d'un de ses doiz que nous avons, et le donner par devocion à aucune eglise de saint Berthelemy. Si voulons que, ou cas que en nostre vivant n'en aurions ordené, que noz diz executeurs le baillent et delivrent de par nous à l'eglise de Saint Berthelemy devant le palais de Paris, ou cas que il n'y en auroit point, ou autre part où ilz verront que bon sera à faire."] (Delisle 530)	A church of Saint Bartholomew

Description of the gifts of reliquaries to individuals excerpted from the bequests, in the order listed in the will (followed by the number in Delisle's edition of the will)	Recipient
I leave to the king of France a belt of gold braid with lozenges decorated with pearls and the fleur-de-lis of France, and these lozenges open, and inside there are many relics; this belt was given by the queen Jeanne of Burgundy to her spouse Philip VI, to wear into battle. ["Premierement nous laissons à nostre très chier et très amé sires et filz le roy de France une sainture de bisete d'or trait à losenges de perles aux armes de France à ys d'or, qui se euvrent, et y a pluseurs bonnes reliques; laquelle sainture nostre très chiere dame madame la royne Jehanne de Bourgongne fist faire pour nostre très chier seigneur et espoux le roy Phelippe, que Diex absoille, pour porter sur lui quant il aloit en guerre."] (Delisle 192) *Discussed in chapter 5.*	Charles VI
Gold pendant cross with five balas rubies, four sapphires, and nine pearls, that opens and inside is a relic of the True Cross. ["Item nous laissons à nostre très chiere fille la royne de France une croix d'or à pendre à un clotet, où il y a cinq balais, quatre saphirs et neuf perles, laquelle se euvre, et y a dedens de la vraie croix."] (Delisle 194)	Isabeau of Bavaria
And a gold brooch that Philip VI attached to his chest and hung his relics on there each day. And I pray that, for love of my husband, who was his godfather, and also of me, he will keep it during his life. ["un fermail d'or que mon dit seigneur et espoux attachoit à sa poitrine, et y pendoit ses reliques chascun jour. Et lui prions que, pour l'amour de mon dit seigneur, qui fu son parrain, et de nous aussi, il le vueille garder durant sa vie."] (Delisle 201) *Discussed in chapter 5.*	Philip, duke of Burgundy

GIFTS AND THEIR RECIPIENTS   217

Description of the gifts of reliquaries to individuals excerpted from the bequests, in the order listed in the will (followed by the number in Delisle's edition of the will)	Recipient
And also a reliquary which has the hair of Our Lady, and behind it has a cameo and there are many good relics. ["Et aussy un reliquiaire, lequel est garny des cheveux Nostre Dame; et par derriere a un camahieu; et y a pluseurs bonnes reliques."] (Delisle 215)	Marie of Valois (1344–1404), Duchess of Bar
And also a tablet of gold, which has outside two cameos on both sides, and above two hands which hold a diamond; and each tablet has relics, and it was given by the king Charles to my daughter Jeanne de France. ["Et aussy unz tableaux d'or, où il a par dehors deux camahieux aux deux costez, et par dessus deux mains qui tiennent un dyamant; et en chascun tableau a reliques; et le donna le roy Charles à Jehanne de France, nostre fille."] (Delisle 217)	Jeanne (1322–1406) Duchess of Brabant
And also a reliquary of gold, that the present king gave to me, which has a piece of the True Cross, of the blood of Christ and milk of the Virgin, that the king took from the Sainte-Chapelle in Paris. ["Et aussi un reliquiaire d'or, que le roy qui à present est nous donna, où il a de la vraie croix Nostre Seigneur, de son sang et du let Nostre Dame, que le roy print en la sainte chapelle du palais à Paris."] (Delisle 219)	Jeanne, duchess of Brittany (1370–1437), became queen of England in 1403
A brooch with a chain of gold, which makes a reliquary and circle, which has a hart in the middle, of which the body is a sapphire, and around are three rubies, three diamonds, three pearls, and six emeralds, and inside there are many relics; and it was given to me by the queen Jeanne. ["Item à nostre très chier cousin le conte d'Estampes, un fermail d'or à une chaenne d'or, lequel fait reliquiaire et fermail, ouquel a un cerf ou milieu, dont le corps est d'un saphir, et autour a trois rubys, trois dyamans, treze perles et six esmeraudes, et dedens pluseurs bonnes reliques; et le nous donna madame la royne Jehanne."] (Delisle 237) *Discussed in chapter 5.*	Louis of Evreux, Count of Étampes (1336–1400)

Description of the gifts of reliquaries, altarpieces, and paintings to individuals excerpted from the bequests, in the order listed in the will (followed by the number in Delisle's edition of the will)	Recipient
A little reliquary, where there is a sapphire in the manner of a heart, and two hands holding it, and above a little Oriental ruby between two pearls, and inside some of the sponge of Our Lord and of the head of John the Baptist; which our lady and aunt the queen Jeanne gave us with great love. ["Et avecques [ce] un petit reliquiaire, où il y a un saphir en maniere d'un cuer, et le tiennent deux mains; et au dessus a un petit ruby d'Oriant entre deux perles; et dedens a de l'esponge Nostre Seigneur et du chief monseigneur saint Jehan Baptiste; lequel nostre ditte dame et tante madame la royne Jehanne nous donna par grant amour."] (Delisle 239) *Discussed in chapter 5.*	Louis of Evreux, Count of Étampes (1336–1400)
Small reliquary with relics of Saint Louis of Toulouse that is in the small *clotet* near my bed. ["Et aussi le petit reliquiaire de saint Loys de Marseille qui est en nostre petit clotet lez nostre lit."] (Delisle 246)	Dame de Préaux
A statuette of Saint Catherine where there are relics that are in the small *clotet* near my bed. ["Une ymage de sainte Katherine, où il a des reliques, qui est en nostre petit clotet lez nostre lit."] (Delisle 260)	Pierre Basin
Large altarpiece of the Nativity, that Blanche put on her great altar at Christmas and on important feast days. ["Item nous laissons à l'eglise Nostre Dame d'Evreux noz grans tableaux de la nativité Nostre Seigneur, que nous avons acoustumé à faire mettre sur le grant autel de nostre chapelle à Noel et aux bonnes festes ..."] (Delisle 38)	Notre-Dame, Evreux
Painting on wood that belonged to the dame de Bailleul. ["Et uns tableaux de bois pains qui furent à la dame de Bailleul."] (Delisle 249)	Dame de Fontenay

GIFTS AND THEIR RECIPIENTS

219

Description of the gifts of paintings to individuals excerpted from the bequests, in the order listed in the will (followed by the number in Delisle's edition of the will)	Recipient
A small round painting depicting heaven and hell that was given to Blanche of Navarre by Blanche, duchess of Orléans. ["Et unz petiz tableaux rons pains, que nous donna nostre fille la duchesse d'Orléans, où est pain[t] paradiz et enfer."] (Delisle 257)	Dame de la Mote
A painted diptych that Blanche put in her *clotet*, with the Crucifixion on one side and the Annunciation on the other. ["Uns tableaux pains, que nous mettons en nostre dit clotet, où il a un cruxifis d'un costé et une adnunciacion de Nostre Dame de l'autre."] (Delisle 261)	Pierre Basin

220 APPENDICES

3   Gifts of Wearable Reliquaries, Metalwork, and Gems

Description of the gifts of wearable reliquaries, metalwork, and gems, from the bequests, in the order listed in the will (followed by the number in Delisle's edition of the will)	Recipient
Belt of gold braid with lozenges decorated with pearls and the fleur-de-lis of France, and these lozenges open, and inside there are many relics; made by the queen Jeanne of Burgundy for Philip VI to wear into battle. ["une sainture de bisete d'or trait à losenges de perles aux armes de France à ys d'or, qui se euvrent, et y a pluseurs bonnes reliques; laquelle sainture nostre très chiere dame madame la royne Jehanne de Bourgongne fist faire pour nostre très chier seigneur et espoux le roy Phelippe, que Diex absoille, pour porter sur lui quant il aloit en guerre."] (Delisle 192) Signet ring worn by Philip VI, which I wear continuously on me, and it belonged to the king Charles [Charles IV] father of my dear daughter the duchess of Orléans, who used it, and also by my spouse after him, and I also wore it in my lifetime ["un signet que portoit mon dit seigneur, lequel nous portons continuelment sur nous, et fu au roy Charles père de nostre très chiere fille la duchesse d'Orléans, que Diex pardoint, qui en usoit, et aussi fist mon dit seigneur après lui, et nous aussi en nostre vivant."] (Delisle 193)	Charles VI
Gold brooch with a large sapphire in the middle, and around rubies, pearls, and diamonds, which belonged to Philip of Navarre [Blanche's brother]["Et aussi lui laissons un fermail d'or ront, où il a un gros saphir un milieu; et autour du fermail a rubis, perles et dyamans, lequel fu beau frère messire Phelippe de Navarre, que Diex absoille ..."] (Delisle 197)	Charles III, king of Navarre
Little diamond, which Philip VI wore, and he loved it greatly and which was given to him by the countess of Hainault, his sister. And we pray that our son for love of us will keep it. ["Et un petit dyamant, lequel nostre dit seigneur et espoux portoit sur lui, et l'amoit moult, et le lui donna la bonne contesse de Henaut, sa suer. Et prions à nostre dit filz que pour amour de nous il le vueille garder."] (Delisle 199)	John, duke of Berry

GIFTS AND THEIR RECIPIENTS 221

Description of the gifts of wearable reliquaries, metal-work, and gems, from the bequests, in the order listed in the will (followed by the number in Delisle's edition of the will)	Recipient
Gold brooch that Philip VI attached to his chest and hung his relics on there each day. And I pray that, for love of my husband, who was his godfather, and also of me, he will keep it during his life ["un fermail d'or que mon dit seigneur et espoux attachoit à sa poitrine, et y pendoit ses reliques chascun jour. Et lui prions que, pour l'amour de mon dit seigneur, qui fu son parrain, et de nous aussi, il le vueille garder durant sa vie."] (Delisle 201)	Philip, duke of Burgundy
Flat [table-cut] diamond that the king gave me at the marriage of madame Catherine of France, his sister. ["Et aussi un dyamant plat, que le roy nous donna aux noces de madame Katherine de France, sa suer."] (Delisle 203)	Louis, duke of Orléans
Crown with stones that had been a gift to Blanche's daughter from a queen Jeanne ["nous laissons à nostre très chiere fille madame Ysabel de France, nostre fillole, un chapeau d'or pierrerie, que nostre très chiere dame la royne Jehanne de Bourgongne donna à Jehanne de France, nostre fille, que Diex absoillle, que fu sa fillole, ainsi que est nostre ditte fillole la dicte madame Ysabel."] (Delisle 205)	Isabelle, daughter of Charles VI
Diamond ring that Philip VI wore on his finger ["Item à nostre très chier et très amé neveu le duc de Bourbon, un anel à dyamant, qui fu nostre dit seigneur et espoux, et le portoit en son doy."] (Delisle 206)	Louis, duke of Bourbon
To the duchess of Berry a ruby ring that my spouse gave to me, and since I gave it to the queen Jeanne d'Evreux, who left it to Jeanne of France my daughter. ["Item à nostre très chiere fille la duchesse de Berry un annel ruby, lequel nostre dit seigneur et espoux nous donna, et depuis le donnasmes à nostre très chiere dame madame la royne Jehanne d'Evreux, que Diex absoille, qui le lessa à Jehanne de France nostre fille."] (Delisle 208)	Jeanne d'Auvergne, duchess of Berry
To the duchess of Burgundy, a paternoster with pearls, with marker beads of rubies and sapphires, and an emerald in the middle, and there it has one hundred [pearls] that	Margaret of Flanders, duchess of Burgundy

Description of the gifts of wearable reliquaries, metal-work, and gems, from the bequests, in the order listed in the will (followed by the number in Delisle's edition of the will)	Recipient
the queen Jeanne d'Evreux left to our daughter. ["Item à nostre très chiere fille la duchesse de Bourgongne, unes patenostres à perles, à saigneaux de rubyz et saphirs, et une esmeraude ou milieu, et y en a cent, que nostre ditte dame madame la royne Jehanne d'Evreux lessa à nostre ditte fille."] (Delisle 210).	Margaret of Flanders, duchess of Burgundy (cont.)
To the duchess of Orléans an emerald in a ring that was given to me by the duke of Berry ["Item à nostre très chiere fille la duchesse d'Orléans, une esmeraude en un annel, que nous donna nostre filz de Berry."] (Delisle 212)	Valentina Visconti, duchess of Orléans
To the duchess of Brabant a gold paternoster with gold marker beads enameled with the arms of France; and there is a ruby in the middle. ["Item à nostre très chiere cousin[e] la duchesse de Breban unes patesnostres d'or à saigneaux d'or esmaillez aux armes de France; et y a un ruby ou milieu."] (Delisle 216)	Jeanne, duchess of Brabant
Diamond that belonged to the count of Evreux, my grandfather, which the queen Jeanne left to me at her death. And I pray that he will keep this diamond all his life for love of this man and me. ["un dyamant qui fu feu monseigneur le conte d'Evreux, nostre ayeul, que nous lessa ma dicte dame la royne Jehanne à son trespassement. Et lui prions que le dit dyamant il vueille garder toute sa vie pour l'amour de nostre dit seigneur et de nous."] (Delisle 226)	Pierre of Navarre
Brooch with a chain of gold, which makes a reliquary and circle, which has a hart in the middle, of which the body is a sapphire, and around are three rubies, three diamonds, three pearls, and six emeralds, and inside there are many relics; and it was given to me by the queen Jeanne. ["Item à nostre très chier cousin le conte d'Estampes, un fermail d'or à une chaenne d'or, lequel fait reliquiaire et fermail, ouquel a un cerf ou milieu, dont le corps est d'un saphir, et autour a trois rubys, trois dyamans, treze perles et six esmeraudes, et dedens pluseurs bonnes reliques; et le nous donna madame la royne Jehanne."] (Delisle 237)	Louis, count of Étampes

GIFTS AND THEIR RECIPIENTS

223

Description of the gifts of wearable reliquaries, metal-work, and gems, from the bequests, in the order listed in the will (followed by the number in Delisle's edition of the will)	Recipient
Little reliquary, where there is a sapphire in the manner of a heart, and two hands holding it, and above a little Oriental ruby between two pearls, and inside some of the sponge of Our Lord and of the head of John the Baptist; which our lady and aunt the queen Jeanne gave us with great love. ["Et avecques [ce] un petit reliquiaire, où il y a un saphir en maniere d'un cuer, et le tiennent deux mains; et au dessus a un petit ruby d'Oriant entre deux perles; et dedens a de l'esponge Nostre Seigneur et du chief monseigneur saint Jehan Baptiste; lequel nostre ditte dame et tante madame la royne Jehanne nous donna par grant amour."] (Delisle 239)	Louis, count of Étampes (cont.)
Cup of gold covered with lilies, decorated with the arms of my aforementioned lady and aunt [this seems to be Jeanne of Evreux, named two bequests prior] and mine. ["un gobelet d'or couvert à ys gregoiz, armoiez des armes de nostre dicte dame et tante et des nostres."] (Delisle 241) *Discussed in chapter 6.*	Charles of Rohan
To the dame de Préaux, a gold paternoster in the manner of a small hollow stick and there is one hundred [beads?], and gold marker beads, where there is a bit of enamel, which belonged to Jeanne my daughter. ["Item à nostre très chiere cousine la dame de Preaulx, unes patenostres d'or en façon de baton creux coppé, et en y a un cent, et les saigneaux d'or parmy, où il y a un poy d'esmail, qui furent à Jehanne de France, nostre fille."] (Delisle 243) Small cross that hangs in my closet, where there is in the middle a cameo and around four sapphires, eight pearls rather large and many small. ["une petite croix qui pent en nostre clotet, où il y a ou milieu un camahieu, et autour quatre saphirs, huit perles assez grosses et pluseurs menues."] (Delisle 244)	Dame de Préaux
One of my best silver-gilt paternosters which they will find in my coffers ["Et unes des meilleurs patenostres dorées qui seront trouvées en noz coffres."] (Delisle 252)	Dame de Gisors

Description of the gifts of wearable reliquaries, metal-work, and gems, from the bequests, in the order listed in the will (followed by the number in Delisle's edition of the will)	Recipient
Silver-gilt cup with a cover worth about 20 francs. ["Et aussi un gobelet d'argent doré à couvercles du pris de environ vint frans."] (Delisle 253)	Dame de Gisors (cont.)
To Blanchete, my goddaughter, daughter of Robert le Grant, my butler, a gold crown weighing five ounces five esterlins, with ten plates with eight pearls in each plate, and ten rubies with emeralds between two little [rubies], and it cost me 72 francs. ["Item à Blanchete, nostre fillole, fille de Robert le Grant, nostre eschanson, un chapel d'or pesant V onces V estrelins, à X assiettes à VIII perles en l'assiette, et X rubis que esmeraudes, assis entre II petis; et nous cousta LXXII frans."] (Delisle 300)	Blanchete, daughter of Robert le Grant
To Blanchete, my goddaughter, daughter of Marguerite de Vymont, my damoiselle, a gold crown weighing five ounces ten esterlins, with ten plates with pearls, in each plate six pearls, and in the middle a small ruby or an emerald, and nine rubies as well as emeralds between two small [stones] and it is precious stonework of Alexandria, and it cost me 46 francs ["Item à Blanchete, nostre fillole, fille de Marguerite de Vimont, nostre damoiselle, un chapel d'or pesant V onces X esterlins, à X assietes piegnes de perles, en chascune assiete VI perles, et ou milieu un petit ruby ou une esmeraude, et IX que rubys que esmeraudes entre deux petis, et est de pierrerie d'Alexandrie, et nous cousta XLVI frans."] (Delisle 302)	Blanchete, daughter of Marguerite de Vymont
To Blanchete, my goddaughter, daughter of Jehan de Poupaincourt, a small gold crown of Alexandrian precious stonework, that I bought to lend to the weddings of my servants and friends. ["Item à Blanchete, nostre fillole, fille de maistre Jehan de Poupaincourt, une petite couronne d'or pierrerie d'Alexandrie, que nous feismes pieça achater pour prester à faire les noces de noz serviteurs et amis."] (Delisle 305)	Blanchete, daughter of Jehan de Poupaincourt

GIFTS AND THEIR RECIPIENTS   225

Description of the gifts of wearable reliquaries, metal-work, and gems, from the bequests, in the order listed in the will (followed by the number in Delisle's edition of the will)	Recipient
To Blanche, my goddaughter, daughter of the sire d'Aumont, a gold crown of Alexandrian stonework and other stonework, and where there are large fleurons and small fleurons of sapphire. And I lend it to my women when they are married in my presence. ["Item à Blanche, nostre fillole, fille du sire d'Aumont, une couronne d'or de pierrerie d'Alexandrie et d'autre pierrerie; et y a grans fleurons et petis florons de saphirs. Et la prestons à noz femmes quant elle sont mariées en nostre presence."] (Delisle 306)	Blanche, daughter of the sire d'Aumont

226 APPENDICES

4 Gifts of Textiles

Description of the gifts of textiles, excerpted from the bequests, in the order listed in the will (followed by the number in Delisle's edition of the will)	Recipient
Set of black liturgical textiles purchased from the archbishop of Sens ["nostre chapelle noire, que nous achatasmes de l'arcevesque de Sens, qui est toute entire et complete."] (Delisle 23)	Notre-Dame, Vernon
Set of black liturgical textiles with three copes ["nostre chapelle de veluau noir à trois chappes seulement."] (Delisle 24)	Saint Hildevert, Gournay
Embroidered image of the Virgin Mary ["un ymage de Nostre Dame qui est de bordure."] (Delisle 31)	Trésor de Notre-Dame, Baudemont
Set of red velvet liturgical textiles decorated with suns and squirrels ["nostre chapelle de veluau vermeil entière semée de souleux et d'escureux."] (Delisle 39)	Notre-Dame, Pamplona
Yellow velvet liturgical textiles embroidered and studded with silver rosettes ["une autre chapelle de veluau jaune entière brodée et semée de rosetes d'argent."] (Delisle 40)	Notre-Dame, Melun
A surplice and an amice ["Item nous voulons que chascun de nos chapellains de nostre chappelle que nous aurons en nostre hostel au jour de nostre tres-passement ait un de noz surpeliz et une aumusse que ilz ont acoustumé de mettre en nostre ditte chappelle, selon l'adviz et ordonnance de noz executeurs."] (Delisle 170)	To each chaplain of her household
Livery for her household servants ["Item nous voulons et ordenons que, se la livrée de noz serviteurs est achatée ou paiée ou la plus grant partie, que elle leur soit livrée senz delay à chascun selon son estat, et tout aussi que nous ferions faire à nostre vivant, et comme nous l'avons acoustumé de faire. Et requerons à noz diz serviteurs que en memoire de nous eulx facent faire leurs robes comme ilz feissent faire à nostre vivant, pour ce que ce sera la derreniere."] (Delisle 173)	Household servants

GIFTS AND THEIR RECIPIENTS

Description of the gifts of textiles, excerpted from the bequests, in the order listed in the will (followed by the number in Delisle's edition of the will)	Recipient
Beds, fully furnished ["Item nous voulons et ordonnons que après nostre trespassement noz damoiselles aient les liz où ilz ont geu en nostre hostel tous garniz, et aussi que ilz aient leurs despens bien et honnestement pour eux en retourner là où ilz verront que bon sera à demourer pour eux, et que ilz y soient conduiz et menez à noz despens."] (Delisle 174)	Ladies-in-waiting, each gets the bed she had used
My room hangings embroidered with lions and the arms of France, Burgundy, and Evreux, complete. "...nostre chambre broudée a lyons, des armes de France, de Bourgongne et d'Evreux toute entière." (Delisle 197)	Charles III
A pair of loose bedclothes, best, to put on women in labor ["une paire de noz draps à lit deliez, des millieurs, à mettre à dames pour leurs gesines."] (Delisle 220)	Jeanne, duchess of Brittany
Complete set of gray room hangings ["nostre chambre encendrée toute entiere."] (Delisle 221)	Agnes, countess of Foix
Complete set of room hangings with a banded or diamond pattern ["nostre chambre fretée entiere."] (Delisle 224)	Pierre of Navarre
Red quilted room hangings without armorials (this bequest changed in 1398, see below) ["nostre chambre vermeille pourpointée senz armoierie."] (Delisle 227) A textile made of red quilted fabric that had angels holding the arms of France and Navarre ["les tappis de mesmes, où il a en aucuns angres qui tiennent les armes de France et de Navarre."] (Delisle 228) A pair of loose bedclothes, the best after the ones given to the duchess of Brittany ["une paire de noz draps à lit deliez, les milleurs après ceulx dessus diz."] (Delisle 231)	Jeanne, viscountess of Rohan
Complete set of green room hangings decorated with roses and the arms of Blanche ["nostre chambre vert entiere à rosiers armoiés de noz armes."] (Delisle 232) Breviary with a purple satin cover embroidered with gold and pearls, on one side the Annunciation and on the other the Crucifixion ["un breviare à l'usage de Romme, qui fu achaté à Paris, et est la couverture brodée sur satarin ynde d'or et à perles, et est d'un costé	Marie of Navarre

Description of the gifts of textiles, excerpted from the bequests, in the order listed in the will (followed by the number in Delisle's edition of the will)	Recipient
l'adnunciacion, et d'autre le cruxifis."] (Delisle 233). *This breviary is discussed in chapter 3.* A hat hanging with strings of pearls, diasper of gold on black camacas ["un chapperon pendant à troches de perles, dyapré d'or sur un camocas noir. Et voulons que se le dit chapperon n'estoit fourré que on le face fourrer en letesses."] (Delisle 234)[1] A set of loose bedclothes, "my best" ["une paire de noz milleurs draps deliez à lit"] (Delisle 235)	Marie of Navarre (cont.)
A complete set of green room hangings, the one that is put up in my house when my friends come before me, and it has five circles in each a lozenge of my arms that is surrounded by white and purple leaves ["nostre chambre vert entiere, que l'en tent en nostre hotel quant noz amis viennent devers nous; et est à v compas, en chascun une losenge de noz armes qui est environnée d'un compas fueilleté de feuilles blanches et yndes."] (Delisle 240)	Charles of Rohan
A set of loose bedclothes, best after those already mentioned ["Et une paire de noz draps à lit deliez, après les lessiez dessus diz."] (Delisle 245)	Marguerite, dame de Préaux
Long robe that she should choose ["une robe longue de nostre corps, celle que elle vouldra choisir."] (Delisle 248)	Dame de Fontenay
A robe, the best that she would like to choose after the one previously mentioned ["une robe de nostre corps, la meilleur que elle vouldra choisir après la dessus dite."] (Delisle 255)	Dame de la Mote
A set of liturgical textiles of three parts, the frontier, dossier, and chasuble of gold of Lucca, the orphreys embroidered with field of gold of Blanche's arms and with birds ["une chapelle des trois garnemens, c'est assavoir frontier, dossier et chasuble d'or de Luques; et est l'orfrois de la ditte chapelle de broudure à champ	Pierre Basin

---

1 In his edition, Delisle noted that the scribe made a mistake here, attaching the phrase starting "Et voulons que le dit chapperon ..." to the discussion of the book of the pilgrimage of Christ a few lines down (no. 236); "Testament de Blanche de Navarre," p. 32.

GIFTS AND THEIR RECIPIENTS 229

Description of the gifts of textiles, excerpted from the bequests, in the order listed in the will (followed by the number in Delisle's edition of the will)	Recipient
d'or de noz armes et à papegaux."] (Delisle 262) Altar textiles ["... un corporalier et les corporaux, six touailles d'autel plaines et une touaille parée ..."] (Delisle 263) A set of red serge room hangings ["une chambre de sarge vermeille."] (Delisle 264)	Pierre Basin (cont.)
A complete robe, the best after that given to the dame de la Mote ["une des noz robes entiere, la milleur après celle de la dame de la Mote"] (Delisle 273) A set of blue room hangings made of serge de Caen ["Et aussi une chambre azurée des sarges de Caen."] (Delisle 275)	Jeanne la Besaine, first lady-in-waiting
A robe, the best after the ones previously mentioned ["une de noz robes, la milleur après les dessus dittes."] (Delisle 276) Two common beds, two sets of bedclothes for each, two covers for them (with the bed where she sleeps that was left to her above), six table linens, twelve towels the best to take from the office of the pantry; two dozen pewter bowls, a dozen plates, two quarts and two pewter ewers to take from the sauce kitchen and butler's kitchen.] ["Item lui laissons pour son mesnage les choses qui ensuivent: c'est assavoir deuz liz communs de nostre fourriere, deux paires de draps pour chascun, et deux couvertoirs de connins pour iceulx, avecques le lit où elle gist, que nous lui laissons en nostre grant testament, item six nappes, douze touailles des milleurs à prendre en l'office de panneterie; deux douzaines d'escuelles d'estain, une douzaine de plas, deux quartes et deux aiguieres d'estain à prendre en la sausserie et eschançonnerie."] (Delisle 282) Room hangings of green toile ["Et aussi une chambre de toille vert."] (Delisle 285)	Jeanne de Rouières
A complete robe ["une robe entiere de nostre corps."] (Delisle 287)	Blanche, dame de Troussy
A robe ["une de noz robes après celles devant dictes."] (Delisle 290)	Jeanne du Mesnil

Description of the gifts of textiles, excerpted from the bequests, in the order listed in the will (followed by the number in Delisle's edition of the will)	Recipient
A long robe ["une de noz robes longues."] (Delisle 292)	Marguerite de Vymont
A long robe ["une de noz robes longues."] (Delisle 295)	Margot le Grant
A long robe ['une de noz robes longues."] (Delisle 298)	Agnote
The models, gold, and silk that ... are in the little coffers ... ["les exemplaires, l'or, et la soie que nous aurons à ovrer qui seront en noz petiz coffrets, à departir entre elles."] (Delisle 308)	Jeanne du Mesnil, Marguerite de Vymont, Margot le Grant, Jeanette Sante, and those who work on the silk
Short robe ["une de noz robes courtes."] (Delisle 311; affirmed in the 1398 codicil, Delisle 426)	Washerwoman; in the 1398 codicil she is called Jeanne
Short robe ["une de noz robes courtes."] (Delisle 312; affirmed in the 1398 codicil, Delisle 427)	Symmonete, healer ['Symonnete qui sert les malades"; in the 1398 codicil she is called a chambermaid ["femme de chambre"]
Short robe ["une de noz robes courtes."] (Delisle 313; affirmed in the 1398 codicil, Delisle 428)	Gilete, chambermaid
In place of the red quilted room hangings from the 1396 will, room hangings with sections with blessed lilies and the pots are decorated with Blanche's arms, recently made ["Item, pour et en lieu de la chambre vermeille pourpointe senz armoierie, que nous lessions à nostre très chier seur madame Jehanne de Navarre, vicontesse de Rohan, nous lui laissons par ce present codicille nostre chambre toute entiere à pos à liz benoists passans dedens; et sont les pos armoiez de noz armes, laquelle nous avons nagaires fait faire. Et neantmoins voulons que elle ait les autres choses que nous lui laissons en nostre dit premier codicille, si comme en icellui est contenu"] (Delisle 409)	Jeanne, viscountess of Rohan
Room hangings with a B, decorated with Blanche's arms, recently made entirely new ["Item nous laissons par ce present codicille à nostre très chiere niece madame Blanche de Navarre, fille de nostre neveu le roy de Navarre, nostre chambre entiere à B, armoiée de noz armes, laquelle nous avons nagaires fait faire toute neufve."] (Delisle 410)	Blanche of Navarre, daughter of Charles III

Bibliography

Primary Sources

Paris, Bibliothèque nationale, MS fr. 20684, pièce 214 (record of birth of Jeanne of France, daughter of Philip VI and Blanche of Navarre).
Pau, Archives départementales des Pyrénées-Atlantiques, E 525 (contemporary copy of the testament of Blanche of Navarre).
Pau, Archives départementales des Pyrénées-Atlantiques, E 519 (1330 financial records for the household of Philip and Jeanne of Navarre).

Internet Sources

ARLIMA, Archives de littérature du Moyen Âge. <http://www.arlima.net>.
Europeana Regia website on the collection of Charles V. <http://www.europeanaregia. eu/en/historical-collections/library-charles-v-family>.
Testaments enregistrés au Parlement de Paris sous le règne de Charles VI. <http://corpus. enc.sorbonne.fr/testaments>.

Secondary Sources

Ackley, Joseph. "Re-approaching the Western Medieval Church Treasury Inventory, c. 800–1250." *Journal of Art Historiography* 11 (December 2014), 1–37.
Acres, Alfred. "The Middle of Diptychs." In *Push Me, Pull You*, 1:595–621.
Adams, Jenny. *Power Play: The Literature and Politics of Chess in the Late Middle Ages.* Philadelphia, 2006.
Adams, Tracy. *The Life and Afterlife of Isabeau of Bavaria.* Baltimore, 2010.
Alcouffe, Daniel. "Camées et vases pierres dures." In *Les fastes du gothique: le siècle de Charles V*, pp. 204–19. Paris, 1981.
Allirot, Anne-Hélène. *Filles du roy de France: princesses royales, mémoire de saint Louis et conscience dynastique (de 1270 à la fin du XIVe siècle).* Turnhout, 2010.
———. "Longchamp and Lourcine: The Role of Female Abbeys in the Construction of Capetian Memory (Late Thirteenth Century to Mid-Fourteenth Century)." In *Memory and Commemoration in Medieval Culture*, edited by Elma Brenner, Meredith Cohen, and Mary Franklin-Brown, pp. 243–60. Farnham, Surrey, UK, 2013.
Angenendt, Arnold. "Relics and Their Veneration." In *Treasures of Heaven*, pp. 19–28.
Anselme, P. *Histoire généalogique et chronologique de la maison royale de France.* 9 vols. Paris, 1726–33.

Appadurai, Arjun. "Introduction: Commodities and the Politics of Value." In *The Social Life of Things: Commodities in Cultural Perspective*, edited by Arjun Appadurai, pp. 3–63. Cambridge, 1986.

Armstrong, C.A.J. "The Piety of Cicely, Duchess of York: A Study in Late Medieval Culture." In *England, France, and Burgundy in the Fifteenth Century*, pp. 135–56. London, 1983.

L'art au temps des rois maudits: Philippe le Bel et ses fils, 1285–1328. Paris, 1998.

Art from the Court of Burgundy: Patronage of Philip the Bold and John the Fearless, 1364–1419. Cleveland, 2004.

The Art of Illumination: The Limbourg Brothers and the Belles Heures of Jean de France, Duc de Berry. New York, 2009.

Autrand, Françoise. *Charles V: le Sage.* Paris, 1994.

Bagnoli, Martina. "The Stuff of Heaven: Materials and Craftsmanship in Medieval Reliquaries." In *Treasures of Heaven*, pp. 137–47.

———. "Dressing the Relics: Some Thoughts on the Custom of Relic Wrapping in Medieval Christianity." In *Matter of Faith*, pp. 100–109.

Baron, Françoise. *Sculpture française: Moyen Âge.* Paris, 1996.

Bearne, Catherine. *Lives and Times of the Early Valois Queens: Jeanne de Bourgogne, Blanche de Navarre, Jeanne d'Auvergne et de Boulogne.* London, 1899.

Beaune, Colette, and Elodie Lequain. "Marie de Berry et les livres." In *Livres et lectures de femmes en Europe entre Moyen Âge et Renaissance*, edited by Anne-Marie Legaré, pp. 49–65. Turnhout, 2007.

Bell, Susan Groag. "Medieval Women Book Owners: Arbiters of Lay Piety and Ambassadors of Culture." In *Women and Power in the Middle Ages*, edited by Mary Erler and Maryanne Kowaleski, pp. 149–87. Athens, Ga., 1988.

Benz St. John, Lisa. *Three Medieval Queens: Queenship and the Crown in Fourteenth-century England.* Basingstoke, 2012.

Bernau, Anke. "A Christian *Corpus*: Virginity, Violence, and Knowledge in the Life of Saint Katherine of Alexandria." In *Saint Katherine of Alexandria: Texts and Contexts in Western Medieval Europe*, edited by Jacqueline Jenkins and Katherine Lewis, pp. 109–30. Turnhout, 2003.

Berné, Damien. "L'action mémorielle des princesses capétiennes à Saint-Denis au XIVe siècle." *Histoire de l'art* 63 (Oct. 2008), 35–44.

Binski, Paul. "The English Parish Church and Its Art in the Later Middle Ages: A Review of the Problem." *Studies in Iconography* 20 (1999), 1–25.

Blick, Sarah, and Laura Gelfand, eds. *Push Me, Pull You*: vol. 1, *Imaginative and Emotional Interaction in Late Medieval and Renaissance Art*; vol. 2, *Physical and Spatial Interaction in Late Medieval and Renaissance Art.* Leiden, 2011.

———. "Introduction to Volume 1." In *Push Me, Pull You*, pp. xxxvii-lii.

———. "Introduction to Volume 2." In *Push Me, Pull You*, pp. xxxv-liv.

BIBLIOGRAPHY

Boehm, Barbara Drake. "Jeanne d'Évreux: Queen of France." In *The Hours of Jeanne d'Évreux. Acc. No. 54.I.2 The Metropolitan Museum of Art, The Cloisters Collection, New York: Commentary*, pp. 35–87. Lucerne, 2000.

———. "Le mécénat de Jeanne d'Évreux." In *1300 ... l'art au temps de Philippe le Bel. Actes du colloque international, Galeries nationales du Grand Palais, 24 et 25 juin 1998*, edited by Danielle Gaborit-Chopin and François Avril, with Marie-Cécile Bardos, pp. 15–31. Paris, 2001.

Bonde, Sheila, and Clark Maines. "The Heart of the Matter: Valois Patronage of the Charterhouse at Bourgfontaine." In *Patronage: Power & Agency in Medieval Art*, edited by Colum Hourihane, pp. 77–98. Princeton, 2013.

Booton, Diane. *Manuscripts, Market, and the Transition to Print in Late Medieval Brittany*. Farnham, Surrey, UK, 2010.

Bouchot, Henri. *Inventaire des dessins exécutés pour Roger de Gaignières et conservés aux Départements des Estampes et des Manuscrits*. Paris, 1891.

Bozzolo, Carlo, and Ezio Ornato. *Pour une histoire du livre manuscrit au Moyen Âge: trois essais de codicologie quantitative*. Paris, 1980.

Brayer, Édith, and Anne-Françoise Leurquin-Labie. *La somme le roi, par frère Laurent*. Paris, 2008.

Brown, Cynthia. *The Queen's Library: Image-Making at the Court of Anne of Brittany*. Philadelphia, 2010.

Brown, Elizabeth A.R. "Death and the Human Body in the Later Middle Ages: The Legislation of Boniface VIII on the Division of the Corpse." *Viator* 12 (1981), 221–70.

———. "The King's Conundrum: Endowing Queens and Loyal Servants, Ensuring Salvation, and Protecting the Patrimony in Fourteenth-century France." In *Attitudes to the Future in the Middle Ages*, edited by John Burrow and Ian Wei, pp. 115–65. Woodbridge, UK, 2000.

———. *Saint-Denis: la basilique*. Paris, 2001.

———. "La mort, les testaments et les fondations de Jeanne de Navarre, reine de France (1273–1305)." In *Une histoire pour un royaume (XIIᵉ-XVᵉ siècle)*. *Actes du colloque Corpus Regni en hommage à Colette Beaune*, edited by A.H. Allirot, M. Gaude-Ferragu, et al., pp. 124–41, 508–10. Paris, 2010.

———. "The Parlement de Paris and the Welfare of the Dead." In *Le parlement en sa cour. Études en l'honneur du Professeur Jean Hilaire*, edited by Olivier Descamps, Françoise Hildesheimer, and Monique Morgat-Bonnet, pp. 47–73. Paris, 2012.

———. "Jeanne d'Évreux: ses testaments et leur exécution." *Le Moyen Âge* 119 (2013), 57–83.

———. "The Testamentary Strategies of Jeanne d'Évreux: The Endowment of Saint-Denis in 1343." In *Magistra Doctissima: Essays in Honor of Bonnie Wheeler*, edited by Dorsey Armstrong, Ann W. Astell, and Howell Chickering, pp. 217–47. Kalamazoo, MI, 2013.

Brunel, Ghislain. *Images du pouvoir royal: les chartes decorées des Archives nationales, XIIIe-XVe siècle.* Paris, 2005.

Bubenicek, Michelle. "Une princesse en politique et son entourage: Yolande de Flandre, comtesse de Bar et dame de Cassel (1326–1395)." In *Positions des thèses de l'École Nationale des Chartes*, pp. 28–34. Paris, 1994.

————. *Quand les femmes gouvernent. Droit et politique au XIVe siècle: Yolande de Flandre.* Paris, 2002.

Buettner, Brigitte. "Profane Illuminations, Secular Illusions: Manuscripts in Late Medieval Courtly Society." *Art Bulletin* 64, no. 1 (March 1992), 75–90.

————. "Women and the Circulation of Books." *Journal of the Early Book Society* 4 (2001), 9–31.

————. "Past Presents: New Year's Gifts at the Valois Courts c. 1400." *Art Bulletin* 83, no. 4 (Dec. 2001), 598–625.

————. "Le système des objets dans le testament de Blanche de Navarre." *CLIO: Histoire, Femmes et Sociétés* 19 (2004), 37–62.

————. "From Bones to Stones – Reflections on Jeweled Reliquaries." In *Reliquiare im Mittelalter*, edited by Bruno Reudenbach and Gia Toussaint, pp. 44–59. Berlin, 2005.

Burgess, Clive. "Late Medieval Wills and Pious Convention: Testamentary Evidence Reconsidered." In *Profit, Piety, and the Professions in Later Medieval England*, edited by Michael Hicks, pp. 14–33. Gloucester, 1990.

Burkholder, Kristen M. "Threads Bared: Dress and Textiles in Late Medieval English Wills." In *Medieval Clothing and Textiles*, vol. 1, edited by Robin Netherton and Gale Owen-Crocker, pp. 133–53. Woodbridge, UK, 2005.

Busby, Keith. *Codex and Context: Reading Old French Verse Narrative in Manuscript.* 2 vols. New York, 2002.

Bynum, Caroline Walker. *Christian Materiality: An Essay on Religion in Late Medieval Europe.* New York, 2011.

Calmette, Joseph. *The Golden Age of Burgundy: The Magnificent Dukes and Their Courts.* Translated by Doreen Weightman. New York, 1963; repr. London, 2001.

Camille, Michael. *The Medieval Art of Love.* New York, 1998.

————. "'For Our Devotion and Pleasure': The Sexual Objects of Jean, Duc de Berry." In *Other Objects of Desire: Collectors and Collecting Queerly*, edited by Michael Camille and Adrian Rifkin, pp. 7–32. Oxford, 2001.

Campbell, Marian. *Medieval Jewellery in Europe, 1100–1500.* London, 2009.

Camus, Jules. *La venue en France de Valentine Visconti, duchesse d'Orléans, et l'inventaire de ses joyaux apportés de Lombardie.* Turin, 1898.

Capetian Women. Edited by Kathleen Nolan. New York, 2003.

Carpenter, Jennifer, and Sally-Beth McLean, eds. *Power of the Weak: Studies on Medieval Women.* Urbana, IL, 1995.

BIBLIOGRAPHY

Caskey, Jill. "Whodunnit? Patronage, the Canon, and the Problematics of Agency in Romanesque and Gothic Art." In *A Companion to Medieval Art: Romanesque and Gothic in Northern Europe*, edited by Conrad Rudolph, pp. 193–212. Oxford, 2006.

Cassagnes-Brouquet, Sophie. "Decor of the Ducal Residences." In *Art from the Court of Burgundy*, pp. 140–41.

Castro, J.R. "El matrimonio de Pedro IV de Aragón y María de Navarra." *Estudios de Edad Media de la Corona de Aragon* 3 (1947–48), 55–102.

Catalogue de comptes royaux des règnes de Philippe VI et de Jean II: 1328–1364. Edited by Raymond Cazelles. Paris, 1984.

Catalogue des livres et documents historiques du cabinet de M. de Courcelles. Paris, 1834.

Caviness, Madeline H. "Patron or Matron? A Capetian Bride and a *Vade Mecum* for Her Marriage Bed." *Speculum* 68 (1993), 333–62.

———. "Anchoress, Abbess and Queen: Donors and Patrons or Intercessors and Matrons?" In *The Cultural Patronage of Medieval Women*, pp. 105–54.

Cazelles, Raymond. *La société politique et la crise de la royauté sous Philippe de Valois*. Paris, 1958.

———. "Le parti navarrais jusqu'à la mort d'Étienne Marcel." *Bulletin Philologique et Historique* 1 (1960), 839–69.

———. "Peinture et actualité politique sous les premiers Valois: Jean le Bon ou Charles, dauphin." *Gazette des Beaux-Arts* (September 1978), 53–65.

———. *La Société politique, noblesse et couronne sous Jean le Bon et Charles V*. Geneva, 1982.

Cazilhac, Jean-Marie. *Jeanne d'Evreux, Blanche de France, deux reines de France, deux douairières, durant la Guerre de Cent ans*. Paris, 2010.

Chambers, Mark. "Surcote/surcoat." In *Encyclopedia of Dress and Textiles in the British Isles*, pp. 566–67.

———. "Serge." In *Encyclopedia of Dress and Textiles in the British Isles*, p. 503.

Chambers, Mark, Elizabeth Coatsworth, and Gale R. Owen-Crocker. "Camaca." In *Encyclopedia of Dress and Textiles in the British Isles*, pp. 108–9.

Champion, Pierre. *La librairie de Charles d'Orléans*. Paris, 1910.

Chartraire, Eugène. *Les tissus anciens du trésor de la cathédrale de Sens*. Paris, 1911.

Christine de Pizan. *The Book of the City of Ladies*. Translated by Rosalind Brown-Grant. London, 1999.

Chronique de Jean le Bel. Edited by Jules Viard and Eugène Déprez. 2 vols. Paris, 1905.

Chronique des quatre premiers Valois (1327–1393). Edited by S. Luce. Paris, 1862.

Chronique des règnes de Jean II et Charles V. Edited by Roland Delachenal. 2 vols. Paris, 1917–20.

Chronique du Religieux de Saint-Denys, contenant le règne de Charles VI, de 1380 à 1422. Edited by L. Bellaguet. 6 vols. Paris, 1839–52.

Ciresi, Lisa Victoria. "Of Offerings and Kings: The Shrine of the Three Kings in Cologne and the Aachen Karlsschrein and Marienschrein in Coronation Ritual." In *Reliquiare im Mittelalter*, edited by Bruno Reudenbach and Gia Toussaint, pp. 165–83. Berlin, 2005.

Clanchy, Michael. "Did Mothers Teach Their Children to Read?" In *Motherhood, Religion, and Society in Medieval Europe, 400–1400: Essays Presented to Henrietta Leyser*, edited by Conrad Leyser and Lesley Smith, pp. 129–53. Farnham, Surrey, UK, 2011.

Clark, William W. "Signed, Sealed, and Delivered: The Patronage of Constance of France." In *Magistra Doctissima: Essays in Honor of Bonnie Wheeler*, edited by Dorsey Armstrong, Ann W. Astell, and Howell Chickering, pp. 201–16. Kalamazoo, MI, 2013.

Coatsworth, Elizabeth. "Cushioning Medieval Life: Domestic Textiles in Anglo-Saxon England." *Medieval Clothing and Textiles* 3 (2007), 1–12.

————. "Amice." In *Encyclopedia of Dress and Textiles in the British Isles*, pp. 36–37.

Cockerell, S.C. "Horae of Jeanne II, Queen of Navarre." In *A Descriptive Catalogue of the Second Series of 50 Manuscripts in the Collection of Henry Yates Thompson*, pp. 151–83. Cambridge, 1902.

Coilly, Nathalie. "La reliure d'étoffe en France dans les librairies de Charles V et de ses frères, fin XIVe- début XVe siècle." In *La reliure medieval: pour une description normalisée. Actes du colloque international (Paris, 22–24 mai 2003) organizé par l'Institut de recherche et d'histoire des texts (CNRS)*, edited by Guy Lanoë and Geneviève Grand, pp. 277–86. Turnhout, 2008.

A Companion to Medieval Art: Romanesque and Gothic in Northern Europe. Edited by Conrad Rudolph, pp. 193–212. Oxford, 2006.

Comptes de l'argenterie des rois de France au XIVe siècle. Edited by L. Douët d'Arcq. Paris, 1851.

Continuator of Guillaume of Nangis. *Chronique latine de Guillaume de Nangis.* Edited by H. Géraud. Paris, 1843.

The Cultural Patronage of Medieval Women. Edited by June Hall McCash. Athens, Ga., 1996.

Curry, Anne, and Elizabeth Matthew. "Introduction." In *Concepts and Patterns of Service in the Later Middle Ages*, edited by Anne Curry and Elizabeth Matthew, pp. xi-xxiii. Woodbridge, UK, 2000.

Couton, Docteur. "L'église Notre-Dame de Vernon." *Bulletin Amis monuments de rouennais* 11 (1911–12), 89–104.

Crist, Larry S. "The Breviary of Saint Louis: The Development of a Legendary Miracle." *Journal of the Warburg and Courtauld Institutes* 28 (1965), 319–23.

Dalas, Martine. *Corpus des sceaux français du Moyen Âge: les sceaux des rois et de regence.* Paris, 1991.

Deane, Jennifer Kolpacoff. "Medieval Domestic Devotion." *History Compass* 11, no. 1 (2013), 65–76.

BIBLIOGRAPHY 237

———. "Pious Domesticities." In *The Oxford Handbook of Women and Gender in Medieval Europe*, pp. 262–78.

de Cessoles, Jacques. *Le jeu des eschaz moralisé: traduction de Jean Ferron (1347)*. Paris, 1999.

Dehaisnes, Chrétien-César-Auguste. *Documents et extraits concernant l'histoire de l'art dans la Flandre, l'Artois, et le Hainaut avant le XV siècle, 1374–1401*. Lille, 1886.

Delachenal, Roland. *Histoire de Charles V*. 5 vols. Paris, 1909–31.

de la Selle, Xavier. *La service des âmes à la cour: confesseurs et aumôniers des rois de France du XIIIe au XVe siècle*. Paris, 1995.

de Linas, Charles. *Rapports sur les anciens vêtements sacerdotaux et les anciens tissus conservés en France*. Paris,1860.

Delisle, Léopold. "Testament de Blanche de Navarre, reine de France." *Mémoires de la Société de l'histoire de Paris et de l'Ile de France* 12 (1885), 1–64.

———. *Notice de douze livres royaux*. Paris, 1902.

———. *Recherches sur la librairie de Charles V*. 3 vols. Paris, 1907.

Depoin, M.J. "La reine Blanche à Pontoise." *Bulletin de la Commission des Antiquités et des Arts de Seine-et-Oise* 11 (1889), 159–63.

de Vaivre, Jean-Bernard. "Les vitraux de la Maison de Navarre à la cathédrale d'Évreux." *Congrès archéologique* (1980), 314–40.

———. "Sur trois primitifs français du XIVe siècle et le portrait de Jean le Bon." *Gazette des Beaux-Arts* (April 1981), 131–56.

de Vic, Claude, and Joseph Vaissete. *Histoire générale de Languedoc, avec des notes et les pièces justificatives*. 5 vols. Toulouse, 1872.

Dewick, Edward S. *The Coronation Book of Charles V, Cottonian Ms. Tiberius B. VIII*. London, 1899.

de Winter, Patrick. *La bibliothèque de Philippe le Hardi, duc de Bourgogne (1364–1404)*. Paris, 1985.

Documents normands du règne de Charles V. Edited by M. Nortier. Paris, 2000.

Doquang, Mailon. "Status and the Soul: Commemoration and Intercession in the Rayonnant Chapels of Northern France in the Thirteenth and Fourteenth Centuries." In *Memory and Commemoration in Medieval Culture*, edited by Elma Brenner, Meredith Cohen, and Mary Franklin-Brown, pp. 93–118. Farnham, Surrey, UK, 2013.

Doublet, Jacques. *Histoire de l'abbaye de S. Denys en France*. Paris, 1625.

Dressler, Rachel. "Continuing the Discourse: Feminist Scholarship and the Study of Medieval Visual Culture." *Medieval Feminist Forum* 43, no. 1 (2007), 15–34.

Dubosc, Michel Georges. *Inventaire–sommaire des Archives départementales de la Manche antérieures à 1790*. Saint-Lo, 1865.

Duchesne, Henri-Gaston. *Histoire de l'Abbaye de Longchamp*. Paris, 1905.

Duffy, Eamon. *Saints & Sinners: A History of the Popes*. New Haven, 1997.

————. *The Stripping of the Altars: Traditional Religion in England, 1400–1580.* New Haven, 1992; 2nd ed. 2005.

Dutton, Anne M. "Passing the Book: Testamentary Transmission of Religious Literature to and by Women in England, 1350–1500." In *Women, the Book and the Godly: Selected Proceedings of the St. Hilda's Conference, 1993,* edited by Lesley Smith and Jane Taylor, pp. 41–54. Woodbridge, UK, 1995.

Earenfight, Theresa. *Queenship in Medieval Europe.* Basingstoke, 2013.

Eames, Penelope. *Furniture in England, France and the Netherlands from the Twelfth to the Fifteenth Century.* London, 1977.

Easton, Martha. "Uncovering the Meanings of Nudity in the *Belles Heures* of Jean, Duke of Berry." In *The Meanings of Nudity in Medieval Art,* edited by Sherry Lindquist, pp. 149–82. Farnham, Surrey, UK, 2012.

Encyclopedia of Dress and Textiles in the British Isles, c. 450–1450. Edited by Gale R. Owen-Crocker, Elizabeth Coatsworth, and Maria Hayward. Leiden, 2012.

Evans, Joan. *Magical Jewels of the Middle Ages and of the Renaissance, particularly in England.* Oxford, 1922.

————. *English Medieval Lapidaries.* London, 1933; repr. 1960.

————. *A History of Jewellery, 1100–1870.* Mineola, NY, 1953; rev. ed. 1970.

Facinger, Marion. "A Study of Medieval Queenship: Capetian France, 987–1237." *Studies in Medieval and Renaissance History* 5 (1968), 3–48.

Famiglietti, Richard. *Royal Intrigue: Crisis at the Court of Charles VI, 1392–1420.* New York, 1986.

Les fastes du gothique: le siècle de Charles V. Paris, 1981.

Feigenbaum, Gail. "Manifest Provenance." In *Provenance: An Alternate History of Art,* edited by Gail Feigenbaum and Inge Reist, pp. 6–28. Los Angeles, 2012.

Félibien, Michel. *Histoire de l'abbaye royale de saint Denys en France.* Paris, 1706.

————. *Histoire de la ville de Paris.* 2 vols. Paris, 1725.

Féry-Hue, Françoise. "*Sidrac* et les pierres précieuses." *Revue d'histoire des textes* 28 (1998), 93–181.

————. "*Sidrac* et les pierres précieuses: complément." *Revue d'histoire des textes* 30 (2000), 315–21.

Field, Sean. *Isabelle of France: Capetian Sanctity and Franciscan Identity in the Thirteenth Century.* South Bend, IN, 2006.

————. "Marie of Saint-Pol and Her Books." *The English Historical Review* 125, no. 513 (2010), 1–24.

Fliegel, Stephen. "The Hours of Charles the Noble." In *Sacred Gifts and Worldly Treasures: Medieval Masterworks from the Cleveland Museum of Art,* edited by Holger Klein, p. 217. Cleveland, 2007.

Flora, Holly. "Patronage." In *Medieval Art History Today: Critical Terms,* edited by Nina Rowe, special issue of *Studies in Iconography* 33 (2012), 207–18.

BIBLIOGRAPHY

Fourrier, Anthime. "La destinataire de 'La Dame a la Licorne.'" In *Mélanges de langue et de literature médiévales offerts à Pierre Le Gentil*, pp. 265–76. Paris, 1973.

Freeman, Margaret. *The Unicorn Tapestries.* New York, 1976.

French, Katherine L. "'I leave my best gown as a vestment': Women's Spiritual Interests in the Late Medieval English Parish." *Magistra* 4 (1998), 57–77.

———. *The Good Women of the Parish: Gender and Religion after the Black Death.* Philadelphia, 2008.

———. "Genders and Material Culture." In *The Oxford Handbook of Women and Gender in Medieval Europe*, pp. 197–212.

Fresne du Cange, Charles du. "Robe de corps." In *Glossarium novum ad scriptores medii aevi*, vol. 4, p. 90. Paris, 1766.

Gaborit-Chopin, Danielle. "The Reliquary of Elizabeth of Hungary at The Cloisters." In *The Cloisters: Studies in Honor of the Fiftieth Anniversary*, edited by Elizabeth Parker, pp. 327–54. New York, 1992.

Gaposchkin, M. Cecilia. *The Making of Saint Louis: Kingship, Crusades and Sanctity in the Later Middle Ages.* Ithaca, 2008.

Gaston Fébus: Prince Soleil, 1331–1391. Paris, 2011.

Gatouillat, Françoise. "La Vierge de Blanche de Navarre et quelques vitraux inédits de la cathédrale d'Évreux." In *Pierre, lumière, couleur: études d'histoire de l'art du Moyen Âge en l'honneur d'Anne Prache*, edited by Fabienne Joubert and Dany Sandron, pp. 309–25. Paris, 1999.

Gaude-Ferragu, Murielle. *D'or et cendres: la mort et les funérailles des princes dans le royaume de France au bas Moyen Âge.* Villeneuve-d'Ascq, 2005.

———. "Les dernières volontés de la reine de France. Les deux testaments de Jeanne de Bourgogne, femme de Philippe VI de Valois (1329, 1336)." *Annuaire-Bulletin de la Société de l'histoire de France, année 2007* (2009), 23–66.

Gay, Victor, completed by Henri Stein. *Glossaire archéologique du Moyen Âge et de la Renaissance.* 2 vols. Paris, 1882–1928.

Geary, Patrick. *Phantoms of Remembrance: Memory and Oblivion at the End of the First Millennium.* Princeton, N.J., 1994.

Gerevini, Stefania. "Christus crystallus: Rock Crystal, Theology and Materiality in the Medieval West." In *Matter of Faith*, pp. 92–99.

Goehring, Margaret. "The Representation and Meaning of Luxurious Textiles in Late Medieval Franco-Flemish Manuscript Illumination." In *Weaving, Veiling and Dressing: Textiles and Their Metaphors in the Late Middle Ages*, edited by Barbara Baert and Kathryn Rudy, pp. 121–55. Turnhout, 2007.

Goldberg, P.J.P., and Maryanne Kowaleski. "Introduction. Medieval Domesticity: Home, Housing and Household." In *Medieval Domesticity: Home, Housing and Household in Medieval England*, edited by Maryanne Kowaleski and P.J.P. Goldberg, pp. 1–13. Cambridge, 2008.

The Good Wife's Guide. Translated by Gina Greco and Christine Rose. Ithaca, 2009.

Grandes chroniques de France. Edited by Jules Viard. 10 vols. Paris, 1920–53.

Graves, Frances M. *Deux inventaires de la maison d'Orléans (1389 et 1408)*. Paris, 1926.

Green, Karen. "From *Le miroir des dames* to *Le livre des trois vertus*." In *Virtue Ethics for Women, 1250–1500*, pp. 99–114.

———. "What were the Ladies in the *City of Ladies* reading? The Libraries of Christine de Pizan's Contemporaries." *Medievalia et Humanistica* 36 (2011), 76–100.

Green, Monica. "Books as a Source of Medical Education for Women in the Middle Ages." *Dynamis* 20 (2000), 331–69.

Grévy-Pons, Nicole, and Ezio Ornato. "Qui est l'auteur de la chronique latine de Charles VI dite Religieux de Saint-Denis?" *Bibliothèque de l'École des Chartes* 134 (1976), 85–102.

Grove Encyclopedia of Medieval Art & Architecture. Edited by Colum Hourihane. Oxford, 2012.

Guest, Gerald. "A Discourse on the Poor: The Hours of Jeanne d'Évreux." *Viator* 26 (1995), 153–80.

Guiffrey, Jules. *Inventaires de Jean, duc de Berry (1401–1416)*. 2 vols. Paris, 1894–96.

Hablot, Laurent. "The Use of Emblems by Philip the Bold and John the Fearless." In *Art from the Court of Burgundy*, pp. 81–83.

Hahn, Cynthia. *Strange Beauty: Issues in the Making and Meaning of Reliquaries, 400-circa 1204*. University Park, PA, 2012.

Hallam, Elizabeth. "Philip the Fair and the Cult of Saint Louis." *Studies in Church History* 18 (1982), 201–14.

Hamilton, Tracy Chapman. *Pleasure and Politics at the Court of France: The Artistic Patronage of Queen Marie de Brabant (1260–1321)*. Turnhout, forthcoming.

———. "Pleasure, Politics, and Piety: The Artistic Patronage of Marie de Brabant." Ph.D. diss., University of Texas, Austin, 2004.

Hamling, Tara, and Catherine Richardson, eds. *Everyday Objects: Medieval and Early Modern Material Culture and Its Meanings*. Farnham, Surrey, UK, 2010.

Harris, Jim, "Digest of Documents." In *"No equal in any land": André Beauneveu, Artist to the Courts of France and Flanders*, pp. 190–205.

Havard, Henry. *Histoire de l'orfèvrerie française*. Paris, 1896.

Hayward, Maria. "Lettice." In *Encyclopedia of Dress and Textiles in the British Isles*, p. 324.

———. "Liturgical Textiles: post-1100." In *Encyclopedia of Dress and Textiles in the British Isles*, pp. 333–37.

———. "Squirrel Fur." In *Encyclopedia of Dress and Textiles in the British Isles*, p. 542.

———. "Squirrel Robe of Queen Philippa." In *Encyclopedia of Dress and Textiles in the British Isles*, p. 543.

Heck, Christian. *Le Ci Nous Dit et le manuscrit de Chantilly: l'image médiéval et la culture des laics au XIVe siècle. Les enluminures du manuscript de Chantilly*. Turnhout, 2012.

BIBLIOGRAPHY

Hedeman, Anne D. "The Commemoration of Jeanne d'Évreux's Coronation in the *Ordo ad Consecrandum* at the University of Illinois." *Essays in Medieval Studies: Proceedings of the Illinois Medieval Association* 7 (1990), 13–28.

———. *The Royal Image: Illustrations of the* Grandes chroniques de France, *1274–1422*. Berkeley, 1991.

Henwood, Philippe. *Les collections du trésor royal sous le règne de Charles VI (1380–1422), l'inventaire de 1400*. Paris, 2004.

Herlihy, David. "Tuscan Names, 1200–1530." In *Women, Family and Society in Medieval Europe, Historical Essays, 1978–1991*, pp. 330–52. Providence, RI, 1995.

Hervier, Dominique. *Pierre le Gendre et son inventaire après décès: une famille parisienne à l'aube de la Renaissance: étude historique et méthodologique.*Paris, 1977.

Higonnet, Anne. "Afterword: The Social Life of Provenance." In *Provenance: An Alternate History of Art*, edited by Gail Feigenbaum and Inge Reist, pp. 195–209. Los Angeles, 2012.

Holladay, Joan. "The Education of Jeanne d'Évreux: Personal Piety and Dynastic Salvation in Her Book of Hours at the Cloisters." *Art History* 17 (1994), 585–611.

———. "Relics, Reliquaries, and Religious Women: Visualizing the Holy Virgins of Cologne." *Studies in Iconography* 18 (1997), 67–118.

———. "Fourteenth-century French Queens as Collectors and Readers of Books: Jeanne d'Evreux and Her Contemporaries." *Journal of Medieval History* 32 (2006), 69–100.

———. "Jean Pucelle and His Patrons." In *Jean Pucelle: Innovation and Collaboration in Manuscript Painting*, edited by Kyunghee Pyun and Anna Russakoff, pp. 17–26. Turnhout, 2013.

Honeycutt, Lois. "Intercession and the High Medieval Queen: The Esther Topos." In *Power of the Weak*, pp. 126–46.

The Hours of Jeanne d'Evreux. Acc. No. 54.I.2 The Metropolitan Museum of Art, The Cloisters Collection, New York: Commentary. Lucerne, 2000.

Howell, Martha. "Fixing Movables: Gifts by Testament in Late Medieval Douai." *Past & Present* 150 (1996), 3–45.

———. *The Marriage Exchange: Property, Social Place, and Gender in Cities of the Low Countries, 1300–1550*. Chicago, 1998.

Hughes, Muriel. "The Library of Philip the Bold and Margaret of Flanders, First Valois Duke and Duchess of Burgundy." *Journal of Medieval History* 4, no. 2 (June 1978), 145–88.

Husband, Timothy. *The Art of Illumination: The Limbourg Brothers and the* Belles Heures *of Jean de France, Duc de Berry.* New York, 2008.

———. "Jean de Fance, duc de Berry." In *The Art of Illumination*, pp. 10–31.

Idoate, Florence. "Inventario de los bienes de la Reina Dona Maria, esposa de Pedro IV, Rey de Aragón." *Principe de Viana* 28 (1947), 417–35.

242 BIBLIOGRAPHY

L'inventaire du trésor du dauphin futur Charles v (1363): les débuts d'un grand collection-neur. Edited by Danielle Gaborit-Chopin. Nogent-le-Roi, 1996.

Inventaire-sommaire des Archives départementales antérieures à 1790: Basses-Pyrénées. Edited by Paul Raymond. 6 vols. Paris, 1863–79.

Inventaire sommaire des Archives départementales antérieures à 1790, Orne: Archives ecclé-siastiques. Série H (No. 3352–4738). Edited by Louis Duval. 4 vols. Alençon, 1899.

Jékely, Zsombor. "Maiolica Jugs in Late Medieval Painting." In *The Dowry of Beatrice: Italian Maiolica Art and the Court of King Matthias,* edited by Gabriella Balla and Zsombor Jékely, pp. 55–66. Budapest, 2008.

Jenkins, Jacqueline, and Katherine Lewis. "Introduction." In *Saint Katherine of Alexandria: Texts and Contexts in Western Medieval Europe,* edited by Jacqueline Jenkins and Katherine Lewis, pp. 1–18. Turnhout, 2003.

Jones, Michael. "Joan of Navarre." *Oxford Dictionary of National Biography.* Oxford, 2004.

Journaux du trésor de Philippe vi Valois. Edited by Jules Viard. Paris, 1899.

Jung, Jacqueline. "The Tactile and the Visionary: Notes on the Place of Sculpture in the Medieval Religious Imagination." In *Looking Beyond: Visions, Dreams, and Insights in Medieval Art and History,* edited by Colum Hourihane, pp. 203–40. Princeton, 2010.

Keane, Marguerite. "Remembering Louis ix as a Family Saint: A Study of the Images of Saint Louis Created for Jeanne, Blanche, and Marie of Navarre." Ph.D. diss., University of California, Santa Barbara, 2002.

———. "Most Beautiful and Next Best: Value in the Collection of a Medieval Queen." *Journal of Medieval History* 34 (December 2008), 360–73.

———. "Memory and Identity in the Chapel of Blanche of Navarre at Saint-Denis." In *Citation, Intertextuality and Memory in the Middle Ages and Renaissance,* vol. 2: *Cross-Disciplinary Perspectives on Medieval Culture,* edited by Yolanda Plumley and Giuliano di Bacco, pp. 123–36. Liverpool, 2013.

Kessler, Herbert, *Seeing Medieval Art.* Peterborough, Ont., 2004.

———. "The Eloquence of Silver: More on the Allegorization of Matter." In *L'allégorie dans l'art du Moyen Âge. Formes et fonctions. Héritages, créations, mutations,* edited by Christian Heck, pp. 49–64. Turnhout, 2011.

Kornbluth, Genevra. "Active Optics: Carolingian Rock Crystal on Medieval Reliquaries." *Different Visions: A Journal of New Perspectives on Medieval Art* 4 (Jan. 2014), 1–36 (each article separately paginated).

Koslin, Désirée. "Value-Added Stuffs and Shifts in Meaning: An Overview and Case Study of Medieval Textile Paradigms." In *Encountering Medieval Textiles and Dress: Objects, Texts, Images,* edited by Désirée Koslin and Janet Snyder, pp. 235–49. New York, 2002.

———. "Wimple." In *Encyclopedia of Dress and Textiles in the British Isles,* pp. 629–30.

Labarte, Jules. *Inventaire du mobilier de Charles v, roi de France.* Paris, 1979.

Laborde, Léon de. *Les ducs de Bourgogne.* 2 vols. Paris, 1849–51.

BIBLIOGRAPHY

———. *Musée des Archives (de l'Empire) nationales, Actes importants de l'histoire de France*. Paris, 1867.

———. *Glossaire français du Moyen Âge: à l'usage de l'archéologue et de l'amateur des arts, précédé de l'inventaire des bijoux de Louis, duc d'Anjou, dressé vers 1360*. Paris, 1872.

Lachaud, Frédérique. "Les textiles dans les comptes des hôtels royaux et nobiliaires (France et Angleterre, XIIᵉ-XVᵉ siècle)." *Bibliothèque de l'École des Chartes* 164 (2006), 71–96.

Lafond, Jean. "Les vitraux royaux et princiers de la cathédrale d'Évreux et les dessins de la collection Gaignières." *Bulletin de la Société nationale des antiquaires de France* (1973), 103–12.

Lagabrielle, Sophie. "Agnès de Navarre: l'amour des beaux objets." In *Gaston Fébus: Prince Soleil, 1331–1391*, pp. 52–67.

Lahav, Rina. "A Mirror of Queenship: The *Speculum Dominarum* and the Demands of Justice." In *Virtue Ethics for Women, 1250–1500*, pp. 31–44.

Leach, Elizabeth Eva. *Sung Birds: Music, Nature, and Poetry in the Later Middle Ages*. Ithaca, 2007.

Leber, Constant. *Collection des meilleurs dissertations, notices et traits particuliers relatives à l'histoire de France*. 20 vols. Paris, 1838.

———. "Le compte de l'execution du testament." In *Collection des meilleurs dissertations ...*, 19:120–69.

Lebeuf, Jean. *Histoire de la ville et de tout le diocèse de Paris*. 3 vols. Paris, 1863–67.

Legaré, Anne-Marie. "La reception du *Pèlerinage de Vie humaine* de Guillaume de Digulleville dans le milieu angevin d'après les sources et les manuscrits conservés." In *Religion et mentalités au Moyen Âge: mélanges en l'honneur d'Hervé Martin*, edited by Sophie Cassagnes-Brouquet et al., pp. 543–52. Rennes, 2003.

Le Grand, Léon. "Episodes de l'occupation de Melun par l'armée du roi de Navarre (1358)." *Annuaire de la Société historique et archéologique du Gatinais* 7 (1889), 285–92.

Lehugeur, Paul. *Histoire de Philippe le Long, roi de France (1316 -1322)*. 2 vols. Paris, 1897–1931.

Leisterschneider, Eva. *Die französische Königsgrablege Saint-Denis. Strategien monarchischer Repräsentation, 1223–1461*. Weimar, 2008.

Lescournay, Jacques. "Testament de Louys, Comte d'Estampes." In *Mémoires de la ville de Dourdan*, pp. 103–11. Paris, 1624.

Lesort, André. "La Reine Blanche dans le Vexin et le Pays de Bray." *Mémoires de la Société historique et archéologique de l'arrondissement de Pontoise et du Vexin* 54 (1948), 35–67.

———. "La Reine Blanche dans le Vexin et le Pays de Bray." *Mémoires de la Société historique et archéologique de l'arrondissement de Pontoise et du Vexin* 55 (1954), 9–88.

Lewis, Katherine. "Female Life-writing and the Testamentary Discourse: Women and Their Wills in Later Medieval England." *In Medieval Women and the Law*, edited by Noël James Menuge, pp. 57–75. Woodbridge, UK, 2003.

La librairie de Charles V. Paris, 1968.

Lightbown, Ronald. *Secular Goldsmiths' Work in Medieval France*. London, 1978.

———. *Medieval European Jewellery, with a Catalogue of the Collection in the Victoria & Albert Museum*. London, 1992.

———. "Cameos, Gems, Nomenclature, Sources and Value." In *Medieval European Jewellery*, pp. 23–32.

———. "Girdles and Belts." In *Medieval European Jewellery*, pp. 306–41.

Lindquist, Sherry C.M. "Gender." In *Medieval Art History Today: Critical Terms*, edited by Nina Rowe, special issue of *Studies in Iconography* 33 (2012), 113–30.

Lord, Carla. *Royal French Patronage of Art in the Fourteenth Century: An Annotated Bibliography*. Boston, 1985.

———. "Jeanne d'Évreux as a Founder of Chapels: Patronage and Public Piety." In *Women and Art in Early Modern: Europe Patrons, Collectors, and Connoisseurs*, edited by Cynthia Lawrence, pp. 21–36. University Park, Penn., 1997.

Lowe, Nicola A. "Women's Devotional Bequests of Textiles in the Late Medieval English Parish Church, ca. 1350–1550." *Gender & History* 22, no. 2 (August 2010), 407–29.

Maddocks, Hilary. "The Rapondi, the Volto Santo di Lucca, and Manuscript Illumination in Paris c. 1400." In *Patrons, Authors, and Workshops: Books and Book Production in Paris around 1400*, edited by Godfried Croenen and Peter Ainsworth, pp. 91–122. Louvain, 2006.

Maddox, Donald, and Sara Sturm-Maddox, eds. *Melusine of Lusignan: Founding Fiction in Late Medieval France*. Athens, GA, 1996.

Maerten, Michel. "The Germolles Château." In *Art from the Court of Burgundy*, pp. 146–47.

Mandements et actes divers de Charles V. Edited by Léopold Delisle. Paris, 1874.

Manion, Margaret. "Women, Art and Devotion: Three French Fourteenth-century Royal Prayer Books." In *The Art of the Book: Its Place in Medieval Worship*, edited by Margaret Manion and Bernard Muir, pp. 21–66. Exeter, 1998.

Marcon, Susy, et al. *Libro de horas de la reina Maria de Navarra*. Barcelona, 1996.

Mariaux, Pierre. "Collecting (and Display)." In *A Companion to Medieval Art: Romanesque and Gothic in Northern Europe*, edited by Conrad Rudolph, pp. 213–32. Oxford, 2006.

Martin, Therese, ed. *Reassessing the Roles of Women as 'Makers' of Medieval Art and Architecture*. 2 vols. Leiden, 2012.

———. "Exceptions and Assumptions: Women in Medieval Art History." In *Reassessing the Roles of Women as 'Makers' of Medieval Art and Architecture*, 1:1–33.

Martinez de Aguirre, Javier. *Arte y monarquia en Navarra, 1328–1425*. Pamplona, 1987.

Matagne, Robert. "Philippe VI ou Jean II le Bon?" *Archivum Heraldicum* 1 (1958), 7–8.

BIBLIOGRAPHY

Matter of Faith: An Interdisciplinary Study of Relics and Relic Veneration in the Medieval Period. Edited by James Robinson, Lloyd de Beer, and Anna Harnden. London, 2014.

McCash, June Hall, ed. *The Cultural Patronage of Medieval Women.* Athens, Ga., 1996.

McIver, Katherine. "Material Culture: Consumption, Collecting and Domestic Goods." In *The Ashgate Research Companion to Women and Gender in Early Modern Europe,* edited by Allyson Poska, Jane Couchman, and Katherine McIver, pp. 469–88. Farnham, Surrey, UK, 2013.

Meale, Carol M. "'... alle the bokes that I haue of latyn, englisch, and frensch': Laywomen and Their Books in Late Medieval England." In *Women and Literature in Britain, 1150–1500,* edited by Carol Meale, pp. 128–58. Cambridge, 1993.

Meiss, Millard. *French Painting in the Time of Jean de Berry: The Late Fourteenth Century and the Patronage of the Duke.* 2 vols. New York, 1967.

Mémoires et notes de Auguste Le Prévost pour servir à l'histoire du département de l'Eure. Edited by Léopold Delisle and Louis Passy. 3 vols. Evreux, 1862–69.

Mercure de France. "Extrait d'une letter écrite d'Auxerre à M. de la R. le 1 octobre 1728, sur une nouvelle découverte de Médailles faite à cinq lieuës de cette ville," pp. 52–59. Paris, 1729.

Mertes, R.G.K.A. "The Household as a Religious Community." In *People, Politics and the Community in the Later Middle Ages,* edited by Joel T. Rosenthal and Colin Richmond, pp. 123–39. Gloucester, 1987.

Mews, Constant. "The *Speculum Dominarum (Miroir des dames)* and Transformations of the Literature of Instruction for Women in the Early Fourteenth Century." In *Virtue Ethics for Women, 1250–1500,* pp. 13–30.

Meyer, Edmond. *Histoire de la ville de Vernon et de son ancien chatellenie.* 2 vols. Les Andelis, 1876.

Meyer, Paul. "Notice sur le ms. du Musée britannique add. 20697." *Bulletin de la Société des anciens textes français* 18 (1892), 94.

Michel, Edmond. "La reine Jeanne d'Evreux à Brie-Comte-Robert." *Bulletin et compte-rendu des travaux de la Société d'histoire et d'archéologie de Brie-Comte-Robert* (Brie-Comte-Robert, 1898), 9–16.

Millin, Aubin-Louis. *Antiquités nationales, ou Recueil des monumens pour servir à l'histoire générale et particulière de l'Empire françois.* 5 vols. Paris, 1791.

Miranda Garcia, Fermín. *Reyes de Navarra: Felipe III y Juana II de Evreux.* Pamplona, 1994.

Mirot, Léon. "Paiements et quittances de travaux exécutés sous le règne de Charles VI (1380–1422)." *Bibliothèque de l'École des Chartes* 81 (1920), 183–304.

Mollat, Guillaume. "Clément VI et Blanche de Navarre, reine de France." *Mélanges d'Archéologie et d'Histoire* 71 (1959), 377–80.

Monnas, Lisa. "The Furnishings of Royal Closets and the Use of Small Devotional Images in the Reign of Richard II: The Setting of the Wilton Diptych Reconsidered." *Fourteenth- Century England* 3 (2004), 185–206.

———. "Cloth of Gold." In *Encyclopedia of Dress and Textiles in the British Isles*, pp. 132–33.

———. "Some Medieval Colour Terms for Textiles." In *Medieval Clothing & Textiles* 10, edited by Robin Netherton and Gale R. Owen-Crocker, with Monica L. Wright, pp. 25–57. Woodbridge, UK, 2014.

Montaiglon, Anatole de. "Joyaux et pierreries données au couvent des Grands Carmes de la place Maubert à Paris par la reine Jeanne d'Évreux en 1349 et 1361." *Archives de l'art français*, 2nd ser. (1861), 448–53.

Montesquiou-Fezensac, Blaise de, and Danielle Gaborit-Chopin. *Le trésor de Saint-Denis*. 3 vols. Paris, 1973–77.

Morand, Kathleen. *Jean Pucelle*. Oxford, 1962.

Moreau-Néret, André. "Philippe VI de Valois et la Chartreuse de Bourgfontaine où son coeur fut déposé." *Mémoires de la Fédération des Sociétés d'histoire et d'archéologie de L'Aisne* 13 (1967), 149–63.

Moret de Bourchenu, Jean P. "Testament de Clémence de Hongrie reyne de France, seconde femme de Louis Hutin." In *Histoire de Dauphiné et des princes qui ont porté le nom de dauphins*, 2 vols., 2:217–21. Geneva, 1722.

Morganstern, Anne McGee. *Gothic Tombs of Kinship in France, the Low Countries, and England*. University Park, PA, 2000.

Morice, Pierre-Hyacinthe. "Testament de Jeanne de Navarre, vicomtesse de Rohan." In *Mémoires pour servir de preuves à l'histoire ecclésiastique et civile de Bretagne*, 3 vols., 2:716–22. Paris, 1742–46.

Morse, Mary. "Alongside Saint Margaret: The Childbirth Cult of Saints Quiricus and Julitta in Late Medieval English Manuscripts." In *Manuscripts and Printed Books in Europe, 1350–1550*, edited by Emma Cayley and Susan Powell, pp. 187–206, nn. 273–81. Liverpool, 2013.

Mulder-Bakker, Anneke, ed. *Sanctity and Motherhood: Essays on Holy Mothers in the Middle Ages*. New York, 1995.

———. "Jeanne of Valois: The Power of a Consort." In *Capetian Women*, pp. 253–69.

Musacchio, Jacqueline. *The Art and Ritual of Childbirth in Renaissance Italy*. New Haven, 1999.

Muthesius, Anna. "Silk in the Medieval World." In *The Cambridge History of Western Textiles*, edited by David T. Jenkins, pp. 325–54. Cambridge, 2003.

Narbona Cárceles, María. "La 'Discreción Hermosa': Blanca de Navarra, reina de Francia. Una dama al servicio de su linaje." In *La dama en la corte bajomedieval*, edited by Martí Aurell et al., pp. 75–116. Pamplona, 2001.

BIBLIOGRAPHY

———. "Ladies in waiting." In *Women and Gender in Medieval Europe, an Encyclopedia*, edited by Margaret Schaus, pp. 447–48. New York, 2006.

Nash, Susie. "'Adrien Biaunevopt ... faseur des thombes': André Beauneveu and Sculptural Practice in Late Fourteenth-century France and Flanders." In *"No equal in any land," André Beauneveu: Artist to the Courts of France and Flanders*, pp. 30–65.

Naughton, Joan. "A Minimally-Intrusive Presence: Portraits in Illustrations for Prayers to the Virgin." In *Medieval Texts and Images: Studies of Manuscripts from the Middle Ages*, edited by Margaret Manion and Bernard Muir, pp. 111–25. Chur, Switzerland, 1991.

Newton, Stella Mary. *Fashion in the Age of the Black Prince: A Study of the Years 1340–1365*. Woodbridge, UK, 1980.

———. "Queen Philippa's Squirrel Suit." In *Documenta Textilia: Festschrift für Sigrid Müller-Christensen*, edited by M. Flury-Lemberg and K. Stolleis, pp. 342–48. Munich, 1981.

"No Equal in Any Land," André Beauneveu: Artist to the Courts of France and Flanders. Edited by Susie Nash, with contributions by Till-Holger Borchert and Jim Harris. London, 2007.

Nolan, Kathleen. *Queens in Stone and Silver: The Creation of a Visual Imagery of Queenship in Capetian France*. New York, 2009.

———, ed. *Capetian Women*. New York, 2003.

Nuechterlein, Jeanne. "The Domesticity of Sacred Space in the Fifteenth-Century Netherlands." In *Defining the Holy: Sacred Space in Medieval and Early Modern Europe*, edited by Andrew Spicer and Sarah Hamilton, pp. 49–79. Aldershot, UK, 2005.

O'Meara, Carra Ferguson. *Monarchy and Consent: The Coronation Book of Charles V of France*. London, 2001.

Orlin, Lena Cowen. "Empty Vessels." In *Everyday Objects: Medieval and Early Modern Material Culture and Its Meanings*, edited by Tara Hamling and Catherine Richardson, pp. 299–308. Farnham, Surrey, UK, 2010.

Orme, Nicholas. *Medieval Children*. New Haven, 2001.

The Oxford Handbook of Women and Gender in Medieval Europe. Edited by Judith Bennett and Ruth Mazo Karras. Oxford, 2013.

Palazzo, Éric. "Relics, Liturgical Space, and the Theology of the Church." In *Treasures of Heaven*, pp. 99–110.

Paris 1400: les arts sous Charles VI. Paris, 2004.

Paris, Paulin. *Le premier volume des Grandes Chroniques de France: Selon que elles sont conservées en l'église de Saint-Denis en France*. Paris, 1836.

Parsons, John Carmi, ed. *Medieval Queenship*. New York, 1993.

———. "Introduction: Family, Sex, and Power: The Rhythms of Medieval Queenship." In *Medieval Queenship*, pp. 1–11.

————. "Mothers, Daughters, Marriage, Power: Some Plantagenet Evidence." In *Medieval Queenship*, pp. 63–78.

————. "The Queen's Intercession in Thirteenth-century England." In *Power of the Weak*, pp. 147–77.

————. "Of Queens, Courts, and Books: Reflections on the Literary Patronage of Thirteenth-century Plantagenet Queens." In *The Cultural Patronage of Medieval Women*, pp. 175–201.

Penketh, Sandra. "Women and Books of Hours." In *Women and the Book: Assessing the Visual Evidence*, edited by Lesley Smith and Jane H.M. Taylor, pp. 266–81. Toronto, 1996.

Perkinson, Stephen. "Courtly Splendor, Urban Markets: Some Recent Exhibition Catalogues." *Speculum* 81, no. 4 (Oct. 2006), 1150–57.

————. *The Likeness of the King: A Prehistory of Portraiture in Late Medieval France*. Chicago, 2009.

Perret, Noëlle-Laetitia. *Les traductions françaises du "De regimine principum" de Gilles de Rome: parcours matériel, culturel et intellectuel d'un discours sur l'éducation*. Leiden, 2011.

Petit, Ernest. *Histoire des ducs de Bourgogne de la race capétienne*. 10 vols. Paris, 1901.

Pietri, François. *Chronique de Charles le Mauvais*. Paris, 1963.

Pinder, Janice. "A Lady's Guide to Salvation: The *Miroir des dames* Compilation." In *Virtue Ethics for Women, 1250–1500*, pp. 45–52.

Pinoteau, Hervé. "Tableaux français sous les premiers Valois." *Cahiers d'héraldique* 2 (1975), 119–76.

Pitte, Dominique. "Bus-Saint-Rémy. Sondages archéologiques à l'abbaye Notre-Dame-du-Trésor." *Bulletin monumental* 165, no. 4 (2007), 381–83.

Plagnieux, Philippe. "Une fondation de la reine Marie de Brabant: la Chapelle Saint-Paul Saint-Louis." In *Mantes médiévale: la collégiale au coeur de la ville*, pp. 110–16. Paris, 2000.

Plaisse, André, and Sylvie Plaisse. *La vie municipale à Évreux pendant la guerre de Cent Ans*. Évreux, 1978.

Power of the Weak: Studies on Medieval Women. Edited by Jennifer Carpenter and Sally-Beth McLean. Urbana, Ill., 1995.

Pradel, Pierre. "Les tombeaux de Charles V." *Bulletin monumental* 109 (1951), 273–96.

Pritchard, Frances. "The Uses of Textiles, *c*. 1000–1500." In *The Cambridge History of Western Textiles*, pp. 355–77. Cambridge, 2003.

Proctor-Tiffany, Mariah. "Lost and Found: Visualizing a Medieval Queen's Destroyed Objects." In *Queenship in the Mediterranean: Negotiating the Role of the Queen in the Medieval and Early Modern Eras*, edited by Elena Woodacre, pp. 73–96. New York, 2013.

BIBLIOGRAPHY

———. "Transported as a Rare Object of Distinction: The Gift-giving of Clémence of Hungary, Queen of France." *Journal of Medieval History* 41, no. 2 (2015), 208–28.

Prost, Bernard, and Henri Prost. *Inventaires mobiliers et extrait des comptes des ducs de Bourgogne de la Maison de Valois (1363–1477)*. 2 vols. Paris, 1902–8.

Push Me, Pull You: vol.1, *Imaginative and Emotional Interaction in Late Medieval and Renaissance Art*; vol. 2, *Physical and Spatial Interaction in Late Medieval and Renaissance Art*. Edited by Sarah Blick and Laura Gelfand. Leiden, 2011.

Reassessing the Roles of Women as 'Makers' of Medieval Art and Architecture. Edited by Therese Martin. 2 vols. Leiden, 2012.

Rees-Jones, Sarah. "Public and Private Space and Gender in Medieval Europe." In *The Oxford Handbook of Women and Gender in Medieval Europe*, pp. 246–61.

Reinburg, Virginia. 'For the Use of Women': Women and Books of Hours." *Early Modern Women: An Interdisciplinary Journal* 4 (2009), 235–40.

———. *French Books of Hours: Making an Archive of Prayer, 1400–1600*. Cambridge, 2012.

Rey, Fabrice. "Princely Piety: The Devotions of the Duchesses Margaret of Flanders and Margaret of Bavaria (1369–1423)." In *Art from the Court of Burgundy*, pp. 81–83.

———. "The Tapestry Collections." In *Art from the Court of Burgandy*, pp. 123–25.

Richard, Jules-Marie. *Une petite-nièce de Saint Louis, Mahaut, comtesse d'Artois et de Bourgogne (1302–1329). Étude sur la vie privée, les arts et l'industrie, en Artois et à Paris au commencement du XIVe siècle*. Paris, 1887.

Robinson, James. "From Altar to Amulet: Relics, Portability, and Devotion." In *Treasures of Heaven*, pp. 111–15.

Rodrigues, Ana Maria S.A. "The Treasures and Foundations of Isabel, Beatriz, Elisenda, and Leonor. The Art Patronage of Four Iberian Queens in the Fourteenth Century." In *Reassessing the Roles of Women as 'Makers' of Medieval Art and Architecture*, 2:903–35.

Rollo-Koster, Joëlle, and Kathryn Reyerson. "Introduction." In *'For the Salvation of my Soul': Women and Wills in Medieval and Early Modern France*, edited by Joëlle Rollo-Koster and Kathryn Reyerson, pp. 1–2. St. Andrews, 2012.

Rosenthal, Joel T. "Aristocratic Cultural Patronage and Book Bequests, 1350–1500." *Bulletin of the John Rylands University Library of Manchester* 64 (1982), 522–48.

Rosenwein, Barbara. "Thinking Historically about Medieval Emotions." *History Compass* 8, no. 8 (2010), 828–42.

Rouse, Mary. "Archives in the Service of Manuscript Study: The Well-Known Nicolas Flamel." In *Patrons, Authors and Workshops: Books and Book Production in Paris around 1400*, edited by Godfried Croenen and Peter Ainsworth, pp. 69–90. Louvain, 2006.

Rouse, Richard H., and Mary A. Rouse. *Manuscripts and Their Makers: Commercial Book Producers in Medieval Paris, 1200–1500*. 2 vols. Turnhout, 2000.

―――. "Marie de St-Pol and Cambridge University Library, MS Dd.5.5." In *The Cambridge Illuminations: The Conference Papers*, edited by Stella Panayatova, pp. 187–91. London, 2007.

―――. "French Literature and the Counts of Saint-Pol, ca. 1178–1377." *Viator* 41, no. 1 (2010), 101–40.

Sabatier, Étienne. *Histoire de la ville et des évêques de Béziers*. Paris, 1854.

Salamagne, Alain. "Le Louvre de Charles V." In *Le palais et son décor au temps de Jean de Berry*, pp. 73–138. Tours, 2010.

Sand, Alexa. "*Materia Meditandi*: Haptic Perception and Some Parisian Ivories of the Virgin and Child ca. 1300." *Different Visions: A Journal of New Perspectives on Medieval Art* 4 (2014), 1–28 (each article separately paginated).

―――. *Vision, Devotion, and Self-representation in Late Medieval Art*. Cambridge, 2014.

Sauvage, Hippolyte. "Documents relatifs à la donation du comte-pairie de Mortain à Pierre de Navarre par Charles VI." In *Mélanges de la Société de l'histoire de Normandie* 5 (1898), 226.

Scher, Stephen. "Bust of Marie de France." In *Set in Stone: The Face in Medieval Sculpture*, edited by Charles T. Little, pp. 138–40. New York and New Haven, 2006.

Schimansky, Dobrila-Donya. "The Study of Medieval Ecclesiastical Costumes – A Bibliography." *Metropolitan Museum of Art Bulletin* 29, no. 7 (March 1971), 313–17.

Schleif, Corine. "St. Hedwig's Personal Ivory Madonna: Women's Agency and the Powers of Possessing Portable Figures." In *The Four Modes of Seeing: Approaches to Medieval Imagery in Honor of Madeline Harrison Caviness*, edited by Evelyn Staudinger Lane, Elizabeth Carson Pastan, and Ellen M. Shortell, pp. 382–403. Farnham, Surrey, UK, 2009.

Scott, Margaret. *Medieval Dress & Fashion*. London, 2009.

Sécousse, Denis-François. *Mémoires pour servir à l'histoire de Charles II, roi de Navarre et comte d'Évreux, surnommé le Mauvais*. Paris, 1758.

―――. *Recueil de pièces servant de preuves aux mémoires sur les troubles excités en France par Charles II, dit le Mauvais, roi de Navarre et comte d'Évreux*. Paris, 1775.

Shadis, Miriam. "Piety, Politics, and Power: The Patronage of Leonor of England and Her Daughters Berenguela of León and Blanche of Castile." In *The Cultural Patronage of Medieval Women*, pp. 202–27.

―――. "Blanche of Castile and Facinger's 'Medieval Queenship': Reassessing the Argument." In *Capetian Women*, pp. 137–61.

―――. "The First Queens of Portugal and the Building of the Realm." In *Reassessing the Roles of Women as 'Makers' of Medieval Art and Architecture*, 2:671–701.

Sheingorn, Pamela. "'The Wise Mother': The Image of St. Anne Teaching the Virgin Mary." *Gesta* 32 (1993), 69–80.

Sherman, Claire Richter. *The Portraits of Charles V of France (1338–1380)*. New York, 1969.

BIBLIOGRAPHY

———. "The Queen in Charles v's *Coronation Book*: Jeanne de Bourbon and the *Ordo ad Reginam Benedicendam*." *Viator* 8 (1977), 255–97.

———. "Taking a Second Look: Observations on the Iconography of a French Queen, Jeanne de Bourbon (1338–1378)." In *Feminism and Art History: Questioning the Litany*, edited by Norma Broude and Mary Garrard, pp. 100–117. New York, 1982.

Sill, Gertrude Grace. *A Handbook of Symbols in Christian Art*. New York, 1975; repr. 1996.

Skemer, Don. *Binding Words: Textual Amulets in the Middle Ages*. University Park, Penn., 2006.

Spiegel, Gabrielle. *The Chronicle Tradition of Saint-Denis: A Survey*. Brookline, Mass., 1978.

Stanton, Anne Rudloff. "From Eve to Bathsheba and Beyond: Motherhood in the Queen Mary Psalter." In *Women and the Book: Assessing the Visual Evidence*, edited by Lesley Smith and Jane H.M. Taylor, pp. 172–89. London, 1997.

———. *The Queen Mary Psalter: A Study of Affect and Audience*. Philadelphia, 2001.

———. "Isabelle of France and Her Manuscripts, 1308–1358." In *Capetian Women*, pp. 225–52.

Sterling, Charles. *La peinture mediévale à Paris, 1300–1500*. 2 vols. Paris, 1987–90.

Stones, Alison. "Some Portraits of Women in Their Books, Late Thirteenth-Early Fourteenth Century." In *Livres et lectures de femmes en Europe entre Moyen Âge et Renaissance*, edited by Anne-Marie Legaré, pp. 3–27. Turnhout, 2007.

Stratford, Jenny. *Richard II and the English Royal Treasure*. Woodbridge, UK, 2012.

Strohm, Paul. "The Queen's Intercession." In his *Hochon's Arrow: The Social Imagination of Fourteenth-century Texts*, pp. 95–119. Princeton, 1992.

Stuard, Susan Mosher. *Gilding the Market: Luxury and Fashion in Fourteenth-century Italy*. Philadelphia, 2005.

Sumption, Jonathan. *The Hundred Years War I: Trial by Battle*. Philadelphia, 1990.

———. *The Hundred Years War II: Trial by Fire*. Philadelphia, 1999.

———. *The Hundred Years War III: Divided Houses*. Philadelphia, 2011.

Surget, Marie-Laure Lemonnier. "Les 'ennemis du roi': parenté et politique chez les Evreux-Navarre, 1298–1425." Ph.D. diss., Université Paris Ouest Nanterre La Défense, 2004.

Tabbagh, Vincent. *Gens d'église, gens de pouvoir: France, XIIIe-XVe siècle*. Dijon, 2006.

Taylor, Jane H.M. "Le Roman de la Dame a la Lycorne et du Biau Chevalier au Lion: Text, Image, Rubric." *French Studies* 51, no. 1 (January 1997), 1–18.

Thalamus parvus. Le petit thalamus de Montpellier. Edited by La Société Archéologique de Montpellier. Montpellier, 1841.

Thompson, Henry Yates. *Thirty-two Miniatures from the Book of Hours of Joan II, Queen of Navarre*. London, 1899.

Tilley, Christopher. "Introduction." In *Handbook of Material Culture*, pp. 1–6. London, 2006.

Treasures of Heaven: Saints, Relics, and Devotion in Medieval Europe. Edited by Martina Bagnoli *et al.* Baltimore, 2010.

Le trésor de la Sainte-Chapelle. Paris, 2001.

Le trésor de Saint-Denis. Edited by Daniel Alcouffe. Paris, 1991.

Tucoo-Chala, Pierre. "L'histoire tragique d'un couple au XIVᵉ siècle: Agnès de Navarre et Gaston Fébus." *Homenaje a José Maria Lacarra de Miguel* 2 (Pamplona, 1986), 741–54.

Vale, Malcolm. *The Princely Court: Medieval Courts and Culture in North-West Europe, 1270–1380.* Oxford, 2001.

Vallet de Viriville, Auguste. *La bibliothèque d'Isabeau de Bavière, femme de Charles VI, roi de France.* Paris, 1858.

Van Buren, Anne. *Illuminating Fashion: Dress in the Art of Medieval France and the Netherlands, 1325–1515.* New York, 2011.

Van Houts, Elisabeth, ed. *Medieval Memories: Men, Women, and the Past, 700–1300.* Essex, 2001.

Van Kerrebrouck, Patrick. *Les Valois.* Villeneuve d'Ascq, 1990.

Van Os, Henk. *The Art of Devotion in the Late Middle Ages in Europe, 1300–1500.* Princeton, 1994.

———. *The Way to Heaven: Relic Veneration in the Middle Ages.* Amsterdam, 2000.

Viard, Jules. "Compte des obsèques de Philippe VI." In *Archives historiques, artistiques et littéraires,* vol. 2, pp. 49–53. Paris, 1890–91.

———. "Philippe de Valois: la succession à la couronne de France." *Le Moyen-Âge* 23 (1921), 219–22.

———. "Philippe de Valois avant son avènement au trone." *Bibliothèque de l'École des Chartes* 91 (July-December 1930), 307–25.

Vidier, A. "Notes et documents sur le personnel, les biens et l'administration de la Sainte-Chapelle du XIIIe au XVe siècles." *Mémoires de la Societé de l'histoire de Paris et de l'Ile-de-France* 28 (1901), 332–33.

Vignat, Gaston. "Testament de Blanche, duchesse d'Orléans." *Mémoires de la Société archéologique de l'Orléanais* 9 (1866), 115–44.

Viollet, Paul. "Comment les femmes ont été exclues en France de la succession à la couronne." *Mémoires de l'Academie des Inscriptions et Belles-Lettres* 34 (1895), 125–78.

Viollet-le-Duc, Eugène. *Dictionnaire raisonné de l'architecture française du XIe au XVIe siècle.* 9 vols. Paris, 1858–68.

Virtue Ethics for Women, 1250–1500. Edited by Karen Green and Constant Mews. Heidelberg, 2011.

Vitry, Paul, and Gaston Brière. *L'église abbatiale de Saint-Denis et ses tombeaux: Notice historique et archéologique.* Paris, 1925.

Von Falke, Otto. *Kunstgeschichte der Seidenweberei.* 2 vols. Berlin, 1913.

BIBLIOGRAPHY

Walker-Meikle, Kathleen. *Medieval Pets.* Woodbridge, UK, 2012.

Wardwell, Anne. "The Stylistic Development of 14th- and 15th-century Italian Silk Design." *Aachener Kunstblätter* 47 (1976–77), 177–226.

Webb, Diana. "Domestic Space and Devotion." In *Defining the Holy: Sacred Space in Medieval and Early Modern Europe,* edited by Andrew Spicer and Sarah Hamilton, pp. 27–47. Aldershot, 2005.

Weigert, Laura. "The Art of Tapestry: Neither Minor nor Decorative." In *From Minor to Major: The Minor Arts in Medieval Art History,* edited by Colum Hourihane, pp. 103–21. Princeton, 2012.

Whiteley, Mary. "Royal and Ducal Palaces in France in the Fourteenth and Fifteenth Centuries. Interior, Ceremony and Function." In *Architecture et vie sociale. L'organisation intérieure des grandes demeures à la fin du Moyen Âge et à la Renaissance, Actes du colloque tenu à Tours du 6 au 10 juin 1988,* edited by Jean Guillaume, pp. 47–63. Paris, 1994.

Wieck, Roger. *Time Sanctified: The Book of Hours in Medieval Art and Life.* New York, 1988.

———. *Painted Prayers: The Book of Hours in Medieval and Renaissance Art.* New York, 1997.

Wildenstein, Georges. "Deux primitifs du temps de Jean le Bon." *Gazette des Beaux-Arts* (September 1961), 121–26.

Williamson, Beth. "Material Culture and Medieval Christianity." In *The Oxford Handbook of Medieval Christianity,* pp. 60–75. Oxford, 2014.

Wixom, William. "The Hours of Charles the Noble." *Bulletin of the Cleveland Museum of Art* 52 (1965), 50–83.

Women and Gender in Medieval Europe, an Encyclopedia. Edited by Margaret Schaus. New York, 2006.

Woodacre, Elena. *The Queens Regnant of Navarre: Succession, Politics, and Partnership, 1274–1512.* New York, 2013.

Woolgar, Christopher. *The Great Household in Late Medieval England.* New Haven, 1999.

———. "Treasure, Material Possessions and the Bishops of Late Medieval England." In *The Prelate in England and Europe: 1300–1500,* edited by Martin Heale, pp. 173–90. York, 2014.

———. "Queens and Crowns: Philippa of Hainaut, Possessions and the Queen's Chamber in mid-XIVth-century England." *Micrologus* 22 (2014), 201–28.

Wraight, Gilly. "Books: Covers." In *Encyclopedia of Dress and Textiles in the British Isles,* p. 88.

Wray, Shona Kelly, and Roisin Cossar. "Wills as Primary Sources." In *Understanding Medieval Primary Sources: Using Historical Sources to Discover Medieval Europe,* edited by Joel T. Rosenthal, pp. 59–71. New York, 2012.

Wright, Georgia Sommers. "The Tomb of Saint Louis." *Journal of the Warburg and Courtauld Institutes* 34 (1971), 65–82.

———. "A Royal Tomb Program in the Reign of Saint Louis." *Art Bulletin* 56 (1974), 223–43.

Wyss, Michaël, et al. *Atlas historique de Saint-Denis: des origines au XVIIIe siècle.* Paris, 1996.

Yonan, Michael. "Toward a Fusion of Art History and Material Culture Studies." *West 86th: A Journal of Decorative Arts, Design History, and Material Culture* 18, no. 2 (Fall 2011), 232–48.

Index

Agnes of France, duchess of Burgundy 13, 25, 42–43, 89, 91–92, 95, 192, 209, 227

Agnes of Navarre, countess of Foix 25, 95, 192, 209, 227

Agnote 110, 112, 199, 211, 230

Albertus Magnus 154

Alfonso of Aragon, spouse of Marie of Navarre 104

altarpieces 116–17, 120, 126, 218

altar textiles 113, 178–79, 183–85, 189–90, 198, 229

amice 183–85, 226

angels 1, 23, 83, 86, 93, 99, 134–35, 138, 141–42, 194, 214, 227

Aragon 2–3, 25, 42–43, 56–57, 86, 104, 154, 195

Aubery Gosset 184

Bailleul, dame de 126, 218

Basin, Pierre 6, 39, 40, 55, 65, 113–14, 120, 124, 126, 135–36, 149, 184–86, 192, 210, 218–19, 228–29

Baudemont, Abbey Trésor Notre-Dame 69, 191, 213, 226

Baudin, Colin 184

Beaubec, abbey of 69, 117, 213

Beauneveu, André 28, 47

beds and bedding 1–2, 17, 110, 121–22, 135, 143–44, 149, 178, 180–83, 192, 195, 201, 218, 227–29

Belin 70; see also Bolin

Belles Heures of the duke of Berry 7, 78, 94, 122–24, 135–37, 162, 203, 207

Belote 109

Bellozanne, abbey of 69, 144–45, 213

belts 1, 12, 43–45, 129–30, 151–56, 163, 170–1, 177, 216, 220

Béziers 2–3, 50

    Saint-Nazaire, cathedral 2–3

Blanchart 175, 177

Blanche d'Aumont 176, 225

Blanche of Castile, queen of France 12, 89, 92–93, 158, 209

Blanche of France, daughter of Philip V, nun at Longchamp 51, 102–3, 105–6, 142, 207–8

Blanche of France, duchess of Orléans xi, 10, 17, 33, 37–41, 67–71, 99, 101, 119, 126, 163, 166, 177, 184, 194, 201, 203, 215, 219–20

Blanche of Navarre, queen of France

    book collection of 10, 13, 45, 51, 57–59, 66, 70–71, 77–117, 206–211

    chapel of Saint Hippolyte at Saint-Denis 3, 5, 9, 11, 19–36, 51, 56–57, 73, 116, 186, 194

    coat of arms of 23, 28–29, 32, 45, 103, 134, 183, 185–89, 193–97, 214–15, 227–30

    confessor of 45, 55, 113, 120, see also Pierre Basin

    death of 39, 65

    devotional practices 19, 64, 82–84, 116–50, 166–69, 178–79, 183–91, 202–203

    executors of her will 36, 39–41, 58, 64, 68, 111, 127, 133–134, 173, 184–85, 200

    funeral instructions 33–36, 200

    goddaughters of 170–177

    liturgical textiles of 125, 178–79, 183–91, *see also chapelles*

    as mediator 4, 8, 9, 12, 51–61, 71, 75, 76, 91, 115, 142, 152, 202

    residences of 33, 55, 59–60, 121, 178–79, *see also* Neaufles

    room hangings of 87–88, 110, 113, 135, 160, 178–80, 192–98, *see also chambres*

Blanche of Navarre, queen of Navarre (Blanca I), daughter of Charles III of Navarre 196–198, 201, 205, 230

Blanchete (several goddaughters with this name) 170, 173–75, 177, 224

Boisseau, Robert 45

Bolin 70; see also Belin

Bonne of Luxembourg 43

books

    as contact relics of Saint Louis 70–1, 81, 83–93, 151, 206–7, 209

    commemorative rebinding 57, 80, 103–4

    for education of children 62, 77–8, 80, 89–93, 207, 209

    wedding gifts 17, 56-7, 80, 104, 195, 209

    see also books of hours, breviary, missal, psalter, *romans*

books of hours   9, 15, 17, 38, 70, 71, 81–82,
    83–84, 87, 92, 94–95, 97–98, 105, 106,
    116, 122, 152, 162, 207, 209
Bourgfontaine, charterhouse of   34, 47, 69,
    130–31, 212
Braquemont, Regnault de (Renaud)   39, 55,
    58, 62, 65, 113
breviaries   38, 56–58, 73, 77, 79–81, 83–88, 92,
    98–99, 101–5, 180, 195, 206–10, 227–28
Brie-Comte-Robert   44
brooches   12, 44–5, 87–8, 117, 129, 151–54,
    156–59, 163, 167, 169, 177, 194, 216–7,
    220–2

cameos   129, 146, 148–49, 217, 223
Carmelites of Paris   34, 36–41, 58, 64, 117, 163,
    171, 215
chambermaid   79, 178, 199, 230
chambre   87, 125, 181, 192-7, 199, 227-30, *see
    also* room hangings
chapeau d'or (gold head ornament)   170–72,
    175, 221
chapel
    domestic, in the queen's residences   113,
        117–21, 135, 178, 184–85, 210, 218
    Saint-Michel in the Palais de la Cité
        45–47
    see also Blanche of Navarre, chapel of
        Saint Hippolyte
chapel d'or (gold head ornament)   170–75, 224
chapelles (sets of liturgical textiles)   125,
    183–191, 226, 228
chaplains   109, 183–84, 226
chapperon (hat, also *chaperon*)   195, 228
Charlemagne   37
Charles de Trie   71
Charles of Evreux, count of Étampes   67, 157
Charles of Rohan   109, 193-4, 210, 223, 228
Charles of Spain   53
Charles of Valois   16, 47, 131
Charles I, king of Sicily (Charles of Anjou)
    25
Charles II, king of Navarre   4, 5, 9, 16–17, 25,
    32, 42–44, 52–57, 68, 75, 86–88, 91,
    102–4, 109, 146, 157, 180, 194, 209
Charles III, king of Navarre   1, 17, 62, 84,
    87–88, 99, 106, 156, 180, 194, 196, 206–7,
    220, 227, 230

Charles IV, king of France   1, 17, 25, 33, 40–41,
    67, 71, 101, 126, 135, 169, 220
Charles V, king of France   2–5, 10, 11, 15-17,
    25, 28, 33, 45-47, 52–58, 67-69, 72, 74–75,
    78–79, 88–89, 99–100, 103-4, 106–7, 121,
    141, 143–44, 148–49, 154–57, 159, 164, 170,
    172, 174, 179, 192, 195, 202–4, 207, 217
Charles VI, king of France   1, 10, 12, 15–17, 35,
    37, 58, 60–61, 72, 74–75, 101, 106–7, 144,
    148-49, 153–56, 159, 162, 164, 169–70, 172,
    207, 216, 220–21
chasuble   183, 185–89, 191, 228
chess   106, 114, 207
childbirth   128, 141, 168, 182–83, 201, 227
Christine de Pizan   99
Christmas   120, 189, 218
Chronique d'Outre-mer   106, 160, 209
Clémence of Hungary, queen of France   12,
    72, 80, 82–3, 139, 143, 199, 201, 203–4
clotet   37–8, 119, 121–22, 124–25, 135–36, 139,
    143–46, 149, 178, 191, 203, 212–16, 218–9,
    223
cloth of gold   34, 121, 154, 171–72, 190, 200
couronne (gold head ornament)   170–72,
    175–76, 224–5
crowns   8, 12–13, 22–23, 25–26, 44–45, 55, 66,
    69, 74, 117, 151–53, 169–72, 199–200, *see
    also chapeau d'or, chapel d'or, couronne*
    wedding gifts to goddaughters   172–77,
    179
crystal   7, 116, 118, 128–31, 135, 140–42, 145, 191,
    212–14

Dame à la licorne   82-83
damoiselles   109–113, 181, 199, 227, *see also*
    ladies-in-waiting
De regimine principum   107
diamond   1, 12, 15, 40, 45, 71, 87–88, 101, 129,
    149, 152–54, 156–66, 170, 204, 217,
    220–22
Dieudonné, Jean, bishop of Senlis   65
diptych   116–17, 122, 126, 135, 149, 203, 219
dogs   26–27
Doublet, Jacques   23, 25, 28–29

Edward II, king of England   139
Edward III, king of England   162, 199
emblems   197, 240

INDEX

emerald   43, 154, 157–59, 164–67, 169–70, 173–74, 217, 221–22, 224
enamel   45, 131, 141, 147, 168, 222, 223
Estienne Gieuffron   65
Evreux, cathedral of Notre-Dame   5, 55, 58, 68-69, 120, 133-34, 142, 215, 218

Felibien, Michel   23, 29, 39, 40, 50, 60, 68
fleur-de-lis   3, 23, 29, 116, 130–31, 153–54, 156, 171, 212, 216, 220
Fontenay, dame de   82, 109, 126, 198–99, 210, 218, 228

Gace de la Buigne (Gasse de la Buyne)   109, 210
Gaignières, François Roger de   5, 23–24, 28–31, 45–48, 131
gemstones   7, 88, 101, 104, 128–30, 144–46, 88, 148–49, 151–57, 159, 161–67,169, 171, 174–75, 220–25
   loose   151–52;
   see also crystal, diamond, emerald, sapphire, pearl, ruby
gender   13, 18, 77–78, 106, 203
Gieffroy Grioires   184
Gilete   199, 230
gisant (recumbent tomb effigy), *see* tombs, tomb figures
Gisors   33, 55, 59, 68, 139,191, 213
Gisors, dame de   109, 168–69, 210, 223–24
gobelet (drinking cup)   193, 223–24
gold   13–14, 37–40, 45, 87–88, 104, 117, 127–30, 144–146, 148, 150, 153–54, 156–57, 160–61, 166, 168, 170–76, 183, 185–86, 193, 195, 215–17, 220–25, 227–28, 230; *see also* cloth of gold
Gomerfontaine, Cistercian convent   17, 69, 139–40, 213
Grandes Chroniques   5, 44, 53–54, 106, 207
griffin   183, 186
Guillaume de Chartres   83
Guillaume de Degulleville   97, 99
Guillaume de Dormans, Archbishop of Sens   189, 226
Guillaume de la Porte   40
Guillaume de Nangis   42

Havard, Henry   131, 133

heart tomb   5, 47–50, 131
Hours of Charles the Noble   87
Hours of Jeanne of Navarre   92, 95–96
Hours of Marie of Navarre   84, 85
household   1-2, 18, 19–20, 57, 59–60, 70, 74, 116, 117–19, 121–22, 150, 175–76, 178–85, 193–94, 201–2
   members of   15, 51, 58–59, 64–65, 70, 74, 77, 81, 107, 109–11, 113–14, 136, 178, 181–82, 192, 198–99, 201
Hundred Years War   4, 16, 52-56

Ingeborg Psalter   89
inventories   xi, 6–7, 23, 72, 78–79, 82, 87–89, 102, 128, 154–57, 170–172, 179–82, 192, 194, 203–4
Isabeau of Bavaria, queen of France   8, 16–17, 35, 37, 74, 78, 94, 98–100, 130, 144–46, 149, 190, 206, 216
Isabelle of France, queen of England   78–79, 113
Isabelle of France, daughter of Charles VI   170–74, 176, 221
Isle-Dieu, abbey (abbey of l'Isle-Dieu)   69, 138, 212

Jacobins, Paris monastery   1, 5, 34, 47–50, 202
Jacqueline de Dammartin   2
Jacques de Bourbon   143
Jean de Liège   25, 33
Jean Le Bel   44
Jean Le Noir   95
Jean Mauger   40
Jean Menart   62
Jean Miélot   122, 125
Jean Pucelle   105
Jeanne de Harcourt   70, 105, 177
Jeanne de Rouières   58–59, 65, 92, 109–11, 182, 194, 199, 210, 229
Jeanne, duchess of Brabant   148–49, 168, 217, 222
Jeanne du Mesnil   109, 111, 149, 199, 211, 229–30
Jeanne la Besaine   109–10, 199, 210, 229
Jeanne of Auvergne, duchess of Berry   17, 74, 105, 124, 165, 207–8, 221
Jeanne of Auvergne and Boulogne, queen of France, wife of John II   44, 91, 173–74

Jeanne of Bourbon, queen of France   7, 17,
    57, 106, 154, 164, 172, 174–5, 207
Jeanne of Burgundy, queen of France, wife of
    Philip V   33, 142
Jeanne of Burgundy, queen of France, wife of
    Philip VI   10, 13, 17, 33, 43–45, 47, 53,
    66, 69–70, 79, 89, 91–94, 98–100, 139,
    153–55, 172–73, 190, 198–99, 201, 203,
    206–8, 216, 220
Jeanne of Evreux, queen of France   xi, 4-5,
    9–10, 16–17, 19, 25, 33-35, 38–41, 44, 51,
    53, 55–58, 61–62, 65–72, 77–84, 88–89,
    93, 96, 99–103, 105, 107, 119, 121, 128,
    131–32, 135, 141, 153–54, 157–61, 163,
    165–68, 171–73, 177, 186, 193, 200, 202–4,
    208, 215, 217–18, 221–23
Jeanne of France, daughter of John II, and
    wife of Charles II, king of Navarre   4,
    17, 25, 52, 55
Jeanne of France, daughter of Philip VI and
    Blanche of Navarre   2–4, 11, 17, 19–20,
    22–29, 31, 34, 50–51, 56-57, 66, 77, 79, 92,
    110, 144, 148–49, 153, 165, 167–68, 172–74,
    176, 195, 217, 221, 223
Jeanne of Navarre, duchess of Brittany, queen
    of England after marriage to Henry IV
    (Joan of Navarre)   17, 103, 144,
    146–148, 180–83, 192, 201, 208, 217, 227
Jeanne of Navarre, nun at Longchamp
    42–43, 51, 70, 79–80, 102–3, 105, 142, 180,
    208
Jeanne of Navarre, queen of France and
    Navarre (Jeanne I of Navarre), wife of
    Philip IV   96
Jeanne of Navarre, viscountess of Rohan
    (Jeanne la Jeune)   4, 42-43, 51, 67–68,
    70–71, 97–98, 109, 128–29, 176, 179, 181,
    190–91, 193–96, 201, 203–4, 209, 227, 230
Jeanne of Valois, countess of Hainault
    162–63
Jeanne II, queen of Navarre   17, 25–26, 28,
    42–43, 47–50, 86, 88, 92–98
Jeanette Sante   112, 211, 230
Jehan de Poupaincourt   175, 224
Jehan Heudain   184
John, duke of Berry   xi, 7, 10, 16, 17, 25, 72, 74,
    78–79, 92, 94, 99, 100, 104-107, 123, 129,
    135–36, 162, 164, 202-03, 207, 220

John, duke of Brittany   148
John, duke of Girona   2, 56
John II, king of France   xi, 15, 17, 28, 43–45,
    50, 52–53, 69, 74, 82–83, 91–92, 109, 155,
    173
John, viscount of Rohan   67
joyaux   7
    see also enamel, gemstones, gold, silver

knights   2, 39, 55–56, 113, 194

ladies-in-waiting   58, 74, 79, 92, 109–10, 112,
    181, 192, 210-11, 227, 229; *see also*
    damoiselles
Lapidary of King Philip   161
lapidaries   88, 161
Lent   179, 192
lettice (white fur)   195, 228
lion   87–88, 154, 183, 186
Longchamp, abbey   42–43, 51, 70, 79–80,
    102–3, 105, 142, 180, 190, 207–8
Louis IX, *see* Saint Louis of France
Louis X, king of France   25, 28, 42, 52, 80, 139
Louis, duke of Anjou   10, 17, 25, 91, 99–100
Louis, duke of Bourbon   16, 17, 106, 164, 207,
    221
Louis, duke of Orléans   16, 17, 35, 71, 101, 107,
    111, 149, 162, 164–65, 207, 221
Louis of Evreux, count of Étampes (d. 1400)
    67–68, 70–71, 92–93, 101, 157–59, 163,
    209, 217–18, 222–23
Louis of Evreux, son of King Philip III of
    France, grandfather of Blanche of
    Navarre   47, 160–61
Louis of Navarre, brother of Blanche of
    Navarre, deceased in early childhood
    42
Louis of Navarre, count of Beaumont-le-
    Roger, brother of Blanche of Navarre
    16, 25, 42–43
Louis of Vernon   39
Lucca,
    textiles from   183, 185–86, 228
    Volto Santo of   29

Mahaut of Artois   7, 139, 204
Marbode of Rennes   161
Margaret of Artois   33, 47, 56

INDEX

Margaret of Burgundy, duchess of Flanders 17, 72, 78, 100, 107, 194, 197, 208, 221-22

Margaret of Burgundy, wife (repudiated) of King Louis X of France 42, 91

Margot le Grant 109–10, 112, 199, 211, 230

Marguerite d'Alencon 158

Marguerite de Vymont 74, 109–10, 112, 174, 199, 211, 224, 230

Marguerite, dame de Préaux 143–44, 146, 149, 168, 181, 218, 223, 228

Marie of Blois 17, 99, 100, 207

Marie of Brabant, queen of France 47, 71, 84, 86, 91, 101–102, 139, 206, 208

Marie of Evreux, sister of Jeanne and Philip of Evreux, aunt of Blanche of Navarre 168

Marie of France, daughter of Jeanne of Evreux 17, 26, 33

Marie of Luxembourg, queen of France 101–102, 208

Marie of Navarre, daughter of King Charles II of Navarre, niece of Blanche of Navarre 17–18, 79-80, 97–98, 104–105, 180–81, 194–95, 198, 209, 227-28

Marie of Navarre, queen of Aragon, wife of Peter IV, sister of Blanche of Navarre 25, 42–43, 84–85, 154

Marie of Saint-Pol 71, 72, 78–80, 83, 113

Marie of Valois, duchess of Bar 99–100, 148, 208, 217

Marion le Grant 74

material culture, study of 7, 14–15, 19, 41, 117–18

Melun 53, 55

Notre-Dame of Melun, collegiate church 68–69, 131, 134, 142, 189, 215, 226

Memling, Hans 196

Millin, Aubin-Louis 5, 47, 131, 133

Miracles de Notre-Dame 58, 110, 210

Miroir des dames 96–97, 209; see also *Speculum Dominarum*

missal 81–82, 109, 113, 121, 126, 184, 210

monogram 192, 196–97

Mortemer, abbey 69, 134–35, 212

Mote, dame de la 109, 113, 126, 199, 210, 219, 228, 229

nail relic 36–41, 58, 215

Navarre, kingdom of 3–5, 17, 19–32, 41–43, 47–50, 52–56, 61–62, 75, 84–89, 91–93, 103, 196–98

Neaufles, château of Blanche of Navarre 33, 41, 55, 57, 59, 64, 68, 109, 114, 122, 171–72, 179, 189, 200

Nicolas Moysy 184

Nicole de Rueil 184

Notre-Dame, Evreux, cathedral 5, 55, 58, 68-69, 120, 133-34, 142, 215, 218

Notre-Dame, Melun, collegiate church 68–69, 131, 134, 142, 189, 215, 226

Notre-Dame, Pamplona, cathedral 47, 189-91, 198, 226

Notre-Dame, Paris, cathedral 34, 170–72, 200

Notre-Dame, Vernon, collegiate church 189, 226

orphreys (*orfrois*) 185, 228

Oudart de Venderez (Oudart le Gendre) 39–40, 58, 62, 65, 112, 211

Pamplona 204–5

Notre-Dame, cathedral 47, 189-91, 198, 226

Paris 2–5, 17, 33–69, 87, 104, 126–29, 141, 163, 204

Carmelites, monastery 34, 36–41, 58, 64, 117, 163, 171, 215

Chapel of Saint-Michel in the Palais de la Cité 45–47

Jacobins, monastery 1, 5, 34, 47–50, 202

Notre-Dame cathedral 34, 170–72, 200

Sainte-Chapelle 146, 148–49, 217, 252

Saint Bartholomew ("Saint Berthelemy") near the Palais de la Cité 127

Saint-Jean-en-Grève 33, 60, 172

paternoster 100, 117, 144, 151–53, 166–69, 177, 202, 221–223; *see also* rosary

patronage 1, 3–4, 6–13, 19–60, 77

pearl 40, 43, 87, 104–5, 145–48, 153–54, 156, 158–59, 167, 169, 173–74, 190, 195, 216–18, 220–24, 227–28

Pèlerinage de Jésus Christ 97, 104, 209

Pèlerinage de vie humaine 97, 99

Pèlerinage du monde 97, 209

Peter IV, king of Aragon (Pedro IV) 42, 154

Peter I, king of Castile (Pedro "the Cruel") 44, 50

INDEX

Philip, duke of Burgundy   10, 13, 16, 17, 25, 72, 75, 78–79, 89, 91–92, 100, 106, 109, 156–57, 173, 177, 197, 203, 207, 216, 221
Philip, duke of Orléans   3, 67, 166
Philip of Evreux, king consort of Navarre, father of Blanche of Navarre   16, 25, 42–43, 47, 49, 88, 160
Philip of Navarre, count of Longueville   6, 16, 42–43, 52, 55, 87-88, 220
Philip III, king of France   16, 25, 47, 86, 107, 168
Philip IV, king of France (Philip the Fair)   5, 16, 25, 50, 77, 96, 107, 108, 111, 149, 160, 207
Philip V, king of France   33, 51, 103, 105, 142
Philip VI, king of France   1, 2, 4, 5, 12, 15, 16, 17, 20, 22–23, 28–30, 34, 36, 43–48, 52–53, 66–67, 70–71, 75, 91, 117, 130–31, 143, 152–57, 162–67, 169, 177, 192, 198–99, 216, 220–21
Philippe de Villiers   2
Philippa of Hainault   162, 190
Pierre Aymé   2
Pierre de Venise   184
Pierre Gautier   184
Pierre Hesterel   184
Pierre of Navarre, count of Mortain   17, 60, 61, 106, 160, 162, 180, 209, 222, 227
Pintoin, Michel (*Religieux* of Saint-Denis)   35–41, 44, 74
plague   43–44
Pontoise   41–42, 55, 68–69, 135, 212, 214
Pope Clement VI   50
Pope Gregory XI   4
Préaux, dame de, *see* Marguerite, dame de Préaux
provenance   13–14, 37, 41, 45, 66, 70, 81, 86, 89, 91–93, 101, 110, 113–14, 117, 148–49, 153, 160–61, 165–66, 173, 177
psalter   5, 13, 45, 81, 83, 88–92, 95, 97–98, 100, 105–6, 109, 177, 207, 209–10
purse   154, 156–57

queens
   dowager   2, 4, 8, 12, 33, 51-56, 66, 155, 169, 202
   patronage of   1, 3–4, 6–13, 19–60, 77
   piety of   13, 32, 35, 77, 92, 94, 171, 180, 191, 201–202

power of   1, 8, 12–13, 15, 52, 61, 75, 202
regalia of   12–13, 155, 169, 171
role as mediator   4, 8–9, 12, 51–56, 61, 71–72, 75–76, 91, 115, 142, 152, 202
role as mother (symbolic)   8, 35, 61, 71–72, 74–76, 80, 92, 114–15, 142, 152, 177, 180, 202

relics and reliquaries   93, 115–59, 212–23
   architectural reliquaries   129, 138-40
   books of Saint Louis   70–1, 81, 83–93, 151, 206–7, 209
   display of, *see* chapel and *clotet*
   nail   36–41, 58
   True Cross   130, 144–46, 213, 216–17
   wearable   151–59, 177
   wrapping of loose relics   128
Religieux of Saint-Denis, *see* Pintoin, Michel
Richard II, king of England   72, 191
rings   12, 44, 71, 117, 151–53, 160–61, 164–67, 169–70, 204, 220–22
Robert Cresserel   107, 211
Robert le Grant   112, 173, 224
robes   183, 198–99, 226, 228–30
rock crystal, *see* crystal
romans   81–83, 99, 109–10, 161, 210
Roman de Mélusine   99
Roman de Renart   82
Roman de Sidrac   126, 161
Roman des déduis   109, 210
Romance of the Panther   82
room hangings   7, 11, 64, 73, 88, 110, 113, 135, 160, 178–79, 183, 192–98, 205, 227–30, *see also chambre*
rosary   166–68 *see also* paternoster
roses   192–94, 198, 227
Rouen   128, 135, 170, 172
ruby   40, 43, 87, 101, 129, 145, 153–54, 156–59, 163, 164–70, 173–74, 177, 216–18, 220–24

Saints
   Agnes   119
   Bartholomew   65, 73, 126–27, 134, 215
   Catherine   6, 105, 113, 122, 124, 128, 135–37, 139–140, 149, 184, 203, 213, 218
   Christine   139–140, 213
   Christopher   134–35, 212
   Denis   20, 45–46, 119, 160–61
   Didier   134–35, 212

INDEX

Elysabel   112, 210–11
Elysael   105, 208
George   157
Gile   112, 210–11
John the Baptist   20, 28, 33, 101 116–17, 120,
  122, 128, 158–59, 213–14, 218, 223
John the Evangelist   100
Lawrence   122, 136, 138, 213
Leonard   122, 191, 213
Louis of France   1, 5, 13–14, 25, 29, 31–32,
  37, 45–46, 70, 75, 79-94, 98–100, 116, 128,
  141-42, 158, 162, 177, 204, 206-9, 214
Louis of Toulouse (Saint Louis of
  Marseille)   122, 128, 131, 134, 143–44,
  146, 149, 214, 218
Loup   122, 186, 189, 191, 213
Maurice   122, 139, 212
Margaret   128, 139–41, 183, 213–14
Michael   129
Valentine   138, 212
Saint-Denis, abbey   1–3, 5, 9, 11, 13, 19–41, 47,
  50–51, 56–57, 60, 67–68, 71, 116, 128,
  131–32, 148, 171–72, 199–200
  chapel of Saint Hippolyte   3, 5, 9, 11,
    19–36, 51, 56–57, 73, 116, 186, 194
  chapel of Saint John the Baptist   33
Saint Hildevert, Gournay   69, 189, 226
Saint-Laurent, priory   69, 136, 213
Saint-Nazaire, cathedral of Béziers   2–3
sapphire   40, 87–88, 129, 145–46, 152, 154,
  156–59, 163, 167, 176, 216–18, 220–23, 225
Sausseuse, priory   69, 140, 214
silk   57, 121, 154, 183, 185–87, 189, 190, 195, 230
silver   3-4, 8, 13–14, 45, 55, 93, 95, 116–17, 120,
  122, 128–31, 134–136, 138–40, 142, 144–45,
  150, 154, 176, 178, 191, 212–14
silver-gilt   3, 13, 121, 128–31, 134, 136, 144, 150,
  166, 168–69, 178, 212, 223–24
Somme le roi   5, 77, 81, 106-8, 111, 149, 164, 207,
  211
Speculum Dominarum   96–97; see also
  Miroir des dames
squirrel   183, 190–91, 198, 226
  squirrel suit of Philippa of Hainault   190

stag   120, 129, 157–58
surcote   25–26, 29, 198
surplices   183–85, 226
Symmonete   81, 99, 112, 198–99, 230

tableaux   120, 126, 218–19
tableaux d'or   149, 217
testaments   1–4, 6–17, 38–41, 44–45, 58,
  60–80, 82–83, 98, 101, 105, 156–58,
  160–61, 176–79, 190–92, 201–4
Thibaut Roussel   62
Three Kings amulets   154-5, 157
tombs   2–3, 5, 8, 13, 23–28, 32–33, 47, 50, 57,
  103, 143
  tomb figures   23, 25–26, 28, 33
Troussy, Blanche, dame de   175, 199, 210–11,
  229
True Cross relics   130, 144–46, 213, 216–17

Valentina Visconti, duchess of Orléans   17,
  79, 97, 101–2, 165–66, 177, 208, 222
Vernon   39, 55–56, 68–69
  Franciscans of   69, 143, 214
  Hôtel-Dieu   69, 93, 106, 116, 142, 206, 214
  Notre-Dame, collegiate church   5, 68–69,
    131, 133–34, 142, 189, 215, 226
  Sausseuse, priory   69, 140, 214
vestments   7, 64, 69, 113, 135, 178–79, 181, 183,
  185–87, 189–91, 193, 195, 197, 199, 201–3
Vie de Saint Louis   116, 206
Viollet-le-Duc, Eugene   119
Virgin Mary   5, 65, 100, 116, 130–31, 134, 178,
  189, 191, 196, 212, 215, 226
Virgins (the 11,000 Virgins)   122, 130, 139–40,
  212, 214
Volto Santo of Lucca   29–30

Wautriquet de Couvin   97
weddings   2-4, 17, 42, 44, 80, 104, 151, 163–65,
  170–77, 195, 224
  gifts   17, 56, 104, 164, 170–77, 180, 195
Wight, Matilda   190
wimple   22, 25–26, 29, 199